THE STORY OF THE
JODHPUR
LANCERS
1885–1952

Published by
NIYOGI BOOKS
Block D, Building No. 77,
Okhla Industrial Area, Phase-I,
New Delhi-110 020, INDIA
Tel: 91-11-26816301, 26818960
Email: niyogibooks@gmail.com
Website: www.niyogibooksindia.com

English Text © Brigadier M.S. Jodha

Editor: K.E. Priyamvada
Design: Shraboni Roy

ISBN: 978-93-86906-63-2
Publication: 2018

Printed at: Niyogi Offset Pvt. Ltd., New Delhi, India

An aerial view of Jodha Squadron lines at Ratanada, Jodhpur, 1903

Dear Michael,

Both your book & this
one by Brig. M.S. Jodha
have finally brought to
life the gallant feats
of the Jodhpur Lancers
in the Centenary year their
"finest hour" the fall
of Haifa, Israel.
With my thanks &
appreciation of your
work.
With warm greetings
for the New Year

Bapji Jodhpur

Jan. 2019.

THE STORY OF THE
JODHPUR
LANCERS
1885–1952

BRIGADIER M.S. JODHA

NIYOGI
BOOKS

It gives me immense pleasure to pen down the Foreword for the book *The Story of the Jodhpur Lancers*. The genesis of the Jodhpur Lancers and its subsequent rise to stellar heights of glory before and during the Great Wars makes for very interesting reading.

It was on 23rd September 1918 that they had their finest hour, when in a daring, daylight, uphill, full-blown cavalry charge, facing the enemy's machine guns and artillery fire, they captured the fortified town of Haifa. Today Haifa Day is commemorated on 23rd September, both in India and Israel. The 'Teen Murti-Haifa Chowk' memorial in New Delhi, stands in grand testimony to this unparalleled feat at arms and excellent horsemanship.

Such historical campaigns fought by Indian soldiers encapsulating acts of valour across the world should be authentically and meticulously documented for future generations to become aware of our rich heritage in warfare. Such compilations serve as inspirations to our youth.

I feel immensely proud in dedicating this book to the bravehearts of the Jodhpur Lancers who created such a great legacy with their toil, sweat and blood. I compliment Brigadier M.S. Jodha, whose grandfather led the charge at Haifa, in producing this excellent book with a personal touch.

'Jai Hind'

Bipin Rawat
General
Chief of the Army Staff

I am delighted to write a Foreword to *The Story of Jodhpur Lancers*, raised in 1889 by my great-great-grandfather Maharaja Jaswant Singh II. During the Great War the Jodhpur Lancers covered themselves with glory more than once, but most famously at Haifa on 23rd September 1918, when they carried out what many describe as one of the last and the finest successful cavalry charges ever made. It is appropriate, we mark the centenary of this battle so that their services, which have been largely forgotten, can be recalled and remembered.

It is a pity that it has taken nearly a hundred years to record their famous exploits. I hope that this exhaustive and painstaking compilation done over a period of a decade, by Brigadier M.S. Jodha, whose grandfather Lieutenant Colonel Aman Singh Jodha, OBI, IOM, led the daring charge at Haifa after their leader, the gallant Major Dalpat Singh, MC, was killed, will not only pay rich tributes to our gallant war heroes, but will also inspire and enthuse the present and future generations to read more about the glorious past of their ancestors in the service of their country. The Brigadier has taken the skeins of Jodhpur history and woven them expertly with rare photographs and documents to create an interesting story, which is both illuminating and fascinating.

I trust that this book will be read widely, not only for its own absorbing interest, but also for the detailed information it contains. May it also be cherished as a priceless memento by those who lost near and dear relatives, who gave up their lives for their King and country and now lie buried in a far distant land. I am proud of the Jodhpur State Forces and my family owes them a great debt of lasting gratitude.

GAJ SINGH
MAHARAJA OF JODHPUR

01 March 1939, Viceroy Linlithgow and Maharaja Umaid Singh inspect the guard of honour by the Jodhpur Lancers.

Photo courtesy: Mehrangarh Museum Trust

Contents

Acknowledgements

© Nathfoundation, Sweden

The arm badge that the Jodhpur Lancers' men wore, on the upper right arm of the ceremonial white kurta, was a magnificent brass badge of the *cheel* (kite), facing right with wings outstretched, some 2½ inches high, resting on a scroll with the inscription 'Marwar', the ancient name for the kingdom of Jodhpur. It is also seen on the Jodhpur Lancers' statue at the 'Teen Murti-Haifa Chowk' memorial in New Delhi.

Photo courtesy: Professor (Capt) Ashok Nath, FRGS, Nath Foundation, Sweden

The Story of the Jodhpur Lancers has taken several years to write and could not have been written without the generous assistance and goodwill of numerous friends, well-wishers and colleagues. While working on an assignment which is very close to one's heart, emotions overide professionalism. I was afflicted with this sense of drift in good measure during the initial stages of the project. I was at a loss as to where to start and where to end; each incident and anecdote seemed to be important enough to find a place in the volume. It was with a heavy heart I gave precedence to reality and professionalism and after that the journey, though tumultuous, was fortunately on track. The book is essentially a historic and pictorial rendition of the journey of the Jodhpur State Forces.

I freely acknowledge my indebtedness to the various public and private archives, books, publications and other documents that I have consulted. I am also indebted to several members of the Jodhpur Lancers and Jodhpur Sardar Infantry for their valuable assistance, without which, obviously, it would have been very difficult to have given an adequate account of any particular incident, at which I was not present in person. It is, after all, the collective achievements of many that I write about. Beyond doubt, many brave deeds, fully deserving of mention in these pages, must have been unavoidably overlooked, in which case the leniency of readers is requested.

There is, alas, not room to list all the people who have helped and guided me on this long, long trail, but I would like to extend my thanks to Squadron Leader Rana Chhina, MBE (Retd), and Major General Ian Cardozo, AVSM, SM (Retd), Centre for Armed Forces Historical Research at the United Service Institute (USI), New Delhi, who encouraged me to write and helped source material from abroad, while I was a research scholar with them and special thanks to Mr Jon Lee, a research scholar in UK, who uncovered invaluable material about the regiment and Dr Yashaswini Chandra for her advice on publishing the book. Thanks to Mr Dominiek Dendooven of the 'In Flanders Fields Museum' Ypres (Ieper); Tony McClenaghan in UK; Igal Graiver in Haifa and Professor (Capt.) Ashok Nath, FRGS, a military historian who maintains a magnificent private Indian Army heritage collection, who allowed me to use the entire range of Jodhpur badges and uniform paintings from his collection. A special thanks to the Archives of the Royal Palace of Belgium.

I am extremely grateful to the many people in Jodhpur who have made this book possible and I commence my long list of thanks with my late parents Ganga Singh and Ugam Kanwar, my in-laws Bhairon Singh Rajawat and Tej Kanwar, my wife Vijay Laxmi and my two sons—Captain Karamveer Singh and Lieutenant Manveer Singh—and the many friends who gave me both information and encouragement whilst writing this. I thank my brothers Narayan Singh, Balu Singh, Shyam Singh, Daulat Singh, Shiv Charan Singh and sister Pushp Kanwar for sharing the story umpteen number of times. I also thank Maharaj Daleep Singh, Maharaj Dushyant Singh Raoti, Raoraja Bijay Singh, Raoraja Daljeet Singh, Raoraja Vijay Singh, Mr Narpat Singh Bhati Banasar, Aditya Singh Galthani, Colonel Devpal Singh Rathore, Maharaj Hari Singh Zalim Niwas, Maharaj Dalpat Singh Bhopalgarh, Rajat Singh Bhati and Colonel Daulat Singh Utamber, Thakur Man Singh Kanota, Thakur Pradhuman Singh Chandelao, Gajendra Singh Sankhwas, Mr Daulat Singh Pannai Niwas, Vasant Singh Rodla and Colonel Rajendra Singh Damoi, who all helped shared their material with me. I would like to thank all of them who allowed me access into their private space and also extended their most generous and gracious hospitality. Their enthusiasm has been infectious. To them my deepest gratitude. For me the journey has been an extremely rich and rewarding one.

I have often quoted other people's words, as they not only add authenticity but also a valuable and interesting insight into the person. Thus I would particularly like to thank all those who have been kind enough to allow me to quote them and I am similarly obliged to the research done by many authors, some of whose descendants I have not been able to track down.

Many people were kind enough to put up with the infliction of having to 'force read' my manuscript. Without exception, all of them contributed significantly to improving what I had written. It only remains, then, to acknowledge with the deepest gratitude the kindness of those who have been good enough to help with criticism and advice, and to submit the pages that follow to the judgement of those for whom chiefly they have been compiled.

I also express my sincere gratitude to Lieutenant General Hanut Singh, PVSM, MVC (Retd), the doyen of armoured warfare in the South Asian region and hero of the Battle of Basantar, in the 1971 War, whose father Lieutenant Colonel Arjun Singh had served with the Jodhpur Lancers, to read through my draft copy of the book. In spite of his advanced age and ill health, he was kind enough to draw a title page for the book and, unable to write much, he left behind for me a 30-minute video recording, giving some invaluable suggestions about the book, weeks before his death in April 2015.

Picture Credits: My thanks go to Kunwar Karni Singh Jasol, Director Mehrangarh Fort Jodhpur and to Umaid Bhawan Palace, Jodhpur, who allowed me to access their archives and helped source photographs from abroad. The rest of the photographs are from the private collections that I was kindly shown during my numerous visits to the families of erstwhile Jodhpur State Forces. I also thank Mr Pradeep Soni, Additional Chief Engineer (Retd) of Jodhpur who photographed many objects for the book.

I would like to give a very special word of thanks to late Dr Mahendra Singh Nagar, Mehrangarh Museum Trust, Jodhpur for initially helping me in my research in every possible manner. I also thank Kunwar Jagat Singh Raoti, Secretary to H.H. Jodhpur for sharing many important documents from his great-grandfather's personal collection, and Dr Mahendra Singh Tanwar, Dr Sunayana Rathore and Mr Sunil Laghate at Mehrangarh Fort. My special thanks to Shri Gajendra Singh Shekhawat, Union Minister of State for Agriculture and Farmers' Welfare (Member of Parliament from Jodhpur). I also thank Dr B.K. Modi, Mr Ravi Kumar Iyer and Ms Nazneen Rowhani for their enthusiasm and wholehearted support towards the centenary commemoration of the Battle of Haifa. I thank both the present Commanding Officers of the successor units of the Jodhpur Lancers and Jodhpur Sardar Infantry, Colonel Ravi Rathore of the 61st Cavalry and Colonel S.K. Singh of the 24th Mechanised Infantry (Jodhpurs) respectively.

I would like to express my gratitude and thanks to the Niyogi Books team for giving me the opportunity to work on this project. I thank K.E. Priyamvada for her very thorough and professional work on editing, Shraboni Roy and Shaju K. Anthony for doing such a wonderful job with the design of the book and making it so special. I also thank Mr Nirmal Kanti Bhattacharya and Mr Niyogi for showing confidence to publish my first book at very short notice.

I am especially grateful to the Chief of Army Staff General Bipin Rawat, UYSM, AVSM, YSM, SM, VSM, ADC, for sparing his valuable time to write a Foreword for my book.

Finally, I owe an immense debt of gratitude to Maharaja Gaj Singh, affectionally known throughout Jodhpur as 'Bapji' (respected father). Without his approval, encouragement and support, this book could not have been written. He very kindly agreed to write a foreword to this book, and provided me access to extremely rare photographs and documents, for which I am incredibly grateful. He helped open the door of Princely India and I gained a privileged access which enabled me to witness and photograph the otherwise hidden world of the Maharajas.

The author with Maharaja Gaj Singh of Jodhpur.
Photo courtesy: Kunwar Narendra Singh Nathawat

The author highlighting the role of the Jodhpur Lancers at the 'India and the Great War'
International Conference, at USI, New Delhi, in March 2014. L to R: Tony McClenaghan,
Squadron Leader Rana Chhina, the author and Andrew Kerr.
Photo courtesy: USI, New Delhi

Lest We Forget

To reduce the expenditure of the Government of India, Viceroy Lord Dufferin (1884–1888) introduced the scheme of 'Imperial Service Troops' (IST), i.e. forces raised in, and paid for by, the princely states. There was a special romance attached to the IST and the States Forces because they comprised troops of the Indian Princes themselves—indeed the Jodhpur Lancers popularly addressed as the '*Jo Hukum Lancers*', were supposedly the most aristocratic unit in India at that time. In Jodhpur, the regiment was known as the Sardar Rissala (named after Maharajkumar Sardar Singh), but when serving outside the state it was called the Jodhpur Lancers.

In 1888 Maharaja Jaswant Singh of Jodhpur ordered his trusted brother Maharaj Sir Pratap Singh to undertake the raising up of the Jodhpur Lancers (The term Maharaja is used for a ruling prince, Maharajkumar for heir apparent and Maharaj for a brother or son of the ruler who do not inherit the throne). The British spelt and pronounced his name as Pertab Singh, but he was universally referred to by them as 'Sir P'. In Jodhpur particularly, and among his Indian contemporaries in Rajputana and the rest of India, he was known as 'Sarkar'. Sir Pratap was an accomplished soldier and sportsman, as well as the Prime minister, and three times the Regent of Jodhpur.

This little book aims at giving a bird's eye-view of the Jodhpur Lancers—their origin, their deeds and dash, and their part in the armies of the British India and the Rajas. This book would allow their friends and relations to obtain some idea of their experiences the officers and men of the Jodhpur Lancers went through, whilst they were serving in the many wars that they fought.

The Jodhpur Lancers duty took them to North West Frontier Province during the Hazara Expedition (1891), Mohmand and Tirah Campaign (1897–98), to Transvaal South Africa (1900–1902), to China during the Boxer Rebellion (1900–01), to France and Flanders and to Palestine and Syria during the whole of the Great War (1914–1920) and to Italy, Iraq, Syria and Hongkong during the Second World War from 1939–46.

However, it was on 23rd September 1918 that they had their finest hour, when in a daring, daylight, uphill, full-blown cavalry charge, in the teeth of machine guns and artillery fire, they captured the fortified town of Haifa (now in Israel) from Turkish German Forces. The Jordan Valley, Haifa and Aleppo have since been the names honoured in the annals of the Indian Cavalry arm. The massed machine guns of Haifa now decorate the formidable Mehrangarh Fort of Jodhpur and the 61st Cavalry Regiment at Jaipur. Similarly, the 'Teen Murti-Haifa Chowk' memorial situated at one of the busiest roundabouts of New Delhi, with a column and three statues of uniformed lancers, stands in mute testimony to this unparalleled feat at arms and excellent horsemanship.

During the Second World War, the Jodhpur Lancers was the first Indian State Cavalry or Infantry unit to leave its state to join an Indian army formation, and was the first state cavalry regiment to be selected for mechanisation, whilst the men of the Jodhpur Sardar Infantry were the first Indian troops to land on the mainland of Italy, at Salerno, on 09 September 1943. Besides the above firsts, it can be said that the Jodhpurs were the first among other IST units whose personnel were awarded the first ever India General Service (IGS) Hazara 1891, Indian Order of Merit (IOM), a Military Cross (MC), a Distinguished Service Order (DSO), a Victoria Cross (VC) and post-independence the Param Vir Chakra (PVC)!

On 01 April 1951, it was decided to take over these State Forces and merge them with the existing Indian army. The inevitable result of this was the destruction of the identity of these forces, quickly and irrevocably. Contemporary developments in India have tended to draw a veil over the history and exploits of the State Forces, a history that is full of glory and deeds of valour, a history that has its beginnings in years long before the Indian Army came into existence. The Jodhpur Lancers was amalgamated into the 'D' Squadron of 7th Light Cavalry in 1951. However, in 1956 this squadron was split into to the 8th Cavalry and 20th Lancers, and through Durga Horse to the 61st Cavalry Regiment. The Jodhpur Lancers are still remembered with reverence by the Indian Army almost 130 years after its raising and each year 23rd September is commemorated as Haifa day, both in India and Israel.

This is the story of great endeavour and much hard work, loyalty, devotion to duty, and self-sacrifice, of great difficulties met with and overcome. It is a proud record. But surprisingly the regimental history of these regiments was never written and the material for this book is based largely upon my own research. A book on the history of the Jodhpur State Forces in the War, 1939–45 was written by Brigadier R.C. Duncan, Commandant Jodhpur State Forces, at that time. Unfortunately this book, now rarely available, covers only the period of 1939 to 1945. There are many works, official and otherwise, which deal with Jodhpur Lancers in part, but the writer knows of no single work, which presents to the reader a brief survey of

23 September 2010, Haifa. Left to right: Ambassador Navtej Sarna; Major General Amos Gilas, Israeli Defence Forces; the Author; and Group Captain Ajay Rathore, VM (Now Air Commodore), on the occasion of Commemoration of the First Haifa Day in Israel.
Photo courtesy: Alex Ringer

the whole story. It is in the hope of supplying this want that I pierced together a complete story from fragments for the reader. The interesting nature of the subject and the difficulty of acquiring information about the military history of Jodhpur made me curious to look for more. I then began to search more and found there was more, much more.

However, there were problems in compiling this history, largely because original records are inadequate, or have since been lost or destroyed. Sadly, though inevitably, many of those who could have contributed from first-hand knowledge to the compilation of such a history, are no longer with us. I have put myself to extra pains and trouble in writing this book, by acquiring much previously unpublished material including first-hand accounts such as letters, maps, documents and rare photographs to personalise and reconstruct the story. Luckily I have unearthed many letters exchanged between the British and Jodhpur Lancers' officers that reveal much about their experiences, motivation and state of mind in various phases of war in China, France, Palestine and elsewhere.

The memories of the war still linger in families and army regiments and thus, in my attempt to better understand some of the challenges faced by the Jodhpur troops during the Great War, I first took a trip to Haifa, Israel, in September 2010, again

Centenary Commemoration of the Great War in Brussels, Belgium, in October 2014.
From left: Ambassador Manjeev Puri; General Van Caelenberge, Belgium Chief of Staff;
the Author; Mr Dominiek Dendooven of In Flanders Field Museum Ypres; and Squadron
Leader Rana Chhina, MBE (Retd) USI, New Delhi.
Photo courtesy: Embassy of India, Belgium

in November 2017 and September 2018 and proudly walked through the last few
kilometres of the same route of 'Belled el Sheikh–Tel Abu Huwam–Mount Carmel–
German Street–Haifa', as was taken by the Jodhpur Lancers that memorable
afternoon of 23rd September 1918. Then to the Western Front of Belgium and
France in October 2014. Travelling between Ypres and Lille in France, I visited
the villages that dot the countryside and learned that Indian war heroes such as
Govind Singh, VC, are household names there, and that each family has a story to
share about the warmth and bravery of the Indian troops stationed in that region.
I walked along the fields of Flanders, where one can still pick out the pieces of
spent bullets and horseshoes embedded in the soil. I was moved by the sight of the
tricolour and Ashoka's Lions at Menin Gate, Ypres, and was pleasantly surprised
to learn that the look of the Indian War Memorial at Neuve Chapelle (designed
by Sir Herbert Baker, who also co-designed New Delhi) is identical to that of the
Sanchi Stupa.

This work is what I would call a labour of love. It required several years of persistent and patient research. It also required travel to several places in order to obtain data, photograph collections and consult archives. In the process I met many interesting people, some of whom have become my good friends.

I had the privilege of hearing this oral story literally from the horse's mouth since childhood, as my grandfather and both his sons had served in the Jodhpur State Forces continuously from 1889 till 1950. Over the years, in order to lend credence to this oral history, I have studied the work of several historians, delved through National Archives in New Delhi, State Archives in Bikaner, Sumer Public Library and Maharaja Man Singh Pushtak Prakash, Jodhpur and referred to tons of unpublished manuscripts in private collections. The more I learnt, the more inquisitive I became. The happiness I derived, in reading through those original collections in Jodhpur and elsewhere was extremely satisfying. In fact wherever I went, I got either a good picture or the relevant material that I was looking for. Many a time I wondered if some power was guiding me to all these places where I had no intention of going! Slowly it became a passion and over the years I collected so much material that I did not know what should I do with it all. Somewhere, deep down, I was aware that now the onus to compile and present this wonderful story rested on me and on no one else; otherwise the story of this fine regiment would be lost forever!

So one memorable day, during my posting at Shimla in 2005, while glancing at a photograph of my grandfather, I announced that I am going to write a book on it. A few people, including some freinds, laughed at the idea. This was enough to steel my resolve to complete this project at any cost.

For almost a century the story of the Battle of Haifa of 1918 was a forgotten chapter in India and unknown in Israel. However, I can derive immense pride and satisfaction from the fact that my personal quest to unearth this story has finally paved the way for both Prime Ministers of India and Israel recently visiting each other's countries, to pay their personal respects to the Haifa heroes of 1918. In fact an interesting incident had led to uncovering of this tale, which is covered in greater detail later in the book.

The Story of the Jodhpur Lancers is a richly illustrated kaleidoscope packed with historical data assembled from a wide variety of sources, much of it previously unavailable, that represents a wealth of history, culture and knowledge that's often been difficult to uncover. Steeped in history as it is, the book unfolds the saga of that glorious era supported by more than 500 rare photographs and letters sourced from personal collections of erstwhile royal families, museums and archives the world over. The reader must look with pride at the gallants standing proud with their gem encrusted weapons and arms...through the annals of history, and capture the magic, sensuality, romance and glory that was the Jodhpur Lancers in this sumptuously illustrated volume. However, it is now both part of the history of the Indian Army, and a record of a bygone era.

The book endeavours to preserve the deeds of our veterans and valiant martyrs for posterity. Their story needed to be told, lest we forget the sacrifice that they made a hundred years ago. Their forgotten faces needed to be seen again and their courage remembered and commemorated. This story brings them to life again.

I have spent almost every spare moment of the last 10 years in uncovering the tale—hoping that the story would indeed live up to its rich legacy. For me personally, though I did not have the good fortune to know him, my grandfather remained the unique inspiration and I am immensely proud of him and his services.

Dedication

The author (extreme right) explaining the Jodhpur Lancers story to Maharaja Gaj Singh of Jodhpur (second from right) after the opening of the photo gallery dedicated to the Haifa heroes of 1918, in Mehrangarh Fort, Jodhpur, on 12 May 2018.

Photo courtesy: Dr Sunayana Rathore

As they say, 'Those were the times' and 'The time moves in one direction while the memory in another'. The past seems to haunt all of us at some point in time. This book began as a personal quest to trace the events that led to the award of Indian Order of Merit (IOM) during the Battle of Haifa, now in Israel, on 23rd September 1918 to my grandfather. My search for his IOM citation continued for many years, till I found it in the National Archives in New Delhi, in 2007. Along the way, this book was conceived, and I began to collect all additional material on the subject from time to time.

For me personally the whole story is so glorious, so stimulating and so rich that it has been a privilege to tell the tale. I therefore humbly dedicate this book to all gallant Marwaris, and in particular to the memory of my grandfather Lieutenant Colonel Aman Singh Jodha, Sardar Bahadur, OBI, IOM, who served the Jodhpur

Captain Aman Singh took this photo in 1915 at Paris. On the right is the studio's seal on the rear of this photo—Photographie Henri, 25 Rue d'Amsterdam, Paris, France. In fact my first interest in the Jodhpur Lancers was fired after seeing this photograph of his in Paris. I wondered what made him go there.

Photo courtesy: Shivcharan Singh Jodha, Digarana

A hundred years later, in October 2014, following the footsteps of my grandfather, I reached the very doorstep of 25 Rue d'Amsterdam, Paris, photo studio, holding the same photograph of my grandfather that he had taken here in 1915! Standing there on the cobbled streets, looking at the buildings all around, it was very easy to be transported 100 years back in time.

Photo courtesy: The author

State Forces for 40 long years (1889–1929) and had the honour to lead the Jodhpur Lancers in that memorable charge at Haifa, on 23rd September 1918.

To be a soldier in 19th-century Jodhpur was to be a member of an honourable profession, as the soldier caste enjoyed high status and respect. My grandfather, like many men of his generation, was excited by romantic ideals of war and a chance to see the world. He was trained to fire a machine gun and charge on horseback with a sword and lance. He took part in a number of overseas operations on the North West Frontier, China, France, Flanders, Palestine and Syria with the Jodhpur Sardar Rissala, popularly called as the Jodhpur Lancers, in the era of Imperialism where Indian troops served British Imperial interests. The notion of *izzat*, of honour, was a crucial part of the soldier's way of life. *Along the way, I often wondered what it would have been like to believe in God and King and Country and to have those beliefs tested in various theatres of war, which were not yours.*

My grandfather built this handsome *haveli* (stately house, usually with a courtyard) during the Great War, in our village Digarana, Pali, Marwar.
Photo courtesy: Anurag Singh Jodha, Digarana

How could anyone find the courage to charge a machine gun with only a lance or sword in hand? And what does it truly mean to kill another man?

This book on the Jodhpur Lancers is inspired by the remarkable story of my grandfather who rose from a Syce (groom) to Commanding Officer. A brief bio-sketch of him follows.

A remarkable story of a man who rose from a syce to Commanding Officer in the era of imperialism. The photo is taken against a handpainted background depicting a natural setting. He wears a khaki uniform with turban and tunic, with standing collar and four patch pockets with a waist and shoulder belt.

Photo courtesy: Daulat Singh Jodha, Digarana

Lieutenant Colonel Aman Singh was born as the second son to Thakur Raj Singh Jodha at Digarana, Pali Marwar, in 1875. His two sons also joined the Jodhpur State Forces, Major Madho Singh (Jodhpur Sardar Infantry, 1927–1950) and Ganga Singh Jodha (my father, who briefly served Jodhpur Sardar Infantry in 1943–44). Already the fifth generation, including both my sons, are officers in the Indian Army and I do hope this tradition of serving in the army, uninterrupted since 1889, continues.

Major Madho Singh and Officer Cadet Ganga Singh in 1943.
Photos courtesy: Colonel M.S. Jodha, 74 Armoured Regiment

The story goes that one fine morning in 1889, Aman Singh heard the news that the Maharaja of Jodhpur was seeking the services of loyal and brave Rajputs to enlist in the Jodhpur Imperial Service Lancers. He immediately rushed to Jodhpur, which was about 90 kms from his village, but to his dismay, the required numbers were already filled up, by the time he reached there. It would have been an insult to go back to his village now, so he got himself enlisted as a Follower (Syce) and waited for any vacancy that may occur in future. In Marwar of yore the economy was shorn of any gainful employment and the army provided one of the best job opportunities—and with an assured pension too.

Aman Singh was a quick learner; having learned the rudiments of riding on buffalo back at his native village, he quickly adapted himself to ride the horse in the most accomplished manner. Then one fine morning (probably 07 February 1893), the troops were marched off for their routine morning exercises and Aman Singh, who as a syce, was not allowed to ride a horse, took the opportunity to master a horse, which would normally not allow anyone to ride it. Sir Pratap, passing by, was so impressed with the 'rider'—for he knew the horse well—that he at once asked who he was. Quickly dismounted (fearing he was being pulled-up for riding the horse) and with folded hands, he replied '*Hukum*, I am syce Aman Singh Jodha'. Sir Pratap, impressed with his riding skills, at once waved his hand to direct him to join the Jodha Squadron and he became a Sowar! The official list of Jodhpur Imperial Service Lancers has 07 February 1893 as the date of Aman Singh entering service. Having achieved his first promotion that morning there was no looking back for Sowar Aman Singh. Soon with his ability, courage and hard work, he became a renowned rider in his Jodha Squadron and the Regiment and went on to become the Commanding Officer.

Another interesting episode happened during the battle of Henu Bridge in Jordan Valley on 14 July 1918 during the Great War. It illustrates the value system and the bond that existed between the officers and men in the Rissalas at that time. The Jodhpur Lancers was operating along with the Poona Horse that day, when suddenly Aman Singh, who was commanding the 'B' Squadron of Jodhpur Lancers, came across a critically injured man of the Poona Horse. The man, Daffadar Peerdan Singh, was in tears as to how his daughter Rassal Kanwar would be married after his death and asked Aman Singh to take care of her. Much later, after the war, Lieutenant Colonel Aman Singh married his elder son, Captain Madho Singh to Daffadar Peerdan Singh's daughter, to fulfil the promise that he would have made that day to his fellow soldier. Such were the times and the men and their value systems!

Aman Singh had qualified at Musketry School, Meerut, and in the Equitation Course at Saugar Cavalry School. Aman Singh first saw active service on the

Aman Singh as Rissaldar Major in February 1914.
Photo courtesy: Mehrangarh Museum Trust

North West Frontier in the Mohmand and Tirah Campaign in 1897 and was awarded the India General Service Medal Tirah 1897–98. Then followed service in China, during the Boxer Rebellion 1900–01 for which he received the China Medal. He became Rissaldar Major 2nd Lancers Sardar Rissala on 01 June 1914. He later served throughout the Great War 1914–18 in France, Flanders, Palestine and Syria as Squadron Commander.

He was promoted to the rank of Captain and made Squadron Commander in France on 10 December 1915. He had the honour of being presented to the King George V, in Buckingham Palace, on Wednesday, 07 June 1916, while on a short arranged leave in London from 01 to 13 June 1916.

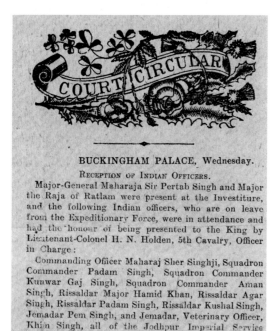

The Court circular Buckingham Palace, Wednesday 07 June 1916. Squadron Commander Aman Singh with other Jodhpur Lancers officers had the rare honour of being introduced to King George V in Buckingham Palace.
Newspaper courtesy: Maharaj Dushyant Singh Raoti

He was awarded the Order of British India 2nd Class for distinguished conduct on the field with the title of 'Bahadur' on 20 April 1917, for Field Service in France ('Gazette of India' No. 596, dated 20 April 1917).

Next he saw active service in Palestine and Syria and was awarded the Indian Order of Merit for commanding the leading 'B' Squadron in the famous charge at Haifa on 23 September 1918 ('Gazette of India' No. 848, dated 26 April 1919). His 'B' Squadron played the most critical role and helped gallop the Turk out of Haifa.

After the war the Jodhpur Lancers remained on active service in Aleppo, Syria, during the Egyptian Rebellion of 1919, where Aman Singh, promoted to the rank of Major, remained as Officiating Commanding Officer. He later received the 1914 Star, British War Medal and Victory medals for the Great War.

My grandfather's medals. **First row, left to right:** The sleeve badge *cheel*, the Indian Order of Merit (IOM) 2nd Class, Order of British India (OBI) 1st Class, OBI 2nd Class.
Second row, left to right: India General Service Medal Tirah 1897–98, China 1900–01, 1914 star, British War medal, Victory medal and 1935 Jubilee medal. The OBI instituted in 1837, consisted of two classes. The first class carried with it the title 'Sardar Bahadur'—literally 'the brave one' or 'valiant chief' and the second class carried the title 'Bahadur'.
Photo courtesy: Captain Karamveer Singh Jodha, 2/11 Gurkha Rifles

After the Great War the Maharaja of Jodhpur rewarded Major Dalpat Singh, MC, and Captain Aman Singh, for heroics at Haifa, by granting a Jagir or Estate as due reward, under the scheme of granting 'Land, Jangi Inams and Jagirs' in Marwar to the members of the Imperial Service Troops, who had rendered 'Specially Distinguished Service' during the Great War. (*Vide* Jodhpur Regency Council No. 1, dated 16 February 1920).

The gold cufflinks presented to Aman Singh by the Prince of Wales on 30 November 1921 at Jodhpur during the investiture ceremony for the award of IOM.

Photo courtesy: Colonel Vikram Singh Rathore, Army Aviation Corps

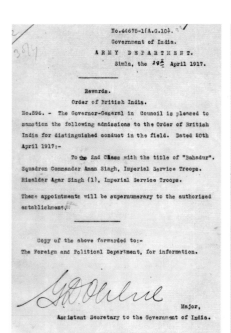

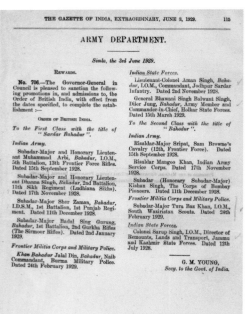

The Government of India letter of 28 April 1917 and the *Gazette of India Extraordinary* of 03 June 1929 for Award of OBI 2nd and 1st Class to Lieutenant Colonel Aman Singh with titles of Bahadur and Sardar Bahadur respectively.

Photo courtesy: The author

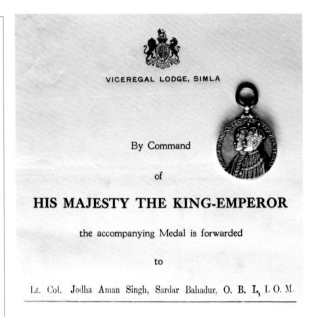

The citation for the award of IOM at Haifa on 23 September 1918. On the right is the 1935 King's Silver Jubilee Medal to Lieutenant Colonel Aman Singh Jodha, OBI, IOM.
Photos courtesy: The author

On 28 August 1922 Aman Singh was selected as the first Commanding Officer of the newly raised Jodhpur Sardar Infantry (later 20 Rajput and now 24 Mechanised Infantry Battalion). On 18 February 1924 he was promoted to the rank of Lieutenant Colonel. On 02 November 1928 he was again decorated with Order of British India 1st Class with the title of Sardar Bahadur (*Gazette of India*, Extraordinary No. 706 dated 03 June 1929). He also received the 1935 Silver Jubilee Medal (Govt of India No. F 77 (3)-H/34 dated, 15 May 1935).

In appreciation of his exceptionally meritorious services, he was bestowed with 'Tazim, Gold, and Hathi Saropa' by the Maharaja of Jodhpur in January 1948 on the occasion of the birth of the present Maharaja Gaj Singh (*Vide* HQ Part II No 326, dated 27 January 1948).

He hung up his spurs on 08 August 1929, after serving the Jodhpur State Forces for 40 glorious and memorable years. On his retirement, a special Marwar Gazette

Left: As a mark of special recognition during the Centenary year of the Battle of Haifa (1918–2018), the honour of *Marwar Ratan* and Rs 1 lakh was conferred on Lieutenant Colonel Aman Singh Jodha for his gallantry at Haifa on the occasion of the 560th foundation day of Jodhpur on 12 May 2018. **Right:** Lieutenant Colonel Aman Singh, OBI, IOM, in 1948. By his dash and gallantry at Haifa he won everlasting glory for himself and the Jodhpur Lancers.
Photos courtesy: (L) Mehrangarh Museum Trust, (R) Thakur Shyam Singh Jodha, Digarana

was published in *'Ijlas-I-Khas'*, Notification Number 57, dated 07 September 1929, by the then Maharaja Umaid Singh, acknowledging his immense contribution to the Jodhpur State Forces, from 1889 to 1929. Lieutenant Colonel Aman Singh passed away on 05 May 1950.

And 100 years later, the Mehrangarh Museum Trust conferred the prestigious Major Dalpat Singh, Marwar Rattan Award 2017 to Lt Colonel Aman Singh for his exceptional gallantry during the Battle of Haifa. The award with a citation was received from Maharaja Gaj Singh of Jodhpur, on 12 May 2018 during the solemn ceremony that marked the 560th foundation day of the city of Jodhpur. The event also kickstarted the centenary commemoration of the Battle of Haifa in Jodhpur, with the opening of a photo gallery dedicated to the Jodhpur Lancers.

Winners of Rajputana State Forces Football Shield 1928. **Seated left:** Chand Singh Bagawas;
centre: Lieutenant Colonel Aman Singh Jodha, OBI, IOM, Commanding Officer JSI 1922–1929,
extreme right: Captain Chattar Singh Osian and **front row centre:** Nahar Singh Hariadana.
The players are seen wearing jerseys with the letters SI (Sardar Infantry) and the *cheel* logo.
Some of the players are proudly showing off their wristwatches while others have tactfully covered
their wrists.
Photo courtesy: Thakur Balu Singh Jodha, Digarana

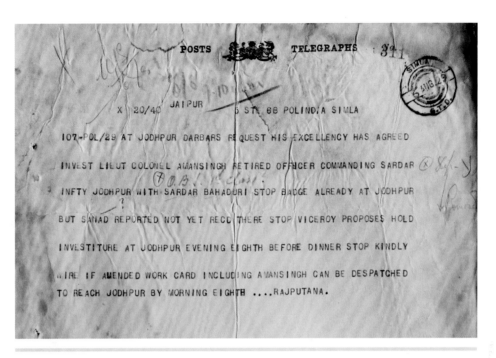

Telegram from Viceroy's office Simla, dated 06 August 1929, to Maharaja of Jodhpur, about Investiture of Lieutenant Colonel Aman Singh with OBI 1st Class, on 08 August 1929.
Photo courtesy: The author

Lieutenant Colonel Aman Singh Jodha, OBI, IOM, hung up his spurs on 08 August 1929, after 40 glorious years in the Jodhpur State Forces, from 1889 to 1929.
Photo courtesy: The author

No. N. 114

MARWAR GAZETTE

Published by Authority.

Vol. 64.	JODHPUR.—SATURDAY SEPTEMBER 7, 1929.	No. 57
जिल्द ६४	जोधपुर शनिश्चरवार ता॰ ७, सेप्टेम्बर सन् १९२९.	नम्बर ५७

IJLAS-I-KHAS NOTIFICATION.

In wishing farewell to Lt. Col. Jodha Aman Singh, Sardar Bahadur, O. B. I., I. O. M., on the occasion of his relinquishing the command of the Sardar Infantry and retiring on pension, I wish to place on record my great appreciation of his long and loyal services to the State Military Forces extending over 39 years.

After a successful career in Sardar Rissala, where he held relieving command for some time at the front in the Great World-War, he was selected and transferred in 1922 as Commanding Officer for the newly-raised Rajput and Jat Companies. He had all the difficulties of a pioneer in organising the Sardar Infantry, and its present state of efficiency does great credit to his high ability and experience.

He saw active service in China, on the North-West Frontier, and in France and Palestine throughout the recent Great War. The gallant deeds of his Squadron in the memorable actions at Jordon Valley, Haifa and Allepo have been mentioned in War Diary and Despatches. His brilliant exploit at Haifa in capturing Turkish prisoners and Machine guns won for him the I. O. M. In recognition of his long and faithful services he was decorated with the Order of British India. I wish he may be spared long to enjoy his well-earned rest and honours.

इजलासे—खास—नोटिफिकेशन.

जोधा अमानसिंह सरदार बहादुर O. B. I., I. O. M., के सरदार इन्फेन्ट्री से रिटायर्ड होने पर मैं विदा देते हुए उसकी स्टेट मिलिटरी फोर्स में ३९ साल से अधिक और वफादार खिदमत की वहरीरी कद्रदानी करना चाहता हूँ ।

पिछली लड़ाई में बहुत अर्से तक सरदार रिसाले में रिलिविंग कमेन्डर की हैसियत से अच्छी तरह से काम किया और १९२२ को नई कायम हुई राजपूत और जाट कम्पनियों का कमेन्डर मुकर्रर किया गया । उस को सरदार इन्फेन्ट्री के सुधारने में बहुतसी तकलीफें पेश आई और सरदार इन्फेन्ट्री की मौजूदा तरकी की हालत उसकी काबलियत और तजुर्बें की वायस है, पिछली लड़ाई में वो चीन नोर्थ वेस्ट फ्रोन्टीयर और फ्रान्स और पेलेसटाइन में शामिल था । जोरडन वेली हाइफा और अलेपो में उसकी फौज की बहादुरी की तारीफ वार डायरी व डिस्पेच में की गई है ।

अलेपो में तुर्की कैदी और मशीनगन्स पकड़ने में बहादुरी दिखाने के सबब से उसको I. O. M. का खिताब दिया गया । उसकी दराज और वफादार खिदमत के सिलसिले में O. B. I. का खिताब दिया गया ।

अब मैं चाहता हूँ कि वह अपनी बाकी की जिन्दगानी अमन चेन से बसर करें ।

Raikabagh Palace.	UMAID SINGH,
Dated, 14th August 1929.	Maharaja.

Special Marwar Gazette published on the retirement of Lieutenant Colonel Aman Singh Jodha, by Maharaja Umaid Singh of Jodhpur, on 14 August 1929.

Photo courtesy: Lt Manveer Singh Jodha

Historical Overview of the State of Marwar and its Troops

Jodhpur, the second-largest city in the Indian State of Rajasthan, was formerly the capital of a princely state known as Marwar (Land of Death), one of the three principal states in Rajputana, which comprised 22 princely states prior to 1947. During the closing years of the 12th century, Jaychand Rathore, the ruler of Kanauj, was expelled from his capital by Mohammed Ghori in 1194 AD and Siaji, the great-grandson of Jaychand, roamed about with his followers, but eventually succeeded in planting the standard of the Rathores in the sand-hills of the Luni in 1212 AD. One of his successors, Rao Jodha, laid the foundation of the present city of Jodhpur in 1459 AD, the offshoots of which included Bikaner, Kishengarh, Ratlam, Idar, Jhabua, Sitamau and Sailana states.

Today, Jodhpur known as 'Sun City' and 'Blue City' is a popular tourist destination, featuring many palaces, forts and temples, set in the stark landscape of the Thar desert. The word 'pur' used as a suffix means 'city' and appended to the name of Jodha, it denotes '**Jodha's City**'. The nearby town of Mandore, initially served as the capital of Rao Jodha; eventually he decided to shift base to a safer spot and moved from Mandore to Jodhpur in May 1459 and laid the foundation of what was destined to become one of the mightiest forts of all time—**the Mehrangarh Fort**. Most of the chiefs since Jodha had done something to enlarge or renew some part of this majestic fort.

Map showing Marwar Region. Marwar, an arid kingdom on the edge of the Great Thar desert with Jodhpur as its capital, was the domain of the Rathore dynasty.
Photo courtesy: Mehrangarh Museum Trust

The crests of Marwar State and the Jodhpur Lancers. According to local lore, Goddess Chamunda assumed the form of a kite (*cheel*) to warn Rao Jodha (founder of Jodhpur) on several critical occasions of impending dangers. The kite, the symbol of Marwar's guardian spirit, was thus incorporated into the royal insignia of Marwar, when the coat of arms of Jodhpur was designed and formalised by the College of Arms, London, when Queen Victoria was ordained Empress of India.
Photo courtesy: (left) Virendra Singh Rajawat, Mayo College, Ajmer and
(Right) Colonel Ravi Rathore, 61st Cavalry Regiment

Mehrangarh (Fort of the sun) Fort, Jodhpur—a view of the Clock Tower in 1913. The Clock Tower was built in March 1910.
Photo courtesy: Mehrangarh Museum Trust

View of Mehrangarh Fort from Gulab Sagar Tank, built by Gulab Rai, a favorite concubine of Maharaja Vijai Singh (1752–93). Many of Jodhpur's large water tanks were funded by royal consorts for the benefit of the public. A steam force pump, installed in 1890, lifted water from the tank to the top of the fort.
Photo courtesy: Mehrangarh Museum Trust

The Jodhpur coat-of-arms. The colours salmon-pink, white, red, yellow and green represent the five-coloured *panchranga* state flag. The three ears of millet record Sher Shah's saying that in trying to conquer Marwar he had 'nearly lost the empire of Hindustan for a handful of *bajra*'. The kites or *cheel*s represent the winged Goddess Durga who had appeared on several critical occasions to assist the state, in this form. They are, therefore, 'supporters' to the state arms. The moto '*Ran banka Rathore*' means 'Rathore invincible in battle'.
Photo courtesy: The author

Sir Samuel Swinton Jacob, designed the Jubilee Courts (*Mehkma Khas*) Jodhpur, in celebration of Queen Victoria's Jubilee in 1887, at a cost of Rs Three lakhs (Jodhpur Lancers Troops seen in foreground, in February 1914). He also designed St Stephens College, Delhi; Rambagh Palace and Albert Hall Museum, Jaipur; and Lalgarh and Laxmi Niwas Palace at Bikaner.

Photo courtesy: Mehrangarh Museum Trust

A view of the Mehrangarh Fort Jodhpur in 1885. Kipling wrote of it, 'It might have been built by Titans and coloured by the morning sun'.
Photo courtesy: The author

The formidable Mehrangarh Fort, considered the finest in Rajasthan, stands on an isolated outcrop of sandstone rock which rises abruptly from the surrounding plain. The fort commanding the city is built on a sandstone formation rising to the height of 245 feet above the level of the city. The walls and building of the fort rise to a height of 207 foot from its base. This rock is at the end of a ridge that extends for about 25 miles across the desert, and it is made to seem doubly impregnable by the quarrying of sections of its face so that it rises sheer like dressed stone. On this rock lived an old 'sadhu' (sage), 'Cheeria Nathji' and when his tranquility was broken by Jodha's masons, he cursed him, 'Jodha! May your citadel always suffer a scarcity of water!' The terrible curse was much dreaded in this harsh and inhospitable land.

It is said that the rock on which the Fort stands is four miles in circuit. The high sheer walls of both the fort and palace, are built by large blocks of stone, well cemented and sometimes pinned together with iron spikes, dominate the city and can be seen for miles around. Within the fort are the old palaces, a series of beautiful courtyard buildings, barracks and magazines which date from the 17th century onwards. The fortified area stands to the south, with a long wide rampart for working artillery supported by battlements with massive towers. The palace of the maharaja is approached by a steep path along the east side of the cliff which passes through seven arched gateways. The royal complex consists of a series of varied apartments displaying elaborate stone-carving in its arches, windows and balconies, which are both elegant and beautiful in artistic design and finish, with the extensive use of *jalis*, perforated stone screens carved with intricate patterns.

The majestic Mehrangarh Fort of Jodhpur guards the blue-coloured city like a falcon perched on its 400-feet sheer rock face. The fort also served as the residence of Marwar rulers from Rao Jodha (1459–89) to Maharaja Takhat Singh (1873). Maharaja Jaswant Singh (1873–1895) moved out of the fort to Rai ka Bagh Palace. What makes it so dramatic is the way successive generations between 1459 and 1880 raised an exotic palace above the ramparts. These pleasure buildings that project above the ramparts rise for two or three storeys in a series of symmetrical groups of open half-octagons and bows.
Photo courtesy: PixelDo.com

The old city of Jodhpur is surrounded by a thick stone wall, which is massive and strong. It is 24,600 feet long, three to nine feet thick and 15 to 30 feet high, strengthened by towers, buttresses and ramparts with loopholes for defence. There are about a 100 towers and six huge gates in this wall. Each gate bears the name of the place to which it leads, i.e., Merati, Sojati, Jalori, Siwanchi, Chandpole and Nagauri.

The history of the erstwhile state of Jodhpur is a record of heroic exploits, epic victories and magnificent gallantry. The story of Jodha's city is as much a ballad of her kings and queens and warriors, as it is a tale of the Jodhpur's heroic struggle with, and victory over, the elements; her character shaped as much by the blood and passion of her protectors, the enterprise of her merchants and the sheer grit of her peasants, as by the hot sands lashing at her spirit. Much of the prosperity of Marwar was due to trade by naturally enterprising and industrious Marwari banias.

In the early 19th century the British recognised the military potential of the Rathores and other Rajput Princes and co-opted them as allies and thus, in

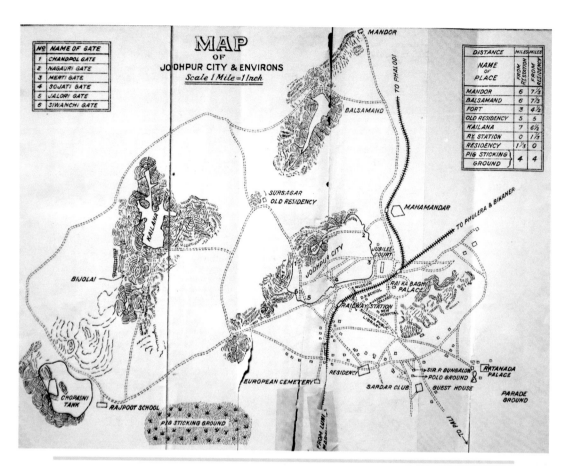

An old map of Jodhpur city of 1920. Besides other places the map shows a pig-sticking, polo and parade ground. Jodhpur was famous for the sports of polo and pig-sticking.
Photo courtesy: Himmat Singh Chauhan

January 1818, during the reign of Maharaja Man Singh (1803–1843), Jodhpur was brought under British control. Jodhpur became a princely state in the Rajputana Agency of British India. The over-seeing British 'Residents' directed Rajput rulers to introduce modern governance to what they perceived as medieval feudal kingdoms. They also chose to address each of the rulers and his kingdom by the name of his capital city. And so, Marwar became Jodhpur. The British took direct control of Ajmer, which became the province of Ajmer-Merwara. A large number of other Rajput states in central and western India made a similar transition. Most of them were placed under the authority of the Central India Agency and the various states' agencies of Kathiawar.

Maharaja Takhat Singh ruled Marwar from 1843 to 1873. He was adopted from Ahmednagar when Maharaja Man Singh died issueless. He supported the British during the Uprising of 1857. His sons were Maharaj Jaswant Singh (who became Maharaja in 1873), Zorawar Singh (his two sons Lieutenant Colonel Sher Singh and Major Akhey Singh served with the Jodhpur Lancers), Sir Partap (his daughter's son Captain Prithi Singh Bera and his two Raoraja sons, namely Sagat Singh and Hanut Singh served with the Jodhpur Lancers), Kishore Singh (he was Commander-in-Chief of Jodhpur State Forces before Sir Pratap. He died in 1898), Bhopal Singh (he and his son Rattan Singh commanded the Jodhpur Sardar Infantry till 1916), and Zalim Singh (he was assistant *Musahib Ala*, Prime Minister, under Sir Pratap until 1902. His sons Captain Guman Singh and Gaj Singh served with the Jodhpur Lancers).

Queen Victoria was proclaimed *Kaiser-i-Hind* (Empress of India) at an Imperial Assemblage held at Delhi in January 1877. The silken banner incorporating eccentric mix of symbols—five colours of Marwar and the kites, symbols of the Rathores' patron Goddess Chamunda, alongside the British Crown—was presented to Maharaja Jaswant Singh on that occasion. On the reverse are embroidered the words *Kaiser-i-Hind Victoria ke huzoor se* (By the grace of Empress Victoria). Ninety shield-shaped banners embroidered with European style crests were designed for Indian Princely States by Robert Taylor and John Lockwood Kipling.
Photo courtesy: Umaid Bhawan Palace

Maharaja Takhat Singh died at midnight on 12 February 1873 in Mehrangarh Fort, Jodhpur. Next morning at sunrise the mortal remains of the Maharaja were placed in a '*janpan*', the body was dressed in state costume and secured in a sitting position; the front of the '*janpan*' was open, so that all could see the face. A grand procession was formed and followed by an immense crowd, ever increasing, the late Maharaja was carried out for the last time from his fort to the old capital, Mundore, where from time immemorial the cremation of his ancestors had always taken place. It was a sight not easily to be forgotten, men threw off their turbans, beat their breasts, and shared every outward sign of grief. He had left 28 legal and 15 illegal wives, but for the first time no attempt at *sati* was made on his death!

His successor, **Maharaja Jaswant Singh** (1873–95), was a progressive ruler. During his investiture two companies of infantry and one and half troops of cavalry of Erinpoora Irregular Force along with one company of infantry and one troop of cavalry of Deolee Irregular Force came to Jodhpur for participation in various ceremonies (since there was no Jodhpur Lancers at the time). He was specially honoured personally by the Prince of Wales who invested him with the Insignia of the Grand Cross of the Star of India (GCSI) at Calcutta in 1876.

Grand chapter of the Star of India at Calcutta, 01 January 1876. The Prince of Wales investing the Maharaja Jaswant Singh of Jodhpur with GCSI. Like the Mughals, the British instituted a complex scheme of ceremonies, titles, and presentations through which Indian royals were incorporated into the imperial hierarchy. New orders of chivalry, such as the Order of the Star of India, were instituted to reward loyal Indian princes.
Photo courtesy: Umaid Bhawan Palace

Left: Maharaja Takhat Singh (1843–1873) and **right:** his son Maharaja Jaswant Singh (1873–1895).
Photos courtesy: (left) Maharaj Hari Singh, Zalim Niwas and (right) Thakur Praduman Singh Chandelao

Subsequently his gun salute was raised to 19, and then to 21 guns. It was during his reign in 1882 that he constructed the Jodhpur railways and in 1889 undertook the raising of the Jodhpur Lancers. He had one son Maharaj Sardar Singh born in 1880 and two Raoraja sons, Sawai Singh (Residency Vakil)—whose son Lieutenant Colonel Sujjan Singh became Commanding Officer (CO) of Jodhpur Sardar Infantry (JSI) from 1929 to 1939—and Tej Singh, who was CO of JSI till 1919.

Maharaja Jaswant Singh died at 04:30 PM on 11th October 1895 at Rai ka Bagh Palace Jodhpur. Lieutenant Colonel T. F. Mullen, the Civil Surgeon Bikaner, wrote in his medical report that,

> For several days in the end of September and beginning of October 1895 the late Maharaja suffered from rather severe malarial remittent fever. He was clear of fever on the 3 and 4 October, but on the 5 after the taking of some strong native medicine (it is said) the fever returned. On the

Maharaja Jaswant Singh had desired that his cremation be performed at Deokund in front of the Fort instead of Mandore in Jodhpur. This beautiful white marble structure called Jaswant Thada (cenotaph) was built by his son Maharaja Sardar Singh in 1899 at cost of Rs 2,84,678 and since then it continues to serve as the cremation ground for the royal family of Jodhpur.

Photo courtesy: Mehrangarh Museum Trust

Rai ka Bagh palace was built by Maharaja Jaswant Singh and he died in this palace on
11 October 1895.
Photo courtesy: The author

6 instant there was pain in the lower part and front of the chest on the right
side which became extremely severe and resisted the various remedies tried
by Deputy Superintendent of Dispensaries and Vaccination, Ali Murdan
Khan, until cupping with the drawing off of a little blood was resorted to.
This measure lessened the pain.

On the night of the 06 instant, while I was at Marwar junction on my way
to Bombay, I received a telegram from Sir Pratap Singh, telling me the
Maharaja was ill and asking me to return by next train, which I did, and
got to Jodhpore at 2 AM of the 7 October. I drove at once to the palace
and examined His Higness. I found him suffering from inflammation of the
capsule of the liver and with, as I believe, a small portion of the lower and
front part of the right lung inflamed (Labular pneumonia in fact). He was
also suffering from fever.

The Maharaja soon showed signs of improvement and on the 9 instant he
asked me not to cure him too quickly lest the cure might not be perfect
and the disease return. I was satisfied with His Highness' progress untill at
1 PM on 11 October the Deputy Superintendent Ali Murdan Khan thought
the pulse showed that a stimulant was necessary and it was given. About
an hour later the pulse was again found to be failing and I was sent for

about 2.20 PM. There were then serious signs of heart weakness which our measure temporarily relieved. Up to twenty minutes before his death he was able to use a handkerchief to wipe perspiration from his face and later helped to hold a glass placed to his lips, the contents of which he swallowed without difficulty. When he spoke, he spoke rationally and knew each of us around him. Quite suddenly the heart stopped, there were three or four gasps and all was over. Cause of death heart failure.

The next day little after sunrise the remains of the Maharaja were carried in a grand procession through the Paota garden and the Nagouri gate to the hill above the Deo Kund lake near the fort where the ceremony of cremation was performed at the express wish of the Maharaja instead of at the usual place, Mandore. Tens of thousands of mourners lined the roads by which the procession passed and all the hills in the neighbourhood of the place of cremation were crowded.

Maharaja Jaswant Singh was succeeded by his minor son Sardar Singh, but Sir Pratap Singh, conducted the administration until his nephew; **Maharaja Sardar Singh** (1898–1911) came of age on 18 Febuary 1898. In order to impart 'English' education to the new ruler, Captain A.B. Mayne of Central India Horse (CIH) was appointed as tutor during the minority of Sardar Singh at a gross salary of Rs 1,000 from 01 May 1896.

Left: Maharaja Jaswant Singh (ruled 12 February 1873–11 October 1895) **Right:** His son, Maharaja Sardar Singh (born on 11 February 1880 and ruled from 18 February 1898 to 20 March 1911).
Photos courtesy: Mehrangarh Museum Trust

His rule was full of incidence and on 10 March 1911, Maharaja Sardar Singh caught fever while motoring in the rain from Meerut to Delhi and on 20 March 1911, he died due to pneumonia at Ratanada Palace, Jodhpur at 4.30 PM (incidently at exactly the same time his father Maharaja Jaswant Singh had died). He was succeeded again by his minor son, Sumer Singh on 5 April 1911.

Maharaja Sumer Singh ruled from 1911–1918. Sumer Singh was sent to Wellington College in England from September 1911 to August 1913 under the guardianship of Major A.D. Strong. Sumer Singh was the first prince from Marwar to have been educated in the United Kingdom. History repeated itself yet again when Sumer Singh died suddenly on 03 October 1918. In September 1918 he visited Poona for the races and came back to Jodhpur seriously ill with influenza; double pneumonia and enteric supervened and after a brief illness he died on 03 of October. He was succeeded on 14 October 1918 by his younger brother Umaid Singh, who again was a minor.

Left: Maharaja Sumer Singh (1911–1918) and **right:** Maharaja Umaid Singh (1918–1947) were brothers.
Photo courtesy: Mehrangarh Museum Trust

Maharaja Umaid Singh, born on 08 July 1903, was the second son of Maharaja Sardar Singh and the younger brother of Maharaja Sumer Singh. He ruled Marwar from **1918 to 1947**. He sat on the Marwar Gaddi (throne) on 14 October 1918 and was invested with full ruling powers on 27 January 1923. He was married on 11 November 1921.

WORK-CARD.

—

INVESTITURE OF HIS HIGHNESS THE MAHARAJA OF JODHPUR.

27th January 1923.

His Excellency will leave his residence on foot at 12·45 P.M., and will be met at a short distance from the Durbar pavilion by the Resident and His Highness' principal Sardar, and by His Highness at the pavilion.

2. His Excellency and the Maharaja will proceed to the *dais*. His Excellency will be on His Highness' right hand.

3. On arriving at the *dais*, His Excellency will take his seat on the right hand throne.

4. After the presentation of the *khilat* His Excellency will, after a short conversation with the Maharaja, rise and address His Highness. After the address His Excellency will resume his seat.

5. On the conclusion of the reading of the translation of His Excellency's address, His Excellency and the Maharaja will both rise, and His Excellency taking His Highness by the hand will say :—

"**I declare Your Highness to be invested with full ruling powers.**"

6. After the Political Secretary has recited His Highness' full titles, His Excellency and His Highness will resume their seats.

7. After the Maharaja has replied to His Excellency's address, certain of His Highness' attendants will be presented to His Excellency, and will offer the usual *nazar*, which will be touched and remitted.

8. On conclusion of the presentations, *itr* and *pán* will be given by His Highness to His Excellency, to the Agent to the Governor-General, the Political Secretary and to the Resident, and by Maharaja Sri Zalim Singhji to the other British Officers present.

9. His Excellency will then rise and leave the Durbar pavilion.

On 27 January 1923 Maharaja Umaid Singh was invested with full ruling powers by Viceroy Reading in Jodhpur. Above is the investiture work card of Maharaja Umaid Singh
Photo courtesy: Mehrangarh Museum Trust

He was made an Honorary Captain in the Army (17 Poona Horse) on 24 October 1921, was promoted to the Honorary rank of Major on 02 June 1923, Honorary Lieutenant Colonel on 18 August 1933 and Colonel in September 1936.

The rank of Air Commodore was bestowed upon him in March 1939 and Honorary Air Vice Marshal in the Royal IAF in 1945, as a tribute to his personal interest in flying. He was made Honorary Lieutenant General on 15 October 1946. Thus he was bestowed with both ranks of a Honorary Lieutenant General and Honorary Air Vice Marshal, a rare distinction indeed. He was created a KCVO (Knight Commander of the Royal Victorian Order) on 17 March 1922, a KCSI (Knight Commander of the Order of the Star of India) on 03 June 1925, a GCIE (Knight Grand Commander of the Order of the Indian Empire) on 01 January 1930, a GCSI (Knight Grand Commander of the Order of the Star of India) on 23 June 1936 and an Aide-de-Camp (ADC) to the King George VI in January 1937.

27 January 1923, Viceroy Reading (fifth from left) at Maharaja Umaid Singh's (sixth from left) Investiture at Jodhpur.

Photo courtesy: Maharaj Dushyant Singh Raoti

A silver trumpet with the Jodhpur coat of arms presented to the Poona Horse by Maharaja of Jodhpur.

Photo Courtesy: Colonel Ashish Singh Pundhir, 17 Poona Horse

Maharaja Umaid Singh was bestowed with the Honorary Rank of Air Vice Marshal in 1945. He was perhaps the only prince to be granted both the honorary ranks of Lieutenant General and Air Vice Marshal.
Photo courtesy: Umaid Bhawan Palace

Maharaja Umaid Singh with his ADCs in 1929. **Standing left to right:** Raoraja Abhay Singh, Kishore Singh Indroka, Dalpat Singh Rohet, Maharaj Akhey Singh, Raoraja Narpat Singh, Maharaj Guman Singh, Pirthi Singh Bera, Kalyan Singh Bhanwari and Raoraja Hanut Singh.
Seated left to right: Maharaj Ajit Singh (brother of H.H. Umaid Singh), Maharaja Umaid Singh and Maharajkumar Hanwant Singh (1947–1952).
Photo courtesy: Umaid Bhawan Palace

Among other things, Maharaja Umaid Singh was a pioneer in the field of aviation in India and he built one of the first airports in the country at Jodhpur. He is remembered as the monarch who skillfully and sensitively brought the fabled desert kingdom from the camel tracks of the past to the international aviation maps of the future. His contribution towards reorganisation of the Jodhpur State Forces in 1922 and 1939, as also steering them through World War II is commendable. He truly was the builder of the modern Jodhpur. He died on 09 June 1947, due to a ruptured appendix, at Mount Abu.

The 'Raj-Tilak' ceremony of Maharaja Hanwant Singh was performed on 21 June 1947 at Mehrangarh Fort, Jodhpur. On 11 August 1947 when he signed the instrument of accession, he flourished a tiny revolver—cunningly hidden in a pen—at Sardar Patel, saying that he would shoot him if he betrayed the people of Jodhpur. He retained his title and an annual Privy Purse from the Government of Rs 17,50,000.
Photo Courtesy: Umaid Bhawan Palace

Maharaja Umaid Singh's son, Group Captain **Maharaja Hanwant Singh (1947–1952)**, born on 16 June 1923, was a keen aviator as well, but tragically died in an air crash on 26 January 1952 at the age of 29. He was married to Maharani

Krishna Kumari of Dharangdhra, Gujarat, on 14 February 1943. She passed away, on 03 July 2018, at the grand old age of 92 years. In those dramatic years Maharaja Hanwant Singh, with a 700-year-old legacy, acceded to the Government of India in 1949 and in 1950 Rajputana, a geographical combination of erstwhile princely states, became the new state of Rajasthan.

Left to right. Seated: Maharaj Devi Singh, Maharaj Himmat Singh, Maharaja Hanwant Singh, Maharaj Ajit Singh, Maharaj Kumar Gaj Singh and Maharaj Dalip Singh in 1951. **Standing:** Rao Bahadur Sawai Singh Lodha, Chanod Gurasa, Govind Singh Mehta, Maharaj Hanut Singh, Rajkumar Sobhag Singh, Maharaj Guman Singh, Maharaj Rattan Singh, Baldev Singh Bhati Satasar, Thakur Rattan Singh Bikamkor, Thakur Bhawani Singh Pokhran, unknown, unknown, Thakur Aidan Singh Pal, Lieutenant Colonel Dungar Singh, MC, Ranjitmal Bhandari, Manikchand Mutha Pal, unknown.
Photo courtesy: Surendra Singh Rajawat

Maharaja Hanwant Singh, who had merged his kingdom into the Indian Union, was contesting the first general election in 1952. On the day of the counting on 26 January 1952, certain of a win, the Maharaja took off for a celebratory flight in his two-seater Beechcraft Bonanza plane with Zubeida (his second wife). He was flying dangerously low and buzzed a *tonga* (horse-driven cart) trotting in the dry riverbed below. But as he pulled up, the aircraft hit power cables and crashed, killing both passengers instantly. Tragically, the Maharaja's independent party had won a landslide, taking 31 of 35 seats. A film called *Zubeidaa* written by Zubeida's son from her previous marriage, Khalid Mohamed, became a Bollywood hit in 2001. The details of the crash are covered elsewhere in the book.

President Dr Rajendra Prasad recognised **Gaj Singh, born on 13 January 1948,** as the 38th Maharaja of Jodhpur, in 1952, when he was only four years

Maharaja Gaj Singh at the age of four years when he was formally installed as the Maharaja of Jodhpur on 12 May 1952. He was recognised by the President of India under article 366 (22) of the Constitution with customary titles of 'His Highness Raj Rajeshwar Maharajadhiraja Maharaja Shri Gaj Singhji Bahadur, Maharaja of Jodhpur', with a Privy Purse of 10 lakhs a year. The Privy Purses were abolished in 1971.
Photo courtesy: Mehrangarh Museum Trust

old. Maharaja Gaj Singh fondly called as 'Bapji' by the people of Jodhpur, still rules in their hearts. The Jodhpur residents still see the family as their royals, and Gaj Singh as their Maharaja.

It was thanks to the efforts of these rulers that when Marwar became part of the Indian union after independence, it was not only Rajasthan's biggest state, but also its most modern.

The State of The Troops of Marwar in 1885

The origin of the Jodhpur State Forces goes back to long before the Indian Army came into existence in 1795. The Marwar army had a reputation going back to the early period of its history—a reputation signified during the Mughal period

Who are these remarkable men and what gave generations of them their exceptional courage?
A group of warriors called Rajputs in 1902. For more than 500 years the Rathores ruled the state
of Marwar. According to a Marwari quatrain in praise of the clans, 'In arms none surpasses the
Rathore'. Most grew strong bushy beards, parted in the middle and brushed stiffly upward and
towards the ears. The military was mainly represented by the Rajputs, who were the lords of the soil.
These old warriors lament the days that are passing by in words of Sir Alfred Lyall's verses, 'I cannot
learn in an English school, yet the hard word softens and change is best. My sons must leave the
ancient ways, the folk are weary, the land shall rest, and the gods are kind for I end my days'.
Photo courtesy: Mehrangarh Museum Trust

by the saying that their chief could command the services of one lakh swords,
'*Lakh Talwaran Rathoran*'. This force was largely composed of light cavalry and
formed an obedient and homogeneous army. Every soldier was the son of the soil
and most of them were proud of being the descendants of the same ancestor as

their chief. Their battles have now passed into the realms of song and story, which are still narrated dramatically by bards with patriotic enthusiasm. Numerous stories abound of its army clad in saffron robes fighting to the last man against frequently terrible odds and when inevitable defeat came, their women immolating themselves in a mass holocaust in faithfulness to their dead. Such astonishing sacrifices, known as *Johar*, are not to be found in the annals of any other country.

Richard Head and Tony McClenaghan in their book, *The Maharajas' Paltans* have said that, the armed forces of Marwar were formed from the feudal contingents provided by *Jagirdar*s (nobles) when needed, until Maharaja Vijay Singh's reign (1753–1793). However, the growing power of these nobles and increasing menace of the Marathas led Maharaja Vijay Singh to raise a small force of his own, chiefly composed of the foreign mercenaries—Rohilas, Afghans, Nagas and Purbias. At the time when the Maratha power was in the ascendant and the Pindaris were ravaging India, the Jodhpur forces numbered some 12,000 men, of whom 4,000 were Jagirdar Sowars. The latter, were called out to aid in time of war whilst the remainder, were a mixed force including guns, cavalry and infantry. The foreign mercenaries were still employed at this time and cost the state exchequer about two lakhs of rupees. Only half of the 8,000 were on duty at a time, the others being allowed leave, etc. These mercenaries were more unscrupulous and less faithful than the indigenous force. Thus, the Marwar army degenrated into a heterogeneous, indisciplined and poorly equipped force till conclusion of the treaty of 1818, whereby the state was freed from all fear of external attack, the necessity of maintaining a large standing army for the defence of the Raj disappeared.

Some of these men were habitual consumers of opium, which they consumed just before going to war. The Rajputs always fed some to their horses as well, so as to make them immune to fear and to permit them to better endure the fatigue of battle. Opium, which made the warriors fearless and oblivious to danger and increased their force and courage tenfold, worked as a cure-all for their soul. This excessive consumption of opium at the time of war led to a habit of daily consumption. Sanctioned by its usage, comes the Rajput expression of 'sharing of opium,' to ratify a solemn engagement, an inviolable promise. (The consumption of opium was not illegal and it was consumed openly and distributed to users while on active service even during the Great War. This practice was, however, completely eradicated during the inter-war period of 1919 to 1939).

On 06 January 1818 a treaty was signed with the British at Delhi, thereby bringing the State fully under British protection. Under article 8 of the Treaty of 1818, the Jodhpur Maharaja was required to furnish a contingent of 1,500 horse for the service of the British Government whenever required. This proved unsatisfactory and it was revised on 07 December 1835 by substituting the payment of 1.15 Lakhs annually for the obligation to furnish a contingent of 1,500 Horse.

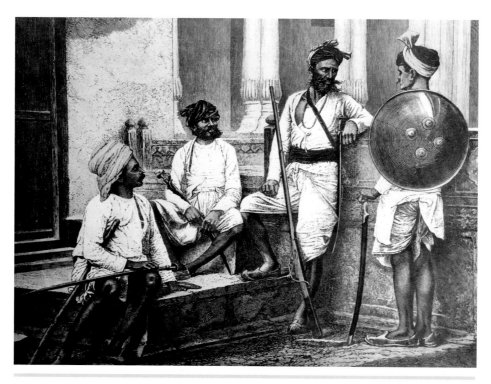

The Rajput warriors. A popular saying described the Rathore warrior: Horse, dress, turban, moustache and sword. These five things were inseparable from a Rajput.
Photo courtesy: Mehrangarh Museum Trust

This sum was at first devoted to the formation and maintenance of a Corps known as the Jodhpur Legion Cavalry and stationed at Erinpura. Recruitment for this force started in January 1836 at Ajmer, but in November of the same year the force moved to Erinpura, about 78 miles south of Jodhpur. The Jodhpur Legion was a composite force of cavalry, infantry and artillery. Subsquently the sum of Rs 1.15 Lakhs was also utilised for the upkeep of 43 Erinpura Regiment. In 1921 the 43 Erinpura Regiment was also disbanded.

As per *Hakikat Bahi* (record of events) with Maharaja Man Singh Pushtak Prakash, Jodhpur, Lieutenant Colonel James Tod who had the political duties of Marwar added to his portfolio, paid a visit to Jodhpur on 18 November 1818. He was received at the 'Daulat Khana' courtyard of the fort by Maharaja Man Singh who presented him with some books from his personal library. He noted that,

> Some years ago, Raja Man Singh had a corps of three thousand five hundred foot, and fifteen hundred horse, with twenty-five guns, commanded by Hindal Khan, a native of Panipat. There was also a brigade of those monastic

militants, the Bishanswamis, under their leader, Kaimdas, consisting of seven hundred foot, three hundred horse, and an establishment of rockets (*baan*), a very ancient instrument of Indian warfare. At one period the Raja maintained a foreign force amounting to eleven thousand men, of which number two thousand five hundred were cavalry, with fifty-five guns, and a rocket establishment.

In 1839 the military administration of the state's own forces was effectively re-organised under the supervision of the then Political Agent, Captain Ludlow. Until this time the soldiers were generally armed with matchlocks and swords, or pistols in the infantry. Mostly they were without officers, with a resultant lack of discipline and efficiency, to the extent that many of the soldiers mortgaged their weapons to money lenders. In 1841, acting on Ludlow's advice, Maharaja Man Singh disbanded two-thirds of his force, leaving only 4,000 as the total number of troops serving under him. In addition, there was a substantial force employed on guard duties in the palace, in escorting treasure and on other confidential duties. They were not included in the regular military force of the state and the payment of their salaries was also made separately.

1840, the Political Agent Captain Ludlow's signed seal of Jodhpur *Kucheri* (Government office) to reorganise Jodhpur forces.
Photo courtesy: Maharaja Man Singh Pustak Prakash

Some changes were made during the reign of Maharaja Takhat Singh (1843–73) as, at the time of the 1857 Uprising, the Raj troops numbered 3,200 and the Jagirdar horses 4,000. On 21 August 1857 the Jodhpur Legion revolted. They operated in Jodhpur State for some time and cooperated with Thakur Kushal Singh of Auwa until 10 October 1857, where they also defeated a local levy of the pro-British Maharaja of Jodhpur. Maharaja Takhat Singh was created GCSI for his support during the uprising.

In 1866 Maharaja Takhat Singh made a request for the services of a British officer, on a salary of Rs 500 per mensem, to drill the troops of his state. Interestingly, his request was denied on the grounds that the despotic power of the sovereign is largely checked by the knowledge of the inability of his ill-paid and ill-disciplined troops to coerce the Thakurs. If an officer were to be given, then, in a brief space the efficiency of his troops will be so much increased that the fear of opposition to the mandates of the Durbar would be removed, and who knows how the despotic power thus placed in the hands of the Chief would be used ?

At the beginning of the reign of Maharaja Jaswant Singh, in 1873, the Marwar military force consisted of 8,000 to 9,000 cavaliers and footmen and a sum of Rs 6,00,000 or so was spent every year on its maintenance. This motley rabble employed on police and escort duties was poorly equipped, undisciplined and undependable. The Maharaja entrusted its charge to his brother Maharaj Kishore Singh. He tried to introduce designations, uniform, drill and discipline on the British model, but could make little headway. Thus, till 1885, the Jodhpur state troops were a motley and untrained rabble, with officers who called themselves Colonels, Majors and so on, but training, discipline and proper equipment were non-existent. But while Maharaj Kishore Singh failed, his younger brother Pratap Singh succeeded with the introduction of the Imperial Service Troops Scheme.

FORMATION OF IMPERIAL SERVICE TROOPS

The Panjdeh incident in March 1885, when the Russians attacked an Afghan force on the North West Frontier, led to fear of an an impending war with Russia. This led Viceroy Dufferin to announce on 17 November 1888, the scheme of Imperial Service Troops (IST) i.e., the troops held for the support of the Imperial interests. He asked the Indian Princes to locally recruit their troops, train and equip them at their own cost, to a standard of regular army, so as to be available to the Government of India in times of war. Great care was taken that these troops should be the real state troops and not resemble the old contingents of

The C-in-C Jodhpur State Forces, (left) Maharaj Kishore Singh, (right) Maharaj Sir Pratap.
Photo courtesy: Maharaj Dalpat Singh Bhopalgarh

foreign mercenaries. It was hoped, incidentally, that these troops would furnish interesting and more active employment for young nobles and gentry to whom the life within the State might fail in affording a career, and to a certain extent it had these results.

After few months, on 16 November 1885, just after the completion of the railway from Marwar Junction to Jodhpur, on the Rajputana-Malwa line, **Viceroy Dufferin**, visited Jodhpur for the first time and stayed at camp in Paota. A cavalry squadron from Erinpura acted as escort with Sir Pratap and Hurjee (ADC to Sir P) riding on either hand of the Viceroy from Jodhpur station to the Paota Camp.

After the Viceregal visit in 1888, Maharaja Jaswant Singh expressed a strong desire to raise one regiment of cavalry and one of infantry as Imperial Service Troops, at once. The former proved an easy task and in 1889 the First Lancers Sardar Rissala, 600 strong was raised, but the Rajput of Marwar had no leanings for foot soldiering (Since cavalry had dominated the battlefield and the elitist cult of a horseman, with special rules and traditions always attracted Rajputs). It was then decided to raise a second regiment of cavalry instead of infantry. This offer was accepted and the following year, in 1890, the 2 Lancers Sardar Rissala

Maharaj Kishore Singh seated on a chair (centre), with his Jodhpur *Top Khana* (Gunnery) in 1888. The Indian State troops clothed themselves in a colorful blend of traditional European military uniforms and Indian items, such as elaborate turbans and kept up a military tradition.
Photo courtesy: Hemant Sharma, Udaipur

Jodhpur Camp Paota in 1885. The Ship House built in 1885 is on the left.
Photo courtesy: Dr Mahendra Singh Tanwar

600 strong was raised. By 1893 Jodhpur had two cavalry regiments called as 1 and 2 Lancers Sardar Rissala (also called as Jodhpur Imperial Service Lancers). Since the formation of these troops meant an increased expenditure, so subsequently, in 1893, the irregulars (all foot soldiers) were disbanded as being of no military value, thus leaving the Jodhpur army consisting of the Jodhpur Imperial Service Lancers and some traditional units consisting of artillery, cavalry, infantry and the Jagirdar militia for ceremonial purposes at much reduced numbers.

The British Government offered up-to-date arms, and lent officers to train these troops. An officer was appointed Inspector-General of IST, with a staff of inspecting officers and assistant inspecting officers, to assist in the training of these troops and to advise the Durbar on military matters connected with the troops. The technical training in the use of rifle and lance was given through the means of the IST Musketry School and by Annual courses of instruction in signaling by the Signaling Inspector of IST.

The various Imperial Service units were often superbly dressed, designed and changed at the whim of individual state rulers. When mobilised for active service the plain khaki drill service dress of the regular Indian Army was worn. It was emphasised that however you may dress your troops in glory for gala occasions, the war dress must be as simple and easy as possible.

A Musketry Class: Recruits at sword practice. Reliable men with a sharp sword or *tulwar*, a sharp lance, sharp pair of spurs and, above all, a good heart was the desperate requirement of the times in Marwar during 1888–89.
Photo courtesy: The Council of the National Army Museum, London

Types of the Imperial Service Cavalry at the Delhi Durbar, 1911. The Jodhpur Lancers trooper is second from right. Uniforms were a key element in regimental identity and pride. Each regiment cherished its own traditions and they all were magnificently different in their full dress uniforms.
Photo courtesy: The author

Soon after their raising some of these Imperial Service Troops, including the Jodhpur Lancers, took part in early campaigns on the North West Frontier of India and during the Boxer rebellion in China in 1900–01. By 1914, some 29 states were involved in Imperial Service Troop's (IST) scheme, providing strength of some 22,479 men, of which some 18,000 eventually served overseas, and throughout the four years of the Great War they were maintained in the field at the expense of their Rulers. To each unit of IST, as it was mobilised for service were attached two or three British 'Special Service Officers' (SSO) to advise and help the Indian Commandants.

Sir Pratap Singh— the Man Behind the Jodhpur Lancers

Born at Mehrangarh Fort, Jodhpur, on 22 October 1845, as the third son of Maharaja Takhat Singh, Sir Pratap Singh (1845–1922) was the best-known and most popular Indian of his day. Basically, he was a soldier—and a prince only incidentally. He was the Prime Minister of Jodhpur from 1878 to 1895 for his brother, Maharaja Jaswant Singh, and thereafter served as Regent of Jodhpur three times, during the minority of three young rulers of Jodhpur.

Sir Pratap began the first of his three terms as Regent of Jodhpur, when Maharaja Jaswant Singh died on 11 October 1895 and was succeeded by his minor son Sardar Singh. Sir Pratap remained Regent until 18 February 1898 when his nephew Maharaja Sardar Singh was invested with ruling powers. He then became the Maharaja of a small Rathore state of Idar, a position he held from 12 February 1902 to 05 April 1911. While serving at Idar, Sir Partap's heart was still in Jodhpur and he would often try and visit the state, but Viceroy Curzon (with whom Sir P did not enjoy particularly good relations) had left a note in 1902 that 'Sir Pratap must not on any account be allowed to get his foot at Jodhpur. To Idar is where I sent him and at Idar he will remain'.

However, on 20 March 1911, Maharaja Sardar Singh died suddenly, and was succeeded by his minor son, Sumer Singh. This necessitated Regency and Sir Pratap at once wrote from Idar, 'Taking into consideration my experience of four generations at Jodhpur and my own humble services to Government, I hope

The colourful, exotic, picturesque and striking figure of Sir Pratap in Jodhpur Lancers' uniform in 1887. He was a leading figure at Queen Victoria's Golden Jubilee of 1887 and Diamond Jubilee of 1897. He became the Victorian and Edwardian era's most admired prince, 'the beau ideal' of the Indian prince. In this photograph Sir P wears a turban of a blue-grey hue, with narrow stripes of dark red and off- white, heavily laced with gold; on his left there is a 'puff-ball' of black and gold threads from which emerges a 9" tall hooked ornament decorated with gold and black tufts and objects. The white kurta has no facing colour, but collar, cuffs and shoulder panels (reaching half way to the elbows) and the bottom of the kurta are all heavily laced with gold. There are gold shoulder cords and a gold aiguillette on the right shoulder. The breeches are white, and knee-boots black, with gold spurs. The cummerbund is scarlet with a line of gold embroidery in a Kashmiri pattern along the upper edge and a similar pattern, also in gold, on the hanging ends. The belt is gold lace with a central white stripe and gold buckles. The sword has a gold scabbard and guard, white ivory and gold sword knot and slings.

Photo courtesy: Umaid Bhawan Palace

and trust the Government will certainly be pleased to recognise my right to be appointed regent and serve my head family.' His request was accepted and he gave up his throne in April 1911 to return to Jodhpur as Regent to his young grand-nephew, and he was allowed to retain the title Maharaj Bahadur, with a personal salute of 17 guns. The term lasted from 06 April 1911 to 26 February 1916.

Sir Pratap Singh as Colonel of the Imperial Cadet Corps during the Delhi Durbar in 1911 and on the right is the original water colour painting by Simpkin in 1912. Sir Pratap was a dominant figure in princely India during the late 19th and early 20th Century. He counted amongst his friends the kings and queens of England including Queen Victoria, even the viceroy deferred to him. He was a dashing handsome man whose imperfections added to his appeal: his limp reminded of hunting accidents, his trademark Jodhpur ('band gala') coat and 'jodhpurs' were well worn and rumpled (he was the designer of the 'Jodhpur breeches', which became well known as 'Jodhpurs', and which became the approved habit of polo players the world over). He was also a daring and skillful *shikari* (hunter) and an extraordinary horseman. Sir P received a fixed salary and held no *jagir*.
Photos courtesy: (Left) Mehrangarh Museum Trust;
(right) Professor (Capt) Ashok Nath, FRGS, Nath Foundation, Sweden

History repeated itself yet again when Sumer Singh died suddenly at 1300 hours on 03 October 1918, at the young age of 21 years and was succeeded by his younger brother Umaid Singh, who again was a minor. Sir Pratap, still a Raj favourite, was recalled from the war in Palestine, and again became Regent of Jodhpur from 03 October 1918 to 04 September 1922, when this time Sir Pratap himself passed away.

In fact Sir Pratap was the de-facto ruler of Jodhpur State (off and on for 44 years and that is how he got the appellate *Sarkar*, meaning government or ruler) and he was the life and soul of Jodhpur public affairs; coercing wild tribes and handling truculent barons in his effective, summary fashion. He ruled Jodhpur with an iron hand. R.B. Van Wart, Sir P's admiring biographer, wrote: 'Not one person but received his orders, and woe betide him who failed to carry them out to his mentor's satisfaction. Before the lash of his tongue, strong man quailed and crept away like terrified children.'

He was quite a character. A born soldier, straight talking, efficient, with immense administrative ability, he was seen as the ideal embodiment of the Rajput prince. He was a favourite among the British, and he was knighted in 1885. He became an intimate friend of three British sovereigns. At Queen Victoria's durbar in 1887 he is said to have presented her not with mere jewels, like everyone else, but with his own sword, his most valuable possession as a Rajput warrior. Sir Pratap was one of the most famous of the Indian soldiers, and had rendered conspicuous service to the British Crown.

Despite his various responsibilities in Jodhpur and Idar, Sir Pratap participated in several British expeditions into Afghanistan and elsewhere. He was commissioned in the Jodhpur Lancers and accompanied General Neville Chamberlain's mission to Kabul in 1878. He was promoted Honorary Lieutenant Colonel in the British Army on 21 June 1887. He served in the Mohmand expedition on the staff of General Elles in 1897 and in the Tirah campaign as ADC to General William Lockhart in 1898, where he was wounded.

Sir Pratap Singh in 1911 at the Delhi Durbar.
A favourite of Queen Victoria, he always wore the miniature of Queen Victoria, set in pearls, presented to him by the queen herself on his turban.
Photo courtesy: Mehrangarh Museum Trust

He was promoted to Honorary Colonel on 20 May 1898. When it was decided to send a force from India to China in 1900 to relieve the foreign embassies besieged in Peking, Sir Pratap at once offered the services of the Jodhpur Lancers, and he accompanied them to take on the Boxer Rebellion.

Sir Pratap was promoted Honorary Major General on 09 August 1902. Furthermore, he was Honorary Commandant of the Imperial Cadet Corps (ICC) in 1903, and Chief of Indian Staff to the Prince of Wales during his tour of India in 1905–06.

He served in the Great War in France and Flanders 1914–17, and in Palestine and Syria in 1918. He was promoted to Honorary Lieutenant General on 03 June 1916.

He was Honorary Colonel of 34th Prince Albert Victor's Poona Horse from 19 November 1912, and Honorary ADC to the Prince of Wales from 24 May 1887 and to the King Edward VII from 11 January 1902–10, and to King George V from 03 June 1910 to 04 September 1922. (On 20 October 1922 Maharaja Bhupinder Singh Patiala was appointed Honorary ADC to the King on the vacancy occurring due to the death of Sir Pratap. There were only four who could be appointed ADCs to the King, the other three were Maharaja of Gwalior, since 29 November 1900, Maharaja of Bikaner and Nawab of Rampur, since 03 June 1910).

He received the Grand Commander of the Order of the Nile of Egypt in 1918 and Grand Order of the Legion of Honour of France and Star of Rumania in 1918. He received numerous other medals—Golden Jubilee 1887 and Diamond Jubilee bar 1897, Coronation 1902 and 1911, Delhi Durbar gold medal 1903 and 1911. He became the only Indian Military Knight Commander of the Most

January 1918: Sir Pratap took this photo before leaving France for Egypt and Palestine during the Great War. Jodhpur's history throughout the last years of the 19th century and early decades of the 20th century is dominated by the colourful and enigmatic character of Sir Pratap. Though never officially the Maharaja of Jodhpur, he was often regarded as such, having served as a minister to his brother and as regent for his nephew and two great-nephews. He had an untiring zeal for reform and he was determined to put the state in the forefront in every walk of life.
Photo courtesy: Raoraja Daljit Singh

Left: Hurjee, ADC and favourite of Sir P. Hurjee was given the *jagir* of Deoli in 1892. **Right:** Sir P wearing the splendid white and gold uniform of the Jodhpur Lancers during the Diamond Jubilee of Queen Victoria in June 1897. He looks every inch a soldier with flashing eyes, clear cut profile with a proud curl to the nostril, stern mouth with its touch of humour lurking in the corner. His name was a household word in England and India. Sir Pratap held no *jagir* and received a fixed salary of Rs 6,000 per month, out of which he gave Rs 500 each to his daughter and Hurjee every month.

Photos courtesy: Mehrangarh Museum Trust and Maharaj Dalpat Singh, Bhopalgarh

Honourable Order of the Bath (KCB) on 24 July 1901, Companion of the Most Honourable Order of the Bath (CB) on 20 May 1898, Knight Grand Commander of the Most Exalted Order of the Star of India (GCSI) on 22 June 1897, Knight Commander of the Most Exalted Order of the Star of India (KCSI) on 1 January 1886, Companion of the Most Exalted Order of the Star of India (CSI) on 29 July 1879, Knight Grand Cross of the Royal Victorian Order (GCVO) on 12 December 1911, (*Kaisar-i-Hind*) KIH 1 Class on 23 May 1900, besides the campaign medals. He was awarded the Knight Grand Cross of the Most Honourable Order of the Bath (GCB) on 1 January 1918.

Sir Pratap was over 70, probably one of the oldest men in the field during the Great War, and he came to Europe with the avowed intention of dying a soldierly death, 'To die in battle is not to die. A soldier's death, wherever won, is the best and greatest gift of life,' he would say.

The shrewd effective broken English of his speech was the delight of all who knew him. Sir Pratap had used the same directness when he first came to London on 20 June 1887 to attend Queen Victoria's Golden Jubilee at the formal invitation of the Queen Empress: Most of the rulers in those days used to stay at the Savoy or

Hurjee, Sir Pratap and Dhonkal Singh, in London, 1887, during Queen Victoria's Golden Jubilee. Dhonkal and Hurjee were as fine polo-players as India had ever produced. Hurjee died on 06 March 1903 and his son Major Dalpat Singh, MC, was killed in action at Haifa in 1918.
Photo courtesy: Maharaja Man Singh Pushtak Prakash

in Claridges or one of the great hotels of London, but Sir Pratap, when he arrived in England, said he would stay at Buckingham Palace. Somebody politely told him that Her Majesty had not invited him to stay in Buckingham Palace, to which he replied, 'Supposing I were to invite Her Majesty to Jodhpur would I expect her to stay in somebody else's house or hotel? So, obviously, Her Majesty will not expect me to stay in somebody else's house or hotel'. Upon which he forthwith entered Buckingham Palace. During the Diamond Jubilee of Queen Victoria in 1897 Sir Pratap was created a Grand Commander of the Star of India (GCSI) and the Queen herself did the honours and pinned the badge on Sir Pratap. Cambridge University also conferred the degree of Honorary LL.D on him.

Sir Pratap had his linguistic disabilities—his English reading and writing skills were indifferent. Although a lover of England and things English, he never became truly fluent in the language which *he spoke in a very idiosyncratic fashion*. He had wonderful English language replete with Marwari syntax and artful malapropisms which he ultimately evolved for himself. *He was famous for speaking in broken ungrammatical English that Britishers found charming.* His knack of summing up the situation in a most apposite and original phrase of broken English proved so entertaining to his hearers that he clung to it throughout his life (though his biographer suspected that this trait was a bit of an act that Sir Pratap played up when he found that it amused people). It became one of his trademarks and citing 'Sir P' became a minor industry in Raj publications! It was considered fashionable in the Raj establishment to admire Sir Pratap.

Stories concerning his peculiar brand of spoken English are legion. His quaint sayings are yet treasured and still recounted by generations of people in Jodhpur and the number of good stories attributed to him are endless. Here is one interesting tale. During a garden party, the Vicerene was talking to some of her guests, standing next to a duck-pond, in which some domesticated ducks were also paddling around. Sir P walked up to her and remarked conversationally, 'Your Excellency, you have beautiful *bataks*!'. The Vicerene blushed deeply, thinking that Sir P had remarked about her posterior. Her embarrassment was only relieved when one of the ADCs explained that *batak* was the Rajasthani word for a duck!

According to another anecdote that happened in Jodhpur in 1920, there was a strike at the Jodhpur railway workshop. A large number of strikers were sitting about quite peacefully near the entrance, and Sir Pratap rode that way. 'Very good thing, you liking striking, I liking shooting', was his way of dealing with the situation; and needless to say the words sufficed, and the strike was over. In another of his trademark remarks, while at Idar he would often be invited to participate in many polo tournaments and whenever he did not wish to participate, then he would simply wire, '*Me catching income, so sorry cannot come*' (Idar was a backward state and Sir Pratap was under pressure to improve its economy).

Beneath his native chivalry, he was a shrewd and critical judge of woman; and a delightful story is told by many about his remark at a big Calcutta reception when the woman he was talking to said, '*Sir Pratap, I want to introduce you to that lady over there.*'
Sir Partap gave one glance, shook his head, and said, '*No thank you; I not want. I thinking not very gentlemanly lady.*'
There is another story, dating back from the Great War, of an Englishman who saw a sturdy figure in a khaki great-coat standing near Buckingham Palace. Impressed by the look of him, the Englishman said:
'*May I ask what is your name?*'
'*Pertab Singh,*' was the answer.
'*What!, the Pertab Singh?*'
'*Yes, I the Pertab Singh,*' he said quite simply, but with quiet assurance.

He was celebrated for his bluff manner, his eccentricities, his skill as a soldier, his sportsmanship and his fine polo skills. At the same time he was a staunch defender and lover of Indian customs and manners. In private life he was modest, upright and staunch, a keen observer of men, and remarkable for character and intelligence. Sir Pratap's gallantry and old world charm won him many admirers, (Sir Walter Lawrence, Private Secretary to the Viceroy was his most important and influential friend) but he never ceased to speak frankly when the situation demanded it as on 22 February 1890, when Prince Albert Victor came and stayed for three days at Paota Camp in Jodhpur. The Prince was not a good horseman but he was keen on pig-sticking, so a reliable and well trained beautiful bay horse was made pig-shy for him. The Prince then went out with Sir Pratap at his side, watching him closely. Sir Partap was not satisfied with his manner of riding, and said promptly: *'Sir, you not riding like that, you riding like this. You riding like that you spoiling my mare.'*

The Prince said, *'Thank you, Sir Pertab, it is good of you to tell me the truth as people never tell me things, always saying I do perfectly.'*

Then again on the occasion in November 1921 when the Prince of Wales came to Jodhpur and was taken pig-sticking, a favorite and dangerous sport among the Jodhpur horsey set, at which Sir Pratap excelled. The Prince (the future King Edward VIII), although an accomplished polo player, was much less experienced

A rare signed copy by Prince of Wales (future King Edward VIII) with his first 'kill' at pig-sticking at Jodhpur on 30 November 1921. Sir Pratap (centre) and Maharaja Umaid Singh (right) are seen.
Photo courtesy: Mehrangarh Museum Trust

at the pig-sticking business, and made a careless mistake; he dismounted during the hunt that left him exposed, before the pig had been killed, which could have cost him dearly. Sir Pratap immediately admonished the headstrong prince to immediately remount, with the words: 'I know you (are the) Prince of Wales, and you know you (are the) Prince of Wales, but the pig doesn't know you are the Prince of Wales!'

There are many wonderful stories about Sir Pratap, his courage, his chivalry, his courtesy and **Sir Henry Newbolt** has turned one such story into a poem—'**The Ballad of Sir Pertab**':

> A young Englishman came to stay with Sir Pertab in Jodhpur. They went out shooting and pig-sticking together and there in 1901 he died of some sudden fever and a terrible problem arose. There were not enough Englishmen in the place to carry his body out to burial—there were three but a fourth was needed—and Sir Pertab said, 'I will be the fourth bearer of my friend's corpse',
>
> The Englishman said, 'You will lose caste if you touch his body', but Sir Pertab refused to pay any attention. Next morning the Brahmin priests were on his doorstep and said to him, 'You will have to do very severe purification.' Sir Pratap told them to go away and never speak of it again, because **there is a caste that is higher than any other caste and that is the caste of the soldier.**

> *In the first year of him that first*
> *was emperor and king,*
> *a rider came to the rose-red-house,*
> *the house of Pertab Singh.*
> *Young he was and an Englishman,*
> *and a soldier, hilt and heel,*
> *and he struck fire in Pertab's heart*
> *as the steel strikes on steel.*
> *Beneath the morning stars they rode,*
> *Beneath the evening sun*
> *And their blood sang to them as they rode*
> *That all good wars are one.*
> *They told their tales of the love of women,*
> *their tales of east and west,*
> *but their blood sang that of all their loves*
> *they loved a soldier best....*

It was Sir Pratap who raised the Jodhpur Lancers and created a polo team that, for a time, held the Indian Championship, besides winning laurels at Hurlingham and Ranelagh in England. Sir Pratap had invented the famous 'Jodhpurs' (riding breeches). He personified in his life and character the traditional virtues of the Rajputs but nevertheless managed to bridge the gap between the old ways and the new. During his last few years and close to 80 years he still lived mainly in riding boots and breeches and could still be described as '**the hardest nut one could ever wish to meet**'. Still he believed in 'making a boy hard', insisting on the disciplined life for all the young Sardars and Princes, turning them out at dawn on to the polo ground or pig-sticking field, discouraging all tendency to softness, as unworthy of a great fighting race.

The last New Year Card for Sir Pratap from his friend Field Marshal Haig, whom he described as the best of British Generals during the Great War. Haig sent this autographed childhood photo card of himself playing with his toy cavalry!
Photo courtesy: Raoraja Daljit Singhji

THE LAST WISH

Sir Pratap lived through rapidly changing times and finally died in the complex aftermath of the First World War. Once, he became ill in 1920 and at that time he prepared himself for death, by dressing himself in his finest uniform and sat on a chair with sword in hand, but despite these preparations he was two years too early to die.

However, when it was finally decided to invest Maharaja Umaid Singh with full ruling powers during the cold weather of 1922, Sir Pratap secretly expressed his last wish to Viceroy Reading in a private letter, on 18 July 1922 that he may be allowed to serve for a limited period in the Council of Maharaja Umaid Singh. He wrote:

> *My Most Esteemed and Valued Friend,*
> *I am glad that the minority administration is shortly to come to an end, and that Maharaja Umaid Singh, by close and steady application to his studies and work, has duly qualified himself to be placed in charge of his ancestral state.*

Sir Pratap in 1902.
Photo courtesy: The author

He would no doubt require assistance of old and experienced hands to begin with at least for a couple of years and a competent council will be placed at his service.

To serve the interest of the state of my birth as also to loyally help the descendants of my kind brother Sir Jaswant Singh Bahadur of beloved and revered memory I had abdicated the Idar 'gaddi' and am still anxious to pass my remaining days in serving the state and the illustrious head of my clan.

I have sanguine hopes that in consideration of my life-long services to the Jodhpur State and to the supreme Government, Your Excellency will be so good as to see your way to find a suitable place for me in the council that may be proposed to serve the Durbar for a limited period.

With sentiments of high esteem and regard, I beg to remain, Your Sincere friend, Pratap Singh.

However, on 12 August 1922 the Viceroy in a curt reply to the old veteran mentioned that 'it is really for the young Maharaja Umaid to decide the composition of his Council without my advice, unless he chooses to solicit it.' Viceroy Reading replied:

My dear Sir Pratap,

I share Your Highness' gratification that Maharaja Umed Singh has qualified himself for the exercise of ruling powers and I look forward to visiting Jodhpur some time in the cold weather for the purpose of performing the ceremony of investiture.

My friend, you ask me to find a place for you on the council which will assist him in conducting the administration after he has received his powers.

I think the best answer I can give you is to explain the position as I see it. The constitution of the council is a matter for Maharaja to decide and I feel that I must leave it to him to make his own selections with the advice of his Political

Officers and that it would be a mistake for me to attempt to influence his choice at the outset. You will, I know, realise how difficult it might be for all concerned if I were to say anything which the Maharaja might take as indicative of a desire on my part that he should appoint to his council someone on whom his own choice had not fallen.

I am deeply sensible of the great services which you have rendered to the ruling house and the State of Jodhpur, and I am mindful in particular of the sacrifice which you made in 1911 when you resigned the 'gaddi' of Idar in order to serve your much loved Marwar in her hour of need. His Highness will, I am sure, never forget what you have done for Jodhpur but it is really for him to decide the composition of his Council without my advice, unless he chooses to solicit it.

Sincerely Yours,
Reading.

Unfortunately, Sir Pratap died within days of receiving this curt reply from the Viceroy Reading.

THE END

Finally the end, when it came, was sudden; he took ill in the night and death claimed him in the early hours of the morning at 0700 Hrs on **04 September 1922**. The written report dated 05 September 1922 by Lieutenant Colonel J. W. Grant, IMS, the Residency Surgeon, Western Rajputana States says,

> Sir Pertab retired to rest on the evening of the 3rd instant, in his usual health, about 0230 AM on the 4th, Captain Hanut Singh called for me, saying that Sir Pertab had an attack of pain in the chest. I went to his house immediately but before my arrival the attack was over. I examined him, and heart, lungs and temperature presented nothing abnormal. He was talking as usual, and appeared at ease. I stayed with him till after 3 AM, when he went to bed, and expressed himself as feeling quite well. At 7 AM a telephone message came that Sir Pertab had another attack. I arrived shortly afterwards but found him dead. In my opinion death must have been instantaneous, and due to heart failure. Sir Pertab had no organic disease of the heart. There were signs of cardial weakness after his illness in January last, but no more than that to be expected at this advanced age.

King George V in a telegram dated 06 September 1922 wrote,

> I am grieved to hear of death of my old and valued friend Sir Pratap Singh and I assure you and people of Jodhpur and Idar of my sincere sympathy in their loss, which loss is also my own for His Highness was to me a true,

The marble memorial of Sir Pratap stands next to the small plain marble memorial stone of his ADC, Hurjee. Sir Pratap wanted to be cremated, not in the royal enclosure, but facing the polo ground next to his house.
Photo courtesy: Pradeep Soniji

devoted friend as he had been to Queen Victoria and to King Edward. He rendered gallant services to the Empire in the Tirah Expedition, China and in the Great War. His attendance upon me as ADC during my two visits to India gave me special opportunity for genial companionship.

Sir Pratap had left full instructions and he wanted to be cremated, not in the royal enclosure at the base of Fort, where he had the right, but facing the polo grounds near his house and next to his closest friend, Hari Singh of Deoli, fondly known as Hurjee. The last rites were performed, it was all very simple. The tiny band of Europeans, his relations and state officials attended. A dismounted escort of the state forces accompanied the cortege and sounded the last post; otherwise the ceremony was of a private nature. Today a simple marble *chattri* on a red sandstone base, without name or inscription, stands by the side of a plain memorial stone to his ADC, Hari Singh (Hurjee) of Deoli, to mark the passing of a great personality of his era. To the left of Sir Pratap's *chattri* is a red sandstone temple dedicated to Sugan Kanwar, who, in 1954, became the last recorded sati of the Rajputs. She was married to Brigadier Zabar Singh, whose maternal grandfather was Sir Pratap.

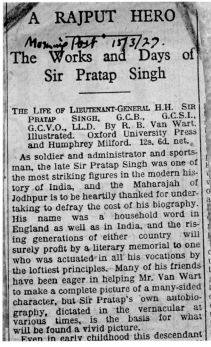

A RAJPUT HERO

The Works and Days of Sir Pratap Singh

THE LIFE OF LIEUTENANT-GENERAL H.H. SIR PRATAP SINGH, G.C.B., G.C.S.I., G.C.V.O., LL.D. By R. B. Van Wart. Illustrated. Oxford University Press and Humphrey Milford. 12s. 6d. net.

As soldier and administrator and sportsman, the late Sir Pratap Singh was one of the most striking figures in the modern history of India, and the Maharajah of Jodhpur is to be heartily thanked for undertaking to defray the cost of his biography. His name was a household word in England as well as in India, and the rising generations of either country will surely profit by a literary memorial to one who was actuated in all his vocations by the loftiest principles. Many of his friends have been eager in helping Mr. Van Wart to make a complete picture of a many-sided character, but Sir Pratap's own autobiography, dictated in the vernacular at various times, is the basis for what will be found a vivid picture. Even in early childhood this descendant

Left: A portrait of Sir Pratap Singh made by Mr J. P. Gangooly in 1927 still proudly hangs in the assembly hall of the RIMC, Dehradun. Sir Pratap had left behind to Jodhpur a memory and example which can never be forgotten. **Right:** A tribute published after his death.
Photos courtesy: Commandant RIMC and Mr Jon Lee

After Sir Pratap's death a committee was formed at Delhi with Commander-in-Chief as President, to collect funds to **'Perpetuate the memory of one of the most picturesque and striking figures in the modern history of India.'** A circular dated 17 October 1923, outlined the object of the Memorial Fund, and said:

> As a soldier and administrator, and a sportsman, Sir Pertab's record was unique, and made his name a household word in England as well as in India...It is unlikely that a reputation thus built up could ever fade, and it is in the interests of posterity, rather than in any apprehension that the name of 'Sir P', may be forgotten, that the idea of a definite and lasting tribute to his memory is put forward. By such a memorial the rising generations may be helped to keep in view the lofty principles and indomitable spirit which animated him.

In the last meeting of the committee held on 02 February 1926, the secretary of the committee announced that a sum of Rs 96,655 was collected (including 135 Pounds sent by King George V) and allocated among four projects: Rs 76,000 to endow three annual scholarships for Indian Cadets at the Royal Military

College, Sandhurst; Rs 17,000 for prizes to cadets at the Prince of Wales's Royal Indian Military College, Dehradun; and a portrait by Mr J. P. Gangooly, Calcutta to be hung in Dehrundun Military College at a cost of Rs 3,000; and production of a biography by Mr R.B. Van Wart (the cost of the biography was borne by the Maharaja of Jodhpur).

THE RAISING OF THE JODHPUR SARDAR RISSALA

The crest of the Jodhpur Lancers was a *cheel* on a brown background. This was not worn on uniforms, its use was restricted to letterheads, cards, mess crockery and vehicles, etc.
Photos courtesy: The author

It was during the reign of Maharaja Jaswant Singh of Jodhpur in 1888 that he ordered his trusted brother Maharaj Sir Pratap Singh to undertake the setting up of the Jodhpur Lancers as Imperial Service Troops (IST) and to do away with the old feudal system where the Jagirdar of the state supplied horses and men to the Maharaja of Jodhpur's personal forces. Sir Pratap, realising the vastness and the magnitude of the job in hand decided to appeal to the Viceroy of India to depute one of their best officers for the raising of the Jodhpur Lancers.

Major Stuart Beatson of the Bengal Lancers was selected to help raise the Jodhpur Sardar Rissala. So the raising of the regiment started with the attachment of Major Stuart Beatson (Later Major General) of the 11th Bengal Lancers, from August 1889, at a salary of Rs 600 per month. For five years Major Stuart Beatson

Perhaps the earliest of the Jodhpur photos. Sir Pratap on the left with his elder brother
Maharaja Jaswant Singh in 1878. Sir Pratap was *Musahib Ala* (Prime minister) of Marwar State
from 1878 to 1895.
Photo courtesy: The author

remained in Jodhpur, where he worked whole-heartedly to raise the Sardar Rissala.
He and Sir Pratap were also instrumental in formulating and popularising modern
polo in north India.

Jodhpur being the home of horses and camels had always produced good strong
horsemen and, with training, good cavalrymen, known for their discipline and
courage. It must be appreciated that a vast amount of recruitment for the Indian
Cavalry was done from this area, both for the cavalry as well as other branches
of the army. In fact three of the Indian Army cavalry regiments, the 16th Light
Cavalry, the famous 17th Poona Horse, and the 18th Cavalry were totally manned
by men from Jodhpur State.

When the IST scheme was introduced, Jodhpur's intention had been to raise
one cavalry unit (600 strong) and one infantry unit (1,000 strong) but, whilst
the cavalry was quickly recruited to its strength, the Rajputs of Jodhpur had no
leanings in the direction of marching on their feet and there were few applications
for infantry service (the Rajputs regards foot service as inferior, and it was thought
derogatory to belong to infantry, when tribesmen were serving in cavalry).
It was therefore decided to raise a second cavalry regiment. The title given to

Left: Sir Pratap as *Musahib Ala* (Prime Minister) Marwar State in 1880. **Right:** Major (Later Major General) Stuart Beatson, 11th Bengal Lancers, in 1891, in Jodhpur Lancers uniform. He was inspecting officer with the Jodhpur Lancers from 20 July 1889 to 19 July 1894. (His son Major C. E. S. Beatson, MC of 105 Royal Field Artillery was killed in Ypres salient on 3rd October 1917 during the Great War).

Photo courtesy: Umaid Bhawan Palace

the regiment was 1st Lancers, Sardar Rissala. From its formation until 1922, it consisted of three squadrons of Rathore Rajputs and one Squadron of Kaimkhanis with a strength of 600. In 1893 the 2nd Lancers, Sardar Rissala was raised, and comprised almost exclusively of Rathore Rajputs clan wise. Initially raised as a full regiment of 600, its strength was reduced to 300 (half regiment) in 1902. The strength of the Second regiment was allowed to fall below the sanctioned strength on account of the indebtedness of the state (it still cost the state Rs 7 lakhs anually, though initially in 1888 it was planned that the cost will be Rs 5.5 lakhs for the two regiments).

On 15th March 1889, just one week prior to his leaving India, after 41 years, **General Sir Frederick Roberts, C-in-C in India, visited Jodhpur** for the first time and spent a couple of days before leaving for Bombay. After reviewing the parade, he mentioned:

The cavalry were specially fine. The gallant Rajput horsemen of Jodhpur had always been famous for their chivalrous bravery, unswerving fidelity, and fearless self-devotion in their wars with the Mahrathas and the armies of the Mughal Emperors, and I felt, as the superbly mounted squadrons passed before me, that they had lost none of their characteristics, and that blood and breeding must tell, and would, if put to the test, achieve the same results now as of old. There could be but one opinion as to the value of the 'Sardar' Cavalry, so named after the Maharaja's son and heir, Sardar Singh, a lad of only nine years old, who led the little army past the saluting flag, mounted on a beautiful thorough-bred Arab.

General Roberts, again, in his banquet speech spoke words both memorable and prophetic. He said,

In the life of Colonel Skinner, which I have been reading again with increased interest since I came to Rajputana, we are told that, if we seek for a picture of chivalrous gallantry, unswerving fidelity, and fearless self-devotion, we have only to turn to the cavalry of the Rajput states, and particularly to that of the Rathores. We shall then find acts of resolute heroism that have not been surpassed by the troops of any age or country. It is the '*Izzat* or *Abroo*' of the Rajput which is dearer to him than life, and which makes him ready to sacrifice everything in defence of his chief and clan. Of one thing I am sure, that what has been done before will be done again should occasion require it, and we may rest satisfied, that no Rajput cavalry were more self-sacrificing to their ruler than the body of Rathore horse, now being raised at Jodhpur....And I can promise the princes, nobles and well-born Rajputs who take service in this cavalry that their birth and grand traditions of the Rajput race will be most carefully respected when the time comes for them to take their place in the field with the troops of the Queen-Empress of India!

Stirring words which were to be borne out in every detail on the fields of France and Palestine during the Great War.

Having arrived at Jodhpur on 07 August 1889, Major S. Beatson made his first progress report on state of the Jodhpur Sardar Rissala on 01 January 1890.

Major Beatson says,

Anything more chaotic than the state of the Sardar Rissala, it is difficult to imagine. No distribution of troops, no appointed officers or non-commissioned officers, no method in the issue of orders, no routine, old-men and smart boys, leggy walers and blood Arab ponies all mixed up without any discrimination, and dressed and harnessed in several different patterns.

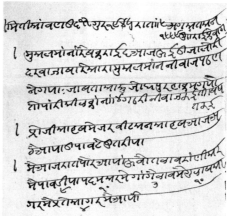

As per *Hakikat Bahi* (the day-to-day account of Jodhpur Court life) No. 35, Major Stuart Beatson was received at Rai ka Bagh Palace Railway Station Jodhpur on 07 August 1889.
Photo courtesy: Maharaja Man Singh Pushtak Prakash

He submits the following report:

ORGANISATION: All the 300 men (average age 22 years) were borne upon one roll, no squadron or troops existing. Certain of them drew higher rates of pay and possessed therefrom authority over the others, but no rules or regulations were in force to control this authority. There were no proper arrangements for cooking of food.

MEN: All men were recruited locally, are well-bred looking, hardy Rajputs of the desert, fond of horses and accustomed to ride from boyhood, they stand privation well, are light, active and ideal horse soldiers; all Rathores, a race amongst which bravery and endurance of hardship and pain are regarded as the highest virtues.

HORSES: The horses (average age 8 years) though all excellent in their class were somewhat uneven both in size and quality, sixteen-hand horses being side by side with thirteen-hand ponies and coarse-bred Walers mingled with high-caste Arabs.

ARMS: The weapons carried by the men were lances and swords, the former being too short to give a lancer the advantage he should have in the length of his weapon when at the 'Engage'; but the latter were light and serviceable *'Tulwars'*, the metal of the blade, however, being, in many cases, of very inferior quality.

SADDLERY: Only a few saddles were in use, the men riding chiefly on the *'Cheoti'*—a folded-up wadded quilt, fastened to the horse with a broad stuff surcingle, to which the stirrup leathers are attached. The bridles were of all sorts

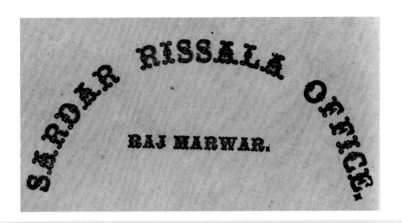

01 January 1890, First Progress Report Sardar Rissala by Major Stuart Beatson.
Photo courtesy: Kunwar Jagat Singh Raoti

and sizes, some men using bits of one, others of another pattern, whilst many rode their horses in chain snaffles.

UNIFORM: The uniform was of a particular neat slate-grey colour, comprising puggri (cloth worn round head as headdress), blouse with silver buttons, kumarband (waist sash), breeches and pattis (cloth worn round legs) with native shoes, the sword in a Sam Brown belt. The colours in the lance pennon were red and white.

MEDICAL ARRANGEMENTS: No medical provision for the care of the sick was at hand, so severe cases were sent to the city hospital, some three miles distant, whilst men suffering from lesser ailments went without treatment of any short.

LINES: The Regiment was not at one place, 160 men being located in one place, the remainder three miles away in another, thus rendering the communication of orders, and exact performance of routine or parade almost impossible. Officers and men had no knowledge of drill or weapons they bore, and there was no one who could teach them. While riding the men imitated riding tricks of the race-course with 'a hunched up back' and 'toes in front of the horses shoulders'.

Since Major Beatson possessed the friendship and confidence of Sir Pratap, so he was speedily able to ascertain his wishes regarding the arming and equipping, etc., of the Jodhpur Sardar Rissala. These were as follows:

- Sardar Rissala, be called after the Maharajkumar Sardar Singh.
- That the officers and men should receive net pay, all the horses, saddlery, arms and equipment being the property of the state.

- Rates of Pay.* Squadron Officers Rs 250; Rissaldars Rs 80; Jemadars Rs 40; Kote-Duffadars Rs 25; Duffadars Rs 18; Trumpeters Rs 14; Sowars Rs 12 per month.
- That the Regiment should be a class one, composed entirely of Rajputs drawn from the state territory.
- That the Regiments should be divided into four clan squadrons of Jodha, Mertia, Gogade, Khichis and Jodha, Kaimkhanis, Mertia, and Khichis Rajputs in 1st and 2nd Regiment respectively.
- That only suitable men be retained in the Sardar Rissala.
- That all unsuitable or undersized horses should be cast, no animal being in future purchased that was over 15 or under 14 hands.
- That the uniform remain the same, a Rajput plume and better quality blouse being added for full dress, whilst the lance pennon be changed from red to orange and grey (the colour of the Jodhpur flag).
- That Government be asked for Snider carbines, carbine buckets and revolvers, and new lances and sword obtained.
- That saddles, on the pattern recommended for the Bengal Cavalry, be obtained as soon as possible.
- That lines, to accommodate men and horses in one place is built on the Bengal Cavalry plan. (Subsequently the Jodha Squadron lines were built at Ratanada and the rest at Shekhawatji-ka-Talao. They received piped water supplied from Balsamand and Kailana lakes respectively).
- The Sardar Rissala will NOT be organised on the Silladar system, as the state is prepared to provide horses, arms, and equipment.

Brass Horse Martingale of the Jodhpur Sardar Rissala worn as part of horse furniture on the bridle. It consists of a garter-like strap bearing the inscription Sardar Rissala Jodhpore. At the centre within the strap the armourial bearings (State coat of arms) of Jodhpur.
Photo courtesy: Professor (Capt) Ashok Nath, FRGS, Nath Foundation, Sweden

*The men received British or '*Kaldar*' and Jodhpur silver coins as pay in rupee, half rupee and quarter rupee pieces. The coins were minted at Jodhpur, Pali, Nagore, Sojat, Jalore, Merta and Kuchawan mints. The Jodhpur coins had special marks of 'Jhar' or the 'Turra' of seven or nine branches and the 'khanda' or the sword. The Gold mohrs, half mohrs and quarter mohrs coined only at Jodhpur were sometimes used as coat buttons by the officers

The Jodhpur Lancers men in their new white uniform. Lord Roberts had remarked about them
'the ranks are smartly turned out in a most picturesque uniform; they are admirably mounted
and steadiness combined with dash shows how carefully the regiment have been instructed'.
Photo courtesy: Mehrangarh Museum Trust

- That Government be asked for the loan of the services of two trained Non-Commissioned drill instructors and one Trumpeter, and that a proper system of drill be introduced at once.
- FULL DRESS. Grey Puggri (lungi) and Silver Head Plume (turra), Grey Serge Blouse (kurta), Orange Kamarband, Breeches, Puttees, Ammunition Boots and Spurs, sword-belts, overcoats, blankets, badges, Grey and Orange Pennon.
- UNDRESS. Cotton Puggri, Grey Cotton Blouse, Grey Kamarband, Breeches, Patees, Boots and Spurs, Grey and Orange Pennon.
- SADDLERY. Bengal Cavalry pattern
- WEAPONS. Lance, Sword, Carbine-Snider, Revolver for Officers.
- STRENGTH OF SARDAR RISSALA.[#] Commandant–01, Squadron Commanders–04, Rissaldars–08, Jemmadars–08, Wordie Major (Adjutant)–01, Kot-Daffadars–08, Daffadars–48, Trumpeters–08, Farriers–08, Sowars–506.

[#] The Officers, Kot-Daffadars, Farrier Major and Trumpeters were armed with Revolvers and Swords whilst Daffadars, Farriers and Sowars had Carbines, Lances and Swords

RECRUITING: The recruits (all inhabitants of Marwar) were enlisted after being examined and pronounced fit by troop officers, the medical officer and the Commandant. Recruits, however, had flocked in and the competition for service in the Regiment had been very keen. The idea of military service was most popular amongst the Rajputs, who were thorough soldiers at heart and by blood. Sometimes the officers with recruiting parties were sent out to get recruits. The kit and uniform was issued to them from regimental stores on admission, the price of which was gradually cut from their pay. The 'Asamis' ('Asami' came to include the cost of horse, saddlery, equipment, accoutrements) amount was Rs 200.

It was the endeavour to spend the state money in the state and almost all the minor articles of equipment had been manufactured in the city, whilst the cloth for the men's blouses had been woven in the Jodhpur jail. After many trials by March 1890 it was decided to **dress the men in white Serge Blouse and white Breeches, with black Puttees and boots.** This was made in Jodhpur; it was durable and cheap, and looked exceedingly smart. In case of active service it could in a few hours be dyed a blue-grey colour of a most serviceable and invisible hue.

1903, an aerial view of Jodha Squadron lines at Ratanada, Jodhpur (now No 3 hostel). It consisted of small rooms with verandahs and horses stood picketed in front of each man's quarters. The rest of the lines were at Shekawatji-ka-talao near the officer's mess of Jodhpur Lancers, now with the Indian Army.
Photo courtesy: Mehrangarh Museum Trust

JODHPUR SARDAR RISALA (I.S.T.)
1912.

©Nath Foundation, Sweden

Jodhpur Sardar Rissala, Rathore Rajput, 1910: probably one of the most photographed and painted uniforms of the ISF included in Lovett's *Armies of India*. On the right a Jodhpur Sardar Rissala sowar in original watercolor by Henry J. Simpkins, 1912. The sowar wears a pale blue turban with yellow and red stripes at intervals, with a very long hanging end reaching below the waist at the back, and white tuft plume, white kurta faced grey; orange-red waist sash with narrow kashmir end border; brown waistbelt and narrow support strap over right shoulder. White breeches; dark blue or black putees. The bamboo lance with steel butt tip and lance head, orange over white swallow-tailed pennant, no wrist loop and gilt-hilted sword in black painted steel scabbard with yellow metal fittings. The colours of the Jodhpur Lancers pennons were saffron over white, depicting self-sacrifice and death with honour before surrender.
Photos courtesy: (left) The Council of the National Army Museum, London; (right) Professor (Capt) Ashok Nath, FRGS, Nath Foundation, Sweden

As per Major Beatson, 'Personnel' and 'material' were both available, and only method and teaching were required to produce in the combination of the Rathore and the Arab a very model for light cavalry. Soon, with the aid of Sir Pratap Singh, a selection of men and horses was made and followed up by a distribution of men into their clan troops. A site for the cavalry lines was also selected, and the building of the lines commenced under the directions of Mr W. Home, the State Engineer.

By this time the drill instructors had arrived. On 08 October 1889 the Government of India sanctioned the empolyment of three Non-Commissioned Officers, namely Daffadar Sudama, Lance Daffadar Narayan Singh and Trumpeter Gurditt Singh of the 11th Bengal Lancers in connection with the organisation of the Jodhpur Lancers. Their services were further extended by one more year on 22 September 1890. Two squads each of 10 specially chosen smart men, were handed over to them, the idea being to teach these men so much of the rudiments of true cavalry horsemanship and drill as would enable them in time to take squads, and thus diffuse the knowledge throughout the Regiment. Later few selected men were sent to Army Veterinary School Poona, Mhow, Arsenal, for instruction and repair of rifled arms, Surveying and Map reading at Roorki Engineering College, Musketry at Imperial Service Troops Central School, Meerut, and a course of physical training at Ambala. A gymnasium was built near the regiment lines for the better health and physique of the men and one man from each squadron of the two regiments had been sent to the 28th Light Cavalry to be trained as Gymnastic Instructors. A well-equipped hospital for the troops was also built on the approved standard plan.

It was the Maharaja's wish that **saddles should be ordered from England** as he doubted anything but the best articles would stand the extraordinary dryness of the Jodhpur climate. An order for saddles was accordingly despatched to a good English firm. Bits had been ordered out from Birmingham. After several trials an admirable lance was decided upon, its length with sufficient lightness whilst the point had great penetrating power and strength. With regard to the **sword there was more trouble, the difficulty being to combine cutting power and lightness,**

One amongst the 100 curved blades purchased in April 1912 from Messrs Mole and Sons, Birmingham, belonging to Aman Singh Jodha.
Photo courtesy: Ransher Singh Rathore, Digarana

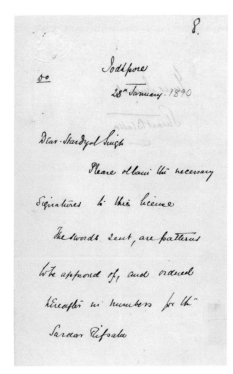

Left: Major Stuart Beatson orders for new pattern swords for Sardar Rissala on 28 January 1890.
Right is Ugam Singh Chandelao, Maharaja Sardar Singh and Captain Dhonkal Singh wearing
embroidered kurta with 'cummerbund' beneath sword belt, Jodhpur Lancers uniform in 1902.
Photos courtesy: (Left) The author; (right) Mehrangarh Museum Trust

but the Maharaja was pleased with the result of various deliberations and the
men highly approved of the weapon. A total of 600 sword blades were imported
from Messer's King King and Company England in September 1890. Another
600 sword blades were imported from Messrs Mole and Sons of Birmingham
in May 1891 (these were better than the earlier consignment of 600) for
2nd Lancers Sardar Rissala. Another 200 sword blades were purchased from
Messrs Mole and Sons in March 1897 to replace the broken blades and further
100 more curved blades purchased in April 1912 from the same firm. In the
meantime the Government had acceded to the request for Snider's Carbines and
38 pistols and that supply was soon provided.

By August 1890 the Sardar Rissala was able to put two squadrons on parade, and
the riding drill of the men had made a good progress. The great test of the cavalry
was to be able to make a long steady advance, with two or three half changes
of front, finishing with a dashing charge, a break-up in disorder and quick rally.
These movements were performed by the Regiment before the Adjutant-General
of the army, winning very high praise from him.

The waist belt plate worn by officers of Jodhpur Lancers on a zari belt. An oak leaves wreath and the monogram, in silver on gilt brass plate. The silver plated initials on the plate can be read as RIC or as RJC. With the passage of time and absence of records, its exact meaning has been lost. According to Prof (Capt) Ashok Nath, an authority on Indian military insignia, there is a possibility that it is based on an earlier design of belt plates worn by the Jodhpur cavalry of the Jodhpur contingent which had been raised in 1835 and disbanded in 1857. The 'R' possibly is for Rashtra or Rastrik which subsequently through general use crystallised into Rathore. Another waist belt plate with similar initials but with slight modifications has been identified as belonging to the Rohilcund Irregular Cavalry.
Photo courtesy: Lt Manveer Singh Jodha

Major S. Beatson writes that the officers had shown signs of assuming the authority of their rank conferred on them, whilst the men yielded themselves most obediently and cheerfully to such discipline as it has been deemed wise to enforce. It was greatly encouraging to see the way in which clan vied with clan and sowar with sowar to accomplish the best possible work. The 11th Bengal Lancers instructors said that all day long the men were running to them to have little intricacies of drill and niceties in the use of weapons explained to them, and night after night when returning home, the men were heard repeating words of command to one another, and the instructors noticed them practising the lance exercise and drill formations en route. Major S. Beatson had spent hours amongst the officers and men talking of the deeds which have won the Indian Order of Merit (IOM), and have had to fully explain all the conditions which regulate the award of these decorations. Such conversations had generally closed with the following expression from one or the other men that, 'Zarur milega ya marjaega' ('I will certainly win it or die').

The Prime Minister of the state, Sir Pratap, a born soldier, spared no time, trouble or money in making the regiment as efficient as possible. Major S. Beatson had received instant assistance and strong support from Sir Pratap. The following incident was one of many, but it would more than suffice to explain how Sir Pratap made his own feelings pervade all under his command. **Music as a profession was not thought highly of amongst the Rajputs. Naturally enough there was some** demur amongst the Rathores when volunteers were called for Trumpeters. On Major S. Beatson casually mentioning this to Sir Pratap, he at once sent off for a trumpet, and in half an hour all were in the lines, **Sir Pratap himself taking a lesson from the 11th Bengal Lancers Trumpeter, in front of all the men.** Next morning during the parade there were a dozen men hard at work, blowing away, all cheery hearts and lusty lungs, proud of their new office. It had always been an axiom that Rajputs would not brook strict discipline, but one and all followed the splendid example of Sir Pratap.

The Viceroy Lord Lansdowne paid a visit to Jodhpur on 05 November, 1890. The Viceroy was received by Maharaja Jaswant Singh, accompanied by the Resident Colonel Powlett and Colonel Sir Pratap, the *Musahib Ala* (Prime Minister), and Maharaj Kishore Singh, the C-in-C Jodhpur State Forces. A guard of honour was drawn up in the railway premises. A detachment of Sardar Rissala, furnished an escort and a royal salute of 31 guns was fired by the artillery from the Mehrangarh Fort as the Viceroy alighted from the special train. This time the Viceroy was housed at the bungalow of Hurjee, instead of at Paota, where distingished visitors had previously been lodged.

The glittering uniform of embroidered coats and lungis with *turras* (gold-headed plumes) were worn by the Sardar Rissala Officers. The sowars wore a neat uniform, white in colour. They were well-equipped and had silver *turras* (gold/silver thread cockade on a turban with ends drooping over), shining over their heads. The horses of the Rissala were mostly Arabs and Walers.

The Viceroy Lord Lansdowne reviews the Sardar Rissala on parade. The princes clung to their armies as signs of prestige and a form of patronage for their clansmen.
Photo courtesy: Mehrangarh Museum Trust

The Sardar Rissala consisting of four squadrons was drawn up in a line and inspected by the Viceroy on the parade ground situated to the east of the new cavalry line with Chittar hill in the South-West as the background. The regiment was under the command of Sir Partap Singh who had on his right the young Maharaj Sardar Singh seated on a chestnut mare. The Squadron Commanders were Maharaj Zalim Singh, Kunwar Arjun Singh (son of Maharaj Kishore Singh), Maharaj Daulat Singh and Kunwar Shivnath Singh of Bera.

The whole troops were armed with lances and swords. The march-past took place, first at a walk and then at a trot. The Sardar Rissala troops put up some skilful riding; they jumped walls and open drains, rode up and down steps, crossed bridges, and rode through a narrow passage between high walls. Sir Pratap Singh by the motion of his hands made the troops follow him at a rapid pace and then the order for 'charge' was given. With it raised a deafening shout of '*Hari-Hari-Hari*' and the horses proceeded at a tremendous pace. The gallop was then slackened into a trot and the trot into a walk. It was then ordered to proceed at a gallop and when the troops were 50 paces from Viceroy, 'Halt' was the order. The whole cavalry came to a stand still and gave a Royal salute. It was very pleasing to see the whole troops performing many difficult movements without any fault.

At five in the evening some sports such as tent-pegging and goat cutting were shown to the Viceroy on the ground adjacent to the camp. It began with a tent-pegging exercise in different orders, sometimes the party proceeding together in a line, at others from opposite directions in divisions. To make the sport more complicated 'tattis' intervened to be jumped over and then the pegs were to be picked up. The goat cutting sport was a still more challenging mock battle exercise. Four or five goats were hung up at equal distance and the players galloped at full speed, cutting each goat with their swords as they passed. Then a handkerchief was picked up from the ground, while the horse was being ridden at full speed. Captain Hari Singh (Hurjee) cut the most prominent figure throughout, and the Maharaj Kunwar Sardar Singh with some other boys of the Nobles School showed their skill in horsemanship.

At six in the morning the next day, the guests went out for Pig-Sticking, the sport of Jodhpur. Two parties were formed. The first consisted of the Viceroy; Lord William Beresford; Colonel Digby; Colonel Powlett; Sir Partap and Major S. Beatson. The second consisted of Maharaj Zalim Singh, Mr Charles Harbord, Captain Streatfield, Captain Cornish and Mr Erskine. They went to 'Khema-ka-kua', 'Bolia-Bhakar' and Soorpura bund preserve, near Jodhpur, where the hogs were brought down the hill in the adjacent plain to be pursued and speared. The Viceroy, mounted on a roan mare, pursued and secured the first four boars (in pig-sticking the privilege of delivering the first spear was given to the most important

Top: The Jodhpur Rissala men jumping a wall.
Copyright: General Amar Singh Library Museum and Trust

Bottom: A boy soldier—Maharaj Kumar Sardar Singh in 1890, wearing Jodhpur Lancers uniform.
Photo courtesy: Colonel Girwar Singh Dakhan

Camel transport carts were extensively used during the pig-sticking meets to ferry the logistic
requirements of the riders.
Photo courtesy: Thakur Praduman Singh Chandelao

person of the hunting party). After a good day's sport the parties returned satisfied
to the camp at about 9 AM.

At night the entire city was picturesquely illuminated with Chinese lanterns and
thousands of tiny earthen lamps containing wicks floating in oil, giving the effect
of a myriad glow-worms shining in the darkness. **At the State Banquet Sir Pratap
Singh, on behalf of Maharaja Jaswant Singh, gave a speech and said as follows:**

> His Highness the Maharaja heartily thanks Your Excellency for having
> honoured Jodhpur with a visit….We cannot suppose that the Sardar Rissala,
> the organisation of which began but a few months ago, is already equal to
> the old cavalry regiments of the British army, but we do claim to have tried
> to do what it was possible to do in a short space of time towards making
> it fit for service, and we are glad to know that Your Excellency considers
> a good beginning to have been made. Your approval and gracious words
> are a great encouragement to us and we look to the future to prove that our
> troops are worthy of the high expectations formed of them.

The Viceroy in replying spoke as follows:

> Your highness has supported the IST Scheme initiated in 1888 by my
> predecessor, Lord Dufferin. I trust that Your Highness will allow me to

express my admiration for the magnificent body of troops which appeared under the command of your highness's brother, Sir Pertab Singh, upon parade, yesterday morning. The Sardar Rissala has, I understand, been for less than a year under special training; and extraordinary smartness of the regiment is only to be explained by the fact that to both officers and men the service is a labour of love. The Chief Inspecting Officer, Colonel Mellis has reported to me that in no state has a greater spirit of enthusiasm been manifested than in this. I trust that the time may be far distant when the Government of India may find itself called upon to ask the Jodhpur state for the use of its troops, but of this I feel sure that should that time ever come, the Sardar Rissala, and the distinguished officer who commands it, will claim a place which will give them an opportunity of showing that chivalrous traditions of the Rathore family have not been forgotten in this state.

The dancing girls dressed in their finery, accompanied by nautch musicians, performed the *Ghumar* dance. The traditional dancing of India was a source of fascination for the British.
Photo courtesy: Mehrangarh Museum Trust

The Viceroy, accompanied by the Maharaja, then witnessed the *Ghumar* dance. The Viceroy left Jodhpur on 08 November 1890.

In 1892–93 the concept of Cantonment system for the Jodhpur Lancers, was initiated. The construction of the Jodhpur Lancers Officers Mess started in 1892 on a high ground, near a *talao* (pond) known as 'Shekhajee Ka Talao' (it was then called mess-house and comprised of an eating room, a sitting room and offices) and the area around it was converted into Lancers lines called as 'Shekajee Ka Talao' lines. The Jodhpur Lancers shifted into the new location in 1893. It may be worth mentioning here that Jodhpur was the first state to start the mess concept for officers, on lines similar to British messes.

Later in 1918 (probably to commemorate the success of the Jodhpur Lancers in the Great War), a small temple was constructed as an extension to the officers mess building, which was operated by the royal priest. In 1951 the mess building alongside other assets was handed over to the Indian army, excluding the temple. This majestic building was declared a heritage building in 1973 and is now known as **'Battle Axe Officers Mess' and serves as Officers Mess for the Infantry Division.** The temple later became an independent operating agency vide a court order and is known as 'Bala Ji Ka Mandir'.

Today a old *chhatri* from the lawns of the erstwhile Sardar Rissala officers mess (a heritage building) overlooks the 'Shekhajee ka talao' and the majestic Umaid Bhawan Palace in the background.
Photo courtesy: the author

On 19 July 1894, the eventful five-year tenure of Major Beatson came to an end, where he not only helped raise the Sardar Rissala but also introduced modern polo in Jodhpur. The request for further extension by one more year was not granted and Major Beatson thus went away on two years of furlough leave to England. Captain H.R. Tate with one assistant officer was attached with Jodhpur after Major Beatson's departure. Around this time when the raising was completed, Sir Pratap would often ask any visiting British official, 'You thinking, Sahib, being more war soon?'. He would ask them anxiously, waiting for a chance to show what his cavalry could do. In 1895–96, two squadrons were deputed to the Sindh border to prevent Hur outlaws from entering Marwar.

On 24 November 1896 the Viceroy Lord Elgin visited Jodhpur and inaugurated the Jaswant Zenana hospital and Elgin Rajput School in Mandore. He inspected the Jodhpur Lancers and took a group photo with their officers.

The view of Jodhpur Fort and bazaar in 1896. In 1896 the Jodhpur city also had a light tramway (two feet gauge) for passengers and a conservancy tramway for removing refuse of the city (the rail tracks can be seen on left side). All the buildings had stonework-latticed windows, mouldings, traceries, cornices overhanging the street—so exquisite that they seem wafted out of a fairy tale. The shrine rises in tiers of jutting eaves like a pagoda, the front has an embroidery of stone screens and at the entrance stands marble elephants.
Photo courtesy: Mehrangarh Museum Trust

	Commandant.	Squadron Commanders.	Rissaldars.	Jemadars.	Duffadars.	Trumpeters.	Sowars.	Total.	Horses.	REMARKS.
PRESENT ON PARADE.	1	4	6	7	48	13	426	505	505	
ABSENT. { Sick and convalescent	...	...	...	...	...	...	30	30	7	
Regimental Duty ...	...	...	...	1	2	1	11	15	15	
Garrison Duty ...	...	...	1	...	1	...	20	22	22	
On Command leave, &c.	...	...	...	...	1	...	32*	33	65	*includes 30 recruits
Short ...	...	...	1	...	4	2	...	7	...	
Total ...	1	4	8	8	56	16	519†	612	614	† excess Sowars 7

Zeatap [signature]

MAHARAJ DHIRAJ LT.-COLONEL, K.C.S.I., Commanding.

Left: Parade State of First Sardar Rissala signed by Sir Pratap Singh, 25 November 1896.

Photo courtesy: British Library, London, UK © British Library Board. All rights reserved/Bridgeman Images

Top: 25 November 1896: a group of proud Marwaris (Marwari refers to people from Marwar). **Seated from left:** Captain A.G. Peyton 9 Bengal Lancers, unknown, Colonel H.R. Tate 15 Bengal Lancers, Sir P, Colonel H. Mellis (Inspector General IST), Major Hari Singh (Hurjee), Captain G.A. Cookson 16 Bengal Lancers, Dhonkal Singh with officers of Jodhpur Lancers. Hari Singh and Dhonkal Singh were the Commandants of 1st and 2nd regiments at the time. Some of the officers are seen wearing the India General Service Medal with clasp Hazara 1891.

Photo courtesy: Raoraja Daljit Singhji

PARADE STATE OF SARDAR RISSALA.
Second Imperial Service Lancers.
Jodhpore, the 25th November 1896.

	Commandant.	Squadron Commanders.	Rissaldars.	Jemadars.	Duffadars.	Trumpeters.	Sowars.	Total.	Horses.	REMARKS.
PRESENT ON PARADE.	1	4	6	8	46	14	424	503	503	
ABSENT { Sick and convalescent.	...	...	...	...	...	...	14	14	34	
Regimental Duty ...	...	...	1	...	1	1	7	10	10	
Garrison Duty ...	...	...	...	...	...	...	...	...	...	
On Command leave, &c.	...	...	1	...	2	1	79*	83	62	*includes 72 recruits
Short ...	...	...	...	...	...	...	7	7	...	
Total ...	1	4	8	8	56	16	524†	617	609	† excess Sowars 12

Major, Commanding.

MEMO.
Sardar Rissala, Jodhpore.
The 25th November 1896.

MEN.		HORSES.	
	yrs. months. days.	Percentage of Caste:—	
Average age ...	23 10 20	Arabs ...	64·93
	ft. in.	Walers ...	8·22
Average height ...	5 6 nearly	Country-Breds ...	26·05
	St. lbs.		yrs. months. days.
Average weight ...	9 11	Average age ...	8 6 2
			hands. in.
Weight in marching order ...	15 5½	Average height ...	14 2

Left: Parade State of Second Sardar Rissala signed by Major Hari Singh (Hurjee), 25 November 1896. **Right:** Memo Sardar Rissala, 25 November 1896. The Squadrons bore the names of the Rajput lineages: Jodhas, Khichis, Mertias, Gogades, Kaimkhanis (originally Rajputs). Out of a total of 1,200 horses, the force had 779 Arabs, 322 country-bred and 98 Waler horses.
Photo courtesy: British Library, London, UK © British Library Board. All rights reserved/Bridgeman Images

A reporter accompanying the Viceroy Elgin filed this report after the visit to the Mehrangarh Fort,

It is a very imposing mass of fortification, rising some hundred feet sheer from the solid rock, and its upper part stands fully four hundred feet above the town. On the top of the wall facing the town is a splendid collection of ancient guns some four hundred years old and of curious workmanship. Some of them are breechloaders and are interesting as showing how old this type of gun is. From this terrace there is a wonderful view of the city and surrounding country. The wall here has no battlements and standing on the edge as on the edge of a cliff one looks down from the dizzy height on the plain beneath. The houses, trees, lakes, palaces and roads, which are seen winding out to the horizon, look like the minute patterns on a carpet which is drawn up beneath one's very feet. There is also in the fort a collection of arms and armour of great worth, and the jewel house is a veritable Aladdin's Cave. Immense quantities of huge emeralds and pearls, necklaces and bracelets, cases of rings and jewels of all sorts, cut and uncut are shown in glass-covered boxes, whilst in others are fine old gold enamel and golden vessels studded with rubbies and precious stones. All around the room are heaped up silver trappings for elephants and horses, silver baths and basins, maces, sticks and umbrellas, all of precious metal. Some of the gold and enamel horse furniture and harness is most gorgeous. Above these buildings is the 'Zenana Mahal' of red stone, beautifully carved and ornamented and of great size.

The rows of ancient guns at Mehrangarh Fort terrace. These big fat guns must have used up elephants on elepahnts to mount here—the antique guns will always look out from the naked rock and hard browed walls of the fort that stand up, steadfast, indestructible, proud, above the dust-veil and the city sheltering at their feet. At sundown they are lambent in every seam and wrinkle with cold violet-blue, at dawn they will glow with hot carmine, but always they will be there. As some Britisher had said 'the city may change, but, night and morning, the fastness of the Rathores will endure for ever'.

Photo courtesy: Mehrangarh Museum Trust

The state elephant in gold-sequin-embroidered scarlet covering with gold howdah and gold-studded straps neck to shoulder, back to tail, made a gorgeous background. The mahout in scarlet with a saffron *puggaree* sits atop as the elephant plods along with natural gravity at Ratanada Palace, which was all decked up during Viceregal visits.

Photo courtesy: Mehrangarh Museum Trust

The Rissala was at times also used to suppress dacoits who could not otherwise be brought to book. On 18 September 1903 a party of the 1st Regiment Sardar Rissala, consisting of an officer and 14 men, had an encounter with dacoits in the village Jamla of the Sankda Pargana. Six of the dacoits with four camels were killed and four were wounded and captured. The gallant services of the officer and men were rewarded by the Maharaja.

Two officers of Jodhpur Lancers with Marwar police. They were armed with Brown Bess and Percussion Muskets.
Photo courtesy: The author

Besides dealing with dacoits the worst problem in Rajputana was draught and consequent famine, such as the one that occurred in 1898–99, when the population of Jodhpur declined by a staggering 500,000, a 20% drop and half of the State's cattle died. The draught often caused severe lack of fodder for the horses at Jodhpur and consequently the squadrons were moved to Bali and Anandpur Kalu farms, etc.

In 1932 Maharaja Umaid Singh instituted the Jodhpur State Police Medal for meritorious service.
Photo courtesy: Rishi Srivastava

The strength of the Marwar Forces in March 1904 stood as under:

Imperial Service Cavalry (Sardar Rissala).......... 732
Local Force*
        Cavalry......................548 (including camel sowars)
        Infantry 2,171
        Artillery 254
In addition, the irregular militia, supplied by the *Jagirdars*, mustered about 2,019, of which 1,785 were mounted men and 234 infantry.

The number of guns was 121, out of which only 75 were serviceable—namely 45 field and 30 fort guns.

---

* The local military forces were principally utilised as local postal escorts and carriers of messages. At the rate of one horse per Rs 1,000 of Rekh, the *Jagirdars* were required to provide 4,179 horses (3978 Sowar + 402 Footmen, two footmen being reckoned as one Sowar in feudal service). Rekh signify the estimated income and tax of a village and Jagirdar had to pay fixed 8 per cent of the rekh as annual stipend to the Durbar in mid-19th century Jodhpur. Military service was rendered at the rate of one horseman for each thousand rupee of the revenue and one camel or footman for fraction of one thousand rupees exceeding Rs 750 and Rs 500 respectively. However in times of emergency the *Jagirdars* were bound to serve the Durbar at their own expense with all their followers.

The Jodhpur Lancers in Early Campaigns from

1891 to 1902–

Hazara (1891); Mohmand and Tirah (1897–98);

Transvaal South Africa (1900-1902)

and China (1900–01)

HAZARA EXPEDITION 1891

In 1890 the Hassanzai and Akazai tribes of Pathans attacked a reconnaissance expedition, in advance of road construction, in the Black Mountain area of Oghi Fort, on the banks of the Indus River, in the Hindu Kush Mountains, on the North West Frontier of India.

The Pathan tribes Jirga (North West Frontier tribal conclave), Black Mountain Area 1891.
Photo courtesy: Mehrangarh Museum Trust

It was decided to send a Black Mountain Expeditionary Force under Major General W.K. Elles to reinforce the provisions of an 1888 treaty with the Hassanzais and Akazais, which permitted British forces to move freely along the border running north-east of the Indus through the mountains. The units selected for the mission included 11 Bengal Lancers then stationed at Rawalpindi, to which unit Major Stuart Beatson belonged.

While the preparations for the expedition were underway, Sir Pratap and Major Beatson hatched a plan at Jodhpur to somehow ensure that some men from Jodhpur Lancers should also be selected for this expedition. A case was moved to attach a few men of the Jodhpur Lancers with the 11 Bengal Lancers, in the garb of training with them.

The soldiers overlooking the Indus Valley, Black Mountain Expedition 1891.
Photo courtesy: Mehrangarh Museum Trust

On 05 January 1891 permission was granted to a squad of 24 officers and
men (including Captain Hari Singh, Dhonkal Singh, Pratap Singh and others)
from the Jodhpur Lancers for training in musketry and routine duties with the
11 Bengal Lancers, at Rawalpindi. And when one Squadron of 11 Bengal Lancers
was detailed in January 1891 to form part of the Third Brigade, under Brigadier
General Sir W.S.A. Lockhart, then special permission was granted to these
24 men of the Jodhpur Lancers to accompany this 11 Bengal Lancers Squadron
for the expedition!

It certainly looks that the plan hatched by Sir Pratap Singh and Major Beatson to
first get Jodhpur men attached with the 11 Bengal Lancers regiment in the garb
of training and then stake claim to participate in their first ever campaign worked
very well! Though not much fighting took place, the Jodhpur men gained some
valuable first-hand lessons.

By the end of November 1891 the units were ordered to return to their garrison
after peace was established with the Pathans. No battle honour was awarded for
this campaign, however the soldiers who had served in the campaign were awarded
the India General Service (IGS) Medal with the clasp 'Hazara 1891'.

Till this time the IST, still under various stages of raising, were not allowed to participate in any active service and thus were not entitled to receive any campaign medals. But on 06 July 1892 the IST was also made eligible to war medals by the Military Department. Subsequently a case was moved and the medal for the Jodhpur Lancers men was also approved on 29 August 1892. Thus, these 24 men of the Jodhpur Lancers earned their first campaign medal, the IGS Medal with clasp HAZARA 1891.

However, the main person who hatched this plan, Sir Pratap was not granted permission to take part in this expedition, upon which he immediately shot off a letter to General Roberts stating that he be allowed to resign his command of the Jodhpur Lancers and his honorary rank of Lieutenant Colonel be taken away. General Roberts, in reply, urged patience and said, should a suitable opportunity arise, Sir Pratap would not be forgotten.

That opportunity came when the Jodhpur Lancers took part in the Mohmand and Tirah Campaign of 1897–98.

MOHMAND AND TIRAH CAMPAIGN (1897–98)

As soon as the news of the projected Mohmand Campaign reached Sir Pratap, in September 1897, at Jodhpur, he lost no time in pressing his claims, which were this time accepted. Within nine hours of receiving orders he was in a special train enroute for Peshawar with a field troop of Jodhpur Lancers.

08 December 1897 at Rawalpindi. Seated first and third from right Captain Pratap Singh Sankhwas and Dhonkal Singh, second from left Captain Maharaj Sher Singh and centre Brigadier C.R. Macgregor, Rawalpindi Reserve Brigade Commander.
Photo courtesy: Tony McClenaghan

Before starting for the front, Sir Pratap wrote a letter to Maharaj Zalim Singh (his younger brother and Assistant *Musahib Ala*) dated 09 September 1897.

> As I am proceeding on active service to the Nort-West Frontiers of India and as I am taking Harji and Dhonkalji with me, I wish you to look after the two regiments of Sardar Rissala in my place until my return. Squadron Officers Bhairon Singh and Jus Singh will have the command of the first and the second Regiment respectively during the period of our absence. They have been ordered to discharge their duties attentively...

A week later the entire Jodhpur Lancers received orders to take the field, and, being ready in anticipation of the summons, had started within three hours for Ferozepur in nine special troops trains, whence they proceeded to Rawalpindi on 10 October 1897 to join the Tirah Reserve Brigade, commanded by Brigadier General C.R. Macgregor, DSO, where it remained until the close of the Tirah Expedition.

After reaching Peshawar Sir Pratap was ordered to join the Mohmand Expedition on the personal staff of General E.R. Elles, Commanding the Mohmand Field Force to whom Captain Hari Singh (Hurjee) and Captain Dhonkal Singh, and 32 sowars were also appointed as escort. They formed part of the Divisional troops and remained with the Field Force until the expedition was concluded at the end of September. However Sir Pratap arrived two days after the battle of Shabkadar, which practically ended the fighting, and the force was back in Peshawar in a fortnight with its purpose achieved.

In his despatch Major General Elles noted, 'The Cavalry escorts of the Jodhpur and Patiala Cavalry did good reconnaissance work on more than one occasion and came under fire'. The operations were carried out in a country totally foreign in nature to Sir Pratap; the bare, rugged, stony hills, intersected with deep ravines, were every bit as inhospitable as the sandy plains of Marwar, but vastly more difficult to negotiate, and the Pathan's mode of fighting differed entirely from that of the Rajput.

On his return to Peshawar Sir Pratap succeeded in getting appointed as extra ADC to Lieutenant General Sir William Lockhart, who was placed in command of the Tirah Expedition. From Peshawar Sir Pratap marched with General Westmacott to join General Lockhart. He took Hari Singh and Bakhtawar Singh of Bera with him.

In November 1897 General Lockhart ordered an expedition into Chamkani territory and, on 29 November, having crossed the Durbi Khel Pass, they established camp at Dargai. A few shots were fired into the headquarters camp on the night of 29 November, resulting into two members of Sir William's escort being wounded, including Sir Pratap.

Sir Pratap Singh's camp at Dargai during the Tirah campaign where he was wounded on his
right hand.
Photo courtesy: General Amar Singh Library Museum and Trust

General Lockhart and his staff were frequently under fire on the march and
several casualties were sustained among them. For a month more the General's
force scoured the country, before the rebellious tribes laid down their arms.
General William Lockhart, in his dispatch regarding the operation of the Tirah
Expeditionary Force from 01 November 1897 to 26 January 1898, wrote:

> I take this opportunity of expressing my thanks to Lieutenant Colonel Sir
> Pertab Singh, who was attached to me throughout the expedition as Extra
> ADC. This very gallant Rajput nobleman was wounded on 29 November
> 1897, and characteristically concealed the fact until I discovered it by
> accident some days after the occurrence.

The Jodhpur Lancers had little opportunity for earning distinction and no real
fighting. One field troop took part in the Mohmand Expedition, a second was
placed on convoy duty between Bara and Landi Kotal, and a third was ordered to
Peshawar; the rest of the regiment was with the Reserve Brigade at Rawal Pindi.
They succeeded, however, in creating a favorable impression, as Brigadier-General
C.R. Macgregor, DSO, the Rawalpindi Reserve Brigade Commander wrote:
'I consider the Jodhpur Rissala to be a first-class regiment; its arrangements were
excellent, and every one of the men gave proof of smartness as a soldier. I believe
that the days they spent out of their own country provided them an excellent
opportunity for training.'

Thereafter, Sir Pratap and Jodhpur Lancers returned to Jodhpur in good health,
and only lost one man (Daffadar Magan Singh) during their absence of five

months, in time for the investiture of Maharaja Sardar Singh with full powers as a ruling Prince on 18 February 1898. Sir Pratap was created a Companion of the Order of the Bath (CB), and promoted to the rank of full Colonel (GoI 627, dated 18 June 1898) for his efforts. Personnel of the Jodhpur Lancers (89 silver medals for sowars and 67 bronze medals for syces) were awarded the IGS Medal 1895 with clasps Punjab Frontier 1897–98 and Tirah, but because the regiment remained in the Reserve Brigade it did not qualify for the battle honour.

JODHPUR'S AID FOR TRANSVAAL WAR IN SOUTH AFRICA– JANUARY 1900

In the South African War of 1899–1902 the combatant employment of any Indian troops was ruled out. But the states sent considerable number of horses and troopers in remount charge. In January 1900, various princely states offered about 1,220 horses from their Imperial Service Cavalry Regiments for service in South Africa where the British Government was engaged in the Transvaal War.

Out of 1,220 horses, Jodhpur supplied the maximum strength of 194 horses from its Imperial Service Lancers. In addition the Jodhpur Maharaja made a gift Rs 2,000 and 16 horses from his private stables for use of the British Mounted Infantry, Lumsden's Horse in South Africa.

One hundred horses, three Daffadars, four Sowars, two Farriers and 25 Syces left for South Africa on 09 January 1900, from Mathura belonging to the 1st Regiment of the Sardar Rissala (it was stationed at Mathura under Major Jus Singh at that time, due to lack of fodder at Jodhpur). Ninety-four horses, five Daffadars, two Farriers, four Sowars and 30 Syces left for South Africa, on 13 January 1900, from the 2nd Regiment of the Sardar Rissala, stationed at Jodhpur.

It was then decided by the Government that it would pay money at the rate of Rs 630 each horse (including line gear and bridle) and Rs 40 each for saddles, a total Rs 670 (compensation decided as per the existing rate of horse and equipment of the Bengal Cavalry) for each horse and gear to the respective state, so as to allow them to make up their deficiencies so caused in their Imperial Service Regiments. The pay of Daffadars at Rs 22, Farriers at Rs 20, Sowars at Rs 15 and Syce at Rs 6 at dismounted rates was also paid by the Government.

These men returned to Jodhpur in June 1902, except one Farrier, Keshar Singh, who died on 26 January 1900, on board the steamer.

Lord Kitchener send a farewell message, 'Please express to the Indian details about to return to India my appreciation of the good work they have done in

South Africa during the last two-and-a-half years. Good-bye and good fortune in India.'

In 1899 an agreement (No LXXII) was made between the British Government and Maharaja Sardar Singh for the effective control and discipline of his IST when serving beyond the states frontier, thus paving the way for their participation in Third China War (Boxer Rebellion) in 1900–01. These IST were subject to the military law of the states both in peace and war, which was assimilated to the Indian Articles of War (later remodelled into the Indian Army Act).

THE JODHPUR LANCERS IN THE BOXER REBELLION: CHINA 1900–01

The Boxer Rebellion (so-called because some of its leaders were members of a secret society that used a clenched fist as a signal of recognition) was a violent anti-foreigner movement that took place in China between 1900 and 1901. On 17 May 1900, the Chinese Secret Society rebelled against the sale of opium and conversions to Christianity. With the connivance of the Imperial Court they

From left: Amar Singh, Hurjee, Sir Pratap, Bakhtawar Singh and Akhai Singh at stables at Shan Hai Kuan Fort, China, 25 January 1901. They are wearing black arm bands due to the death of Queen Victoria on 22 January 1901.
Photo courtesy: General Amar Singh Library Museum and Trust

attacked the missionaries and the foreign legations were surrounded in Peking. Trapped inside were an assortment of diplomats, civilians and a small number of troops. They were then relieved by the combined force of eight-nation military alliance that included troops from France, Germany, Great Britain, Japan, Russia, Italy, Austria and America.

And when it was decided to send a force from India to China, Sir Pratap at once offered the services of the Jodhpur Lancers. On 11 August 1900, a telegram was received that said the Jodhpur Lancers were selected to go to China. The Commandant of the regiment was Maj. Jus Singh. At that time one of the two regiments of Jodhpur Lancers were temporarily quartered in Mathura to replace the 9th Lancers who had been ordered to South Africa, as also the famine had made horse fodder scarce at Jodhpur (the supply of fodder to two regiments at Jodhpur was always a difficult matter and in famine years an impossibility). On 22 August 1900, the Jodhpur Lancers, with its horses and equipment, proceeded direct to Calcutta from Mathura, by special train sent from Jodhpur.

On 25 August 1900, at Calcutta, the Regimental Headquarters with one squadron were detrained, horses watered and loaded on board the *S.S. Mohawk*. They were followed at intervals by the other three squadrons in separate ships. At Calcutta they received orders to embark for Wei-Hai-Wei. The regiment was accompanied by two British Officers, Major Turner and Captain Hughes. General Beatson came to Calcutta to wish Godspeed to his old friend Sir Pratap, and to the regiment which was largely their joint creation.

The Pioneer newspaper from Calcutta, dated 05 September 1900, published the following account about the departure of the Jodhpur Lancers.

> The Jodhpur Imperial Service Lancers left for China in the *S.S. Mohawk* on the 25 August, having arrived from Mathura early this morning. Calcutta had apparently not realised that they would be leaving at once, and it was only after their departure that the public awoke to the fact, otherwise such a gallant corps would have had a more enthusiastic send off. The band of the 7 Rajputs played the troops on board. We have heard so much about the Jodhpur Lancers and their gallant leader, Sir Pratap, that it must have been great disappointment to many not to have had a glimpse of them.

Owing to change in their destination, being sent back from Wei-Hei-Wai to Shanghai and then moved again to North China, they were for 39 days at sea before they disembarked at Shan Hai Kuan, on the coast north of Taku, at the end of the Great Wall of China, but despite the extra long journey the horses were landed in wonderfully good condition and only six horses were lost in all four transports. The men felt much sea sickness for most of them were at sea for the first time in their life. They passed Hong Kong on 09 September and reached Hong-Kew Wharf, Shanghai, via Wei-hai-Wei on 24 September 1900.

They joined the 4th Indian Brigade of China Expeditionary Force under Brigadier J.T. Cummins, DSO. General O'Moore Creagh, Commander British Expeditionary Force, came on board to see Sir Pratap who was a good friend. The Jodhpur Lancers remained in Shanghai for a few days where the crowd would gather around the Rissala, as a cavalry regiment was quite a novelty in Shanghai.

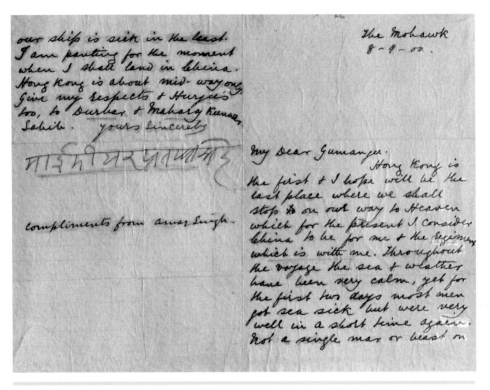

Sir Pratap wrote a letter back home to Jodhpur on board the *S.S. Mohawk,* dated 08 September 1900. The letter has been drafted by Captain Amar Singh Kanota and signed by Sir Pratap as, 'My Dear Pratap Singh'!

Photo courtesy: Thakur Guman Singh Khichi Narwa Collection, Maharaja Man Singh Pushtak Prakash

By the time the Jodhpur Lancers arrived in China in September 1900, most of the serious fighting, associated with the relief of Beijing in August 1900, was over. However a few troops took part in the Nikko, Shimanzai and Funning Expeditions, where they saw some fighting. These sporadic engagements were the remnants of guerrilla warfare that lacked effective direction. At one time the regiment was split into 15 detachments, and some were 60 miles away from the Regimental headquarters. The officers and men had a full share of roughing it, but they were always willing, ready for anything and absolutely uncomplaining. All showed great hardiness and stood the privations and intense cold exceedingly well.

In one of the actions on 12 January 1901, at Lijapoo, a grass cutting party and small escort of nine men from the regiment was attacked by 100 mounted Manchurian bandits. Two sowars were killed (Sowar Mangej Singh Jodha and Sowar Sheoram Singh Mertia) but the Daffadar in Charge, Dal Singh Jodha, drove off the attackers, killing six of them, and covered the retreat of mules and carts until reinforced.

For his coolness and gallantry Daffadar Dal Singh Jodha was awarded the Indian Order of Merit (IOM), Vide G.O. No 419 of 1901. His citation read as:

> Daffadar Dal Singh Jodha, Jodhpur Imperial Service Lancers, was admitted to the 3rd Class IOM for conspicuous gallantry in action near Shanhaikwan, North China, on the 12 January 1901, on which occasion he, with only three men, effectually protected a foraging party of his regiment against a superior body of Chinese, until relieved.

He became the first men amongst the IST troops to get the IOM. Daffadar Dal Singh Jodha was part of the party sent to England for the 1902 Coronation and received his IOM for China from the Duke of Connaught in London.

The Jodhpur Lancers were stationed in Zhili province at the outskirts of Shan Hai Kuan, an ancient fortified city adjacent to the point where the Great Wall meets the sea. The troops were quartered in the Shan Hai Kuan fort during the entire winter. The post ocuppied by the regiment when completed had a perimeter of some 1,100 yards, which necessitated heavy sentry duty and, as the winter advanced and everything was frozen, water for the horses became a serious difficulty as the ice had to be broken. During the first month, all the troop horses had to be used as baggage animals to bring in fodder, as the Commissariat supply was uncertain. Foraging parties visited all villages outside the wall to a radius of 7 or 8 miles. In the same way there was a scarcity of firewood, which had to be brought in.

The forces of Russia, Japan, Germany, America, France and other powers were also present there. Life as garrison troops was almost back to the normal routine, races, polo, tent pegging and all. During their stay Sir Pratap describes that, 'the Russian officers were very fond of drinking. Several times they invited us to their feasts, where cup followed cup without intermission, and everyone was compelled to drink Vodka'. Sir Pratap had nicknamed some Russian Officers as 'Senior Vodka' and 'Junior Vodka' due to their heavy drinking habits!

On 26 February 1901, Major General A.I.F. Reid, Commanding 3rd Brigade inspected the Jodhpur Lancers and he mentioned that, 'the Regiment consisting of Sir Pertab and four staff officers, Regiment Commandant Jus Singh with 21 Jodhpur Officers, 471 fighting men, 370 followers, 525 horses, 296 mules and

Standing from left: Bukhtawar Singh, Hurjee, Sir Pratap, Major J.G. Turner, Japanese officer, Akhai Singh. **Seated:** Amar Singh, Captain Alexander, Captain Hughes and Captain Pinchard. They cover their heads with long scarves of wool and fur wrapped around plain turbans, and coats with fur collars and cuffs, heavy serge Jodhpurs and laced ankle boots, to protect themselves from the severe cold of Shan Hai Kuan's winter.
Photo courtesy: General Amar Singh Library Museum and Trust

ponies is a very fine regiment, animated by a very fine spirit and Sir Pertab is the beau ideal of a native Prince'.

On 26 March 1901, the news of the death of Maharaja of Idar in a newspaper was read over to Sir Pratap (as a routine Sir Pratap always had someone read out newspapers to him every morning) and he immediately sent a telegram to Sir Walter Lawrence (friend of Sir Pratap) the Private Secretary to the Viceroy, 'Hear Maharaja of Idar is dead. Am nearest relation. Hope Viceroy will support my rights'. (Sir Pratap succeeded in this and remained as Maharaja of Idar from 1902 to 1911, when he abdicated the throne of Idar and returned to Jodhpur as Regent due to the death of Maharaja Sardar Singh of Jodhpur in March 1911).

In April 1901 the Jodhpur Lancers took part in a gymkhana at Peking, where the Jodhpur contingent rode off with no less than 11 prizes, no other nationality winning more than two.

Finally, before returning to Jodhpur, Sir Pratap got an opportunity to visit Japan with his staff (including Colonel Jay Gould, IMS, Colonel Hari Singh, Captain Maharaj Akhai Singh, Captain Amar Singh and Bakhtawar Singh Bera). In May 1901 the Japanese Emperor received Sir Pratap, when he visited the Emperor's court and the event was covered in the Japanese newspapers with a photograph of Sir Pratap. The Indian contingent remained in Tokyo and Nagasaki for a month. The party then arrived back at Shan Hai Kwan on 23 June 1901 to join the regiment, which was now ready to leave China for home.

On the return journey the regiment sailed from Taku, China, in three different steamers, viz., *S.S. Itria* on 05 July, *Rajah* on 10 July and *Itinda* on 12 July 1901 and arrived back at Calcutta on 26 July 1901.

The Viceroy in a telegram dated 26 July 1901 wrote,

> Please inform the Jodhpur State Council that I congratulate them upon the safe home-coming of their IST from China. It is with much pleasure that I have learnt that they conducted themselves with much credit in the expedition and have contributed greatly to the good reputation earned by our Indian troops.

Major J.G. Turner, SSO, submitted the following confidential report on the 11-months-performance of the Sardar Rissala Regiment to the Inspector General, IST, dated 23 July 1901, on board *S.S. Itria*:

> **British Officers:** Two British officers were attached to the regiment, viz., Lieutenant Alexander, 6th Bombay Cavalry, and Lieutenant Gaussen, 3rd Bengal Cavalry.
>
> **Horses:** The horses did very well in China. Their fodder consisted for the most part of millet stalks, which we cut up with Chinese chaff-cutters. When living on the country the grain consisted of 'Kowliang' (a kind of bajra), moong and black beans. Including those lost on the voyage out, the total number of horses which became non-effective or unserviceable was 18. These were replaced by Government remounts. Thirty-four additional remounts were purchased from the Government Depot, making a total of 52. Opportunity was taken to sell 72 of the older horses before leaving China. They realised an average of Rs 134. It was very noticeable that old horses are much more liable to suffer from pneumonia on board ship.
>
> **Ponies and Mules:** Including the voyage, four ponies died in China (Eight mules were killed in the attack on a foraging party on 12 January 1901).

Sir Pratap as he appeared in Japanese papers on his visit to Nikko Japan, on 29 May 1901.
On the right is Rissaldar Amar Singh who acted as secretary to Sir Pratap in China.
Photo courtesy: General Amar Singh Library Museum and Trust

Another 56 were sold at an average of Rs 87, others were exchanged for mules and 34 mules were purchased. Altogether 62 mules were added to the transport of the regiment. Although we had not the opportunities of some regiments, still the transport has been much improved and the 'horse chunda fund' (contribution fund) has benefitted as the mules cost $ 40 each.

Clothing and Equipment: The khaki cord pants (Government issue) were no protection against the cold and the men wore 'pyjamahs warm' (Loose trousers worn by cavalry men), which, however, won't stand much wear. The horse clothing taken out did excellently and the special issue of Government jhools to other Silladar regiments was not needed by the Jodhpur Lancers.

Before starting, the men were provided (regimentally) with the new pattern carbine sling. They invariably carried their carbines slung even on the longest days, and never used the carbine buckets.

Ammunition: Our experience was that pouch ammunition deteriorated from the cold and exposure. The carbines, when used in the practices at Shan-Hai-kuan, with ammunition which had been carried in pouches for several months, the shooting was invariably very low (in low temperature cordite gives a lower velocity and therefore less range).

Rank and File: The regiment certainly had its full share of roughing it, but the men were always willing, ready for anything and absolutely uncomplaining. They are hardy and can stand a good deal in the way of privation. They have a great faculty for finding their way about a country, and, lastly, they are more free from the prejudice than any other native troops I have met. Being constantly split up into small foraging parties, they had every temptation to indulge in a little looting, but there was nothing of the sort.

Duffadar Dal Singh Jodha has been awarded the Indian Order of Merit for his conduct on 12 January 1901. This is the first time that this reward has been bestowed on a soldier of the IST.

Health: On the whole the men have kept very well. There were two deaths in addition to the two men killed in action. Four men were returned to India as 'unfits' and 13 were invalided. Unfortunately an epidemic of mumps appeared before even the regiment landed, and it always accounted for 50 percent of the cases in hospital which, however, were never very numerous.

Officers: The following are the officers of the regiment who have been most useful and deserve notice.

Commandant Jus Singh deserves great credit for the working of the regiment, especially since the beginning of this year.

Squadron Commanders—Kunwar Pratap Singh and Thakur Shivnath Singh. Both these officers were on detachment nearly the whole time and looked after their squadrons very well.

Risaldars Sawal Singh and Bahadur Khan.

Jemadars Bhagwant Singh, Mohbat Singh and Pabudan Singh.

Risaldar Amar Singh (Kanota) on Maharaj Sir Pratap Singh's staff was often employed on special patrols when his knowledge of English was very useful.

Maharaj Sir Pratap Singh's presence was a great incentive to all ranks. It is impossible to exaggerate the influence he has over the men, or the veneration with which they regard him. He showed a splendid example, was always up at daylight and made nothing of the severest weather, and I am glad to say his health was excellent. Scarcely a day passed without some foreign officer coming to see the 'Indian Prince', and while they may have been disappointed at the absence of display, they must have been struck by his simple and friendly manner and his almost severe mode of life. Although his presence was a great help, yet at the same time he held aloof from the working of the regiment, which was entirely in the hands of the Commandant Major Jus Singh.'

When the Jodhpur Lancers arrived back at Calcutta on 26 July 1901, many distinguished people from Jodhpur (including Maharaj Zalim Singh, Maharaj Arjun Singh, Thakur Sheonath Singh Bera, Pandit Sukhhdeo Prasad, etc) and Marwari merchants in Calcutta gathered at the Kidderpore Docks, Calcutta, to receive the regiment from China. Sir Pratap, with his staff, went to the Great Eastern Hotel from where he went straight to Shimla, the same night, to meet the Viceroy, to stake his claim to the gaddi (throne) of Idar state, where Maharaja Keshri Singh had died childless in March 1901 (Sir Pratap eventually became the Maharaja of Idar State from 07 January 1902 to 20 March 1911).

The regiment with horses then entrained for Jodhpur by a special train on 27 July 1901. On return from Shimla, Sir Pratap reached Jodhpur on 02 August 1901 via train from Jaipur, wherein at Kuchaman Road the five-year-old Maharaj Kanwar Sumer Singh (Maharaja Sardar Singh was on tour in Europe) and most of the state officials received Sir Pratap. Again at Merta Road Maharaja Ganga Singh of Bikaner came to see Sir Pratap. The same day on 02 August 1901, the regiment also reached Jodhpur where they were received with great fanfare by the people. On 03 August 1901 an address was given by the citizens of Jodhpur and was read by Kavi Raj Murardan and many other poets.

The Regiment had the honour of being allowed by the supreme Government to bear upon its colours and appointments the honorary distinction, 'China, 1900', in commemoration of their gallant conduct and distinguished service during the operations in China under Gazette of India No 276, dated 03 April 1903, and the men the medal with the clasp 'Relief of Peking'. The Jodhpur Lancers also received four guns captured from the Chinese as a trophy presented by Lieutenant General Sir A. Gaselee, Commanding China Expeditionary Force. These obsolete smoothbore guns were received in 1902. Similar guns were also presented to Bikaner, Gwalior, Alwar and Maler Kotla States.

When the regiment returned to Jodhpur, they found Maharaja Sardar Singh on tour from March 1901 onwards to Ceylon and Europe including Carlsbad Austria for spa treatment on medical advice (for a long time he suffered from severe backache, due to numerous falls from his horse). He was on tour till the end of 1901 and would often write home about his journey, health and his horses. Maharaja Sardar Singh had suffered a very severe accident while playing polo on 07 October 1900 and suffered extensive injury to his leg and knees. His health since then continued to be a severe concern till he died in 1911.

The January of 1902 saw the departure of both Sir Pratap to Idar (on 07 January 1902 as Maharaja of Idar) and Maharaja Sardar Singh to Imperial Cadet Corps (ICC) at Dehradun. In November 1901 Viceroy Curzon had invited Maharaja Sardar Singh of Jodhpur to join the ICC for a term of 2 to 3 years. Thus the administration for the next few years in Jodhpur was looked after by a Regency Council.

At the end of the year, Viceroy Curzon visited Jodhpur in the special Vicergal train, for three days, from 22 to 24 November 1902. He was treated royally and all the usual programmes for a visiting Viceroy were carried out, including him reviewing the Jodhpur Sardar Rissala on parade (they had returned from duty during the Boxer rebellion in China).

THE IMPERIAL CADET CORPS (ICC) NOVEMBER 1901

It was established by Viceroy Curzon in 1901, with the main object of providing military training for selected members of the aristocracy of India (between the ages of 17 to 20), who have received education at one of the Chiefs Colleges of Rajkot, Ajmer, Indore and Lahore, so as to be able to take up places in the army as officers. The ICC was not a success as not more than 25 cadets ever enrolled in any of the terms. The graduates received modified King's commissions in the Native Indian Land Forces.

Sir Pratap was made the Honorary Commandant of the Corps, with Major W.A. Watson, CIH as Commandant, Captain Cameroon, CIH as British Adjutant and Captain Deep Singh, Bikaner Camel Corps, as the Indian Adjutant. The Corps functioned from Meerut in winters (01 November to 31 March) and from Dehradun in summers (01 May to 31 August). The Royal Indian Military College (RIMC) was later opened in March 1922 on the campus of the ICC (the area is still called Rajwada Camp).

21 September 1901, Maharaja Sardar Singh at Crystal Palace, London, during his European tour due to health concerns. Seated on either side are Captain and Mrs Bannerman, guardian to the Maharaja and Assistant Inspecting Officer Rajputana Imperial Service Troops from 1901 to 1903. Seated on the ground are Mobji (left) and Dhonkal Singh. Standing: Ugam Singh Chandelao (left) and Thakur of Rian.
Photo Courtesy: Bal Samand Lake Palace, Jodhpur

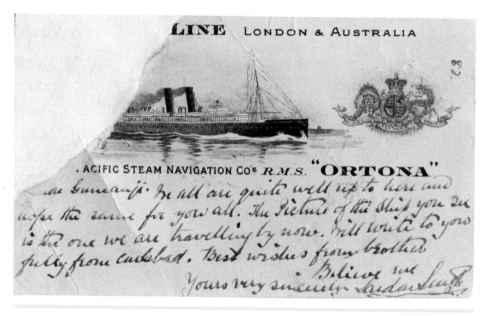

A postcard signed by Maharaja Sardar Singh onboard *RMS Ortona* on his way to Carlsbad, Austria.
Photo courtesy: Thakur Guman Singh Khichi Narwa Collection, Maharaja Man Singh Pushtak Prakash

The first batch beginning in January 1902 had 21 cadets that included Mahraja Sardar Singh of Jodhpur, Madan Singh of Kishangarh, Sujjan Singh of Ratlam and Nawab Iftikhar Ali Khan of Jaora. In addition Bharat Singh of Amleta Ratlam, Ram Singh of Virpoor Kathiawar, Zorawar Singh of Bhojpura Bhavnagar, Samundar Singh of Weir Bharatpur, Khuman Singh and Deo Singh of Kota, Jawahir Singh

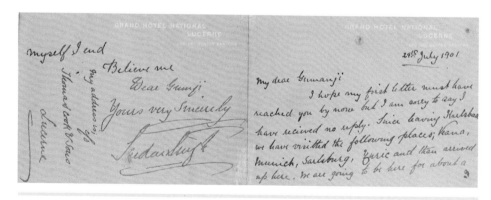

29 July 1901, letter from Maharaja Sardar Singh from Grand Hotel National, Lucerne, Switzerland. He writes that, 'since leaving Carlsbad we have visited Vienna, Munich, Salzburg and Zurich'.
Photo courtesy: Thakur Guman Singh Khichi Narwa Collection, Maharaja Man Singh Pushtak Prakash

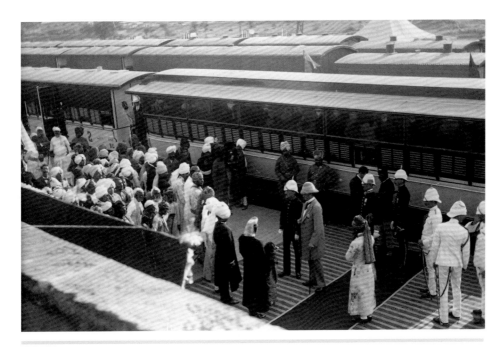

Viceroy Curzon being introduced to prominent persons on arrival at Rai ka Bagh railway station
Jodhpur by Resident Major K.D. Erskine on 22 November 1902. Maharaja Sardar Singh on the
right in white achkan and turban looks on.
Photo Courtesy: Mehrangarh Museum Trust

Viceroy Curzon and Maharaja Sardar Singh drive through the streets to the Ratanada Palace,
as crowds lined the whole route.
Photo courtesy: Mehrangarh Museum Trust

The Regency Council of Maharaja Sardar Singh in 1901. All sporting flowing black/white beards brushed out on either side. **Seated from left:** Sukhdeo Prasad (A Kashmiri Pandit, Judicial Secretary to *Musahib Ala*, was Member of State Council from 1894 to 1926), Kaviraj Murardan (Court Poet and Member of State Council since 1892), Thakur Chain Singh Asop, Thakur Chhater Singh Nimaj, Joshi Askaran (Member of the Council since 1892 and city Kotwal), Munshi Hira Lal (Member of Council since 1892, was hereditary Raj Munshi). **Standing from left:** Bhandari Hanwant Chand (Member of Council Since 1892 and Superintendent of the Appellate Court), Mutha Ganesh Chand (Head of Jawahir Khana), Pandit Madho Prasad (Superintendent of Mallani, Pachbhadra and Sheo Parganas), Pandit Deena Nath (Private Secretary to Maharaja), Singhi Bachraj (Jagir Bakshi), Pandit Jiwa Nand (Assistant Superintendent of Sardar's Courts) and Hamidullah Khan (In charge of Mahkma Tamil—office of legal execution).
Photo courtesy: The author

of Jaisalmer, Pratap Singh of Kama Jaipur, Sardar Singh of Shahpura, Amanat-Ulla Khan of Tonk, Amar Singh of Kanota Jaipur, Sardar Basant Singh of Atari Amritsar, Nawab Wali-ud-Din Khan of Hyderabad, Akhey Singh of Jodhpur, Gopal Singh of Gundoj Jodhpur, Mohammed Akbar Khan of Hoti Mardan and Rai Singh of Chhota Udaipur were selected. The Rajputs comprised 14 cadets out of the 21. The other applicants from Jodhpur, namely Pratap Singh of Sankhwas, Bakhtawar Singh of Bera, Raoraja Amar Singh, son of Maharaj Kishore Singh, Maharaj Rattan Singh, Kishan Singh, Kishore Singh of Bicamkore and Shivnath Singh of Kanota were rejected on various grounds.

The first batch got commissioned on 04 July 1905, where only four cadets were granted commissions in the Indian Land Forces. These cadets were: Amar Singh Kanota (ADC to GOC Mhow Division), Aga Kasim Shah was nephew to Agha Khan (ADC to GOC Poona Division), Wali-ud-Din Khan (Hyderabad Lancers) and Zorawar Singh (Commandant, Bhavnagar Lancers). These officers had a higher status than the Viceroy Commissioned Officers (VCOs) but were not allowed to command European troops. The other cadets got the privilege to wear the ICC uniform. Finally, on 25 August 1917, only nine cadets (all former ICC cadets—Zorawar Singh, Amar Singh, Pirthi Singh Kotah, Bala Sahib Daphle, Raja Jodha Jang Bahadur and Savai Singhji) became the Kings Commissioned Officers (KCO's) in the Indian Army.

Both in 1903 and 1911 at the Delhi Durbar, the cadets of ICC mounted on black chargers in their resplendent strikingly beautiful uniform in white with sky-blue and gold facings, formed a constant contingent in the Viceroy's escort.

Here it becomes important to introduce the name of Captain Amar Singh of Kanota, near Jaipur who had served for six years from 1896 to 1901 with the Jodhpur Lancers and then with the ICC from 1902 to 1905. On 04 July 1905 he was one of the four Indian Officers who were originally granted commission in the

Left to right: Captain D.H. Cameron; Adjutant, Wordi Major Deep Singh; Sir Pratap, Honorary Commandant mounted on his famous horse 'Fitzgerald'; and Major W.A. Watson, Commandant of ICC in 1903.
Photo courtesy: Mehrangarh Museum Trust

Native Indian Land forces and posted as a staff officer to the General Sir Moore O'Creagh, (later Commander in Chief Indian army, after Kitchener, from 1909) GOC 5th Mhow Division, Western Command Headquarters, from 1905 to 1914 (at this time only Eastern, Western and Southern Commands covered India, the Northern Command was added on 01 November 1920).

On 25 August 1917 he was granted a permanent commission in the Indian Army in the rank of Captain, being posted to the 2nd Lancers attached to 16th Lancers. He served as Rissaldar with the Jodhpur Lancers in China from 1900–01 on the staff of Sir Pratap Singh and in France during 1914–15 as ADC to General Officer Commanding (GOC) Sirhind Brigade where he was Mentioned-in-Despatches. During 1916 he served in Mesopotamia and later the same year returned to Bombay as ADC to General Knight. During 1919–20 he served as Squadron Commander 16th Cavalry in Waziristan.

On 04 July 1923 approval was accorded for his retirement with the honorary rank of Major in the army, with the recommendation of Commandant 2nd Lancers and GOC Poona District, following a disagreement with his Commanding Officer. He finished his career as Commandant of the Jaipur State Forces in 1936 with the rank of Major General.

The first batch of ICC Cadets in a camp in 1903.
Photo courtesy: Mehrangarh Museum Trust.

29 December 1902, the state entry at the Delhi Durbar. Sir Pratap riding ahead of the ICC with Major Watson by his side on his black charger Fitzgerald. They wore strikingly beautiful white uniform with sky-blue and gold facings, gold-embroidered knee length ivory coats and sky-blue sash and turbans astride black chargers with snow leopard skins as saddle cloths.
Photo courtesy: Mehrangarh Museum Trust

Amar Singh read and wrote prolifically and from 03 September 1898 to 01 November 1942 (the day he died), kept a diary and wrote in it every single day, except for one day when he fell off his horse and was unconscious. Eighty-nine volumes (800 pages per volume) of Amar Singh's diary now housed at castle Kanota, contain stories about his daily life and also about the general, social, political, military and cultural milieu that existed in the times he lived. His diary provides the most vital source of information about the life with the Jodhpur Lancers in those early years. He was married from the house of Sir Pratap in Jodhpur, in September 1901.

Meanwhile the famine and poor financial state rendered it extremely difficult for the Marwar Durbar to maintain the two regiments of Sardar Rissala to their full strength. Luckily, for the reconstituted regiments of Madras Cavalry, a squadron of the Rajputs of Rajputana was urgently required. Thus one Mertia Rathore squadron of the 2nd Sardar Rissala was transferred to the Third Madras Lancers in October 1902. In 1903, as a result of the Kitchener reforms, the 3 Madras Cavalry was renumbered the 28 Light Cavalry. This measure saved Jodhpur from an embarassing situation. The strength of the two regiments of Jodhpur was thus reduced to a total of six squadrons till the outbreak of the First World War. Incidentally one of the persons who was transferred to the 3rd Madras Cavalry from the 2nd Regiment of Sardar Rissala was none other than Sowar Govind Singh. He went on to win the Victoria Cross during the First World War. The details are given subsequently.

On 01 January 1903, Delhi Durbar gold medal was presented to Maharaja Sardar Singh and three Silver Medals to Thakur Mangal Singh Pokhran, Rao Bahadur Sher Singh of Kuchaman and Thakur Fateh Singh of Ras. At a Durbar held on the 02 January 1904, the Resident, Western Rajputana States, distributed the medals for China and the Delhi Durbar to the First Regiment, 576 silver and 333 bronze medals having been received for China and two for the Delhi Durbar. The recipients of the latter were Major Jus Singh the Commanding Officer of the First Regiment and Duffedar Birad Singh, the senior Non-Commissioned Officer.

Major Jus Singh died in 1907 and Sir Pratap from Idar recommended that Captain Dhonkal Singh should be made the Commanding Officer in his place, but Major Pratap Singh Sankhwas was then made the Commanding Officer on 26 March 1908. Major Pratap Singh had earlier served in Jodhpur Fort Artillery from January 1886 to October 1894 and joined Sardar Rissala in November 1894. He served in China as Squadron Commander of Sardar Rissala. The Commanding Officer of the 2nd Regiment Sardar Rissala was Maharaj Sher Singh since 20 August 1901.

On 1 November 1908, Viceroy Minto, visited Jodhpur and in the romantic setting of the great durbar at Jodhpur, delivered the message of the King. On his arrival the entire route was lined with Jodhpur Lancers, police and 8,000 Jagirdar troops, who wore ancient armour. Some of the horsemen were covered from head to foot in the coats-of-mail used in the time of the early Mughal Emperors; their horses were flanked by mirrors suspended from the saddles; these were used to dazzle and disconcert the enemy in bygone days, and sparkled and flashed in the sunlight as the horses galloped here and there.

Lady Minto's diary describes the scene in Jodhpur:

> It was exactly as if we had gone back at least five centuries. The entire route was lined on each side with the Thakurs and their retinues, each band having their distinctive 'pugrees'. On either side of the road there were caparisoned horses with marvelous trappings, long flowing draperies covering their heads, richly embroidered with gold and silver, all wearing the thick gold bracelet above the right knee, pawing the ground and arching their necks as they are taught to do; elephants completely covered with velvet embroideries and massive silver ornaments; camels galore, some

A 3rd Madras Lancers title worn from 1891 to 1903.
Photo courtesy: Professor (Capt) Ashok Nath, FRGS, Nath Foundation, Sweden

The marriage party of Amar Singh Kanota assembled in front of Sir Pratap's bungalow in Jodhpur on 08 September 1901, prior to departure for thikana of Satheen. All wore uniforms of the Jodhpur Lancers including the groom! The party included the entire Jodha Squadron of the Jodhpur Lancers.
Copyright: General Amar Singh Library Museum and Trust

The *khidmutgar*s (valets), *chuprassi*s (messengers), and other attendants in white with scarlet and gold *cummerbund*s (waist sash) and saffron *puggaree*s (headdress) made a fitting background at Jodhpur during the viceregal visits. The people of Jodhpur as a whole led a hard life and these moments of excitement made bright interludes in their rather drab lives. The buildings en route were bright with buntings, flags and other decorations, and the houses and the roads were thronged with people.
Photo courtesy: Mehrangarh Museum Trust

carrying antediluvian guns which look as if they could never have done much execution; mounted men covered from head to foot with chain armour, wearing the identical suits of mail used in battle at the time of the early Mogul Emperors.

The Viceroy witnessed the Jodhpur Lancers on parade directly under the command of the Maharaja Sardar Singh. He then presented the KCSI badge to Maharaja Sardar Singh and six 9-pounder guns to the Jodhpur Lancers.

On 22 April 1909, the C-in-C Lord Kitchner visited Jodhpur and Maharajkumar Sumer Singh commanded the Jodhpur Lancers on parade. On 01 January 1910, Maharaja Sardar Singh was bestowed with the GCSI badge at Calcutta.

DEATH OF MAHARAJA SARDAR SINGH 20 MARCH 1911

Major J.W. Grant, I.M.S. the Residency Surgeon, Western Rajputana States describes in his medical report that:

Maharaja Sardar Singh standing alongside
Viceroy Minto in Jodhpur on 01 November
1908. The Mehrangarh Fort of Jodhpur is
seen in the background.
Photo courtesy: Mehrangarh Museum Trust

Jodhpur Camel *Bhisti* (water-carrier) with an entire goatskin on his back to supply water. Jodhpur
was always deficient of water and the population had to suffer much toil and hardship in bringing
water from great distances or had to pay exorbitantly for it to the *Bhisti*s, who brough it in on camels
or bullocks for sale.
Photo courtesy: Thakur Praduman Singh Chandelao

Maharaja Sardar Singh's illness was caused by a chill, which he caught while motoring from Meerut to Delhi on the 10 March 1911. He was attacked with fever that night, when travelling by rail to Ajmer. He halted at Ajmer on the 11 March and spent the day in the Maharajkumar's (Sumer Singh) house, in the vicinity of the Mayo College. At 4 P.M. on 12 March with 104 degrees temperature he reached Ratanada Palace Jodhpur by train. He passed a restless night on the 12, but on the 13 his condition greatly improved. He slept well on the 14 and 15, and expressed himself as feeling generally very comfortable.

On the morning of the 15, he showed symptoms of mental aberration and by 16, definite signs of pneumonia were present. On the 15, after consulting with the Minister of the State, I telegraphed to Lieutenant Colonel Roberts, I.M.S. Residency Surgeon, Indore, requesting him to come immediately to Jodhpur. He arrived about 2 P.M. on the 17 and remained until the end. After examining His Highness, he confirmed the diagnosis and expressed himself as being well pleased with his general condition, owing to His Highness taking all the nourishment administered to maintain his strength. All went satisfactory during 18 and 19. On

01 November 1908, Viceroy Minto reviewed the Jodhpur Lancers on parade.
Photo courtesy: Mehrangarh Museum Trust

19 night there were signs of exhaustion but he rallied for a few hours. By 20 morning, he was much worse, his circulation was obviously failing, and respiration became difficult. These symptoms increased in spite of all measures adopted, and His Highness quietly expired at 4.30 P.M. on the afternoon of the 20 March 1911. He lapsed into unconsciousness about an hour before the end came.

The Maharaj Kumar Sumer Singh and his younger brother Umaid Singh, who were at the Mayo College, were wired for early on the morning of the 20 March, but they did not arrive in time to see their father alive. Maharaja Sir Pratap arrived from Idar on 22 March 1911.

On 21 March his remains were carried in a grand procession leaving the palace shortly after sunrise at 7 AM and taking the route through the Rai ka Bagh, Paota gardens and Nagori gate on to the Deo Kund, where the ceremony was performed on a spot adjoining the cenotaph of his father Maharaja Jaswant Singh. His funeral was quite an extraordinary sight as nearly the whole population of 60,000 people of the city, besides people from all the surrounding villages, poured out in grief. The state offices, city gates and all shops were closed as a mark of respect. The funeral rites continued for many hours and the actual cremation was not completed till about 4 PM.

He was succeeded as Maharaja by his minor son, Sumer Singh. This necessitated Regency and Sir Pratap, gave up his throne of Idar in 1911 to return to Jodhpur as Regent to his young grandnephew Sumer Singh, who was only 14 years old.

Immediately on arrival at Jodhpur, alongwith Maharaja Sumer Singh, Sir Pratap went to London to attend the coronation of King George V on 22 June 1911. Both Commanding Officers of the Jodhpur Lancers, Lieutenant Colonel Pratap Singh and Lieutenant Colonel Sher Singh also attended the coronation in London. Both these officers stayed at Hampton Court and incured mess bill expenditure of 21 Pounds for their two months' stay during June and July 1911.

Before returning from London, Sir Pratap admitted Maharaja Sumer Singh for studies at the Wellington College in August 1911, with Major A.D. Strong as his guardian. However, Sir Pratap took alongwith with him to Jodhpur his son Raoraja Narpat Singh and Dalpat Singh (son of Hurjee), who had been studying at Eastbourne College, London, since 1903 and had now completed their education. On arrival at Jodhpur he made Dalpat an officer in the Jodhpur Lancers (he died at Haifa in 1918) and Narpat Singh as Vakil (advocate) in Jodhpur Residency.

Maharaja Sumer Singh then briefly returned to India to attend the 1911 Delhi durbar where, on 14 December 1911, during the military review he personally

Lieutenant Colonel Pratap Singh CO 1st Lancers Sardar Rissala from 1908 to 1925 (standing extreme right) and Lieutenant Colonel Maharaj Sher Singh CO 2nd Lancers Sardar Rissala from 1901 to 1917 (seated extreme left) attended the 1911 Coronation ceremony of King George V in London.
Photo courtesy: Gajendra Singh Sankhwas

commanded the Jodhpur Lancers. A total of 26 Delhi durbar silver medals were received by the men of the Jodhpur Lancers. Maharaja Sumer Singh stayed in Wellington College for about 2 ½ years till the end of 1913, after which he returned to India in time for a visit by Viceroy Hardinge to Jodhpur on 08 February 1914. The Viceroy was received ceremoniously at the Rai ka Bagh railway station and escorted by the Jodhpur Lancers to Ratanada Palace.

Later the Viceroy inspected the Jodhpur Lancers on parade and also visited the Mehrangarh Fort.

Thereafter on 08 February 1914, the Viceroy drove to Chopasani village and inaugurated the Rajput High School at Chopasani.

BRIEF HISTORY OF RAJPUT HIGH SCHOOL CHOPASANI

In 1875, two small schools—the first of their kind in Rajputana—were started for the sons of 'Nobles' (Thakurs and Jagirdars). In 1886 these two schools were amalgamated and named the 'Powlett Nobles School' in honour of Colonel Powlett, then Resident to the Western Rajputana States (it was intended that the boys would proceed to the Mayo College Ajmer from here). The same year, in 1886, a Department of Education was also opened in Jodhpur.

On 27 November 1896 Sir Pratap started a school in Mandore, Jodhpur, for poor Rajput boys. This was opened by, and named after, Viceroy Elgin (intended for boys as recruits for the Jodhpur Lancers) and was amalgamated with the Nobles School in 1899. Later, while Sir Pratap was in Idar, the schools again separated and continued with varying fortunes (the number of pupils dwindled to one boy, who too was generally absent!) until Sir Pratap was appointed Regent in 1911. He promptly rescued it from total eclipse and reunited the two schools in April 1912 and appointed an English Principal, Mr R.B. Van Wart (who wrote the biography of Sir Pratap after his death in 1922).

Photo of Dalpat Singh seated second left and Raoraja Narpat Singh seated second right in their Eastbourne College rugby team at London in 1910.

Photo courtesy: Bill Bowden and Michael Partridge

08 February 1914, a detachment of Jodhpur Lancers and nobles await the arrival of
Viceroy Hardinge at Rai ka Bagh Palace Railway Station.
Photo courtesy: Mehrangarh Museum Trust

The Jodhpur Rissala men escort Viceory Hardinge in the car to Ratanada Palace. By 1914
the Jodhpur State Garage had 51 cars!
Photo courtesy: Mehrangarh Museum Trust

Sir Pratap and Viceroy Hardinge reviewing Jodhpur Lancers on parade on 08 February 1914.
Photo courtesy: Mehrangarh Museum Trust

08 February 1914, Viceroy Hardinge, closely followed by Sir Pratap, visits the Mehrangarh Fort in Jodhpur, as the State troops present a *salami* (salute) to the Viceroy.
Photo courtesy: Mehrangarh Museum Trust

The plans for a new building were prepared (on a chance visit to Jodhpur, Edwin Lutyens approved the design of the school) and the site was selected near the lake and village of Chopasani four miles out of Jodhpur city. In November 1912 the

On 08 February 1914, Viceroy Hardinge opened Powlet Nobles and Elgin Rajput school. Mr C. Skelton, State Engineer and Mr B. Chunilal were incharge as supervisors during the construction of this majestic building during 1912 to 1913. The school was instrumental in sending many boys to Jodhpur State Forces and continues to send them now to the Indian Army. A sum of Rs 91,000 was also collected by Rajput ex-soldiers as pie fund towards its construction.
Photo courtesy: Mehrangarh Museum Trust

first stone was laid and just 15 months later the present imposing building erected at a cost of Rs 4.5 lakhs was inaugurated by the Viceroy Hardinge at 10:30 Hrs on 08 February 1914 by turning the key of a silver padlock. The original design was that of Mr G.J.O'Brien, late State Engineer but it was elaborated and the entire work carried out by his successor Mr C. Skelton.

The main building contained 14 classrooms, library, reading room, principal's and daftry/clerks offices, an imposing hall capable of holding 600 people (then the largest in the state), beside a swimming bath, gymnasium, stables for 30 horses, quarters for 25 teachers, hospital and extensive playgrounds. There

The Elgin School boys in Mandore in 1898. The school during this time was operating from an old deserted palace building of Maharaja Abhey Singh in Mandore. The boys were trained to join as recruits for the Jodhpur Lancers.
Photo courtesy: The author

was a boarding house for the Nobles to hold 50 boys who paid fees of Rs 500 per annum (later these boys joined Mayo College) and three other houses, each could hold 150 boys for the Elgin School and they were fed, clothed and educated at state expense. A contribution of a sum of Rs 91,000 was also collected by Rajput ex-soldiers as pie fund towards its construction.

In March 1949, there was serious trouble in Jodhpur State when it was announced that the Chopasani School will be converted into Military College, that would admit boys irrespective of caste or creed. Several students went on hunger strike against the decision, the Ministry of States intervened and a settlement was effected, whereby it was agreed that the school with its land, buildings and furniture be handed over to Rajput Sabha to be maintained by them as a school with effect from 01 July 1949. As per the terms of the agreement, the Rajput Sabha was to pay to the Jodhpur Government the book value of the buildings of Rs 5,81,534 as assessed from the books of the Public Works Department Jodhpur after deducting a sum of Rs 91,000, the cost of the fourth hostel constructed from the Pie Fund of the Rajputs. The school since then continues to function and has produced some outstanding personalities.

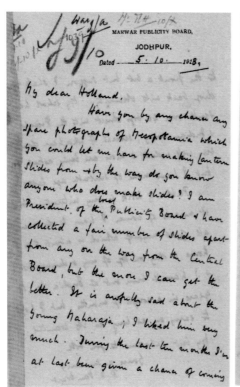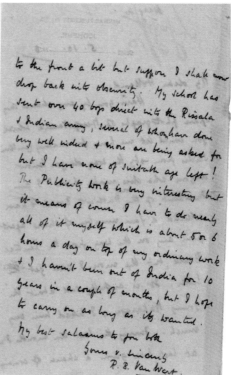

R. B. Van Wart, the principal of Rajput High School Chopasani, writes that his school has sent 40 boys direct to Jodhpur Rissala and the Indian Army during the Great War, several of whom have done very well indeed and more are being asked for, but I have none of suitable age left! The letter was written on 05 October 1918, just two days after the death of Maharaja Sumer Singh. He writes that, 'it is awfully sad about the young Maharaja, I liked him very much....'. In this letter he is seeking photographs of Jodhpur Lancers during the war for the Marwar Publicity Board.

Photo courtesy: Meharangarh Museum Trust

On 08 July 1914, Sir Pratap applied for the services of Major H.N. Holden, 5th Bengal Cavalry. He was commandant of the Viceroy's Bodyguards and at that time Inspecting Officer of the Imperial Service Cavalry and Transport Rajputana in Jaipur from 1911. His services were asked for a period of five years, at a salary of Rs 1,500 plus Rs 100 conveyance allowance per month and rent-free house. His duties included advice on training of Jodhpur Lancers, as well as Marwari Horse breeding and Grass Farm. However, before the matter could be settled the Great War had broken out and eventually Major Holden accompanied the Jodhpur Lancers as Senior Special Service Officer (SSSO) to the Great War, where sadly he was killed in action on 26 October 1918 at Aleppo, just five days before the war formally ended.

Nobles School boys at Chopasani 1913-14. The boy on extreme right in the last row is Raoraja Sujjan Singh, who later became Commanding Officer of Jodhpur Sardar Infantry in 1929. Standing first row left to right: Balwant Singh, Narendra Singh, Prahlad Singh and extreme right Yuvraj Singh.

Photo courtesy: Raoraja Dharmendra Singh

The group photo taken just after the inauguration of Rajput Chopasani High School in February 1914. Sir Pratap (seated third from left) was persuaded to wear his Cambridge LL.D robes. In the centre is Viceory Hardinge and the Vicerine and Maharaja Sumer Singh is seated third from right. Standing first, second and third from right are Major A.D. Strong, Captain E.L. Maxwell and Major H.N. Holden. These three were the SSO's with Jodhpur Lancers during the Great War. Seated on the ground from left are Maharaj Umaid Singh, Raoraja Abhey and Maharaj Ajit Singh.

Photo courtesy: Mehrangarh Museum Trust

The Maharaja's suburban palace—Ratanada Palace was built in 1894, decorated with buntings and flags, as the men of the Jodhpur Sardar Infantry and Jodhpur Lancers present *salami* to the Jodhpur's chief nobles in their full court dresses in February 1914.
Photo courtesy: Mehrangarh Museum trust

Perhaps the last family get together. Major Hyla Holden with his mother in the front seat and his brother in the rear seat in October 1913, outside Steeple Langford Church Salisbury (Hyla was on leave from India from 19 April 1913 to 17 October 1913). Both the brothers died during the Great War on 01 December 1917 and 26 October 1918. There are stained glass windows with their names in this church.
Photo courtesy: Mr Tom Holden

The Jodhpur Lancers in the First World War

(From August 1914 to February 1920)

The news of the outbreak of war between Great Britain and Germany was received at Jodhpur on 05 August 1914. Sir Pratap lost no time in placing the Jodhpur Lancers and the entire resources of the state at the disposal of the King, and then rushed off to Shimla, where he requested Sir Harry Watson, then Inspector-General of the IST, to use all his influence with the Viceroy to further his request to be sent to France. Sir Pratap also sent a telegram to the King for permission to proceed for war. Soon a telegram from C-in-C, Shimla, was received on 20 August 1914 at Jodhpur that said the Government of India had selected the Jodhpur Lancers to proceed on field service to Egypt (not to France) at a very early date.

The fortnight spent after that at Jodhpur was a busy one for all ranks. Mobilisation was not a simple matter for the Silladar Cavalry. Each regiment had to provide, at its own expense, its horses, transport, tents, saddlery, clothing and equipment (except rifles, revolvers, ammunition and signalling equipment). All kits and equipment were checked and overhauled, and transport, sanitary, provost and other regimental establishments were organised on a war footing.

Both the regiments of Jodhpur Lancers were combined to form a composite unit for mobilisation. A squadron of the Alwar Imperial Service Lancers was attached to Jodhpur Lancers as 10 per cent reinforcement. The Strength of Jodhpur Lancers that went to war—British Officers 03, Indian Officers 28, Other Ranks 497, Followers 58, Riding Horses 540, Draught Horses 53, Mules 63 and Wagons 19.

A panoramic view of Jodhpur in 1914. The picture gives a sense of the sprawling town, with soldiers and horses mingling with the crowd, as the historic Mehrangarh Fort looms large in the background.
Photo courtesy: Mehrangarh Museum Trust

Lieutenant Colonels Maharaj Sher Singh (Sir Pratap's nephew) and Pratap Singh, were the Commanding Officer and the Second-in-Command respectively. Major Hyla Holden (5th Cavalry), Major A.D. Strong (10th Lancers) and Captain E.L. Maxwell (11th Lancers), accompanied the regiment as SSOs. (Two or three British officers from the Indian Army were attached to each Imperial Service unit. They were termed SSO and were not sent to command the troops but to advise the Maharaja's own Indian officers who held the command appointments).

Just one week prior to their departure for the war, on 23 August 1914, in a very interesting letter to his sister, Captain E.L. Maxwell, SSO with the Jodhpur Lancers describes the situation in Jodhpur, prior to their departure for the War

.... Practically the whole work of getting this regiment ready for war falls on our shoulders, as none of the Rajput officers know anything about preparing for war, we find ourselves working 14 hours a day. The men look excellent and probably are so, for the Rajputs are one of the great traditional fighting races, but the horses are mostly small Arab ponies, many of them long past the age at which a horse by regulation is cast from the service. The officers are, of course, exclusively Rajput, and are not very highly trained; majority of them are of the ruling family, or are Thakurs. The Commanding Officer, Maharaj Sher Singh is a very smart looking fellow, and wears diamond studs in his ears! A fair number talk English and, as I say, all of them are gentlemen.

I am staying in the house of old Sir Pertab Singh, the Regent of the State, whose name is probably known to you, for he is in his way a famous old gentleman. His idea of the present war is probably something as follows: King George will place himself at the head of his Household Cavalry and the Jodhpur Lancers and leading these invincible troops in person, will hurl himself and them upon the Kaiser, who will likewise be at the head of his Household. The Kaiser and his Guard Cuirassiers, Dragoons and Hussars, will be ridden down like so many dummies by the brigade under George's command; irretrievably broken, they will flee headway from the field, and it will remain for George and his men and the Jodhpur Lancers to finish the war by riding in procession through the streets of Berlin. Something of that sort passes, I imagine, through the not very modern mind of Sir Pertab.

For a man of 80, over or under, old Sir P is little less than a miracle—and yet he can neither read nor write nor count more than 20! In spite of which he is, so I am told, the moving power of the state, and masterful to boot. Imagine a short, squat little man, with legs bowed beyond usual limits; a grey bristly head, bullet-shaped and usually bare, toothbrush moustache dyed a jetty black, and a ferocious eye. A queer little figure, talking broken English, and formerly, even now I daresay, a wonderful man of his hands, certain death to a pig, a mighty hard rider, a fine polo player, a great '*Shikari*' and above all sincerely loyal.

The house (of Sir P) in which I am living is a strange mixture of magnificence and squalor, the latter predominating. We all dine together, British and Rajputs, and it is the pleasure of the host that we do so in 'payjamas'! (being a bit of a snob, I gratify my own snobbish tastes by foregoing these in favour of shirtsleeves and whites). The meal is fairly loathsome, chiefly English dishes but a few native plates added; everything is slovenly and fairly dirty. Greyhounds and Mongrel bull dogs prowl around the table, thrusting soiled noses on to a soiled tablecloth, in quest of the scraps, which are handed to them from the plates of the compassionate. Other meals we get as time permits, and in such company as happens along.

I have a long bath hewn out of solid stone, which looks like marble; it is equipped with taps for hot and cold water. But the hot tap runs cold, the cold tap doesn't run at all, and the waste water hole is plugged with a bundle of rags!

So far as we know at present our plans are as follows—we have to be out of this and at Ahmedabad, where the local metre gauge line meets the broad gauge, by September 1; at Ahmedabad we go into camp, probably for a fortnight, anyway till ships can be found in which to export us—and the delay is horribly galling.... I think I will close this now for we are apt to be too busy to do much writing....

From your affectionate brother
E.L. Maxwell

Captain E.L. Maxwell, was the SSO with the Jodhpur Lancers from August 1914 to January 1916. His mother Sophia Lockhart was sister of General William Lockhart and his brother was F.A. Maxwell, who was a Victoria Cross awardee. Captain E.L. Maxwell was killed in action on 20 July 1916.

On 27 August 1914 Maharaja Sumer Singh wrote a private letter to the Viceroy Hardinge,

This morning I went to see my troops before they leave for the front.... they are going... and that I could not go....and I hope you will consider this request and allow me to go. I am willing to go as anything with anyone, and as for accommodation I assure you I will cause no trouble, and am willing to double up with Sir Pratap or with anyone else. The responsibility of my going will be taken gladly by my men. If I am killed, there are my two brothers behind who can succeed me. I only propose taking one man, that is, Dhonkal Singh Jodha, who can look after my clothes and horse. I sincerely hope you will sanction my going.'

In reply on 01 September 1914 the Viceroy wrote, 'Although I was at first opposed to the idea of your going to the war, I now agree to your doing so with your own regiment of Lancers.... Please look after Sir Pertab and see that he does nothing dangerous.' The Viceroy also approved that the Maharaja may take two horses and three attendants, who should include Guman Singh Khichi and Dhonkal Singh Jodha (Both of whom were created Rao Bahadur in February 1914).

In fact a large number of rulers of Indian Princely States flocked to France to serve in the war (though most of them, except Sir Pratap, were employed on staff or liaison duties well away from the front), among them Maharaja Ganga Singh of Bikaner, who brought with him his famous Camel Corps (which he left behind in Egypt for service on the Suez front, while he himself went on to France with

Meerut Division). The first four Indian princes to land on the soil of France were curiously enough Rathore Rajputs—Maharajas of Jodhpur, Bikaner, Kishengarh and Sir Pratap. In fact *The Times of India* used a phraseology in August 1914: 'The swords of the martial Princes leapt from their scabbards.'

As per the War diary entry (it contains a daily record of events) the Jodhpur Lancers entrained for Sabarmati at 07:30 AM on 29, 30 and 31 August 1914, and, after a few days, embarked at Bombay on 14 September, where there were floods of rain and the regiment was accommodated in goods sheds at Alexandra docks. The horses stood in rain with no chances of lying down.

After the regiment had left Sir Pratap handed over the cares of the state administration to Colonel Windham, the Resident, and on Tuesday, 15 September 1914, he with Maharaja Sumer Singh, along with their attendant Sardars, left Jodhpur for Bombay en route for the front (Sir Pratap also took along his daughter's son, Prithi Singh of Bera and three of his nephews and several noblemen, including his Raoraja sons Hanut Singh and Sagat Singh, a few of them as syce or grooms, and personal servants, as it was impossible for them to go in any other capacity). There was a large gathering of Europeans, and of the leading sardars and officials and people of Jodhpur to see them off. Shortly before the train started Sir Pratap made a speech to all present. He was visibly deeply affected and spoke with strong emotion. He said that, 'he and the Maharaja Sahib and the Jodhpur Lancers were going to the front. While away, they might rest assured that the Britsh Government would, whatever happened, look fully after the interests of the Jodhpur state'. Just as the train was leaving Sir Pratap called on the crowd to call for '*Fateh, Fateh, Fateh, Angrez Badshah ki Fateh*'. The crowd then ran in and embraced his and the Maharaja's knees and feet. Before leaving Jodhpur the Maharaja contributed Rs one lakh to the Indian War Relief Fund.

On reaching Bombay on 16 September 1914, Sir Pratap wrote a letter to Lieutenant Colonel C. J. Windham, Resident Jodhpur that, 'I am not in the least anxious about the Jodhpur State, when I know there is such a Government behind us, and a Viceroy like Lord Hardinge….Maharaj Umaid Singh and Ajit Singh are yet children. You should look after them carefully. You know this very well that, they are Marwar!'

On 16 September 1914 in Bombay, with torrents of rain and cyclone, the Jodhpur Lancers commenced embarking with Headquarters, 'A' and 'B' Squadrons on the *City of Birmingham* and 'C' and 'D' Squadrons on the *S.S. Tactician*, forming part of the same convoy which was proceeding to France under escort. The air in the lower holds of *City of Birmingham* was very foul and several cases of mad staggers and colic among horses was reported, due to bran getting damp while being put on board at Bombay.

Major H. N. Holden, the SSO Jodhpur Lancers in a letter dated 20 September 1914 to Colonel H.D. Watson, Inspector General IST at Shimla, describes the scene at Bombay as,

We got to Bombay on the 14 after a comfortable journey but found a cyclone blowing and rain falling in torrents. Our camp was under water, so they moved the 2nd Gurkhas hurriedly on to their ship and put us in their goods sheds in the dock, we were quite comfortable there except for the horses that were outside standing in water. We three British Officers lived in a railway saloon. It rained heavily and steadily, and when we loaded up on the ship on the 16, it came down in floods so that all our kit came on board with the water running out of it. We have got most of our kits up and dried them a bit. The men are pretty fit, we have some fever but not much.

The horses in the lower decks were in a dreadful atmosphere whilst we were in dock and some of them got 'chukkers' and went mad and knocked themselves about badly. Strange to say they were all Arabs and all Greys. No Whaler or Cleveland Bay yet has shown any sign of that, they stand quiet and eat well, this fact has surprised me very much. The lower horse decks, on which most of the horses are, are below water line and so all the urine etc. has to be brought up in buckets and emptied over the side. I must say the men, who have never been accustomed to doing anything of this sort, have played up very well. I notice that as a rule a horse's leg begin to give out at the end of three weeks, of course, by slinging and getting them out of their stalls and rubbing them down, we can help them, but there is sure to be some grief amongst them. They will require a good three weeks at the other end to get them on their legs again I fancy, whether they will get it or not is another matter...

On 17 September the convoy came out of dock but remained anchored in the harbour till at noon on 20 September when it steamed off from Bombay under naval escort (for an unknown destination, which all hoped and believed would be France) in formation of three-in-line, almost 30 ships in all, with one or other cruiser circling round and round. The convoy presented an imposing sight. For the troops, this was already turning out to be a great adventure and the overall morale among the troops was buoyant. Just to get a glimpse of the sea was for the Jodhpur men an adventure; to sail on it, to see fresh countries on either side, and then to fight against a civilised enemy comprised a succession of unexpected happenings outside of the daydreams of the most imaginative Sowar. Like most initial volunteers across the world, the war might have initially seemed a great adventure. They would get the chance to see vilayat (a foreign country), to meet people from other cultures, to fight alongside European soldiers. This all seemed glamorous to people in India, but one can imagine just what a life-changing (and in many tragic instances, life-ending) journey this must have been for the Jodhpur men who experienced the war. On 23 September the convoy from Karachi joined in. The ships were cooler when underway and the horses were less distressed.

The ships were off Aden at midnight on 27 September and on 30 September received orders to go to Suez full steam. On 02 October, at 6 PM, they arrived at Suez and anchored. On 03 October, orders were received to disembark and go by train to Ismailia and necessary arrangements were being made. However, before leaving Bombay, Sir Pratap took the precaution of wiring to the King a request that the Jodhpur Lancers should be sent to France, (Sir Pratap wanted to fight against the Germans instead of Turks) and not to any lesser theatre of war (originally intended for defence of the Suez Canal). Luckily, the new orders arrived next day and the Jodhpurs then sailed for Port Said on 04 October under new orders. Going through the Suez Canal was a fine sight, one ship following another in a long unbroken line at 5 knots or so. After Port Said, the ships in the convoy were allowed to sail independently, each at her top speed of about 14 knots or 26 kmph; considered fast in those days, when even mail steamers moved at not much over 16 knots.

A troop ship passing through the Suez Canal.
Photo courtesy: Mehrangarh Museum Trust

After a rough, but otherwise uneventful, voyage both the ships arrived at Dock Marseilles (the Indian base port), France on 12 October 1914 at midday. It was cloudy and it drizzled off and on—and quite cold for the south of France. There was considerable enthusiasm amongst the French for the newly-arrived Jodhpurs, who were warmly welcomed by cheering crowds shouting 'Vivent Les Hindous'. The commotion and excitement of the scene were infectious.

In a letter home Captain E.L. Maxwell describes their arrival,

> '... From the dock part of the down we presently came to the better and bigger streets, and here we found ourselves alarmingly popular. All the small boys wanted to shake us by the hand, and ran beside our horses in order to do so; from the big shops the lovely French maidens came darting forth to clap their hands and gave bewitching smiles; all the traffic of the streets turned to stare and to greet, and at the corners little crowds gathered to see our two squadrons pass. Being a shy man, I was embarrassed by all this love of the British and the Indians! From the big streets we passed into suburbs, and for 12 miles we went along an endless paved road, bordered with plane trees and a tram line and little villas ....'

After a magnificent reception the regiment marched to La Peune Camp about 12 miles away from Marseilles Dock and camped in tents, in rain-soaked surroundings. Half the men remained at the port to unload both the ships and left in lorries the following morning for the camp. Except during the monsoon months, rain is conspicuous by its absence in Jodhpur State, so the men had a somewhat rude introduction to the vagaries of the European weather and climate as rain fell almost incessantly, causing much discomfort both to men and animals. The clay soil on which camp was pitched became a morass and it was impossible to rest or exercise the horses and all kit became soaked and saturated in mud. The plight of Jodhpur troops, still in their khaki summer clothing, was pitiful as the camp was flooded by heavy rain. One Officer, three men and a follower had to be sent to hospital, all from effects of exposure to cold. It was not considered advisable that the horses should be ridden at once after six weeks on board ship. Six French and one English interpreter were at first attached to the regiment but afterwards reduced to one, Mr M de Hamel.

The regiment remained at La Peune Camp, Marseilles for nine days, from 12 to 20 October and the men got used to the French weather and their new ration, and the horses got back into condition after the long voyage. All those days at the camp were a strange mixture of East and West. It may be imagined how the Lancers exercising in the park attracted the bourgeois from the city. It particularly attracted the attention of the celebrated Russian battle painter Lady Massia Bibikoff, who was excited to see the Jodhpurs and made some excellent sketches and impressions of the Jodhpur Lancers.

The man marching off from Port Marseilles to La Peune camp. The French crowd extended
a warm welcome with shouts of '*Vivent Les Hindous*'.
Illustration courtesy: Major General Ian Cardozo, AVSM, SM (Retd)

Indian troops decamped at Marseilles on arrival in France. The contemporary picture postcard
gives a sense of the sprawling camp, complete with horses and tents brought over for the war
from India. There was an atmosphere of 'frantic excitement and enthusiasm' on the arrival of the
Jodhpur Lancers in France.
Photo courtesy: The author

She describes the arrival of the Jodhpurs at Marseilles in her own words,

The crowd shouting welcome to the gallant, bronze-faced soldiers who marched by with the dignified yet swinging gait, and smiled with a flash of dazzling teeth when people threw them flowers and children gave them flags. It was a delirious scene. The people in the cafes stood on chairs and shouted, *'Vivent Les Hindous!'* I followed the Jodhpur Lancers right in the midst of the turmoil of their camp, to watch and note all their characteristics and I drew anything and everything that particularly struck me. All over there was nothing but soldiers, carts, empty wagons and limbers, boxes of every imaginable size, rows of white tents and lines of picketed horses, and lances stuck in the ground and tied up like sheaves and all chaos with an accompaniment of shouts and orders and braying mules made up a scene so unexpected, so out of the common. Seldom have I seen such fine men, tall, slender, beautifully proportioned, their expression is gentle and remarkably sympathetic, especially when a kindly smile lights up their bronze faces. They posed merrily, standing stiff, motionless, their arms glued to their

A Sentry at the Jodhpur Lancers camp in La Peune, Marseilles. Lady Massia Bibikoff drew many sketches of the Jodhpurs.
Photo courtesy: Our Indians at Marseilles by Massia Bibikoff

sides! I got fond of the camp smell—a mixture of wood-smoke, new bread, leather and horse-sweat.

I was told that this regiment belongs entirely to a Maharajah and it had nothing but Rajas as officers, about whom I had only imagined in fairy stories. I was taken to the Commanding Officer of the Jodhpur Lancers Lieutenant Colonel Maharaj Sher Singh—never in my life had I seen a handsomer man. As he moved his head, two diamonds, which he wore in his ears, darted out blue gleams, and a radiant smile lighting up his face disclosed dazzling teeth like a row of big pearls. I requested Maharaj Sher Singh, if I could sketch him. He invited us to his tent which was lined with yellow stuff with oriental designs in black, the bed was covered with a fine oriental rug and at the back were piled his portmanteau, his weapons and folding chair. Sher Singh wore a turban that was folded several layers thick over his right temple, cheek and ear, and kept in place by the *puggaree* that went round his head, he wore Eastern slippers of leather with turned up tips. The oval of his face is regular. His nose is slightly aquiline with finely cut, open nostrils, a thick short moustache, black as jet, covers an exquisitely moulded mouth. The large eyes were splendid, with a deep and penetrating look—eyes of smouldering fire under their long lashes. The diamonds in his ears, the flash of his eyes, his brilliant smile, lent a sort of radiance to his face, and from his whole personality issued an impression of force and vigour, and the whole impression most sympathetic.

A signed portrait of Lieutenant Colonel Maharaj Sher Singh drawn by Massia Bibikoff on 17 October 1914. Massia said of him that, 'Never in my life had I seen a handsomer man than him'. Perhaps both fell in love for a brief period of 15 days in La Peune Camp Marseilles!
Photo Courtesy: Our Indians at Marseilles by Massia Bibikoff

At the end of the sketch I gave him our address at Paris and he promised to see me at Paris after the war, if he was still alive, and from there he will take me to India and lodge me in his palace and I will be received as queen and heaped with pearls and diamonds! I said, 'Oh! if only your words could come to pass then my wildest dreams would come true.'

Each day till the departure of the Jodhpur Lancers to the front on 21 October, Massia would come and meet Maharaj Sher Singh for whom she would do all kinds of purchasing like cigarettes, stationery, etc., from the town (the men were not allowed to leave the camp) and then take his permission to draw other characters in the Jodhpur Camp.

Left: The signed sketch of Captain Dalpat Singh drawn by Massia Bibikoff on 18 October 1914.
Right top: Jodhpur Lancers troops in Camp La Peune, Marseilles, France, on 16 October 1914, drawn by Massia Bibikoff.
Right bottom: The most ingenious ovens for making bread drawn by Massia Bibikoff on 18 October 1914.
Photos courtesy: Our Indians at Marseilles by Massia Bibikoff

ENGLAND AND INDIA — COMRADES IN ARMS,
WHERE IS THE FOE WHO SHALL DRAG
FROM THEIR MIGHTY HANDS, THE STAFF ON
WHICH STANDS,
BRITANNIA'S HONOURED FLAG?

Top: The mule carried big leather bags full of water on either side. It was a practical and convenient method of transporting water in camp. Sketch drawn by Massia Bibikoff on 15 October 1914. *Photo courtesy: Our Indians at Marseilles by Massia Bibikoff*

Bottom: The Jodhpur troops gathered at Marseilles station before they entrained for Orleans. They arrived in France armed with *tulwar*s and lances, dressed in cotton, and destined to serve in the freezing conditions of snow and ice for more than three years in France. The Jodhpur Lancers was the only Imperial Service Cavalry regiment to serve in France. On the right is a contemporary British propaganda postcard after the arrival of the Indian Cavalry in France.

Photos courtesy: (left) Jon Lee and (right) Jyotirmay Bareria

On 21 October 1914, the Regiment left La Peune Camp, Marseilles, for Orleans in three trains, starting from Harbour Station, at 12:45 PM. The Russian Lady Massia Bibikoff followed them to the station and hurriedly made some more sketches before their departure from the station.

Turmoils of departure, 21 October 1914—Jodhpur Lancers entraining for the front at Harbour Station, Marseilles. After the Jodhpurs' departure Lady Massia Bibikoff remarked, 'gone are the gallant sons of the land of marvels'
Photo courtesy: Our Indians at Marseilles by Massia Bibikoff

Arriving at Orleans (70 miles south-west of Paris) on 24 October, the troops again received an enthusiastic welcome on their way to the Indian advanced base camp established at La Source (Champs de Cercettes) six miles away from the town. Here they received their equipment, including coats, warm underclothing and bayonets (the issue of bayonets to Jodhpur men was a surprise) from Ordnance and all tents, including officers tents, brought from Jodhpur were valued and taken over by the government. On their arrival here Captain Amar Singh Kanota, now posted as ADC to the Sirhind Brigade Commander came calling and stayed with the regiment till 02 November 1914.

Meanwhile Maharaja Sumer Singh was made Honorary Lieutenant with effect from 02 October 1914 and on 13 January 1915 appointed to the 3rd Skinner's

ARMÉE ANGLO-INDIENNE — Cavalier Indien

Captain Amar Singh Kanota, ADC to the Sirhind Brigade Commander, would often come and meet the Jodhpur Lancers during the war. He had served with Jodhpur Lancers from 1896 to 1901.

Photo courtesy: The author

25. GUERRE 1914 TYPES HINDOUS - En embuscade

The unfamiliar weather and being woefully ill-equipped posed persistent problems for the men. Issue of bayonets was a surprise for Indian Cavalry men.

Photo courtesy: The author

Horse as an Honorary Officer. It was considered that the Maharaja's appointment would have a beneficial effect on recruiting (since 3rd Skinner's Horse was largely recruiting from Rajputana). He was given a nice place to live in at St Omer, the Headquarters of General Sir John French, C-in-C of the British Expeditionary Force (BEF), to whose staff he was now attached.

On 02 November 1914 the regiment railed to Merville in three trains, and further proceeded to Rue de La Croix Marmuse and joined with Deccan Horse and Poona Horse as part of 9th Secunderabad Cavalry Brigade under 1st Indian Cavalry Division (later 4 Cavalry Division). Here the Regiment went into billets

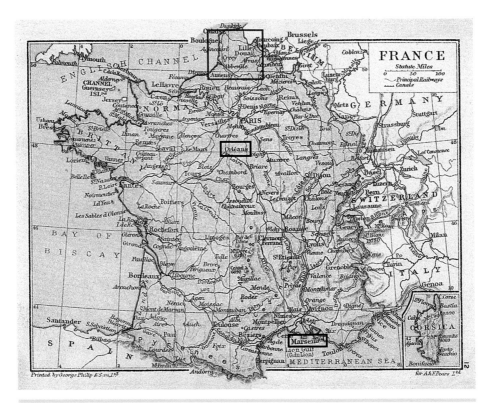

France 1914 to 1917. The Jodhpurs arrived at Marseilles and railed to Orleans and operated further north in the area bounded by The red square.
Map courtesy: Dominiek Dendooven at In Flanders Field Museum, Ypres

about four miles behind the firing line. The sound of gun and rifle fire, heard for the first time, forced the men to realise that they have really made their entry into the Great War. During their stay here the regiment provided 200 men each day for digging trenches and also looked after the horses of XX Deccan Horse who were in the trenches.

Maharaja Sumer Singh of Jodhpur on
24 January 1915, soon after his appointment
as honorary officer with 3rd Skinner's Horse.
Sir Pratap was honorary Colonel of the
34th Poona Horse. Both these high profile
soldiers of Jodhpur Lancers perhaps had the
distinction of being one of the youngest (at
16 years) and the oldest soldier
(at 69 years) of the Great War!
Photo Courtesy: Raoraja Daljit Singhji

At this time Field Marshal Earl Roberts, VC had come over to greet nearly all the units of the Indian Army, as their Colonel-in-Chief, and he was very pleased to see the Jodhpur Lancers on parade. Unluckily, a day or two later on 15 November 1914, he fell ill and died of pneumonia. Earl Roberts was closely connected with the Jodhpur Lancers whom he visited on 15 March 1889 at Jodhpur, just one week prior to his leaving India after 41 years. Sir Pratap was given the honour to escort the corpse of his old friend to England for interment. The funeral was arranged on a grand scale, befitting a great soldier. The day following the funeral, Sir Pratap went to pay his respects to the King in London.

On 17 November 1914 the Regiment left La Croix Marmuse at 11 AM and arrived at Vendin-Les-Bethune at 2 PM and spent the rest of the day in taking up billets, rationing and settling down. Here several important inspections were carried out. On 19 November, Prince of Wales, Prince Arthur of Connaught and Lieutenant General Sir James Willcocks and staff visited the regiment where two squadrons were paraded. Snow fell most of the day and on 20 November, the morning run was taken as weather turned very cold, frost having followed on snow. It is possibly worth recording that it was at Vendin-Les-Bethune that the Jodhpur men saw snow for the first time in their lives. The idea of being in a country where it was known to snow often during winter months filled many of the men with dread and they thought they must surely die. However, the sight of British soldiers and also Indian Sepoys taking part in snowball fights, and thoroughly enjoying themselves in the snow, greatly reassured them.

August 1914, (L to R) Captain Prithvi Singh Bera, Maharaj Ghuman Singh and Dalpat Singh Rohet.
Photo courtesy: Maharaj Hari Singh

The Jodhpur sowar did become the subject of many artists during the war. The distinctive Jodhpur Lancers sleeve badge *cheel* can be seen on the right shoulder. The image on the left is of Sowar Bane Singh (who sadly died during the war). Sketch by the official artist of the French army during the First World War, Lucien Jonas. The image on the right is by Eric Kennington.
Photos courtesy: (left) Dominique Faivre, France, (right) Mr Alasdair Kennington, Estate of Eric Kennington.

During this time the regiment was despatched to Merville and took part in the heavy work of holding the line between Armentieres and Givenchy. During the whole of November the regiment took part in the First Battle of Ypres. This was the first major battle in which Indian troops took part. The First Battle of Ypres, took place at a small market town in Flanders, bordering present day Belgium, where Khudadad Khan of 129 Baluchis became the first Indian recipient of the highest military award for gallantry, the Victoria Cross.

On 23 November the General Officer Commanding (GOC) Secunderabad Cavalry Brigade, inspected the horses of the regiment and on same day, 50 men under Major Strong went into trenches at Gorre (2.5 kms North of Bethune) to act as reserve and another 340 rifles were provided by the regiment in the evening and five days later a slightly smaller group of 36 men with Captain Maxwell joined the Poona Horse in the firing line around Festubert. On 02 December during their stay at the frontline, although the Germans were so close that they could throw hand-grenades across, only two Lancers were wounded, Lance Daffadar Jawahir Singh and Pith Singh.

On 01 December 1914, 50 men under Maharaj Sher Singh and Major Holden were taken out of the trenches and went to Hinges, Headquarters of Indian Corps where they were inspected by the King who had come down to France. The King also invited Maharaja Sumer Singh and Sir Pratap at Merville where they had lunch with King Albert of Belgium, President Poincare of the French Republic, the Minister for War (Viviani), and Marshal Joffre. The King George V, while introducing the Jodhpur Durbar to the King of Belgium, remarked that the young Maharaja Sumer Singh is ruler of an Indian state of Jodhpur which is bigger than Belgium in extent!

On 06 December 1914 the regiment left Vendin-Les-Bethune by 0945 hrs and arrived at Busnes at 1230 hrs and took up billets. Here it took part in the heavy fighting around Festubert and Givenchy. On 21 December at Festubert two squadrons under Lieutenant Colonel Pratap Singh and Major Strong with the remainder of the Secunderabad Cavalry Brigade carried out a dismounted counter attack on the enemy. Heavy rain had fallen and the men had to stand for hours in trenches half full of water before the attack was launched at 04:30 AM. The cold was intense. It was in this attack that four men were killed and six were wounded including Major A. D. Strong and Jemadar Guman Singh. Rissaldar Kesri Singh, also in the trenches that day, had preferred to carry the injured Major A. D. Strong (wounded in the leg) on his back to the reserve lines safely, instead of his own injured uncle Sowar Sardar Singh, for which he was recommended for the IOM. Tragically Sowar Sardar Singh, who was shot by a bullet, died next morning and Risaldar Kesri Singh never got his richly deserved IOM! (Sowar Sardar Singh's name is mentioned on panel 8 at Neuve Chappel Memorial France).

Major A. D. Strong, who had been evacuated to England, wrote a letter dated 09 January 1915 from 10 Carlton House, London, to Maharaj Sher Singh, Commanding Officer, Jodhpur Lancers, saying,

'I hope Jemadar Gumanji was not badly hit and that all our wounded are doing well, I wonder where they are. I am getting on very well but the doctor says it may be some months before I shall be fit for service again. I am very sorry to have left you all so early in the war. I hear you are now with General Remington. I hope you have good quarters and that the horses are under cover. General Turner (he was with Jodhpur Lancers in China) has been to see me several times and asked a great deal about you all. Please thank Keshriji for helping me back. I do not know who the other man was. Daffadar Salim Khan was wounded with me. He behaved very well. You will look after them I know. Please give my *salams* to everyone. Our men had a trying time that night (21 December 1914) and did their best.

Major A.D. Strong, DSO, the SSO with Jodhpur Lancers was evacuated to London after he was injured on 21 December 1914. He was married during his sick leave in March 1915. He later re-joined the Jodhpur Lancers on 26 August 1915.
Photo courtesy: Brigadier David Webb Carter (Retd)

At this time snow fell continually and the men, unaccustomed to this sort of climate, felt the bitter cold intensely and there were many cases of frost-bite. Here they were plastered in mud and wet up to the knees and unshaved, living on hard ration biscuit and tinned meat, sleeping with their clothes on in these cold and damp trenches, but, in spite of all this, Sir Pratap Singh, although 70 years of age, set them an example, deliberately wearing khaki drill uniform instead of serge and helping them in no small way to remain cheerful. Standing in mud and water for long periods in the winter inevitably led to cases of frostbite and trench

Letter dated 09 January 1915 from Major A. D. Strong in England to Maharaj Sher Singh in France. The available postal history provides good insight into what transpired during this pivotal period.

Photo courtesy: Maharaj Jaideep Singh Raoti

A group of Jodhpur men poses for a real photo postcard in a camp shortly after arrival in France. Standing extreme left is Captain Bahadur Singh and extreme right is Rissaldar Umaid Singh. Umaid Singh was the leading troop commander of the leading 'B' Squadron at Haifa in 1918. Right is a field service India postcard in Hindi used by Indian soldiers during the First World War. Indian army personnel on field service had free postage to India.

Photos courtesy: (left) Aditya Singh Galthani and (right) Professor K.C. Yadav

King Albert of Belgium with King George V at the market square of Furnes accompanied
by Sir Pratap Singh walking along with the Prince of Wales (centre) and
Maharaja Ganga Singh of Bikaner (extreme right) on 04 December 1914.
Photo courtesy: Archives of the Royal Palace of Belgium

foot. When the regiment withdrew from the firing line, five Jodhpur Officers were
suffering from frozen feet.

The remnants of the cavalry brigade reformed and re-organised ready to meet
a further German attack. The whole of the Indian Corps was relieved on the
evening of 22 December and the regiment moved to Liettres from Busnes. On
23 December Captain Maxwell and Maharaj Akhai Singh returned from fighting
in the evening by taking a lift in motor lorries.

At Christmas Sir Pratap sent the Jodhpur trademark 'Fulgars' (long padded
dressing gown) with a characteristic letter to the King that he hoped that the King
and Queen would send him some ginger, peppermint, and brandy, which were in
due course dispatched and presented to him, to his delight, with a greeting card
for each officer and men by the Prince of Wales in person on 25 December 1914.
On 27 and 29 December Captain Amar Singh came to meet Sir Pratap and others
at the Chateau of Longheim.

Sir Pratap (left) with Lieutenant General M.F. Remington (centre), Maharaja Sajjan Singh of Ratlam (right), France, 09 January 1915. Seen in the left corner is Captain Prithi Singh Bera and Lieutenant Hanut and Sagat Singh. Photographer H.D. Girdwood.
Photo courtesy: Mehrangarh Museum Trust

On 30 December 1914, 'A' and 'B' Squadrons, HQs and Ambulance Section moved from Liettern to Witternesse at midday. The regiment remained billeted in village Witternesse for the rest of the winter. The ground was too sodden and deep in mud to permit of any mounted work, but an outpost scheme and a scheme of defending a position, followed by dismounted attack, route marches, patrolling and convoy drill were carried out on the roads to keep men and horses fit, while the men were drilled on foot, in musketry and taught to use bayonets and practise bomb throwing, followed by inspection of kit, rifles and saddlery on a daily basis. The regimental scouts went out daily to acquaint themselves with the area occupied by the cavalry corps.

Early in January, 1915 an Indian Cavalry Corps was formed under the command of General Remington, and the Jodhpur Lancers, the only Imperial Service Troops left in France, were withdrawn from the Secunderabad Brigade to join the new corps. On 09 January, 1915, the regiment was inspected by General Remington, and afterwards on 18 January by Field Marshal Sir John French, the C-in-C of the British forces in France. Whenever Sir Pratap met the Generals, he used to ask them when the cavalry charge would take place, and they always said it will come about soon, but it never came about as he wished.

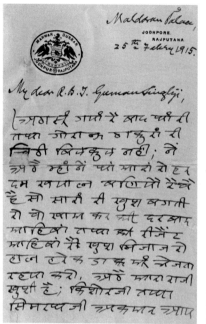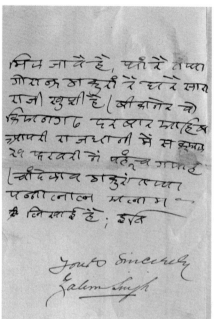

Letter of Maharaj Zalim Singh from Jodhpur, dated 25 February 1915, to Guman Singh, ADC to Maharaja of Jodhpur, in France. He writes, 'May God bless the British Empire with an early victory and the Maharaja and Sir Pratap with honours and awards. May you all come home soon with honours.'

Photo courtesy: Thakur Guman Singh Narwa collection with Maharaja Man Singh Pushtak Prakash

At this time some trouble arose with the men of the Poona Horse, who refused to eat tinned meat having a Bull's head as the trade mark. Sir Pratap was called to satisfy their religious scruples. The men said they will eat it if Sir Pratap first partook of it in their presence, and he did that. They were satisfied, and no further trouble arose.

On 16 January 1915, Captain A.B. Skinner, 5th Cavalry joined the regiment in place of Major Strong who was injured. Between 19 to 29 January 1915 the inoculation of officers and men of the regiment was done against Typhoid fever. The general health of the regiment was good though there was a bout of influenza. On 12 February the regiment was paraded and inspected by the Prince of Wales and General M. F. Remington. On 28 February 1915 Maharaja Sumer Singh and Sir Pratap were both 'Mentioned in Despatches'. On 18 March 1915 Captain P.F. Gell, 14 Lancers joined the regiment on appointment as SSO.

On 27 March 1915 Captain Amar Singh came to see the Jodhpur Lancers at Witternesse where they were still billeted for the winter. Because of the billeting problems, squadrons had their own officers messes. The horses and men lived in

Cultural interactions—a wonderful snapshot of everyday life in France, a rare photograph of
Jodhpur Lancers men posing for the camera with a French soldier and children in 1917. The
war provided Indian soldiers with an opportunity to witness and interact with people of other
nations and that greatly expanded their understanding of other cultures and societies. The war
also afforded social education and opened up relationships far from anything they were used to.
In the midst of madness, men sought ways to cling to the ordinary pleasures of daily existence,
even as the extraordinary events of war intervened. The distinct Jodhpur *cheel* on their right
shoulder sleeves is visible.
*Photo courtesy: Dominique Faivre, France, who holds the largest private collection dedicated to the Indian
Army of the Great War on the Western Front*

barns and outhouses of French farms, while the British and Indian Officers were
billed with French families. The Jodhpur Sowar soon made himself at home
with the French peasantry who came to prefer him to any other troops, including
their own. The Jodhpur Sowar showed remarkable adaptability and innate good
manners when dealing with the French. The men learnt French and some spoke it
extraordinarily well! (The Jodhpur Lancers stayed for almost four years in France
and the men had no serious problems with the French population).

On 04 April 1915 Maharaja Sumer Singh and Sir Pratap along with Captain
Dalpat, Captain Pirthi Singh and Major Holden went to London for a few days
on leave due to health concerns and stayed at the Alexandra Hotel, Hyde Park,
London. Captain Pirthi Singh in a letter described that they all are well and will
get back to France on 04 May 1915.

Meanwhile, in India the Turkish Prisoner of War (PW) camp located at Thayetmyo, in Burma, was full, with 2,629 PWs against its capacity of 2,000. Thus, on 31 May 1915, Colonel C.J. Windham at Jodhpur offered to open a Turkish PW camp at Sumerpur near Erinpura for 2,000 Turkish/Arab PWs. He also offered Jodhpur Jail for 500 PWs and the Nagore Fort to Government of India. The offer for Sumerpur was readily accepted, as more PWs were on the way at Bombay and orders were issued for one Double Company of 75 Carnatic Infantry to move to Sumerpur from Mhow under a British Officer for guard duties on 14 June 1915.

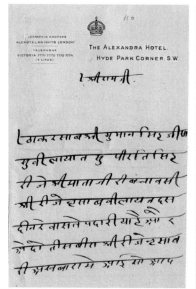
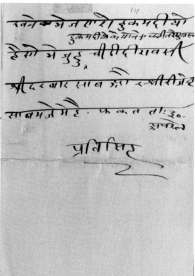

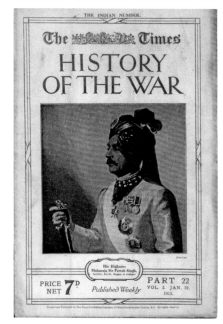

Top: 30 April 1915, Captain Pirthi Singh writes from London. He wrote that I am forwarding photos of Maharaja Regent Sir Pratap Singh published in papers
Photo courtesy: Thakur Guman Singh Narwa collection with Maharaja Man Singh Pushtak Prakash
Left: The cover illustration depicts Sir Pratap Singh of Jodhpur from an early issue of the popular publication *The Times History of the War*, dated 19 January 1915. It was a British weekly publication that gave illustrated news of the war to a wide audience. There was an upswing of awareness and celebration of Britain's colonial connections during the Great War. The war was important for its cultural and political ramifications.
Photo courtesy: The author

A letter written by Sir Pratap Singh to Colonel Windham, the resident at Jodhpur on 21 June 1915 from France. He writes that I am happy to learn that a new Turkish PW Camp is being raised in Sumerpur near Jodhpur. In his typical manner he says, 'Well I saying good bye Germans in France, you saying good bye Turks in Sumerpur!'. The PW Camp cost the state Rs 2,20,568.

Photo courtesy: Thakur Guman Singh Narwa collection with Maharaja Man Singh Pushtak Prakash

Sir Pratap (extreme right), Lieutenant General Remmington (second from right), heir apparent of Belgium (third from right) and Maharaja Sajjan Singh Ratlam (second from left).

Photo courtesy: Archives of the Royal Palace of Belgium

On 22 April 1915 Maharaja Sajjan Singh of Ratlam joined the staff of Sir Pratap in France. He was later promoted Lieutenant Colonel on 03 June 1916 on the recommendation of General Douglas Haig. In July 1915 Captain Raghunath Singh, ADC to Maharaja Sajjan Singh of Ratlam, died of pneumonia and was cremated at Boulogne.

'Somewhere in France', Sir Pratap leading the Jodhpur Lancers on a procession in 1915.
Image drawn by Lionel Edwards and published in the Graphic on 10 April 1915.
Photo courtesy: Jon Lee

The Jodhpur men would often get themselves photographed and send the real photo postcards home. Though portraits of Indian soldiers are seemingly rare but some of these have survived the tide of time. The Sowar wears a khaki *pugree* (short turban), a khaki drill *kurta* (long tunic almost down to the knees), riding breeches, long *puttees*, spurs and black ankle boots. During cold a khaki serge short greatcoat, reaching to the knees, was also worn.

Photo courtesy: The author

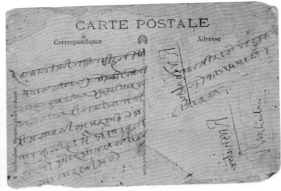

The real photo postcards were made by developing a photograph onto postcard sized photo paper with a postcard backing. Here in this photo the four Karamsot Rajput Sowars of Jodhpur Lancers (perhaps of the same village) namely Sowar Moti Singh, Daffadar Rup Singh, Sowar Mool Singh and Sowar Mangal Singh wrote to their uncle back home that they are all well here and you may kindly frame this photograph. Daffadar Rup Singh and Sowar Mool Singh got IDSM and IMSM medals on 17 February 1917 and 21 September 1918, while Sowar Moti Singh died on 07 April 1915.

Photo courtesy: The author

Another of the Jodhpur Lancers men in France sent these photo postcards back home. The Jodhpur soldier fought for the prestige attached to the honourable profession of arms and for the honour of the regiments to which successive generations of their families belonged.
Photo courtesy: The author

The Jodhpur Lancers men on guard duty at Sir Douglas Haig's chateau in Montreuil.
Photo courtesy: Dr Mahendra Singh Tanwar

The Jodhpur Lancers remained for three months as corps troops under General Remington, later moving on 24 April 1915 with the Corps HQs to Bavinchove near Cassel and on 04 May moved to Linghem (C, D Squadron and HQs) and Liettre (A, B Sqns and Ambulance Section). Again on 17 May they marched

King Albert of Belgium (second from right) with Sir Pratap (third from right) watching the sports by the Indian Cavalry Corps.
Photo courtesy: Archives of the Royal Palace of Belgium

An interested audience of French villagers watching trick riding by the Indian Cavalry.
Photo courtesy: Mehrangarh Museum Trust

Guerre de 1914
Soldat Indien fumant près de sa tente

An Indian veteran enjoying his smoke 'hukkah' in La Peune Camp France, October 1914.
Photo courtesy: The author

to Burbure, when new limber wagons were used for the first time. Further they received orders to move to Hurionville and Ecqvedecques on 18 May and then finally moved back to Linghem on 19 May 1915.

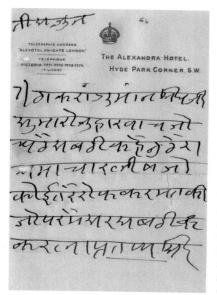

30 June 1915 Sir Pratap writes to Jodhpur from Alexandra hotel London, 'we are all well here'. Since his first visit to the hotel in 1887, he always preferred to stay there.
Photo courtesy: Thakur Guman Singh Narwa collection with Maharaja Man Singh Pushtak Prakash

RAJPUTS' DESIRE TO DIE FIGHTING.

LONGING TO CHARGE AT HEAD OF HIS MEN.

"I hope the time is soon coming when at the head of my men I will die fighting," said that Grand Old Man of India, Lieutenant General Sir Pertab Sing Bahadur who, in his seventieth year, is in the fighting line in France, to the London representative of the "New York Sun." "That is how every Rajput wants to die. If I die fighting I go straight to God. If I die in bed with a doctor looking on I take a long time to get to God. I have not yet had my chance, but soon I hope to charge the Germans at the head of my Lancers and die for the King-Emperor."

His Highness had come from France to attend the memorial service to his old friend Lord Kitchener at St. Paul's, and "The Sun" correspondent was presented to him at the Alexandra Hotel, London. Though a Maharajah of the ancient Rajput blood his Highness is nobility and democracy combined. A Grand Commander of the Star of India, a Knight Commander of the Bath, an A.D.C. to the King-Emperor, an LL.D. from Cambridge, his Highness has been fighting since he could handle a sword. His record in the Tirah campaign and Mohmand expedition, both on the borders of Afghanistan, are well known to every student of Indian history, while Americans who went through the Boxer uprising in China will recall the spectacularly dashing Imperial Service Lancers of which he was in command.

General Sir Douglas Haig, C-in-C of the British forces (centre), introducing General Joseph Joffre, C-in-C of the French Army (right) to Sir Pratap (left) on 05 July 1916, at Montreuil France. Sir Pratap kept pressing the allied commanders for an old-fashioned cavalry charge by the Jodhpur Lancers. Sir Pratap was longing to die in action. He had declared, 'I wish to die leading my men, sword in hand', but had to be restrained many a times during the war.
Picture courtesy: Mehrangarh Museum Trust

Around this time the French Government, in order to give honour to the Indian forces, asked for a procession of Indian troops to pass through Paris, and detachments from all units were selected to take part in the procession. Sir Pratap was placed at the head of this procession, and after its termination he shook hands with President Poincare, who received him very cordially and took him for lunch, where many French Generals were also invited.

On 13 June 1915 the regiment had the honour of supplying a guard of honour under command of Risaldar Guman Singh to the King and Queen of Belgium, who attended the march-past and sports by the regiments of the Indian Cavalry Corps in Aire-sur-la-Lys (Northern France).

On 17 June 1915, after nearly nine months at the front, Maharaja Sumer Singh returned to Jodhpur for his impending marriage and also to receive the full powers of administration of his state from the Viceroy.

In the midst of the war, Lieutenant Hanut Singh wrote a letter home from France, dated 14 August 1915. 'In the first billets we used to get some polo also, but now we don't get to play any polo here but we are trying! (He went on to become the finest-ever polo player of India).

Photo courtesy: Thakur Guman Singh Narwa collection with Maharaja Man Singh Pushtak Prakash

The men of the Jodhpur Lancers, France, 1915. Far away from home, the men were often homesick and ill-prepared for the vagaries of the European winter.

Photo courtesy: Dr Mahendra Singh Tanwar

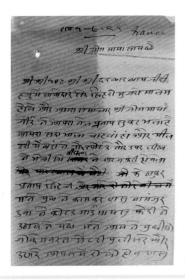

On 01 September 1915 Lieutenant Colonel Sher Singh wrote to Maharaja Sumer Singh at
Jodhpur about affairs of the Sardar Rissala from France.
Photo courtesy: Kunwar Jagat Singh Raoti

On 08 July 1915, about 240 Officers, NCOs and men of the regiment took part,
under command of Maharaj Sher Singh, in the cavalry corps concentration at
the Linghen rifle-range for inspection by Lord Kitchener (Minister of war), who
complimented Major General Sir Pratap Singh on the good condition of men and
horses. From 05 to 17 July, on three occasions, some 250 men were conveyed
in motor buses to NoeuxLes mines to dig trenches and from where they were
billeted at Les Brebis, where on 20 July three men were killed (991 Daffadar Nar
Singh; 905 Daffadar Dool Singh and 1003 Sowar Sumdar Singh) and two men
were wounded (796 Risaldar Guman Singh and 241 Daffadar Khuman Singh).
Major Holden, Captain Skinner and Maharaj Sher Singh visited the wounded
men at St. Venantin Meerut clearing hospital on 22 July and on 23 July Captain
Gell broke his collar bone and was admitted to Lucknow clearing hospital.

On 01 Aug 1915 the regiment marched out from Linghem and Liettres and
moved to Flexicourt and bivouacked in water meadows on the bank of the Somme
Canal. On 26 August Maj. A.D. Strong rejoined the regiment from England,
having fully recovered from his wounds which he had received at Festubert on
21 December 1914.

In September 1915 the Regiment again occupied a sector in the front line trenches
vacated by 17 Lancers at Martinsart and Authuile for a considerable time. Here
the men were issued with box respirators as a defence against gas, which the
Germans had now started to use. While holding this sector, the men were heavily

Somewhere in France, on the left is Lieutenant Colonel Sher Singh and on the right is Captain Gaj Singh. They have marked the trench area they were occupying as 'Jodhpur'! The Indian soldier became an integral part of life and battle on the western front.
Photo courtesy: Dr Mahendra Singh Tanwar

Real photo postcards of Jodhpur men (the distinct Jodhpur *cheel* (kite) can be seen on their right sleeves). The Indian troops mail was censored and monitored by the British and the surviving censored mails provide a sense of the Indian wartime experience, but the descendants of many of these soldiers remain unaware of the contributions made by their ancestors, as there are no records available for most of the soldiers and with no surviving soldiers to narrate their experiences, a treasure trove of information has been lost.
Photo courtesy: The author

Sir Pratap arrives back at Jodhpur from the war. Lieutenant Colonel C.J. Windham, the Resident, is second from left.
Photo courtesy: Meharangarh Museum Trust

shelled and all were glad when the regiment's turn for relief came (they were relieved by 5 Gordon Highlanders) and sent to Hem near Doullens as part of the mobile reserve on 22 September 1915 and while moving Lieutenant Dalpat Singh managed to catch a big pike fish in the backwaters of Somme.

On 25 September Captain P.F. Gell rejoined the regiment from sick leave in England. During the shelling in front line trenches Kot Daffadar Badan Singh, No 1441 Sowar Sheolal Singh, No 35 Cook Sheoji, No 92 Servant Tar Singh and No 23 Sweeper Sheo Kamia were wounded.

On 21 October 1915 the regiment marched off to new billets at Citerne and Frucourt. While here, some men of the regiment were employed in helping farmers to get in their beetroots and turnips! On 10 November and 18 November both Captain E.L. Maxwell and Captain A.B. Skinner left the regiment and proceeded to join 19 Durhams and 10 Battalion Gloucestershire Regiment respectively. Maxwell was killed in action on 20 July 1916 while in command of 23rd Manchesters. They were replaced on 09 December by Major G.R.P. Wheatley, 27 Light Cavalry, as SSO for 'B' Squadron and Captain R.G.A. Trail, QVO Corps of Guides, as SSO for 'D' Squadron. On 15 December the regiment marched to new billets at Tilloy-Floriville, Hinfray, Maigneville and Viamville. The weather consistently remained wet and cold and these villages were almost under water when fatigue parties were employed in clearing up the mud and drains.

On 09 October 1915 Major General Sir Pratap with his son Raoraja Hanut sailed from Marseilles for India first class on P & O Steamer Malwa. He arrived in Jodhpur on 25 October 1915 to attend the marriage (09 December 1915) and later investiture (26 February 1916) of Maharaja Sumer Singh with full ruling powers from the Viceroy (No previous Maharaja of Jodhpur was ever invested by the Viceroy in person).

On 25 November 1915 Major General J.G. Turner (Retd) who was with the Jodhpur Lancers in China, wrote a letter from Westerkirk, Staplegrove, Taunton, Somerset to Lieutenant Colonel Sher Singh.

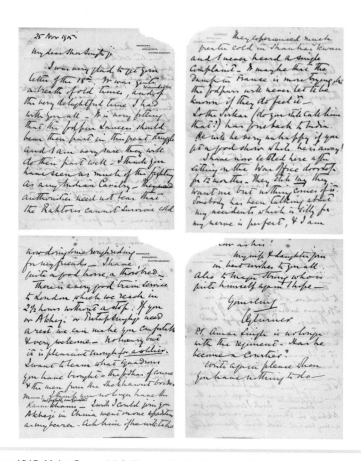

25 November 1915, Major General J.G. Turner (Retd) who was with Jodhpur Lancers in China wrote a letter to the regiment. Knowing Sir Pratap's keenness to participate in battle, he writes, Sir P will be very unhappy if you get a good show while he is away (to Jodhpur)! He means that Sir P will not be able to steal the limelight then.

Letters courtesy: Maharaj Dushyant Singh Raoti

Lieutenant Colonel Panneh Lal Singh, Commandant
Sumer Camel Corps from 1916–1919. He was ADC to
Maharaj Zalim Singh. He collected over 500 recruits
during the Great War and was awarded the
Recruitment badge.
Photo courtesy: Daulat Singh S/O Dr Ratan Singh,
Pannai Niwas, Jodhpur

'I was very glad to get your letter of the 18. It was quite a breath of old times and reminded me of the very delightful time I had with you all. It is very fitting that the Jodhpur Lancers should bear their part in this present struggle and I am very sure they will do their part well. I think you have seen as much of the fighting as any Indian Cavalry. The authorities need not fear that the Rathores cannot survive cold. They experienced much greater cold in Shan Hai Kuan and I never heard a single complaint. It may be that the damp in France is more trying, but the Jodhpurs will never let it be known if they do feel it. So the Sarkar (do you still call him that—Sir Partap was often addressed as Sarkar) has gone back to India. He will be very unhappy if you get a good show while he is away!

I have now settled here after sitting in the War Office doorstep for 12 months. They still say they want me but nothing comes of it. Somebody has been talking about my accidents which is silly for my nerve is perfect and I am now doing some rough riding for my friends-I have, quite a good horse, a thoroughbred. There is very good train service to London which we reach in 2 1/2 hours without a stop. If you or Akhaiji (Sher Singhji's younger brother) or Pratap Singhji need a rest, we can make you comfortable and very welcome—no luxury but it is pleasant enough for a soldier. I want to learn what squadrons you have brought—the Jodhas of course and the men from the Shekhawat border M...? *[Perhaps he meant Mertias]*. I think you no longer have the Kaimkhanis but probably some Ginayatas. I wish I could join you. Akhaiji in China went in one expedition as my bearer. Ask him if he will take me now as his? My wife and daughter join in best wishes to you all. Also to Major Strong who is quite himself again I hope. Captain Amar Singh is no longer with the regiment. Has he become a courtier? Write again, please, when you have nothing to do'. *[The letter shows a shared sense of humour and a strong emotional bond existed between the British and Jodhpur officers].*

While at Jodhpur, on 21 November 1915, Sir Pratap, having returned from active service much impressed by the value of infantry, put forward certain proposals for the reorganisation of the armed forces of Jodhpur. (At this time the Jodhpur

The speech of the Viceroy at Jodhpur on 26 February 1916 at the Maharaja's investiture
lauding the Jodhpur Lancers work at the front.
Photo courtesy: Maharaj Jaideep Singh Raoti

The Viceroy and Maharaja Sumer Singh arriving for the investiture ceremony in the Jodhpur
state buggy on 26 February 1916.
Photo courtesy: Mehrangarh Museum Trust

Maharaja Sumer Singh welcomes Viceroy Hardinge for his investiture ceremony at Jodhpur on 26 February 1916.
Photo courtesy: Mehrangarh Museum Trust

armed forces consisted of two regiments of Jodhpur Lancers; Sardar Infantry Regiment armed with single barrel Enfields; an artillery force quartered in the various forts of the state possessing 56 serviceable and 71 unserviceable guns; the Sumer Rissala mounted on horses and camels; and the Sumer Light Infantry. The last two corps were an ill-disciplined, badly clothed and practically unarmed collection of men, who were scattered over the state and employed as Dak Sowars, guards to local treasuries and lock-ups, and as civil process-servers for the Judicial and Revenue Departments. By no stretch of the imagination could those be regarded as soldiers—their strength, which fluctuated with desertions, was about 1,200 strong.) The proposal was to disperse this crowd of useless irregular force by placing them under the police and civil authorities and to maintain only one regiment of cavalry, one regiment of infantry and to raise a Camel Corps of 400 Sowars. This proposal of the Jodhpur Durbar to the conversion of one of their irregular regiment into a Camel Corps, was approved provided it was not raised as an Imperial Service Unit. It was named as Sumer Camel Corps and Lieutenant Colonel Panneh Lal Singh was made its commandant.

'My good wishes for 1916' Letter from Major General Stuart Beatson (Retd) in England to Lieutenant Colonel Sher Singh.
Photo courtesy: Kunwar Jagat Singh Raoti

A Jodhpur Lancers patrol in action at Linghem, France 28 July 1915. They carried a lance (10 to 12 feet long with a bamboo shaft), sword and rifle. Photographer H.D. Girdwood.
Photo courtesy: Mehrangarh Museum Trust.

General Sir Pratap Singh with a soldierly looking group of Jodhpur Lancers Officers, France, 28 July 1915. Seated on chairs from left Captain Pirthi Singh Bera, Captain A.B. Skinner, Major Hyla Holden, Sir Pratap, Maharaja Sajjan Singh Ratlam, Lieutenant Colonel Sher Singh, unknown. Standing extreme right first and last row are Captain Anop Singh and Captain Aman Singh. Standing first row fourth from right is Captain Dalpat Singh. Lying on the ground in front is 2/Lieutenant Hanut and Sagat Singh. Photographer H.D. Girdwood.
Photo courtesy: Mehrangarh Museum Trust

A troop of Jodhpur Lancers form a firing line at Linghem, France. Photographer H.D. Girdwood.
Photo courtesy: Mehrangarh Museum Trust

01 March 1916 letter from Colonel F.H.R. Drummond (Retd), 11 Bengal Lancers. He was inspecting officer with Kashmir and Punjab Cavalry in 1903—he wrote that 'the name of France in battle honours of Sardar Rissala will be a splendid record to hand over to posterity'.
Letter courtesy: Maharaj Dushyant Singh Raoti

Maharaja Sumer Singh married the sister of the Jam Sahib Ranjit Singh of Jamnagar (the famous cricket legend) on 09 December 1915. Owing to the continuance of the war, there were no festivities and later on 26 February 1916 he was invested with full ruling powers by the Viceroy himself.

In his investiture speech at Jodhpur on 26 February 1916 the Viceroy Hardinge said " ....We all know that for the last year and half, His Highness's Lancers have been at the front in Europe....up to date the state has sent 787 officers and men to the front, of whom over 700 are still on field service...the introduction of superannuation and wound pensions, and family pensions being granted to the heirs of those men who are killed or die of disease on service have contributed to the efficiency and contentment of the Jodhpur Lancers....".

After the investiture of Maharaja Sumer Singh, Sir Pratap left Jodhpur for war on 31 March 1916, and sailed from Bombay on 04 April 1916 for France.

On 28 December 1915 Major General Stuart Beatson (Retd) send his good wishes for 1916 in a letter to Lieutenant Colonel Sher Singh from 75, Portland Court, London West. It reads as, 'Very many thanks for your letter of 22. I was so glad to hear all your news and I first send my good wishes for 1916 to you and all my friends. With Salaams and the very best of good wishes to you and all my friends.

A letter was written by Colonel F.H.R. Drummond (Retd), (he was Inspector General of IST at 1911 Delhi Durbar) from Pitcairns Dunning, Perthshire, on 01 March 1916, to Lieutenant Colonel Sher Singh, saying that,

I was so very glad to receive your letter which you wrote to me from France and to hear that you and the 'Sardar Rissala' are well. The name of 'France' in the battle honours of the regiment will indeed be a splendid record to hand on to posterity and I have no doubt that further honours and glory await the gallant 'Sardar Rissala' in the new field of duty to which it has been called. This Great War has not yet reached a point at which any hope of an early end can be held, but I am firmly convinced that the gallantry of our troops, British, Indian, Colonial and those of our brave allies will ultimately gain a decisive and lasting victory. Your experiences in France must have been very novel and not at all in accordance with the kind of fighting cavalry would long for. Let us hope that in your new sphere of activity you will have a chance to show what the horse men of Jodhpur can do! Please give my kindest remembrances to Thakur Pratap Singh, Maharaj Akhai Singh and all the officers of the regiment and congratulate them from me on the splendid services of the 'Sardar Rissala' in France. With all fond wishes.

On 08 March 1916, Lieutenant General M.F. Remington, on relinquishing the command of the Indian Cavalry Corps, wrote a letter to Lieutenant Colonel Sher Singh.

08 March 1916, Lieutenant General M.F. Remington thanks Colonel Sher Singh, Commandant, Jodhpur Lancers, for gifting him with Jodhpurs famous Fulgar coat on relinquishing the command of the Indian Cavalry Corps.
Letter courtesy: Maharaj Jaideep Singh Raoti

Please accept my best thanks for so kindly sending me the very handsome 'Fulgar' (Jodhpur's famous padded and quilted box-coat) which I shall value as a memento of the good service rendered in the Indian Cavalry Corps by you and your excellent regiment of Cavalry. I have no photos now with me but will not forget to send them in due course on my arrival at home.

Maharaj Sher Singh, Commandant Jodhpur Lancers was re-appointed Honorary ADC to the Viceroy. The Military Secretary to the Viceroy sends him good news in advance on 06 March 1916!
Photo courtesy: Kunwar Jagat Singh Raoti

France 1916: 2nd Lieutenant Hanut, Captain Raghunath, Major A.D Strong, Sir Pratap, Maharaja Sajjan Singh Ratlam and Lieutenant Colonel Sher Singh. Major A.D. Strong was guardian to Maharaja Sumer Singh from March 1911 to August 1914.
Photo courtesy: Camilla Young

In March 1916 the Indian Cavalry Corps ceased to exist as a Corps and the Jodhpur Lancers were attached to the Lucknow Cavalry Brigade and moved to Villeroy and later to Abbeville. It spent the remainder of the year either in the trenches or moving from place to place. Full of incident as were the days for those taking part, trench duty was both wearisome and dangerous. By day, the enemy's artillery gave considerable trouble and both by day and night snipers were active. Constant spadework was necessary both for the repair and improvement of existing trenches and this provided exercise and employment for all ranks. Completely bewildered and amazed when they were first introduced to the network of trenches (deep, damp, muddy and prone to collapse under heavy bombardment), but this, too, soon became a habit with these men.

On 06 March 1916 the Military Secretary to the Viceroy in Delhi wrote a letter to Lieutenant Colonel Sher Singh informing him about his selection as honorary ADC to the Viceroy.

> Thank you for your letter which I received a few days ago. I have put your
> request to the Viceroy who very gladly agrees to it. (Lieutenant Colonel

India's contribution to the war effort in Europe was a source of endless fascination in France and some postcards printed during the war showed the everyday life of an Indian soldier. Here a contemporary postcard depicts an Indian Lancer officer setting off to the town followed by his orderly. Sometimes the Jodhpur Lancers men were allowed to visit Paris for a couple of days of leave, to break the monotony of the war.
Photo courtesy: The author

Sher Singh was made Honorary ADC to the Viceroy on 18 January 1912 for the term of Hardinge's Viceroyalty, but Viceroy Chelmsford approved his reappointment to complete his five-year term as ADC from 04 April 1916 onwards). We were all at Jodhpur last week where the Viceroy invested the young Durbar with ruling powers and we had as usual a very pleasant but too short time there. I am glad to know that you are keeping well and hope perhaps to meet you before long, as I leave India with the Viceroy in four weeks and then go to France.

On 19 April 1916 Lieutenant Colonel Maharaj Sher Singh wrote a letter to Officer Commanding 31 Mule Corps saying that,

> When the Jodhpur Lancers came to France in October 1914, we had with us 'saises' as per the Indian Establishment. The number was reduced and 14 men were transferred as drivers to 31 Mule Corps with 45 mules. These men were 'saises' of this regiment, which is an Imperial Service one and is paid by the Jodhpur Durbar. I do not know what arrangements have since been made about the pay of these men, but I presume, they are now paid by the Government. I would ask you to be so kind to remember these men and keep an eye on them and if possible to give them their proportion of promotion, which should be given to Rajputs or Kaim Khanis.

During the war, leave was arranged for Indian Officers to London and on 01 June 1916 a party of 10 Officers and two Orderlies of Jodhpur Lancers left for England for a few days well-earned break. The party consisted of: No 02 Maharaj Sher Singh; 42 Squadron Commander Padam Singh; 679 Squadron Commander Aman Singh; 1475 Squadron Commander Gaj Singh (son of Maharaj Zalim Singh); 20 Risaldar Major Hamid Khan; 365 Risaldar Agar Singh; 80 Risaldar Padam Singh; 237 Risaldar Kushal Singh; 847 Jemadar Pem Singh; 116 Jemadar Veterinary Khim Singh; 1269 Daffadar Orderly Ummed Singh; 1118 Daffadar Orderly Udai Singh and Major Holden who was promoted Lieutenant Colonel on 03 June. They were very well looked after in London and the party had the honour of being presented to the King in Buckingham Palace, on Wednesday, 07 June 1916, which was much appreciated. The party returned to France on 13 June 1916.

On 08 June 1916 Sir Pratap was promoted to Honorary Lieutenant General and Maharaja Sajjan Singh of Ratlam to Honorary Lieutenant Colonel. While on 15 June 1916 the following were Mentioned in Despatches: Lieutenant Colonel Maharaj Sher Singh; 360 Risaldar Anop Singh; 470 Daffadar Alim Khan; and 151 Daffadar Chiman Singh got IDSM and 1470 Sowar Moti Singh received IOM. From September 1916 Lieutenant Colonel Sher Singh returned to India to take over the command of the Depot at Jodhpur, which had grown to large dimensions, and the command of the regiment fell on to Lieutenant Colonel Partap Singh.

Sir Pratap 'reading' the English paper Daily Graphic! (Sir Pratap was illiterate and thus it remains a mystery whether he is posing for the camera). On his right Maharaja Sajjan Singh of Ratlam smokes on the footsteps of General Douglas Haig's HQ at Montreuil on 17 June 1916.
Photo courtesy: IWM ©

10 August 1916, a letter from Major General Stuart Beatson (Retd).
Letter courtesy: Maharaj Dushyant Singh Raoti

On 10 August 1916 Major General Stuart Beatson (Retd) wrote a letter from Waterloo Hotel, Wellington College, to Lieutenant Colonel Sher Singh telling him that Sardar Rissala is like his own family. He wrote,

Your letter reached me just as I was leaving London this afternoon—so many thanks for it. I am indeed glad to hear that you are all well and the Sardar Rissala doing such excellent work. How proud Maharaja Sardar Singh would have been of you all and also Sir Stuart. It is bad news about the lack of rain in Jodhpur. I pray that the monsoon may break well in time to avert a famine. I was so sorry to miss you when you called with Major Holden. I returned the next day. I shall hope to be more fortunate to see you when you are next in England as I do not expect to be away from London for long, at a time. I watch the papers daily for news of the regiment and you all. It is like members of my own family to me. Please remember me to dear Sir Pratap and to Maharaja of Ratlam and all friends. May you all have a chance of adding fresh glory to the honoured name of Rajputs! My good wishes are always with you. Excuse a scribble on hotel paper and in bad light, Looking forward to seeing you before long when victory is assured. Jai Mata Ji (regimental greeting) to the regiment and salaams to you all, including Major Holden of course.

During the winter of 1916–17 the regiment once again spent most of its time at dismounted training, holding parts of the line, and in construction of defensive works. (During the greater part of 1915 and 1916 the regiment, with the Indian Cavalry Corps, spent most of its time in training behind the lines, wiring certain areas, laying down light railways and preparing a track for a Cavalry advance, should the hostile defence be broken.)

In a yet another letter written by Colonel F.H.R. Drummond (Retd) from Pitcairns Dunning, Perthshire, on 11 August 1916, to Lieutenant Colonel Sher

 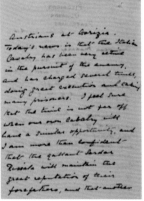 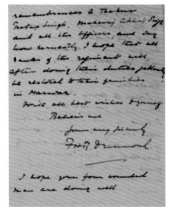

Colonel F.H.R. Drummond (Retd) wrote on 11 August 1916 from Scotland:
'Hope you get the opportunity to charge in France soon'.
Photo courtesy: Maharaj Dushyant Singh Raoti

Singh, he expressed the hope that the Sardar Rissala will soon get a chance to make a Charge.

'Very many thanks for your letter of the 08 instant; I am always so glad to get news of yourself and the gallant Sardar Rissala. Everyone in this country is so proud of the successes, which our brave troops and those of our splendid allies have lately achieved in France, and now we have the intense satisfaction of hearing of the great victory gained by the Italians over the Austrians at Gorizia. Today's news is that the Italian Cavalry has been very active in the pursuit of the enemy and has charged several times, doing great execution and taking many prisoners. I feel sure that the time is not far off when our own cavalry will have a similar opportunity, and I am more than confident that the gallant Sardar Rissala will maintain the great

Left: Major Hyla Holden with his wife Katherine Mary Blackburn at St. Paul's, Knightsbridge, London on 01 February 1917. **Right:** An engraved silver cigarette case presented by Maharaja Sajjan Singh of Ratlam to Major H.N. Holden as a wedding gift.
Photos courtesy: Hyla Holden

reputation of their forefathers, and that another glorious page will be added to the history of Marwar. Once the hostile lines are broken and the enemy forced into the open country, then will be the chance for our cavalry!

I was so sorry I was not in town when you visited London. I live in Scotland where I am now helping to raise a regiment of volunteers. We have already enrolled a large number of fine, sturdy men who will in due course form a couple of useful battalions ready to do their duty whenever called upon. Please give my kindest remembrances to Thakur Pratap Singh,

A party of Jodhpur Lancers in England February 1917. **Seated left to right:** Captain Panne Singh, Captain J.S. Oldham, Sir Pratap, Lieutenant Hanut, Captain Sultan Singh. **Standing first row, second left:** Rissaldar Jatan Singh Ganthiya. **Last row, first and second left:** Jemadar Shaitan Singh (who won IOM in Jordan Valley on 14 July 1918) and Jemadar Bhopal Singh.
Photo courtesy: The author

Maharaj Akhai Singh and all the officers and say how earnestly I hope that all ranks of the regiment will, after doing their duties gallantly be restored to their families in Marwar. With all best wishes to yourself.'

While the war was showing no signs of ending, the senior SSO of Jodhpur Lancers Major Hyla Holden decided that he could wait no longer (he was aged 45 at the time) and decided to get married on 01 February 1917, in England, during a short leave.

Early in 1917 the regiment was ordered to provide one company for the Sialkot Brigade Pioneer Battalion and this company proceeded to Warlincourt on 13 January 1917 but, to the great delight of all, rejoined the regiment in March 1917. On 22 February 1917 Captain H.F.P. Hornsby joined the regiment as SSO. On 25 February another party consisting of 10 officers proceeded on leave to England. They were Squadron Commander Sultan Singh; Squadron Commander Panne Singh; Risaldar Jatan Singh; Risaldar Bahadur Singh; Risaldar Chatar Sal

Real photo postcard dated 01 October 1915 of Sowar Sohan Singh of Jodhpur Lancers with the most common background of a plain drape.
Photo courtesy: The author

Daffadar Bahadur Singh-Signals in-charge Jodhpur Lancers BEF 'A' France sent this real photo postcard on 09 June 1917 to his brother-Havildar Major Simrath Singh of 43 Erinpura Regiment. He was a relative of Captain Keshri Singh. Letters became vital lifelines during the war, providing real information about loved ones and also an imaginative connection between home and the front. Due to prolonged war the men were under constant psychological strain as they were neither defending their home nor had they any chance of leave. They also could not share a language outside their regiment.
Photo courtesy: Aditya Singh Galthani

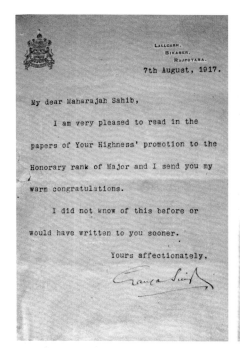

August 1917: Congratulations from Maharaja Ganga Singh of Bikaner to Maharaja Sumer Singh (on the right, wearing Jodhpur Lancers uniform) on his promotion to Honorary rank of Major.
Photo courtesy: Mehrangarh Museum Trust

Singh; Jemadar Keshan Singh; Jemadar Khim Singh; Jemadar Kuman Singh; Jemadar Shaitan Singh and Jemadar Bhopal Singh.

During the summer of 1917, with the Indian Cavalry Corps, the Jodhpur Lancers was held in reserve with the view of seizing a likely opportunity to break through the German line. None occurred and with the advent of winter the regiment once again settled down to trench work and training.

On 01 Aug 1917 Maharaja Sumer Singh was made Honorary Major and Hanut and Sagat Singh (sons of Sir Pratap) were both made Honorary 2/Lieutenants.

On 15 September 1917 at Lemesnil, a party consisting of Maj Reynolds, Captain Hornsby, Lieutenant Daji Raj, SSOs, along with Lieutenant Colonel Partap Singh Commanding Officer and Captain Aman Singh with 5 Indian Officers, 157 Other Ranks and 5 followers, went to the trenches at Vadencourt. However, on 23 September, Lieutenant Daji Raj, 27 Light Cavalry, was killed in action and 1037 Sowar Janak Singh and 1086 Sowar Bahadur singh were wounded. Daji Raj was nephew of Jam Saheb and the son of K.S. Yadvendrasinhji, of Jamnagar, Kathiawar, Bombay. He was cremated in Vadencourt British Cemetery, Maissemy,

Lieutenant Daji Raj, Indian Land Forces, attached 27 Light
Cavalry/Jodhpur Lancers was KIA on 23 September 1917.
Photo courtesy: Jaydev Nancy

France. On the night of 30 September /01 October 1917 the trench party returned
to Lemesnil.

On 20 November 1917, at daybreak General Byang launched his famous attack,
which was preceded by a host of tanks, in the Cambrai Area. The advanced
trenches were taken and part of the Hindenburg line captured, but his last
support line, protected by a canal over which the tanks could not cross, held out,
and the advance was stopped. At this point in time the cavalry divisions were
brought up along the prepared track. Sir Pratap was present with Jodhpur Lancers

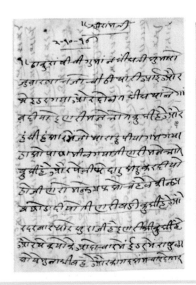 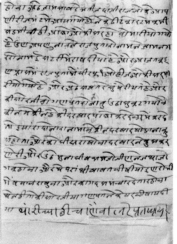

Letter by Sir Pratap, dated 02 October 1917, announcing the death of Lieutenant Daji Raj,
attached to Jodhpur Lancers.
Photo courtesy: Thakur Guman Singh Narwa collection with Maharaja Man Singh Pushtak Prakash

in this advance, but unluckily their progress was prevented by the canal in front. The Jodhpur Lancers bivouacked astride the Hindenburg Line in the vicinity of La-Vacquerie. The horses were kept ready saddled. Next day the Germans still held out, and the cavalry divisions were withdrawn slightly. Fighting continued for several days with varying success, but the cavalry were unable to get through, so they were dispersed and the Jodhpur Lancers returned to their camp.

They had hardly arrived at the camp, however, when the Germans launched a counter attack on 01 December, and all the cavalry regiments were hurried forward to meet it. The Jodhpur took part in a day-long dismounted attack against the Germans at Villers Guislain. Nine tanks were to lead the attack, followed by the 36 Jacob's Horse and the Jodhpur Lancers, the 29 Lancers being in reserve. The attack was due to commence at 06:30 AM, the 36 Jacob's on the right and the Jodhpur Lancers on the left. Owing to the non-arrival of the tanks, due to some unknown reason, the brigade was halted under cover and during the wait some casualties occurred from machine gun fire. The attack commenced at 10:30 AM and the troops were subjected to fairly heavy gun and machine-gun fire in their advance, but by 03:45 PM the Jodhpur Lancers had reached Vaucelette Farm just short of Villiers Guislain with the 36 Jacobs on their left. The regiment that day incurred the loss of five Other Ranks killed and two Officers and 18 Other Ranks wounded. In the ensuing engagements, Captain R.G.A. Trail, Guides Cavalry and the SSO, was killed. He was buried in Tincourt New British Cemetery, France. After a short period in reserve at Devise, the Regiment again took its turn in the trenches. The regiment was kept constantly on the move, often receiving orders to be ready to pursue a retreating enemy but never getting the longed-for charge.

The following important administrative changes took place for the regiment from 1915 to 1917.

Strength. The total number of Officers and men sent to the front up to the close of 1915 was 31 and 665 respectively, and four Officers and 294 men were sent during 1916, making a total of 994. The total number killed or died on the field was 23 and that returned as invalided 191, so at the close of 1916 there were 780 Officers and men on active service in France. A total of 320 men were sent as reinforcement during the year 1917. The strength further rose to 1,005 at the end of September 1917.

Enhancement of Pay and Ration. The pay of Non-commissioned officers and men was considerably enhanced during 1917 so as to make it on equal scale with the enhanced rates of pay in the Government Silladar regiments. Free rations at the scale @ allowed by Government for the Indian Army was sanctioned by the Jodhpur Durbar to all combatants for the duration of the war (@ atta (flour) 680 gms, meat 113 gms, dal (pulses) 113 gms, ghee (clarified butter) 57 gms,

The painting is a water colour by Jean Jacques Berne-Bellecour entitled: The 'guerrilla' of Indian troop—March 1915, which shows an Indian Cavalry Sowar taking aim at the enemy. He was an official French war artist (1874-1939).

Photo courtesy: Squadron Leader Rana Chhina, MBE (Retd)

gur (jaggery) 28 gms, potatoes 57 gms, tea 9 gms, salt 14 gms, ginger, chillies, turmeric, garlic 5 gms and fuel 680 gms per man per day).

Pension. The introduction of the new pension rules for Jodhpur Lancers from 1916 proved a boon, as many old officers and men, who were past active service, were retired, thus promoting the junior and more active men. The enhanced rates of wound, injury and family pensions and gratuities according to rates allowed by the Government of India was sanctioned with retrospective effect from the date on which the Jodhpur Lancers proceeded on active service.

Maintenance charges. The maintenance charges of the Jodhpur Lancers amounted to Rs 6,76,186 during the year 1915, and a portion of the cost incurred on the field was borne by the Government. A grand total of Rs 35 lakhs was spent by the Jodhpur Lancers during the Great War.

Recruiting. Meanwhile the recruitment in Jodhpur was made more attractive by the grant of concessions under the orders of the Maharaja of Jodhpur. The recruiting parties periodically scoured the villages for new recruits by 'beating the drum'. The flow of recruits resulted from an energetic and prolonged recruiting campaign. Many joined due to financial incentives, rank, pensions and medals, all

Posters, leaflets and notices urged Indians to partake in the war economically by purchasing war bonds and certificates. Marwar state 'Our-Day' lottery fete was held at Jodhpur from 10 to 12 December 1917. There was considerable interest to collect funds for the welfare of Indian troops at the front. After the Viceroy's appeal to help 'Saint John's Ambulance' and 'Red Cross Society', Rs 48,785 were raised by 'Our-Day' lottery besides Rs one lakh contributed by Jodhpur towards Indian War Relief Fund. Till 30 September 1917 Jodhpur had raised Rs 8,51,068 from various contributions.
Photo courtesy: The author

designed to make a soldier return to his village on leave or at the end of his service, a figure of admiration and a significant member of society.

Much later, after the war, on 15 April 1923, Lieutenant Colonel B. L. Cole wrote a letter of thanks to Major Dhonkal Singh of Gorau for his services towards recruitment. He wrote,

'I was Recruiting officer in Rajputana from 01 Nov 1916 to 15 June 1921. This period included the dark days of the Great War in which during 1917 and 1918, India was asked to make a very special effort to obtain more and yet more recruits for her armies fighting on the various fronts. Recruiting in Jodhpur was taken up in real earnest and I remember that you were one of the members of the State Recruiting Board, being in a special charge of the Hakumats of Nagaur, Didwana, Parbatsar and Sambhar. Your efforts met with great success and recruits, especially Rajputs, of a good type were forthcoming for the army. The Rajputs of these parts, mostly Jodhas and Mertias, make splendid soldiers and I ascribe this fact to the very good

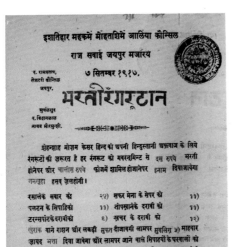

A recruitment poster emphasises the economic benefit with grant of a bonus of Rs 50 to each recruit enlisted and Rs 24 salary per month thereafter. The average pay for a Jodhpur Sowar during the war was Rs 18 (roughly equal to Rs 20,000 a month in today's terms).
Photo courtesy: The author

Daffadar Govind Singh, starting out for his third ride on 01 December 1917.
Photo courtesy: Colonel Jayant Singh 2nd Lancers

example of military qualities that you, yourself have consistently shown since the days of your youth. For your services in this connection you were awarded the honours of an Order of British Empire (OBE) and a Recruiting Badge and the gift of a sword of honour and Sanad.

At the India office on 23 November 1917 the honour of receiving the flag and the shield from Queen Alexandra on behalf of the Indian Army was conferred on Sir Pratap. These were prepared on behalf of the women and children of England for presentation to the Indian Army in recognition of their services. These relics were afterwards, on the conclusion of the war, sent to India where again, on 30 January 1920, Sir Pratap was invited by the Viceroy Chelmsford to Delhi, and they were then placed in the Viceregal Lodge with great ceremony befitting the occasion. These must now be in Rashtrapati Bhawan, New Delhi.

During the end of 1917 the Jodhpur camp received a heartening news when, No 2008 Lance Daffadar Govind Singh, (he was initially recruited and served with the Jodhpur Lancers) of 28 Light Cavalry attached to 2nd Lancers won the Victoria Cross on 01 December 1917 at Ephey in France. On three occasions he volunteered to carry messages between the regiment and brigade headquarters, a distance of 1.5 miles over open ground which was under heavy fire from the enemy. He succeeded each time in delivering the message, although on each occasion his horse was shot and he was compelled to finish the journey on foot. For his great gallantry and devotion to duty Lance Daffadar Govind Singh received

Left: Sir Pratap wrote home from Windsor Castle, London, where he went at the invitation of the King for the investiture of Daffadar Govind Singh, VC.
Photo courtesy: Thakur Guman Singh Narwa collection with Maharaja Man Singh Pushtak Prakash
Right: Large silver salver and gold watch inscribed with his initials 'GS' presented to Jemadar Govind Singh on 06 February 1918 by Alfred Ezra at National Indian Association. Alfred Ezra was born in India to a Jewish family in Calcutta and during the Great War, he served with Indian troops in Europe and earned an OBE for his efforts.
Photo courtesy: Colonel Narpat Singh Rathore and Colonel Rajendra Singh Rathore,
grandsons of Jemadar Govind Singh, VC

the Victoria Cross from King George V's own hands, at Buckingham Palace on 06 February 1918.

After the ceremony an 'At Home' was held in his honour at which Lord Curzon, Lord Hardinge, Lieutenant General Sir Pratap and many other distinguished personages were present. Speeches were made in praise of Govind Singh's dauntless courage, and Sir Partap said that he was indeed proud to hail him a brother Rajput and expressed his pride that another kinsman of his had won the cross, and declared that it was a proud day for the Rathore Rajputs. Subsequently, he attended the reception by the National Indian Association where Gen Sir O'Moore Creagh, VC, late C-in-C in India, presided. Daffadar Govind Singh was then garlanded and presented with an inscribed Gold Watch and Silver Plaque. He pointed out that of the nine Victoria Crosses so far awarded to the Indians in connection with the Great War, this was the second to be won by the gallant Rathore Rajputs, the tribe to which Maharaja Sir Pratap belonged. (Sepoy Chatta Singh, VC, 9th Bhopal Infantry was awarded on 13 January 1916). He added that the Daffadar first began his army career with the Jodhpur Lancers. In October 1902 a squadron of Jodhpur Lancers was transferred to the 3rd Madras Cavalry that included Sowar Govind Singh. Later, as a result of the Kitchener reforms, the 3rd Madras Cavalry was renumbered as the 28th Light Cavalry in 1903.

On 18 February 1918 Sowar Dhonkal Singh of Jodhpur Lancers wrote a letter from France to Suraj Bhan Singh in Marwar, Jodhpur. He wrote '...Daffadar Govind

05 June 1919: Off the saddle at Tel-es-Sherif. Jemadar Govind Singh, VC (standing on left) seen here with Risaldar Krishna Chandra.
Photo courtesy: Colonel Rajendra Singh Rathore

'Gallant were their deeds, undying be their memories'—the Jodhpur Lancers Officers on the eve of their departure from France in February 1918. They are wearing black arm bands due to the death of Lieutenant Colonel Holden's brother O.A. Holden on 01 December 1917 in France. **Seated from left:** Captain Badan, Captain Anop, Captain Dalpat, Lieutenant Colonel Holden, Captain Panai, Captain Aman, Lieutenant Colonel Pratap Singh. **Standing third from right:** Lieutenant Jattan Singh.
Photo courtesy: The author

Singh has won the first prize for bravery, and after this comes your humble servant. Neither he nor I really did anything, but the reputation of our caste for bravery is so great that we win rewards.' (Govind Singh had received the Victoria Cross and Dhonkal Singh had received the Indian Order of Merit). On 08 February 1918 Jemadar Gordhan Singh was selected to proceed to England to form part of the Imperial Mounted Escort on the occasion of the opening of Parliament on 12 February 1918.

The year 1918 came in with rumours of the departure of the Indian Cavalry from France and these rumours were soon confirmed when on 27 February 1918 the Divisional Commander bade farewell to the *Jo-Hukum Lancers*, who had served for nearly three-and-a-half strenuous, anxious years in France. The Jodhpur Lancers were popularly addressed to as *Jo-Hukum Lancers*, (whatever the order or what you ordered will be done) by many British and Indian officers, who had served with the regiment.

On the eve of their departure the Jodhpur Lancers had the honour of receiving the thanks of the King of England for their services in France. During December 1917 Sir Pratap was made Grand Commander of the Bath (GCB) and before leaving France in March 1918, the President of the French Republic conferred the Order of the Legion of Honour (Grand Officer), on him.

For the Jodhpur Lancers the campaign in France was particularly difficult as it waited hopefully for a breakthrough, which never came in the static stalemate of trench warfare. They often found themselves fighting, with newly issued rifles and bayonets as infantry or thrown into hastily planned and ill-conceived counter attacks. Although the Jodhpur Lancers did not suffer the very heavy casualties which their counterparts in the infantry, did yet their losses were not insignificant. On the memorial to the Indian Army at Neuve Chappelle, France, the names of 37 Sowars of the Jodhpur Lancers are inscribed. This is one of the longest list of names on the memorial among the Indian Cavalry regiments, which fought in France and Flanders and perhaps reflects the bitter fighting in which the regiment was involved in the early part of the war, though amongst them some had died of disease rather than wounds.

It remained then, to go and fight elsewhere and this time against the Turks. At last, now the Jodhpur Lancers would find conditions better suited to their abilities, their last hurrah in Palestine, where in a free country, led by the brilliant Allenby, they drove the Turks before them into Syria, demonstrating, once again, their unyielding spirit.

The Neuve Chapelle Indian Memorial in France commemorates more than 4,700 soldiers of the Indian Army who died in the Great War and whose bodies were never recovered. Panel 8 and 9 of memorial carries names of 37 Sowars of the Jodhpur Lancers (in all over 60 men of Jodhpur died in France). On inauguration of this memorial in 1927, the French Field Marshal Ferdinand Foch made a promise that, 'we will watch over their graves with the same devotion that deserves our dead'.

Photo courtesy: The author

The Jodhpur Lancers in Palestine—

Jordan Valley, Haifa and Aleppo 1918 and return home in February 1920

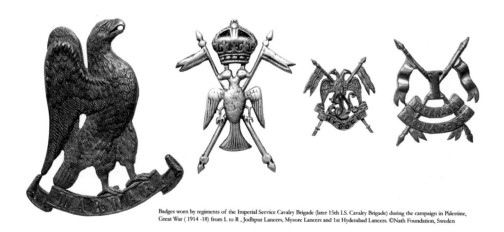

Badges worn by regiments of the Imperial Service Cavalry Brigade (later 15th I.S. Cavalry Brigade) during the campaign in Palestine, Great War (1914 -18) from L to R , Jodhpur Lancers, Mysore Lancers and 1st Hyderabad Lancers. ©Nath Foundation, Sweden

Badges worn by regiments of the 15 Imperial Service Cavalry Brigade during the campaign in Palestine. Left to right: Jodhpur Lancers sleeve badge, two Mysore Lancers badges and Hyderabad Lancers. The Jodhpur Lancers sleeve badge contract was with J.H. Johnson and Co, Aligarh.
Photo courtesy: Professor (Capt) Ashok Nath, FRGS, Nath Foundation, Sweden

On 18 March 1918 the Jodhpur Lancers sailed from Marseilles and disembarked in Egypt on the 28 March, proceeding to Tel-El-Kebir on 29 March to join the 15 Imperial Service Cavalry Brigade, 5th Cavalry Division, Desert Mounted Corps of Egyptian Expeditionary Force (EEF) under the command of General Sir Edmund Allenby. On their arrival in Egypt the Jodhpurs became a subject of interest, as to how would they settle down in this country, after their experience in France. Having spent all those years in Northern France and endured and become accustomed to the rigorous winter climate there, the men felt the heat of Egypt greatly and many went sick for a while but since the surroundings resembled, in some respects, their native Jodhpur, they were soon 'at home'. Here, in more familiar terrain at last, they would cover themselves with glory. Indeed, bored with the trenches of France and itching for some real cavalry fighting, they showed their mettle in their very first action in the Jordan Valley.

They only needed to forget the cramped warfare of the trenches in France and practise real cavalry tactics again, to become a true part of the EEF. Thus the time of next one month spent at Tel-el-Kebir was fully occupied in making adjustments imposed by the new theatre of war. Several officers and men were immediately sent to the Imperial School of Instruction at Zaitoun, near Cairo, to undergo a general course, and to be made conversant with the points especially peculiar to the campaign in Palestine.

Meanwhile Sir Pratap with his staff sailed on 14 April from Toronto onboard HMS 'Liverpool' and arrived at Port Said on 18 April. On the same day he reached at Tel-El-Kebir and Major General Harry Watson who was in command at Cairo, endeavoured to get a good house for Sir Pratap, as he had brought with him 12 young thoroughbreds from Newmarket, but he refused. Sir Pratap, after a brief sojourn at Lord Allenby's headquarter camp at Ramleh, joined the 15 Imperial Service Cavalry Brigade at Deiran under Brigadier-General C.R. Harbord.

While at Deiran Sir Pratap was itching to get some polo and as luck would have it, he saw a fairly level piece of ground but the problem was that it was covered with stones. So the next day the Brigade Headquarters received a peculiar requisition for 400 labourers' baskets for entrenching work! These were soon issued from the Royal Engineers Stores and next morning all the Jodhpuris lined up at one end of the polo ground, each with a basket. They then slowly moved down the ground and collected every stone off it, and afterwards there was some excellent polo that afternoon at Deiran. During this time Sir Pratap would get up at daybreak, and either ride round the posts held by his regiment, or make his son, Raoraja Hanut Singh, put his pony over a 5-foot bar with a blanket hung on it. This was a performance the luckless Hanut had to do every single morning, whatever he or the pony felt like!

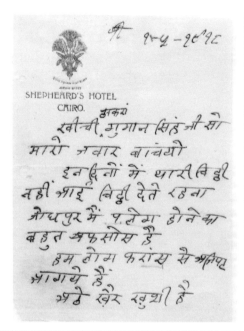

Left: On 01 May 1918 Sir Pratap wrote home from Shepherd's Hotel, Cairo, 'We have arrived in Egypt from France and I was sorry to hear about Plague in Jodhpur!' **Right:** Map of the general area.
Photos courtesy: (Left) Thakur Guman Singh Narwa collection with Maharaja Man Singh Pushtak Prakash (right) Major E.M. Belcher

Here General Headquarters (GHQ) ordered five European Pattern (EP) tents to be drawn for the personal use of Sir Pratap Singh but he kept only one. The regiment soon received marching orders and Major C.O. Harvey, Brigade Major to the 15 Cavalry Brigade described that 'We did our best to persuade Sir Pratap to stay in a hotel in Jerusalem. No EP tents could be taken with us, and we rubbed it into him how uncomfortable he would be. This only made him all the keener to come, and come he did'.

At this time both, Maharaja Sumer Singh and Sir Pratap received the title of the Grand Cordon of the Order of the Nile, from the Sultan of Egypt.

Jordan Valley–July 1918

The regiment was moved by rail through Sinai and marched from Gaza through Askelon, Jerusalem and Jericho to the Jordan Valley on 11 May 1918, where it relieved the New Zealand Mounted Rifles, who left to rejoin their own brigade.

The Jordan Valley was not only decidedly hot in the summer, with temperatures varying from 110 to 125 degrees, but, far worse, it was 1,200 feet below sea level, and terribly depressing. Mosquitoes and flies abounded, the dust was appalling, dysentery and malaria were rife, the Jordan Valley tested the men's endurance and willpower. Raids, rifle fire and enemy shelling broke the daily routine of digging, wiring and standing to arms before dawn. During the time the regiment was in the Jordan Valley enemy aircraft bombed troops four times, but the regiment was lucky and was not visited. Day after day they patrolled, toiled and sweltered in the deathly valley, until malaria, disease, poisonous bites, bullets or bombs claimed them. The valley soon began to affect the health of the regiment. All kinds of fever became rampant, particularly malaria. Men would suddenly become sick, or collapse in a fainting fit, their temperature quickly rising to 104 degrees or thereabouts!

Patrols were frequently sent out and came under machine gun and shell fire. On 16 May the Jodhpur Lancers patrols captured four prisoners from right in front of the Turkish trenches, and on the next day the Brigade was relieved by the 8 Mounted Brigade and it marched off to a bivouac area one mile north of Jericho. On 03 June 1918, the Jodhpur Lancers with the remainder of the Brigade marched to Ras Dieran where it joined the 5th Cavalry Division.

 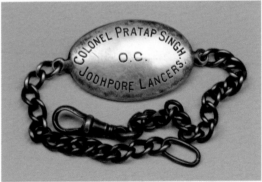

Miniature medals group and silver identification bracelet of Lieutenant Colonel Pratap Singh, Officer Commanding Jodhpur Lancers.
Photo courtesy: Gajendra Singh Shankhwas

On 15 June 1918 Lieutenant Colonel Pratap Singh went away on leave to India and Major Dalpat Singh (son of Hurjee), to whom Sir Pratap was much devoted, became its Officiating Commanding Officer. Mounted training was commenced and reconnaissances were made by officers of all points where the Brigade might be called upon to counter-attack for nearly a month. On the 05 of July the Brigade marched to Latroun, Enab and Talat-Ed-Dum en route for the Jordan Valley, again to camp on the Wadi Nueimah. On the night of 11 July the horses of the Mysore Lancers stampeded, and it was decided to obtain long ropes at once instead of the old system of fore and hind shackles. On 12 and 13 July the regiment marched to Henu Bridgehead, three miles from the Dead Sea. On 13 July early morning Lieutenant Colonel Holden was evacuated very ill with a temperature of 104 and Major P.F. Gell took over as Senior SSO.

On the night of the 13/14 July the Jodhpur Lancers moved from divisional reserve into the portion which included the bridgeheads of Mahadat, Hajla and Henu on the River Jordan, relieving Brigadier-General Godwin's 10 Cavalry Brigade. At 11:58 PM on the 13 July telephone instructions were received from the division to push forward patrols and ascertain if the enemy were occupying their usual positions. For this purpose the bridges were thrown from 03:00 AM to 03:30 AM on the 14, and 'A' Squadron of Jodhpur under Captain Panai Singh and Major Reynolds as SSO, crossed at Henu and another Squadron of Mysore Lancers crossed Hajla bridgehead. In the early hours of the morning 'A' Squadron of Jodhpur Lancers, after crossing Sangsters Ford of the Wadi El Rameh, was reconnoitring forward when it made contact with the enemy. This squadron of Jodhpur Lancers kept working round the enemy's flank, but it could not leave the crossings over Wadi El Rameh unguarded. The enemy appeared to be about 300 strong at 1,200 yards south of Wadi Rameh and were shelling the crossings

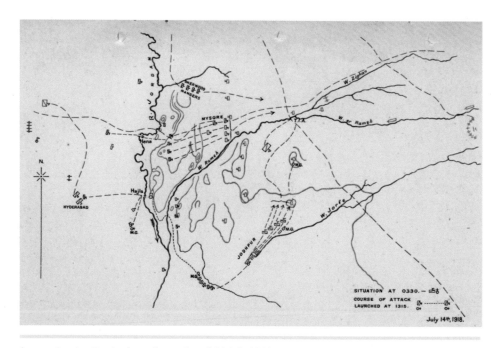

A map showing the Jordan valley action of 14 July 1918.
Map courtesy: Major E.M. Belcher

and rear areas with four camel guns (77 mm) and two 4.2 inch guns. In order to clear up the situation, orders were issued to Captain Anop Singh of 'D' Squadron and Risaldar Shaitan Singh 'C' Squadron through Major Gell to cross over and envelop the enemy's southern flank and secure the approaches to Wadi Rameh towards the Dead Sea with the Mysore Lancers and Sherwood Rangers on their left.

At 12:10 hrs a combined charge was to be carried out on a given signal. The Jodhpur Lancers charged with 125 men (five troops) and Mysore Lancers charged with six troops (also about 125 men). The Mysore Lancers and Sherwood Rangers advanced, at the same time being ably supported by the balance two squadrons of the Jodhpurs and Hyderabad machine gun section which did great damage to the enemy. The advance of the Jodhpur Lancers, less two squadrons, was made in line of troop columns with the troop of Jemadar Khang Singh as advanced guard up the Wadi Jorfe. On reaching open ground, deployment was made in echelon in extended troops, and the high ground in front was galloped. On reaching here the two squadrons right shouldered and galloped down the left bank of the Wadi Rameh where they rallied.

Here the toughest fight took place and many individual fine acts took place and a lot of the enemy were killed and captured and the machine gun section with the help of Hotchkiss guns did great execution. Jemadar Assu Singh and Jemadar Khang Singh seeing a force of the enemy trying to escape, charged them with their troops without hesitation. This force of the enemy turned out to be about two Turkish Squadrons and some Germans also, and the whole of Jemadar Assu Singh's troop were killed, fighting to the last except two men who escaped—both wounded. Both Jemadar Assu Singh and Jemadar Khang Singh were killed. They accounted for a number of the enemy though. Rissaldar Shaitan Singh also attacked a big force of the enemy, estimated at about 50 strong. The Rissaldar killed 4 men and captured 14 prisoners. The Rissaldar and both Jemadars were awarded the Indian Order of Merit (IOM).

Major Dalpat Singh accompanied only by his Trumpet Major Sher Singh, went full-tilt for an enemy machine gun—killing the gunners and capturing the gun. He also captured the Commandant of the 11 Turkish Regiment during the action. Major Dalpat Singh and Trumpet Major Sher Singh were awarded a Military Cross (MC) and an IOM respectively. Major Gell, seeing his Machine gun section Daffadar lying under his (dead) horse, unable to get up and three Turks were closing on him to despatch him, galloped up and despatched all three Turks, winning a Distinguished Service Order (DSO) for himself.

The enemy retreated hurriedly to their original position in the foot hill caves of Wadi Rameh, the Hyderabad Lancers following them up and remaining in touch until 07:30 PM when they withdrew into reserve west of the Jordan. Jodhpur Lancers and Mysore Lancers each then kept three squadrons across the river to picket the enemy.

The action is summarised in the War Diary of the Jodhpur Lancers:

> According to the Prisoner's statements the enemy brought against the Brigade three cavalry regiments (the 9 and 11 Cavalry Regiments of Turks, each 500 strong with the 7 Cavalry Regiment in the reserve) and a machine gun company (of 80 men and eight machine guns). The Commanding Officer, the four squadron commanders, and the adjutant of the 11 Cavalry Regiment were captured. It is estimated that at least 100 of the enemy were killed while 54 wounded and 20 unwounded prisoners and 4 machine guns, 51 captured horses and large quantities of rifle ammunition were left in our hands. Every officer and man who came back out of the fight had blood on his sword or lance, while many used their pistols freely.

The total casualties of Jodhpur Lancers was 28: Two Officers killed and one wounded; 13 Sowars killed and seven wounded; and five men missing. Besides 18 horses killed and 19 wounded and 19 missing.

In all that day Jodhpur Lancers won: One DSO (Major P.F. Gell), One MC (Major Dalpat Singh), Six IOM (Captain Anop Singh, Risaldar Shaitan Singh, Jemadar Assu Singh, Jemadar Khang Singh, Trumpet Major Sher Singh and Daffadar Amar Singh) and Seven Indian Distinguished Service Medals (IDSM), (Jemadar Jowar Singh, 1119 Daffadar Jog Singh, 1361 Daffadar Dhonkal Singh, 1604 Lance Daffadar Bijai Singh, 1316 Lance Daffadar Khang Singh, 1889 Sowar Tagat Singh and 1564 Sowar Guman Singh) for their gallantry in Jordan valley.

CITATION OF AWARDEES—14 JULY 1918

CAPTAIN DALPAT SINGH—MILITARY CROSS

For conspicuous gallantry and devotion to duty. This officer, accompanied only by his trumpeter, charged an entrenched machine gun, killing and scattering the crew and capturing the gun. At the same time he captured the commandant of a regiment and another officer.

NO 1189 TRUMPET MAJOR SHER SINGH— INDIAN ORDER OF MERIT

On the 14 July 1918, he accompanied his Commanding Officer in attacking a post containing a machine gun and the regimental Commanding Officer. He did great execution with his revolver.

Trumpet Major Sher Singh.
Photo courtesy: Dasrath Singh Borunda

CAPTAIN ANOP SINGH—INDIAN ORDER OF MERIT

For conspicuous gallantry in delivering an immediate mounted attack on the 14 July 1918, on the enemy, who were rallying on the flank in formidable numbers. He broke up the formation and rendered it innocuous.

RISALDAR SHAITAN SINGH—INDIAN ORDER OF MERIT

For conspicuous gallantry and initiative on the 14 July 1918, in delivering an immediate mounted attack on the enemy. Accompanied by three men he charged a formed body of about thirty dismounted enemy, killed and wounded fourteen and captured the Officer in Command.

JEMADAR ASSU SINGH—INDIAN ORDER OF MERIT (POSTHUMOUSLY)

On the 14 July 1918, without the slightest hesitation he charged the first enemy he saw, and by his spirit and dash set an inspiring example to all ranks. He was killed fighting. His widow was admitted to the pension of the order with effect from the date of his death.

JEMADAR KHANG SINGH—INDIAN ORDER OF MERIT (POSTHUMOUSLY)

He displayed great gallantry and ability throughout the whole day on the 14 July 1918 and especially in the mounted attack in which he was killed. He set a fine example to all ranks. His widow was admitted to the pension of the order with effect from the date of his death.

NO 1444 DAFFADAR AMAR SINGH—INDIAN ORDER OF MERIT

On the 14 July 1918, he with two other men accompanied his Indian officer and charged a formed body of thirty enemy, killing or wounding fourteen and capturing their officer. Though wounded in several places, he continued fighting.

Brigadier-General CR Harbord, Commanding the 15th I.S. Cavalry Brigade, wrote in his despatch, 'I estimate the strength of the enemy at a minimum of 400 with 20 machine guns. The Jodhpur Lancers charged with 125 men (5 troops) ... I consider that the greatest praise is due to the officers and men of the Jodhpur Lancers for their spirited mounted action....' The success gained was mainly due to the spirited action, dash and able leadership displayed in the mounted attack by the Jodhpur Lancers.

In his letter Jemadar Bir Singh of Jodhpur Lancers described this action as,

> The attack took place in Palestine near the Dead Sea in the Jordan Valley against the Turks in which hand-to-hand fight took place. In this Major General MacAndrew (GOC 5th Cavalry Division) with his own hands took the lances smeared with the enemy's blood from the hands of our jawans and inspected them. He remarked that the jawans of the Jodhpur Lancers were so full of the spirit of valour that they fell upon the enemy in the same manner as a hungry lion falls upon his prey. Here, Jemadar Assu Singh and Jemadar Khangar Singh along with their respective troops embraced death upon the field of battle.

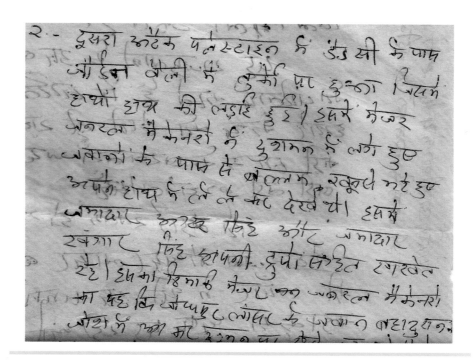

Letter of Jemadar Bir Singh on the action of 14 July 1918. Bir Singh (Gunawati) was with Jodhpur Lancers machine gun subsection as part of the machine gun squadron of the 15 Cavalry Brigade. He was later promoted to the rank of Captain on 16 December 1925.

Letter courtesy: his grand-nephew Colonel Sukhdev Singh Rathore, 61 Cavalry

Major C.O. Harvey the Brigade Major of 15 Cavalry Brigade vividly described the reaction of Sir Pratap in his own words,

> … we did our best to persuade Sir Pratap to stay in an hotel in Jerusalem. This only made him all the keener to come, and come he did. But, luckily, though he thought it most unfortunate, had not come up with us on the night of the relief, and arrived next day, too late to take part in the battle.

> He was delighted with the charge but two things upset him greatly; firstly, his son, 2/Lieutenant Sagat Singh, who was the Adjutant of the Jodhpur Lancers, had been ordered by his SSO, Major Gell, to stay at regimental headquarters at the telephone, in order to coordinate the attack and keep in touch with brigade headquarters. Sir Pratap, when he found out that Sagat had not taken part in the charge, was furious, and, telling him he was no son of his, refused to speak to him for several days. Major Gell told Sir Pratap that Sagat had only acted according to his orders, whereupon Sir Pratap refused to speak to Gell as well!'

> Secondly, 'Only two squadrons of Jodhpur Lancers carried out the charge. The remaining two were supporting the mounted turning movement with fire action. This was not at all to Sir Pratap's liking, and many times a conversation such as this would go on with the Brigadier General Harbord:
> Sir Pratap: 'Yes, very good charge; but why only two squadrons Jodhpur Lancers charge? Why not the whole regiment?'
> General Harbord: 'But, Sir Pratap, the other two squadrons were doing equally good work supporting the charge with fire action, which is most necessary.'
> Sir Pratap: 'That's all very well. Next time you make Mysore and Hyderabad Lancers do fire action, and whole of Jodhpur Lancers charge.'
> Such was his spirit. He had no use for the modern methods of warfare. 'Me not liking propaganda, me fighting man,' was his favourite saying at that time; and his idea of fighting was to get on his horse and charge!

On 25 July 1918, Sir Pratap sent a telegram to Maharaja of Jodhpur through the GOC, EEF, Cairo: Very Glad to inform you that on July 14, Your Regiment made a Gallant Charge.'

The Maharaja wrote back,

> I thank you warmly for your Congratulations on the gallant charge made by my regiment of cavalry at the front on the 14 July. Please convey my warm and grateful appreciation to Sir Pratap Singh and all the rank and file for doing duty … Marwar is proud of the good name and fame that you have kept up and their ruler wishes them all success and glory in the righteous cause.

On 16 July the GOC 5 Cavalry Division (Major General H.J. MacAndrew) and the Desert Mounted Corps Commander (Lieutenant General Harry Chauvel) visited and congratulated the regiment. The C-in-C, EEF General Allenby visited Sir Pratap and the regiment on 27 July and congratulated them and said among other things, 'That the day's operations of the 14 would live as one of the feats of the war'. Later on 10 September General Allenby presented ribbons to the awardees.

On 05 August 1918 Lieutenant Colonel Holden in a letter to Lieutenant Knight (SSO of 'B' Squadron) wrote,

> I got your letter of 12 July 1918 when I returned from hospital on 30 July due to malaria and now today Gell has been evacuated due to malaria! We are losing an average of 9 men per day with fever and today we have 64 down all told! We are in the bridge head south of Ghoraniya, our latitude is minus 1254, the heat is bad and the mosquitoes and flies abound.
>
> You will have doubtless heard of the gallant charge by two Squadrons under Gell on the 14 of July, one of the feats of the war! The two Squadrons together only numbered 125. They took on at least 600 Turks; with the aid of Reynolds and 'A' Squadron holding the Turks in front. They captured the Turkish Commander, five other Officers and 69 Other Ranks and killed over 90. They also brought in four Machine Guns and 52 Turkish horses. They lost two Indian Officers and 19 Other Ranks killed, six missing and seven wounded and about 50 horses killed. Gell got DSO, Dalpat MC, six IOM and seven IDSM and more than these were richly deserved. I was 105 degrees at the time and could only sit at the telephone and was evacuated that night, most unluck. All here send 'Salaams'. Come back to us at Deiran. I hear we go to rest there.
>
> Yours Sincerely, **Holden**

During the next one month the regiment continued to hold the front line trenches in Hajla-Henu Bridgehead. On 06 August 1918 Capain Aman Singh with 'B' Squadron and Lieutenant Chubb, SSO were sent on a special reconnaisance to report on the possibilty of a raid on Er Rameh. The raid was found to be impractible owing to wire, etc. On 16 August the Brigade was ordered to stand to in the morning and 'B' Squadron under Captain Aman Singh and Lieutenant Knight were ordered to cross Henu Bridgehead and to co-operate with Mysore Lancers reconnoitring squadron against the enemy who was holding the Sangstars Ford but on approach of our squadrons the enemy retired.

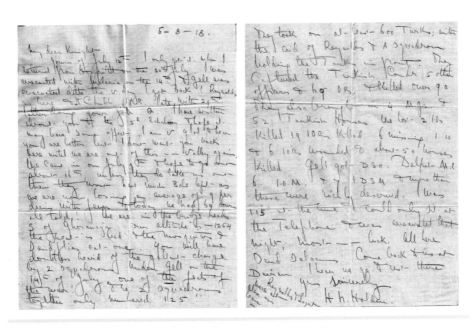

05 August 1918 letter from Lieutenant Colonel Holden to Lieutenant Knight.
Photo courtesy: Major and Mrs Wyndham Knight

On the night of 17-18 August the Brigade was relieved by the 10 Cavalry Brigade and marched out of the valley into bivouacs about two miles west of Talaat-El-Dum. Another night march took the Brigade to Enab at 6 AM on the 19, and a third one to Zernukah (1.5 miles SW of Deiran) at 04:30 AM on the 20. Men and horses were given five day's complete rest, and on the 26 intensive training started with troop and squadron parades. During the month spent at Zernukah, nothing much occurred to disturb the routine of training. Regimental and brigade training was carried on steadily until the middle of September.

During August 1918 the brigade suffered considerably from fever contracted in the valley and Hajla bridgehead, and men started going sick at the rate of about 10 per regiment per diem. Owing to this, the strength of the Mysore and Hyderabad Lancers was greatly diminished. These two regiments, unlike the Jodhpur Lancers, had no reinforcements available in the country, although many were known to be ready in India. The result was that when called upon for active operations a few weeks later, the Mysore Lancers were 100 below establishment and the Hyderabad Lancers over 200 unable to serve due to fever. During August a total of four officers, 97 men and five Followers of Jodhpur Lancers reported sick besides 52 horses evacuated to the Mobile Veterinary Section.

On 16 September 1918 the Jodhpur Lancers marched 18 miles and reached Liketra from Arsuf near Jaffa. On the evening of the 17 September the Brigade marched to the divisional position of readiness at Sommeil, arriving at 1 AM, and bivouacking in orange groves secure from observation by enemy aircraft. This was again left on the 18 and the Brigade reached El Jelil at 1 AM on the 19 and Abu Shusheh on 20 September. The 'B' Squadron team of Captain Aman Singh and Lieutenant Knight laid the advanced watering troughs and cavalry track.

Now the C-in-C, EEF, General Edmund Allenby's historic offensive into Palestine and Syria had began with the 'Battle of Megiddo' on 19 September (The battle of Megiddo was the final Allied offensive of the First world War. The series of battles took place in what was then parts of present day Israel, Syria and Jordan). The brigade then marched straight across the Carmel range to reach El Afule on the 21 September. There was no road and the going was very hilly and stony, and told seriously on the horses. Allenby had decided to attack along the coast, on the Plain of Sharon, where the ground was well suited for cavalry. The way was now open for the capture of the coastal ports of Haifa and Acre.

During the short halts on the march Sir Pratap never got off his horse, as, with his oft-broken legs, he found it hard to mount and dismount. He was, therefore, continuously in the saddle for some thirty hours, except for about five hours rest at Liktera; and this at the age of 73. But it was a bit too much, even for him, and at El Afule he fell ill with fever. In Allenby's words Sir Pratap was,

> Quite knocked up. He went right away, with his regiment, to Nazareth, a 70-mile ride, day and night. I want to send him to convalescent home in Egypt for a few days. A tough old warrior indeed and as keen as a boy. But to that splendid veteran's great disgust he got a bad bout of fever at El Afule on 21 September 1918 and was forced to go to hospital, being evacuated later to Alexandria or else he would have been part of the legendary charge at Haifa.

Guts and Glory with Sword and Lance at Haifa on 23 September 1918

Haifa was an important harbour and railhead and became vital to Allenby's 'Megiddo' plan to secure it as soon as possible to land supplies from the sea. From the Despatch dated 31 October 1918, by General Allenby: item 19 reads: 'I ordered the Desert Mounted Corps to occupy Acre and Haifa. Any force, advancing north-westwards from Haifa along the coast, would have to depend on supplies landed at that harbour. It was necessary, therefore, to occupy the town without delay....'

The Jodhpur Lancers Charge at Haifa.
Sketch courtesy: Major General Ian Cardozo, AVSM, SM (Retd)

On the morning of the 22 September 1918, orders were issued by General Chauvel for the capture of Haifa and Acre by the 5th Cavalry Division next day; but, on a report being received from the air that Haifa was being evacuated, GHQ directed that an attempt should be made to occupy it that afternoon by the 12 Light Armoured Motor Battery (LAM) and the 7 Light Car Patrol. Brigadier General A D'A King, GOC Royal Artillery Desert Mounted Corps, was put in command of the detachment to try and occupy the town. The result was a failure. Three miles short of Haifa, near the village of Belled el Sheikh, the column came under artillery fire, and machine guns opened upon it from the hills. Several tyres were burst, the commander's touring car was damaged, and he had to enter one of the armoured cars. There was nothing for it but to turn back, but this was a matter of difficulty under heavy fire. Eventually, after a critical few moments, the column extricated itself and returned to El Lajjun.

It was clear that Haifa was held. It was necessary, therefore, to carry out an attack in force against Haifa on the 23 September, and this operation was the task of the 5th Cavalry Division comprising the 13, 14 and 15 (Imperial Service) Cavalry Brigades. The 5 Cavalry Division moved in two columns, the 13 Cavalry Brigade on the right against Acre, the 15 Cavalry Brigade, commanded by Brigadier General

C.R. Harbord, on the left against Haifa, followed by the rest of the division. Acre was taken almost without opposition, but Haifa looked to be a far more serious matter, which the Turks went to some pains to defend. The Jodhpur Lancers along with Hyderabad and Mysore Lancers comprised the 15 Imperial Service Cavalry Brigade.

On the 22 September the Hyderabad Lancers were detached to escort over 12,000 prisoners from Lejjun to Kerkur, they reached the brigade late in the afternoon on 23 September, just after Haifa had been captured.

Thus, on 23 September 1918 the stage was set, after four centuries for the crescent moon and star flag of the sprawling Ottoman Empire, which had fluttered over Haifa since 1516, to be hauled down. Haifa is a charming coastal town with splendid site at the foot of Mount Carmel on the southern shores of the Bay of Acre. Carmel is a long narrow ridge, running from the coast to the south-east. Haifa was both strongly defended and easily defensible, commanded as it was by Mount Carmel that rises steeply to a height of about 1,500 feet in the south-west and protected by the River Kishon in the north-east. The approach to Haifa from the plain of Esdraelon is easily defensible; for the road running close under the steep slopes is commanded from the south by Carmel, while to the north the country is broken by the swift and swampy Nahar (river) El Muqatta, or River Kishon and its tributaries and is impassable by reason of its marshy banks. The ground around the river was very soft and its banks were very steep, making it impassable for mounted men.

The road from El Afule to Haifa skirts the North-Eastern edge of the Mount Carmel range. Some two miles before Haifa is reached, the road is confined between a spur of Mount Carmel on the left and the marshy banks of the river Kishon and its tributaries on the right. Thus the access to the town is along a narrow gap (defile) between the ridge and the river Kishon which feeds into the sea. Through this defile runs a road and a railway running north into Acre. Thus the problem for the attacker was the approach to Haifa due to this defile (narrow passage) between the River Kishon and Mount Carmel.

The Turks were strongly posted just outside Haifa to hold the defile thus formed. It was here that the enemy had established themselves, covering every part of the ground with their guns. Their guns were on Mount Carmel, while machine guns at the foot swept the road and approaches.

At 3 AM on 23 September the 15 Brigade with 'B' Battery of Honourable Artillery Company (HAC) moved on to capture strategic Haifa along the Afule-Haifa road. There were only two regiments with the brigade, as the Hyderabad Lancers were absent, escorting prisoners back from Lejjun. No enemy was discovered until the Mysore Lancers, advance guard to the brigade, reached the village of Belled el Sheikh (now called Nesher) about 10 o'clock, and, on emerging from the trees that surrounded the village, came under heavy fire from a battery of 77 mm guns on Mount Carmel, and from machine guns and rifles in the hills north-west of the village, as also from guns sited at the eastern end of the town. Patrols sent out to the north drew fire from a large number of machine guns about Tel Abu Hawam, concealed among trees and shrubs near the main road south of that place. At least 10 machine guns covered the entrance to the town (during the Great War the devastating destructive power of the machine gun influenced events and a couple of well-sited machine guns could hold up the advance of several battalions). It was evident that the position was strongly held.

Brigadier Harbord had arrived at Belled el Sheikh, and received the report of his advance guard. He had a difficult task before him. South of the road the rocky wall of Carmel rose steeply, 1,500 feet above the plain. To the north, the country was flat and open, and afforded little or no cover for troops, except along that portion of the Nahr El Mukatta (the river Kishon), which runs east and west a mile-and-a-half north of Belled el Sheikh, which was bordered with trees and scrub. The Wadi (a watercourse) Ashul el Wavy was practically dry at this time of year, but the Nahr El Mukatta was a perennial stream, the banks of which were very marshy.

The Brigadier decided that the first thing to be done was to silence the guns on Mount Carmel. He accordingly despatched a Squadron of the Mysore Lancers, with two machine guns, to climb Mount Carmel by the steep goat track, which follows the Wadi el Tabil from Belled el Sheikh, with the object of advancing along the track following the crest-line against the guns at the Karmelheim (Religious pension on the crest overlooking Haifa). This squadron was ordered to move along this track to the north, locate the guns, and attack them.

Another squadron of Mysore Lancers was sent up the road running north from near El Harbaj to Tell es Subat, 4.5 miles East of Haifa, with instructions to turn westwards at Tel Es Subat, and advance on the town from the north-east and push along the sea shore, so as to take the enemy positions in reverse.

After giving this movement time to develop, the Jodhpur Lancers were ready to make a mounted attack from the east on the Turks holding the defile, at the enemy positions about Tel Abu Hawam, supported by guns and machine guns from the south-east.

'B' Battery HAC came into action close to the road, about half a mile north of Belled el Sheikh, and the remainder of the machine-gun squadron, with two squadrons Mysore Lancers, a little farther north, along the Acre Railway. The

The River Kishon, Tel Abu Hawam and lower slopes of Mount Carmel are visible in this contemporary photo of the Defile. The winding Kishon river empties itself into the Mediterranean sea, with a glowing sickle at each of its twists and turns.
Photo courtesy: Igal Graiver

Jodhpur Lancers took up a position of readiness, about 500 yards north-east of Belled el Sheikh, preparatory to making a dash for the wooded portion of the Nahr-el-Mukatta. They were to cross this, and then wheel to the left, and charge the enemy on his left flank. These dispositions were soon completed.

The Jodhpur Lancers then set themselves to wait until the Mysore Lancer's squadron had dealt with the enemy guns on Mount Carmel. At 11:45 AM Brigadier Harbord received a welcome reinforcement of the squadron of Sherwood Rangers, which had been sent up from El Harithie. He at once despatched this squadron to the assistance of the Mysore Lancer's squadron on Mount Carmel.

In order not to bring off the mounted attack from the east until these two squadrons were ready to seize the guns on Mount Carmel and the heights overlooking Haifa, orders were issued for the Jodhpur Lancers attack not to commence before 2 PM, by which time they would also get artillery support.

As, however, no news of the squadron on Mount Carmel had yet been received, orders were issued for the remaining troops to stand fast till further orders. The interval of waiting was utilised to despatch several patrols under Lieutenant Knight from both the regiments to reconnoitre the ground and locate the enemy's

The Jodhpur Lancers waiting at Belled el Sheikh.
Sketch courtesy: Major General Ian Cardozo, AVSM, SM (Retd)

The Ottoman Soldiers armed with machine guns lie in wait. The Great War's first mechanised weapon was the machine gun mounted on a tripod that shot out hundreds of bullets in an arc. The lancers, armed with just lances and light weapons, were no match for the rat-rat-rat of the machine gun that mowed down anything that moved. But these men stood up, fought and won!
Picture source: Wikipedia Commons

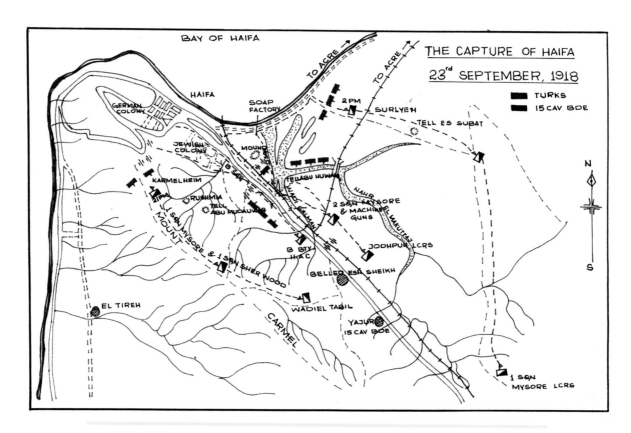

The map of the cavalry charge of the Jodhpur and Mysore Lancers at Haifa on
23 September 1918. This ranks amongst the great cavalry actions in military history.
Map courtesy: The author

position, but they were prevented by machine-gun fire from examining the bank
of the Nahr-el-Mukutta west of the Acre railway, where it was intended that
the Jodhpur Lancers should cross in order to attack the enemy on the far bank.
These patrols however reported the location of many enemy guns and machine
guns along the north side of the wadi. Our artillery and machine guns searched
the palm groves and scrub about Tel Abu Huwam and along the banks of the
Mukatta. Observation was difficult, as the enemy was well concealed. Desultory
firing continued for the next two hours, but there was no sign of any slackening of
the enemy's artillery activity.

At last the Brigadier came to the conclusion that his troops on Carmel had either
been unable to fulfil their task of silencing the enemy guns, or had lost their
way. Time was running on, and he decided that he could wait no longer. The
Jodhpur Lancers were ordered out to the attack at 2 PM. At the appointed hour
the Jodhpores trotted forward in columns of squadrons, in line of troop columns,
their advance being covered by the HAC Battery, four machine guns, and the two

The Jodhpur Lancers dashed over the narrow defile in extended order and galloped over and crashed into the infantry and machine gunners with the lance, killing hundred and wounding as many more. The most critical and daring cavalry charge was brilliantly executed by the 'B' Squadron of the Jodhpur Lancers on the defile that paved the way for victory at Haifa. They had to gallop over exposed ground against heavy rifle and machine gun fire, but they never faltered. The extremely risky 'death ride' on the defile succeeded due to speed, good order and surprise.
Sketch courtesy: Major General Ian Cardozo, AVSM, SM

remaining squadrons of the Mysore Lancers. As they cantered out into the open and crossed the Acre railway line they came under intense enemy fire, but the regiment moved on without a check, changed formation into columns of troops with three paces between them and quickened their pace, left shouldering as they went and suffered little loss, riding straight for the Nahr-el-Mukutta. The fire, however, appeared ill-directed, which was probably due to the vigorous action of the artillery and machine guns supporting the attack.

The plan was to cross the Kishon and attack the town from the north-east, avoiding the dangerous defile but owing to the exposed nature of the ground, it had not been possible to reconnoitre the Kishon beforehand, and, when the Jodhpur Lancers reached there, it was seen that the bank was precipitous and quite impassable. Two ground scouts, forced into the bed of the stream, disappeared instantaneously into the quicksands. It was only too clear that no crossing was possible. The regiment, was, however, now committed to the attack, and it was impossible to turn back. Lieutenant Colonel Hyla Holden, the Senior SSO, ordered the regiment to swing left-handed, cross the narrower wadi beside the El Affule–Haifa railway, and charge the machine guns at 1,000 yards on the lower slopes of Carmel. Thus the regiment changed direction left, except for one squadron, which tried unsuccessfully to find a way over to the right.

It was a ticklish situation as an impassable stream ... forced them to wheel to the left and go through the defile along the main road (which they wanted to avoid). It was a most critical moment, for the regiment was being raked by fire from front and flank, and horses were falling fast. Many casualties occurred at this point in time, including the Officiating Commanding Officer, Major Dalpat Singh, MC, who was hit in the spine by machine gun fire and died of wounds later that night.

Lieutenant Colonel Holden ordered the leading 'B' Squadron Commander Captain Aman Singh, Bahadur, to charge the machine guns on the lower slopes of Carmel, across the railway line towards the defile. Without hesitation, changing direction left, the leading 'B' Squadron (Jodha Rathores) swiftly rallied and turned, galloping over the two branches of the Wadi Ashlul el Wawy, dashed into the enemy machine guns and speared the detachments, killing the crews, and opened the defile, through which ran the main road into Haifa, between the Wadi Selman and the mountain, for the passage of the rest of the regiment. The 'B' Squadron killed 38 of the enemy and captured two machine-guns and two camel guns.

As soon as the critical defile was passed, the 'D' Squadron, (Mertia Rathores) under Captain Anop Singh, Bahadur, was sent half right and charged the 'Mound' east of the road and captured the four enemy machine guns, about Tel Abu Hawam and north of it.

Meanwhile, after clearing the defile, the 'B' squadron made its way along the lower slopes of Mount Carmel, and charged into the German Colony West of

A contemporary postcard showing German Colony (established in 1868), Haifa on 23 September 1918. On the eve of the outbreak of the Great War in 1914, Haifa had some 20,000 residents. The Jodhpur Lancers had galloped into history at Haifa.
Photo courtesy: Igal Graiver

Haifa, capturing several machine guns, and killing large numbers of Turks and Germans. One troop of 'B' Squadron under Rissaldar Kesri Singh reached the first hill and captured two field guns and then made for the top of Mount Carmel, where he captured more guns and prisoners before finally capturing the Turkish Headquarters and the Turkish Commandant.

The 'D' squadron, after clearing up the Tel Abu Hawam area, galloped up the east bank of the Wadi Selman and along the beach, captured the soap factory and entered the town from the north east.

In both engagements the fighting was brisk and Lieutenants Knight and Chubb had their horses killed beneath them as did Captain Aman Singh and Anop Singh. Lieutenant Colonel Hyla Holden then led the two remaining squadrons through the defile straight into the town. Shots were fired by Turks here and there from behind the walls of houses, and a few Turks were actually ridden down in the streets, but the passage of the defile by the 'B' Squadron had practically decided the issue and there was little left to do but round up prisoners. All four squadrons of Jodhpurs thus entered Haifa at about the same moment.

As soon as the charge got home, the Mysore Lancers (less two squadrons), who had supported the Jodhpur attack by fire, mounted as soon as the Jodhpur Lancers masked their fire and followed them at a gallop into the town.

Almost at the same instant as the main attack was launched the left detached squadron of the Mysores charged the enemy's guns south of the Karmelheim. In the course of the very difficult ascent there had been some casualties, and a number of this squadron's horses had dropped out exhausted or lamed. Then after riding nearly six miles over very bad country, they had at last located the enemy guns at Karmelheim, much farther north than had been expected. Dropping his machine guns and all his Hotchkiss rifles on the track, to provide covering fire, the squadron leader led the remainder of his troops away to the left to charge the guns. Owing to casualties on the way up the range, and to some of his men having been delayed by the difficulties of the track, he found that, after providing for Hotchkiss rifles, he had only 15 lances for the charge. Nevertheless, he decided to attack at once, rightly judging that even an unsuccessful charge would probably divert the fire of the enemy guns long enough to permit the Jodhpur Lancers to make their attack in the plain. His machine guns and Hotchkiss rifles had got close to the guns unseen, and now opened a sudden and accurate fire on them. The 15 men then galloped in from the flank and actually succeeded in silencing the battery. About half the squadron of Sherwood Rangers arrived just in the nick of time to follow up the charge and prevent the enemy rallying. One 150 mm naval gun, two mountain guns, and 78 prisoners were taken. By a fortunate coincidence, this charge took place as the Jodhpur Lancers attacked in the plain.

1,350 Turks and German prisoners of war were captured at Haifa.
Sketch courtesy: Major General Ian Cardozo, AVSM, SM

Of the fourth detached squadron of the Mysores, which had been held up by fire about half a mile west of El Suriyeh and two-and-a-half miles north east of Haifa, mounted and advanced as the Jodhpore attack was seen. This squadron charged a strong body of the Turks in position near the mouth of the Nahr el Mukatta, capturing two guns and 100 prisoners.

A large number of the enemy were still hiding in the town disguised as Arabs; those were gradually rounded up. So ended the attack on Haifa.

Described by many as one of the finest cavalry charges ever made, the regiment killed at least 80 of the enemy and captured 1,350 prisoners (including two German Officers and 23 Turkish Officers). As many as 16 Field guns (Two 6-inch Naval guns, Four 4.2-inch Howitzer guns, Six 3-inch Field guns, Four 10-lb Camel guns) and 10 Machine guns, and a large amount of ammunition were collected at Haifa after the action. The captured artillery included two six-inch naval guns, which the Germans had mounted on the top of Mount Carmel, to engage our warships in the event of an attempted landing.

The Brigade casualties were comparatively light given the nature of the operation, seven killed (One Officer and six Other Ranks) and 34 wounded (Six Officers and 28 Other Ranks), and the loss in horses was fairly heavy—60 killed and 83 wounded—it was made up from some unexpectedly good ones captured. The total casualties of the Jodhpur Lancers was six officers and 21 men wounded in this action of which seven subsequently died, and in horses their loss was 26 each killed and wounded and seven missing. Major Dalpat Singh was carried into the town but he died the same night on the operating table. The dead of Jodhur Lancers included Major Dalpat Singh, No 1296 Daffadar Dhonkal Singh,

No 1449 Sowar Gopal Singh, No 1049 Sowar Shazad Singh, No 1189 Trumpet Major Sher Singh, No 1616 Sowar Tagat Singh and No 1470 Sowar Sultan Singh.

In all, that day, the Jodhpur Lancers earned one DSO (Lieutenant Colonel Hyla Holden), three MC (Captain Anop Singh, Lieutenant A.B. Knight and Lieutenant Sagat Singh, son of Sir Pratap), three IOM (Captain Aman Singh, No 1029 Daffadar Jor Singh and Risaldar Kesri Singh of Alwar Lancers attached to Jodhpur Lancers) and 12 IDSM (Jemadar Bishen Singh, Jemadar Bahadur Singh, No 1288 Daffadar Mohbhat Singh, No 1049 Daffadar Doong Singh, No 1321 Lance Daffadar Bhairon Singh, No 1630 Sowar Bagh Singh, No 1427 Sowar Gunpat Singh, No 1559 Sowar Padam Singh, No 1109 Sowar Bhoor Singh, No 1538 Sowar Bhim Singh, No 1353 Sowar Amar Singh and No 1151 Sowar Bishen Singh) for their gallantry in Haifa. In addition two IDSM were won by men of the Alwar Lancers attached with Jodhpur Lancers (No 1150 Lance Daffadar Sowar Singh and No 1143 Sowar Cheyne Singh).

CITATION OF AWARDEES JODHPUR LANCERS AT HAIFA

Lieutenant Colonel Hyla Napier Holden—DSO
For conspicuous gallantry and brilliant leadership at Haifa on the 23 September 1918. He personally led the Jodhpur lancers in a mounted attack by which the town was captured. He galloped his regiment through a narrow defile under heavy fire at close range, directing two squadrons upon certain enemy positions and leading the remainder of the regiment straight through the town. He maintained complete control of his men throughout, and proved himself a most dashing and capable cavalry leader.

Lieutenant A.B. Knight—MC
For conspicuous gallantry and devotion to duty. On the 23 September 1918, during the attack on Haifa, he went out twice under heavy fire on reconnaissance duty to discover if the Wadis in front were passable. He gained valuable information about the ground and the enemy's dispositions, locating accurately the position of four guns and several machine guns.

Captain Anop Singh, Bahadur—MC
On the 23 September 1918, he led his squadron with the greatest dash and ability, when he successfully charged the enemy's position behind a wall, capturing three guns, four machine guns, and many of the enemy. He then led his squadron through the north portion of the town, capturing many more prisoners, and rejoined the regiment at the final objective. He showed throughout the utmost contempt for danger.

Lieutenant Sagat Singh—MC
On the 23 September 1918, during an advance, he twice went back under heavy fire to give orders to squadrons in the rear, afterwards rejoining the remainder of the regiment.

Lieutenant Sagat Singh, MC drawn by
Eric Kennington.
Photo courtesy: Lawrence Hendra

*Throughout the action he gave an example of complete disregard of danger and showed
great coolness.*

Captain Aman Singh, Bahadur—IOM

*On the 23 September 1918, in an attack this Officer commanded the leading squadron
under heavy machine gun and rifle fire. When held up by an impassable wadi in front,
he led his squadron with great dash and gallantry, against the enemy's position on his
left, which he was ordered to take, capturing two machine guns, two camel guns, killing
over 30 of the enemy, and thus opening a way for the regiment through the defile. He
re-organised his squadron and carried the first and second objectives. This officer showed
great courage, coolness and ability throughout the action.*

No 1029 Daffadar Jor Singh—IOM

*For conspicuous gallantry in an attack on the 23 September 1918. Previous to the attack
he twice conducted patrols with great coolness under heavy fire from guns, machine guns
and rifles, each time bringing back reliable information. He accurately spotted gun
flashes and reconnoitred the wadi. During the attack he was the first to reach an enemy
machine gun in action and killed one of the crew. Later on he rendered good service in
capturing guns and prisoners in the upper part of the town.*

Risaldar Kesri Singh, Alwar Lancers (attached with Jodhpur Lancers)—IOM

*For conspicuous gallantry on the 23 September 1918, during an attack. After the forcing
of an entrance to a town, in which his troopers took part, he was sent to capture guns
firing from a higher position. After putting two field guns out of action, he captured
12 Turkish officers and 193 other ranks besides the Turkish Military Headquarters, on
which he left a guard.*

Besides the above, the Mysore Lancers also received: One DSO (Major W.J. Lambert), three MC (Lieutenant H. Horsman, Lieutenant M.N. Meredith and Lieutenant D.G. Mein), one IOM (Jemadar Mir Turab Ali, Mysore Lancers attached with 15 Imperial Service Cavalry Brigade Machine Gun Squadron) and 12 IDSM, (No 911 Sowar Devoji Rao, No 1118 Sowar Sheikh Daoud, No 508 Daffadar Syed Abdul Rahman, No 1185 Sowar Deva Rao Baber, No 1093 Sowar Syed Mohiuddin, No 1232 Sowar Mahdivra Magar, No 753 Daffadar Shanka Rao Nalegay, No 782 Daffadar Annaji Rao, No 958 Daffadar-Major Mir Ashraf Ali, Risaladar Mohammed Hussain Khan, Risaldar Krishne Urs, Risaldar Anand Rao Bhosley). Also one IDSM each won by Bhavnagar Lancers attached with Mysore Lancers (No 707 Sowar Zor Singh) and Kashmir Lancers attached with Mysore Lancers (No 592 Sowar Sham Singh) and Hyderabad Lancers, attached with 15 Imperial Service Cavalry Brigade Machine Gun Squadron (Jemadar Iqbal Ali Beg).

Citation of Awardees Mysore Lancers at Haifa

Major W. J. Lambert, 29th Lancers, Attached Mysore Lancers—DSO

On the 23 September 1918, during the attack on Haifa, Major Lambert commanded the advanced guard of the 15th Imperial Service Cavalry Brigade. He pushed forward and occupied all tactical points close to the enemy's position and led the Mysore Lancers in the attack with great gallantry.

Lieutenant H. Horsman, IARO, Attached Mysore Lancers—MC

In front of Haifa, on the 23 September 1918, he led his squadron under great difficulties over the top of Mount Carmel, placed his automatic guns in position, and delivered a mounted attack from the flank over very rocky and difficult country, capturing two guns, two machine guns, and 76 prisoners. With the utmost gallantry he personally led the charge, and by his skilful leadership contributed largely to the capture of Haifa.

Lieutenant M.N. Meredith, IARO, Attached Mysore Lancers—MC

For conspicuous gallantry in front of Haifa, on the 23 September 1918. As SSO with the advanced squadron he showed skill and determination under heavy fire, and gained much valuable information. Under his leadership his men —who had to remain in the open for four hours under shell fire-captured two guns.

Lieutenant D.G. Mein, 31 Lancers, IA, Attached Mysore Lancers—MC

For gallantry and skilful leadership before haifa on 23 September 1918. He worked his squadron round to the coast about two miles East of Haifa, and charged the enemy simultaneously with the Jodhpur Lancers, capturing two guns, two machine guns and 110 prisoners. He showed himself to be an officer of exceptional gallantry and coolness under fire.

Jemadar Mir Turab Ali, Mysore Lancers (attached to 15 I. S. Cavalry Brigade Machine-Gun Squadron)—IOM

For gallantry and initiative on the 23 September 1918. He brought his machine-gun sub-section across the open under heavy fire and galloped up stony ground to a position which the enemy was just evacuating. He himself was on ahead with his range-taker and killed a Turkish officer with his sword on the way to the position.

It is seen that all the major gallantry awards, specially of Mysore Lancers, went to the British SSOs but unfortunately at least three SSOs from the aforementioned gallantry award winners at Haifa were killed in action in the very next action at Aleppo on 26 October 1918. These included Lieutenant Colonel H.N. Holden, DSO, Lieutenant M.N. Meredith, MC, and Lieutenant D.G. Mein, MC, besides Lieutenant W.D. Raymond attached with Mysore Lancers and few also became wounded.

Lieutenant A.B. Knight the SSO Jodhpur Lancers, in a letter from Syria, dated 10 October 1918, wrote to his father about the battle of Haifa,

> '...Sir P was evacuated on the 21 September and on the 23 we moved down to take Haifa, our brigade leading, Mysore's advanced guard, and I did two patrols getting horse slightly wounded. Then went in the assault with the leading 'B' Squadron (Commanded by Captain Aman Singh). Fairly warm work my poor old horse being finished off with at least two more hits. The men were magnificent, formation column of troops extended trotting up 4,000 yards under heavy gun fire, and the last 2,000 yards under heavy machine gun and rifle fire as well. Held up at less than 400 yards from machine guns on both flanks and front by an impassable wadi; turned and went for the enemy position on the left on the side of a rocky hill almost impossible to get at. However, not a horse fell. I lost my horse on the wadi and ran till I got another horse off the next squadron. They scuppered two Machine Guns, two Camel Guns and killed about 38. As soon as the Turk saw we were across the wadi he began to run.
>
> The second squadron took the right. The 'B' squadron then went on in two halves, one half went through the main street to the second objective near the point where we rallied, other half following up the slopes of Mount Carmel. I followed through with mixtures of all squadrons. One troop took two guns, the Turkish HQ Commandant,

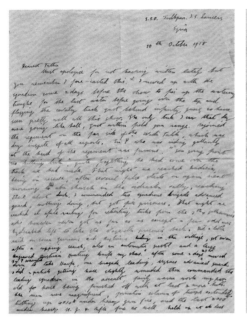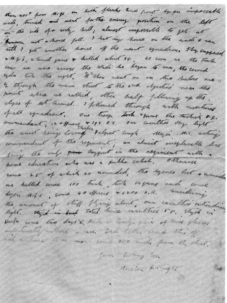

Letter dated 10 October 1918 from Lieutenant Knight written to his father, about the Battle of Haifa.
Photo courtesy: Major and Mrs Wyndham Knight

12 officers and 193 Other Ranks. Our casualties very light, the worst being losing Major Dalpat Singh, MC, acting Commandant of the Regiment, an almost irreplacable loss being the only Rajput in the Regiment with some education who was a '*pucca saheb*'. Otherwise some 25 of which 20 were wounded. The Mysores lost 4 wounded. We killed some 100 Turks, took 14 guns and some dozen machine guns, some 40 officers and 1,200 ORs. Considering the amount of stuff flying about, our casualties extraordinarily light. Total horse casualties 58. We stayed in Haifa some two days. I made a lovely pair of zeiss glasses unfortunately without a case. Had better send this off and continue later, now some 300 miles from the start.......Yours Loving Son, Austin B. Knight.

In another letter written in Hindi, Jemadar Bir Singh of Gunawati near Makrana (he was a machine gunner of Jodhpur Lancers), writes,

While advancing for the world famous battle victory of well fortified Haifa, I have seen Sir Pratap offering wounded enemy soldiers water to drink from his own water bottle...but when and why he went to Cairo with his staff I cannot say but he was not present with the regiment during the Haifa attack....The attack on Haifa took place at high noon, on one side was Mount Carmel upon which the enemy artillery was located and on otherside lay the sea. A single road running along the side of Mount Carmel led into Haifa. Along the road and up to the sea ran a canal full of water that the horses could not cross. About 20 machine guns were sited along the approaches to the town. Ships from the sea also fired upon us, while the rifles and machine guns bullets rained down upon us from the houses as well. I moved up along the left side of the road with the Vickers Machine gun to give fire support, Senior SSO Lieutenant Colonel Holden gave the order to charge on Haifa.

The horses could not cross the canal and Major Dalpat Singh with his orderly, here fell to machine gun fire. Lieutenant Holden ordered us to 'retire', so we retired. I cannot say if it was an *Akash Wani* (Astral Voice or Voice from the Sky) or the inner voice of the warrior spirit; '*Are bhagar kathey javo? Kalo mundo ho jyahi*' (Where do you flee to? Thy faces shall ever be blackened). Upon hearing this, the brave jawans reined in their mounts and turning the horses' heads towards the road to Haifa, charged into the city. The orders to attack, to retire, followed by the charge and entry into Haifa, all happened so swiftly that I was not even able to bring my machine guns into action.

Seeing our comrades gallop into Haifa, we machine gunners drew our revolvers and swords, and mounted, joined up with them. Then amidst a hail of bullets, we sliced through Haifa drawing rein only when we reached the other side. There, in an open *maidan* (field) we planted the Jodhpur Lancers Saffron standard emblazoned with the 'Cheel' (Kite) of Marwar. After a while, what do we see, but large numbers of enemy prisoners being brought and concentrated at that ground. The *maidan* was soon packed with 1,200 prisoners.

The following day we performed the last rites of Major Dalpat Singh and his orderly. I was one of the four men who acted as pallbearer for Dalpat Singh's bier. We took them to Mount Carmel where they were buried in the earth.

The Official History of the War – Military Operations Egypt and Palestine, Volume 2 says,

The Turks made a very stubborn defence of Haifa and but for the dash of Jodhpur Lancers, would have undoubtedly held out for a considerable length of time. The Turks had fought well, firing until they were ridden down, but once our cavalry were through the defile, the fight was practically over. They galloped through the town, riding

28 September 1918, a view of the military camp on the beach of Haifa drawn by James McBey (official war artist to the EEF). The Jodhpur Lancers bivouacked on the beach north of Haifa for two days. Mount Carmel and the harbour of Haifa are seen with small outlines of an olive grove and several ships in the harbour.
Photo courtesy: © Imperial War Museum

down with the lance any bodies of the enemy who showed fight, and, in 20 minutes, had overcome all opposition. A stout-hearted body of men on galloping horses takes a lot of stopping and, within half an hour from the word 'go', Haifa was ours. The attack was well arranged and boldly carried out. The engagement at Haifa gives some brilliant examples of the mounted attack against infantry, artillery and machine guns. This scintillating little victory was won by boldness, speed, and quick thinking. The capture of Haifa was at once used to ease the supply situation, and it was not long before stores landed here could be sent to Semakh by the Turkish railway.

The Official History of the War continues:

the passage of the defile by the 'B' Squadron of the Jodhpur Lancers had practically decided the issue, and there was little left to do but round up prisoners.... No more remarkable cavalry action of its scale was fought in the whole course of the campaign. The position was naturally formidable, with a precipitous hill and an impassable river on either side of a defile; it was held by a well-armed force about a thousand strong which had not yet been engaged, though doubtless in some degree affected by news of the general rout; it was taken in a few hours by a cavalry brigade of two weak regiments and a single 13-pdr battery. Undoubtedly only the boldness and dash of the cavalry combined with skilful flanking movements, made success possible, and there is little likelihood that a dismounted attack by a force of this strength would have had equal fortune. The check on the river bank, which might well have been disastrous, was nullified by the speed and good order in which the leading 'B' Squadron of the Jodhpur Lancers changed direction and charged the enemy on the slopes of Mount Carmel. Machine-gun bullets over and over again failed to stop the galloping horses, even though many of them succumbed afterwards to their injuries.

Here is an extract from the book, *The Indian Army and the King's Enemies 1900-1917* by Charles Chenevix Trench. Description of the action at Haifa,

The charge was led by Major Dalpat Singh... He had as his advisor, as was usual with Imperial Service units, a British Officer, Major Holden.... It was decided to cross the Kishon and attack the town from the North East, avoiding the dangerous defile. But when two ground scouts spurred their horses down the bank, they were engulfed in quicksands. Immediately the order was given to change direction left, the leading 'B' squadron to charge several machine guns on the lower slopes of Mount Carmel. While they did so, supported by fire from some Mysore Lancers, two squadrons galloped straight through the defile into the town. With the loss of three killed and 34 wounded they captured 689 Turks, 16 Field guns and 10 machine guns. It was perhaps the most extraordinary feat of cavalry, on that scale, in that or any war. Probably no regiment but the '*Jo-Hukums*' would have been crazy enough to try it. Sadly, among the dead was the gallant Major Dalpat Singh.

In the main text of his Despatch of 31 October 1918, dealing with capture of Haifa, General Allenby particularly mentioned that,

two miles from the Haifa road, in the passes between the spur of Mount Carmel on the left and the marshy banks of River Kishon, on the right, the 5 Cavalry Division, reaching this point on the 23 September, was shelled from the slopes of Mount Carmel and found the road and the river crossings defended by numerous machine guns. Whilst the Mysore Lancers were clearing the rocky slopes of Mount Carmel, the Jodhpur Lancers charged through the defile, and riding over the enemy's machine guns, galloped into the town, where a number of Turks were speared in the streets. Over 1,350 prisoners and 17 guns were taken in this operation.

A contemporary photo showing Jodhpur and Mysore Lancers riding in triumph through Hamara Square in Haifa on 23 September 1918. The population gave the Indian troops a most enthusiastic reception, including the German colonists who participated in this welcome. It was perhaps the only time in history that a fortified town fell to a charge by horsed cavalry. In a sense it was also the last hurrah of the old Indian Horsed Cavalry. Picture below is the same Hamara Square now known as Paris Square in Haifa today. Seen at the bottom left of the photo is the author with few enthusiasts from India who visited the Paris Square and the Defile in November 2017.

Photos courtesy: (above) © Imperial War Museum (below) The author

In *History of the British Cavalry* written by a British nobleman, the Marquess of Anglesey concludes his description of this action that, 'By 3 PM the battle was over and victory complete. A vital new supply base had fallen into British hands. Four days later the landing of supplies started. Without a doubt this was the most successful mounted action of its scale in the course of the campaign. It was won by a weak brigade of only two regiments and a single 12-pounder battery pitted against about 1,000 well-armed troops who had so far seen no action. These, skilfully deployed, occupied a naturally formidable defensive position with an impassable river on one side of a narrow defile and a steep hill on the other. That they had already received news of the general rout is certain and this may well have affected their behaviour, but there is little evidence to show that they put up less than a respectable resistance. The speed and daring dash and boldness of the two Indian Imperial Service Regiments, in conjunction with the skilful flanking movements were what made the action such a success. The speed and good order demonstrated by the leading 'B' Squadron of the Jodhpurs when it was forced to change direction under heavy fire, were other vital ingredients in what was almost certainly the only occasion in history when a fortified town was captured by cavalry at the gallop.'

An Hebrew story first published in 1920, *Davar* newspaper, weekend edition by Asher Barash, describes the battle of Haifa as,

> ... And precisely at 10 O'clock, the single canon the Austrians had put on top of Mount Carmel began to fire at the Indian cavalry approaching the city....A gallant young Turkish officer defended the city on his own, with that one single gun cannon....And then, out of nowhere, a trio of aeroplanes... circling above the mountain...and when they were gone, everything was quiet. A depressing silence settled on the entire city. Traffic stopped, and everybody was tense in anticipation. Suddenly, from all directions, from Mount Carmel and from all entrances to town, the Indian Cavalry came galloping in battle heat, the end of their scarves flying in the wind, lances smashing, with wild battle cries, and when they came charging, mounted on their thoroughbreds, they looked like a pack of demons. The job was done within an hour, and the populace could now come out and welcome the conqueror. Cavalry jammed all streets in disorder, gently dismounting weaponry and gear, and carrying water for the horses in their fabric palls. And fresh forces continued pouring into the town, hundreds and thousands....their steps were sober and heavy, the large horses and their riders dusty....Indians, Indians and more Indians. All wore dark uniforms, sleeves rolled up above their elbows, their short firearms stashed at sidesaddle, looking like butchers who have just finished their chores....Now, a procession of Turkish prisoners of war is being led, they are among the last...

An artist's depiction of a cavalry charge—*L'arme blanche*—a line of Indian Lancers charge at a Turkish position across the Megiddo valley, tossing lance-point, flying *puggaree*s (turbans) and manes, horse-heads tossing and thunder of hoofs tearing up the earth with clouds of dust streaming towards the defile. The Jodhpur Lancers won everlasting glory for their death-defying charge at Haifa. This was the last major battle in which the cavalry played a decisive part, as slowly the horses had lost their offensive cavalry role as they became more vulnerable to barbed wire, machine guns and artillery. Painting by Thomas Cantrell Dugwell.
Photo courtesy: © *Imperial War Museum*

On the evening of that day, the city was as restless as never before… A hectic night ensued. The last of the Turkish army officers and officials were galloping through the streets on their horses, as if trying to flee the city but to no avail, as all roads were already taken by the enemy. After midnight, all of a sudden, hundreds of feet running down the road, with a few voices calling, warning and reprimanding and then dying down… it was a moonlit night and they saw the Turkish garrison running along the dusty road in total disarray, leaderless….

By any standard, the capture of Haifa, was truly an astonishing spectacle and magnificent feat of arms. Such raw courage the world had rarely seen, nor had death and pain ever been treated with such disdain. These were descendants of men who had fought at Patan, Khanwa and Giri-Sumel, Tunga, and at Merta (when the Rathore horsemen charged upon the more modern and powerful artillery of General De Boigne), Gangwana and Malpura, all legendary Rathore charges, but this was perhaps the finest of them all. Indeed this charge at Haifa is described by many as the most remarkable cavalry action ever in the history of war. That day the '*Jo Hukums*' had to be restrained as they galloped through the streets of Haifa, even after all the machine-gun posts had fallen, spearing and butchering the unfortunate Turks who crossed their path.

Sir Pratap received a number of congratulatory letters and telegrams, including one from the Private Secretary to the King and Queen. General Allenby sent the following telegram to Lieutenant General Sir Pratap Singh at Alexandria.

True copy of the telegram No 675, dated 24 September 1918, sent by General Allenby from the GHQ, Palestine

To, Lieutenant General HH Maharaja Sir Pertab Singh, Alexandria.

Congratulate you on the brilliant exploit of your regiment, the Jodhpur Lancers, who on the 23 September 1918 took the town of Haifa at a gallop, killing many Turks with the lance in the streets of the town,

On 24 September 1918 patrols were sent out to collect enemy field guns and machine guns. In this contemporary painting the Jodhpur Lancers are seen towing away the guns won at Haifa. The guns now decorate the formidable Mehrangarh fort in Jodhpur and the 61st Cavalry Regiment in Jaipur.
Photo courtesy: Raoraja Vijay Singh

and capturing 700 prisoners. Their gallant Major Dalpat Singh, fell gloriously at the head of his regiment. He was buried with full military honours this afternoon. Allenby.

In reply to General Allenby, Sir Pertab simply wrote: 'Dalpat Singh's great day has arrived.'

True copy of the letter dated 24 September 1918 from Major General H.M. MacAndrew, GOC, 5 Cavalry Division, Palestine,

My Dear Sir Pertab,

I am very sorry to tell you that Major Dalpat Singh, MC died of wounds last night. He led the regiment with great dash and was killed by machine gun fire at 100 yards while galloping across the river into Haifa.

The Jodhpur Lancers as usual did splendidly. Their charge across the river with eight machine guns and six guns firing on them was a great sight. I am sorry that you had fever and were not with us but I hope to see you back soon. The enemy here fought better than any we have met yet. Your Regiment had one officer (Dalpat) killed and two wounded, three men killed and 30 wounded.

Yours Sincerely.....*H.M. MacAndrew*

True copy of letter dated, 30 December 1918, Buckingham Palace from Private Secretary to the King.

To, Sir Pertab,

The King and Queen have heard with deep regret of the loss you and the Indian Army have sustained by the death of Major Dalpat Singh, MC, Jodhpur Lancers, in the service of his Imperial Majesty and the Empire.

I am commanded to express Their Imperial Majesties true sympathy with you in your sorrow.

Stamfordham, Private Secretary to the King-Emperor

True copy of letter No 8011/war-2 dated the 13 November 1918, from the Resident, Western Rajputana States, to the *Musahib Ala, Marwar State, Jodhpur.

Sir,

I have the honour to request that you will kindly convey to the Durbar the Hon'ble the Agent to the Governor General's Congratulations on the gallantry displayed by the Jodhpur Lancers in capturing the town of Haifa in Palestine and thus adding fresh laurels to their illustrious record of services.

Colonel Manners Smith will also be glad if you will kindly convey his sincere sympathy to the Durbar and to the family of the deceased at the death of the late Major Dalpat Singh who fell gloriously at the head of his regiment but will live imperishably in the annals of British and Indian military history. I have the honour......

Lieutenant Colonel A.D. Macpherson
Resident, Western Rajputana States

Meanwhile the Jodhpur Lancers men and horses got two days of well-earned rest at Haifa on 24–25 September 1918. The next morning on 24 September the men and horses bathed in the sea! The troops were also allowed to visit the town, which was found to be very interesting, there being many modern houses, superior to any town they had previously visited in the interior. Many of the inhabitants were delighted to see the Indians. The Jodhpur Lancers left behind 30 dismounted men in Haifa before marching off on 26 September 1918.

On recovering from his attack of fever, Sir Pratap returned to Cairo with the view of starting for India at an early date, for the news reached him that Maharaja Sumer Singh was seriously ill at Jodhpur. A few days later on 03 October 1918, he heard that the adorable young ruler was dead. He at once dictated to Sir Harry Watson two telegrams, one to Private Secretary to the King, and the other to the Viceroy, asking that he might again be appointed Regent of Jodhpur during the minority of Maharaja Umaid Singh.

Arrangements were speedily made for his return to India. He wished to spring a surprise by his sudden arrival, as he did not wish anyone in Jodhpur to learn about his arrival details, except the Resident. Colonel Windham, the Resident, received a telegram which puzzled him greatly for a time, it read, 'Arriving by *SS Malwa*', and signed as 'Cunningham'. For some time he was completely at sea as to the interpretation, until he recalled that the name had in the past greatly pleased Sir Pratap, who considered it very expressive, and was fond of saying, 'Lots of Cunninghams in Jodhpur, Sahib!' He used it now with the desired result of informing the Resident and no one else of his arrival (to catch the people who were responsible for the death of the Maharaja Sumer Singh) at Jodhpur on 20 October 1918.

With the capture of Haifa, the first stage of Allenby's advance was complete. There remained the pursuit to Damascus and beyond. Unlike most pursuits by the British Army, this was pressed to the uttermost limits of endurance of horse and man, as though Alexander or Napoleon were in command. All wheeled transport was left behind; only two day's rations and forage were taken; when this was finished, they must live off the land. The next objective for the Jodhpur Lancers was Aleppo, some 300 kms ahead—much of it over rough ground and blown bridges—destroyed by enemy rearguards. The war was now reduced to the pursuit of the remnant of the Turks by the remnants of the 5th Cavalry Division, decimated by malaria and Spanish influenza, past Baalbek, Homs and Aleppo until 31 October when the Armistice with Turkey was signed.

The Last Glory—Gallop to Aleppo—26 October 1918

Following the capture of the ports of Haifa, General Allenby set Aleppo as his next objective. For this purpose the 5th Cavalry Division was split into two columns comprising the Jodhpur, the Mysore and the mechanised units in Column 'A' (15 Cavalry Brigade) and the remainder of the Division in Column 'B' (14 Cavalry Brigade). Only the 15 Cavalry Brigade had the wherewithal in cavalry, armoured cars and guns to undertake the long haul to Aleppo some 300 kilometres to the north. Now the obstacle to the occupation of the rest of Syria after the capture of Haifa was distance, supply and disease. The last was most serious—malaria and an epidemic of influenza 'Spanish flu' added to casualties.

The Jodhpurs two days' halt at Haifa on the 24 and 25 September 1918 gave the horses a much-needed rest. At 5 AM on the 26, the Brigade marched in the main body of the division and bivouacked for the night at Er Reineh. Starting again at 4 AM on the 27 the Brigade marched to Tiberias, arriving at 11:30 AM. After watering horses in the lake, which was very clear and sweet, and feeding, the march was resumed and Kasr Atra was reached at 10:30 PM. This was a very long and wearying march, as the Brigade was frequently held up by the transport of the 14 Brigade which was ahead. On the 27 September Lieutenant Colonel Hyla took over the duties of acting Brigade Commander when Brigadier-General Harbord and his Brigade Major were evacuated sick to Haifa.

Orders were received on 28 September to march again at 5 AM, less the Hyderabad Lancers detached to guard the transport, and the Brigade reached El Kuneitra at midnight of the 28–29. On the 29 the Brigade marched in rear of the division. At 10 PM the whole column halted owing to the advance guard of the Australian Division under General Barrow being held up. At 04:30 AM on 30 September the Australians cleared the road of the opposition and the Brigade halted at 10 AM in Corps reserve six miles south-east of Kaukab, receiving orders to bivouac for the night and concentrate at 6 AM the next day at Deir Khabiye.

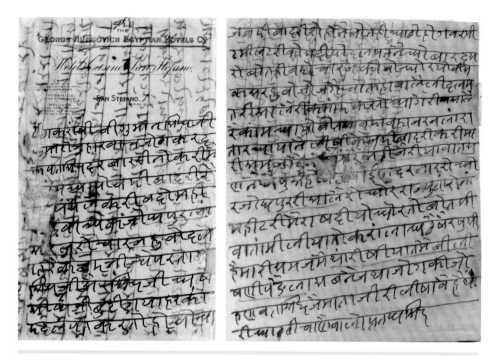

On 23rd September 1918, Sir Pratap staying at Hotel Casino, San Stefano, Alexandria, Ramaleh, Egypt, due to fever, wrote this letter back home to Jodhpur on the hotel letter pad to say, 'Dalpat Singh fought and died bravely while leading the Jodhpur Lancers at Haifa. Dalpat has left a mark in history not only for himself but for the entire Jodhpur Lancers and the Rajputs!'.

Letter courtesy: Thakur Guman Singh Narwa collection with Maharaja Man Singh Pushtak Prakash

At 09:30 AM on the 01 October 1918, the Brigade reached a point two miles north of the Kiswe-Damascus road, and received information that the enemy were holding the gardens round the city. In the meantime the 14th Brigade had entered the city, the majority of the Turks having fled and the rest being only too pleased to give themselves up. On 2 October a composite squadron of the Jodhpur Lancers formed part of the official entry into the city of Damascus, which had been captured the day before by the 14 Cavalry Brigade.

Two days rest followed and Lieutenant Knight in a letter dated 20 October 1918 wrote that, '.....on 04 Oct we lunched at Damascus. Most interesting but a filthy town. Very Easternised, surrounded on all sides by groves and gardens. All our Sherifian friends joined in to lunch, their flags flying everywhere....'

The pursuit of the Turks continued and the Jodhpurs entered Khan Meizelun on 5 October and to Mollaka and Zahle on 6 October. Both places were occupied at dusk without opposition, after a long and dusty march. The inhabitants of Moallaka and Zahle gave the Jodhpurs a most enthusiastic reception. A considerable number of prisoners were captured.

The next four days provided a much-needed rest, and on 11 October the Jodhpurs marched to Tell Esh Sherif, on 13 to Baalbek, 14 to Kebwe, 15 to El Kaa, 16 to El Kusseir, and arrived at Homs at mid-day on 17 October. Henceforward, the 5 Cavalry Division was to become an entirely separate force in its operations. At Homs the nearest troops were at Damascus 100 miles behind, and Aleppo, the next town of any importance, 100 miles ahead, (marching was carried out in accordance with the schedule of 20 minutes trot, one hour's walk, 10 minutes halt). The Jodhpurs had now covered 325 miles in 28 days, and a rest was much needed. Three days were occupied in washing, grazing and cleaning saddles.

Lieutenant A.B. Knight in his letter dated 20 October 1918 continues, '...On 06 October 1918 our Brigade occupied Zahle. Terrific reception—I was nearly blown off my horse by the *feu de joie* (fire of joy). Stayed at Zahle about four days. We then moved on. The ruins at Baalbek are truly magnificent, and some of the Grecian pillars called porticos can be seen for miles—six pillars about 75 feet high....'

Lieutenant Knight continues

> ...Now we have left Homs behind. Since Haifa we have not fired a shot, and have only seen about two Hun planes. We are all getting very tired of this constant marching. We did about 400 miles in the first month from the start, and we have not received a single reinforcement—man or horse—so we are now less than half strength. However not so bad, considering we have left the Australians and General Barrow's outfit behind, paralysed by the roadside. We being right in front now ought to see some fun....Weather has held up magnificently, our only having one days rain so far. It is sometimes quite cold now. Owing to officers going sick I have had to take over Quartermaster again as well as the Squadron. They say the Hun is evacuating Aleppo; however we shall see... Lieutenant Knight

On 19 October 1918 the final advance on Aleppo was launched, but little fighting took place until 26 October. On 19 the Brigade marched to El Rastan to repair a bridge over the Orontes which had been damaged by the Turks. On 20 working parties were furnished to assist the Engineers, and on 21 the Brigade marched to Hama. On 21 October the staff of Sir Pratap started from El Rastan for Cairo to return to India. A week's halt was expected, but in the evening orders were received to continue the march to Aleppo and intercept the further retreat of the Turkish force covering the town. Three light armoured motor batteries and four light car patrols were to go ahead, and the 13 and 14 Brigades were to be one day behind the 15 Brigade. The village of Khan Shaikhun was reached on 22, Seraikin on 24 and Khan Tuman on 25 October.

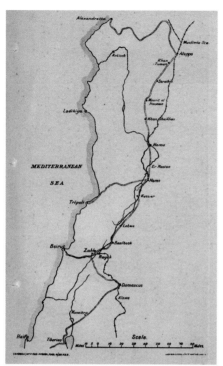

Syria, showing the area of the last stages of the campaign against the Turks. After capturing Haifa, the Jodhpur Lancers moved north to Syria and Lebanon, rolling up the opposing Turko-German forces as they went. The Sinai and Palestine Campaign, culminating in the decisive Battle of Meggido brought to an end the 600-year old Ottoman Empire, and ended the First World War in the Middle East.
Photo courtesy: Major E.M. Belcher

On 25 October, after a blistering two-week march north, the 15 Cavalry Brigade joined the 7 Light Cavalry Patrol at Zi'bre, then 20 kilometres south-west of Aleppo. A report was received here that the enemy were holding a line south and west of Aleppo in large numbers. Advancing a further 10 kilometres northwards, the Jodhpurs bivouacked that night in the region of Khan Tuman, preparatory to the advance on the city the next day, where the last engagement of the campaign was to be fought at Haritan, some eight miles north-west of Aleppo, on 26 October 1918.

26 October 1918—The Affair of El Haritan, Aleppo

On 26 October at 06:30 AM the 'A' and 'B' Squadrons of Jodhpur Lancers, acting as advanced guard to the Brigade, began their last ride as they pushed forward at a trot out of Khan Tuman with one sub-section of the 15 Machine-Gun Squadron (manned by men of the Jodhpur Lancers), to clear the ridge north-west of Aleppo, and got astride the Aleppo-Alexandretta road.

The advanced guard led by Captain Aman Singh of 'B' Squadron, came under fire when it reached the road on its exit from Aleppo and deployed on the ridge overlooking Haritan at 09:45 hrs and halted. At 11 AM, it suddenly came under heavy machine-gun fire from the right side of the road. It thereupon fell back 400 yards, dismounted, and took up a position with two troops on either side of the road with the machine guns on the right.

So far all that had actually been seen of the enemy was a body of a couple of hundred in an enclosed garden south of Haritan. Deeming instant action all important, and in view of the information received, Brigadier Harbord decided to attack at once. He ordered the Mysore Lancers to move round the eastern end of the ridge and charge the enemy. The remaining two squadrons of the Jodhpur Lancers were to follow, while the rest of the machine-gun squadron were sent to reinforce the advanced guard, and get into action to cover the mounted attack.

Meanwhile the Mysore Lancers advancing north-eastward under their Senior SSO Major W.J. Lambert, charged the knoll. The position, held by a party of 150 Turks, was carried, about 50 of the enemy being speared and 20 prisoners taken. The Turks now disclosed far greater strength than had been anticipated, and the regiment, coming under heavy fire, fell back from the ridge. Lieutenant Colonel Holden, who had halted the two Jodhpur squadrons in a fold of the ground in the rear, sent to Major Lambert for news. He was informed that the Mysores would charge again and wanted the Jodhpurs to cover the outer right flank while they rallied. Thereupon the Jodhpur advanced to a position about a half a mile south-east of the knoll, and the Mysores, who were momentarily shaken, rallied a thousand yards in its rear.

The Jodhpurs in their turn however came under heavy fire and at this moment Lieutenant Colonel Holden was shot dead at close range; and the two squadrons likewise began to fall back in some confusion. Then Captain H.P. Hornsby rallied the leading 'D' Squadron under Captain Anop Singh and turned about to charge, Lieutenant Knight promptly swinging round the second 'B' Squadron under Captain Aman Singh and followed them. A moment later Captain Hornsby was shot through the neck and the 'D' Squadron Commander, seeing large numbers of Turkish reinforcements moving up, wisely wheeled the squadron about. Captain Aman Singh with 'B' Squadron then decided to take up his position on the left of the Mysores. The enemy had now disclosed a strength of at least 3,000 infantry, 400 cavalry, with 8 to 12 guns of various calibre, and about 30 machine guns and automatic rifles and for a few moments threatened to counter-attack, but then hesitated and began to dig in. The two Jodhpur Squadrons kept up continuous rifle and machine gun fire and remained in relatively the same position up till 2200 hours. The situation of the Jodhpur and Mysore Lancers remained precarious until relieved at 11 PM by the 34 Poona Horse of the 14 Brigade and marched back to a bivouac area north of Aleppo, where it came into divisional reserve. By midnight the Ottoman force withdrew, ending the last engagement of the war in the Middle East.

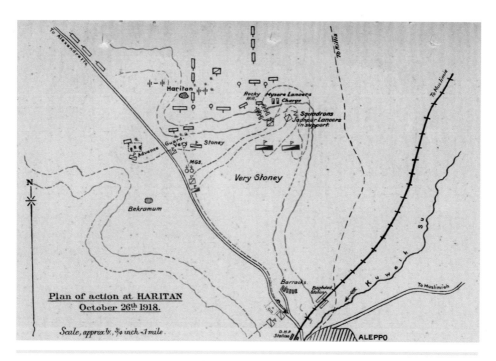

Map of showing the last engagement of the Great War on 26 October 1918 at Haritan, Aleppo.
Map courtesy: Major E.M. Belcher

The enemy's casualties were estimated at 100. The Brigades casualties were one British Officer, one Indian Officer and 16 ORs killed; six British Officers, six Indian Officers, 44 ORs wounded and three ORs missing. The Jodhpur suffered one British Officer and one OR killed and one British officer, two Indian Officers and 17 ORs wounded, besides 13 horses killed and 11 horses wounded/missing.

Captain Hornsby who was wounded, lost consciousness and, on recovery, found himself behind enemy lines. He remained concealed until nightfall and then made his way back to his own lines, winning the Military Cross in the process. His citation reads as, 'During the action of the 26 October 1918, North of Aleppo, when his Commanding Officer was wounded, he went to his assistance. Finding him dead he attempted to recover his horse, but was shot through the neck and rendered unconscious. On recovering consciousness he found himself alone a few yards to the rear of the enemy line. He remained concealed until dark and then made his way back through the enemy outposts to our camp, bringing in most valuable information.'

Captain H.F.P. Hornsby in a letter dated 27 November 1918 to Major W.A.S. deGale, Commanding the 5th Cavalry Depot in India described the death of Lieutenant Colonel Holden who belonged to 5th Cavalry as,

Perhaps you will have heard by this time about Colonel Holden's death. I would have written before, but have been in hospital with a bullet through the neck. Am alright now.

Colonel Holden was killed on 26 October, about six miles north-west of Aleppo. I was standing about ten yards away from him talking to him at the time and he was sitting on his horse. A bullet hit him on the left side of the head, passing out at the right side just above the ear, and he pitched forward in his saddle and rolled over and fell off all of a heap. I ran to him at once and picked him up and called to him but he never answered. He was dead. He had been killed instantaneously.

That night the Turks went back, so the following day the whole regiment went into Aleppo and buried him in the cemetery there. I was in hospital myself so didn't go to the funeral. General MacAndrew was there and all the Divisional and Brigade Staff and the whole of the Jodhpur Lancers.

He was brought up on a gun carriage covered with the Union Jack and his charger was laid behind him. Four British Officers carried him down to the grave and the regiment turned out a firing party and the

Lieutenant Colonel Holden on his charger 'Arab'. He was killed in action at Aleppo while mounted on this horse. Later on 13 March 1919, his charger was transfered to No 1 Remount Depot for further despatch to England to be handed over to his wife as per cavalry tradition.
Photo courtesy: Camilla Young (granddaughter of Major A.D. Strong)

trumpeters sounded the 'Last Post'. The Jodhpur Lancers will feel his loss tremendously. They absolutely worshiped him and would have done anything for him or gone anywhere with him.

We sent a notice to the *Times* and one to the *Pioneer*: 'Lieutenant Colonel H.N. Holden, DSO, 5th Cavalry, Killed in Action on 26 October 1918. Deeply regretted by all officers and ranks with whom he was serving', or words to that effect. I don't know exactly what the wording was. Anyway those are the details if you are publishing a regimental notice.

He had been given the DSO for the Haifa show but never lived to get it, and I now hear that he is to get a bar to his DSO for his consistent good work with the regiment. General MacAndrew told him a few days before he was killed that he was going to get a DSO for the Haifa show, so he knew about it.

His affairs are now being wound up by the committee of Adjustment at Kantara and I expect they will write to you about anything he may have in India. If there is any suggestion in the regiment about getting up a subscription for a memorial tablet please put me down as a subscriber. I would suggest that we might put up a tablet in his father's old church at Steeple Langford or in the Cathedral at Salisbury.

There is not an English Church at Aleppo, only a Syrian Christian one. We have put a cross over his grave in reinforced concrete and have carved on it, 'Lieut Colonel H N Holden, DSO, 5th Cavalry attached Jodhpur Lancers, Killed in Action 26th October 1918. RIP.'

If any of you want to write to his wife, her address is Woodlands, Preston Brighton and now I must stop.

This is from General Sir Edmund Allenby's Dispatch which was published in the *London Gazette* No 31087, dated 30 December 1918,

Early on the morning of 26 October 1918 the armoured cars and the 15 Cavalry Brigade, moving round the west side of the town, followed the enemy along the Aleppo-Katma road and gained touch with him south-east of Haritan. The Turkish rearguard consisted of some 2,500 infantry, 150 cavalry, and eight guns. The Mysore Lancers and two squadrons of the Jodhpur Lancers attacked the enemy's left; covered by the fire of the armoured cars, the Machine Gun Squadron and two dismounted squadrons of the Jodhpur Lancers. The Mysore and Jodhpur Lancers charged most gallantly. A number of Turks were speared, and many threw down their arms, only to pick them up again when the cavalry had passed through, and their weakness had become apparent. The squadrons were not strong enough to complete the victory, and were withdrawn till a larger force could be assembled.

On 30 October, with Palestine, Syria and Iraq lost, the Turks requested an armistice. At noon on 31 October 1918 an Armistice with Turkey came into force, all posts being ordered to remain in the positions occupied at that hour. On 15 November the Jodhpur Lancers marched to Muslimiye Junction and on 30 November to Aleppo. On 11 December 1918 General Allenby made the official entry into Aleppo and inspected the Jodhpur Lancers and said:

> I wish to tell your regiment how much I appreciate the splendid work during the summer and during the advance on Aleppo. I consider your record both in the Jordan valley and in the capture of Haifa as second to none. This I believe is first time in the history that a fortified town has been captured by cavalry at the gallop. I was very sorry to hear of the valuable lives that you have lost but this must be expected in war.

In yet another important letter dated 31 October 1918, Lieutenant Knight wrote to his father,

> '...Since my last letter dated 20 October we have done well over 100 miles, making the total since stunts started well over 550 miles. I had the honour of being SSO of the first squadron (B Squadron) to enter into Aleppo, doing vanguard, which we occupied without resistance, but on the other side bumped against the latest thing in Turco-German troops, fresh from Constantinople, and eight to ten times our number. Being in advance guard we secured the local pivot of manoeuvre, being under very heavy gun, machine gun and rifle fire all day (Just heard that armistice with Turkey in 5 minutes from now). The enemy returning during the night. Again my 'B' Squadron's luck held, in spite of being under the heaviest fire of the lot; a damned sight too heavy and accurate from German guns, machine guns; not to speak of snipers. We had only two men with their clothes cut, though the Indian Squadron Commander Captain Aman Singh and self had one shell burst on the small pile of stones by which we were sheltering behind blown all over us, another two feet and it would have dropped plum on us, then two shrapnel burst about five feet above and to rear of my head and similar escapes.
>
> Meanwhile the rest of the Brigade had been trying mounted operations against several times their number of fresh and unshaken troops without much success, we having no guns at the time. We were relieved at dawn, and came in to rest at Aleppo.

I very much regret to say that Colonel Holden was killed instantaneously by a bullet in the head, his loss is irreparable. I never wish to serve under a more gallant officer and gentleman, who was beloved and respected by all ranks. We recovered his body next morning, and he was buried with full military honours in the Christian Cemetery of Aleppo. I enclose photo. *[on facing page]*

I am the pall-bearer on the left, back view; General MacAndrew right facing. Captain Hornsby was wounded by a bullet through the neck; a most marvellous escape; and got in through the enemy's lines after dark. So we are now reduced to three British Officers, Major Gell and Reynolds and self. Regiment about half strength, mostly 'crocks', no good for charging. Don't know what will happen to us, as we have now marched so far into this country that it is very difficult to get out of it. Aleppo is not a bad town in its way...we all fervently hope and pray to be spared marching out through, hoping that the peace terms will allow us to embark from Alexandretta. I expect they will have us out of it as soon as possible and this Brigade should go before any. Before the war who would have prophesied an Imperial Service Cavalry Brigade first into Aleppo, after having outlasted all the rest, and done the most fighting in this Division....Temperatures here beyond words; nearly freezing at night, and you require a 'topee' (cap) in the heat of the day. Your Loving Son, Austin B. Knight.'

Jemadar Beer Singh wrote in his letter that,

At Aleppo not finding a proper field of fire on top of the mountain, we fixed our machine guns on the slope and opened fire. Brigadier Harbord was watching, I heard him telling Lieutenant Falconer, our Brigade Machine Gun Officer, that till such time as they do not see the enemy, these Jodhpur troops appear very different, but as the enemy appears before them the spirit of valour consumes them.

From 19 September to 26 October 1918 the Jodhpur Lancers as the most advanced troops of the 5th Cavalry Division had actually covered 550 miles in 38 days and had taken part in every cavalry engagement of importance from the breaking of the line to the occupation of Aleppo. Thus the Jodhpur Lancers had completed a march that will be numbered as one of the finest in the annals of war. The greatest exploit in the history of horsed cavalry, and possibly their last success on a large scale, had ended within a short distance of the battlefield of Issus (333 BC), where Alexander the Great first showed how battles could be won by bold and well-handled horseman.

A photo of the funeral of Lieutenant Colonel Hyla Holden on 28 October 1918, West of Aleppo
at Christian Cemetery. It was attended by Divisional and Brigade Commander and Staff and
whole of the Jodhpur Lancers. This photo was sent by Lieutenant Knight to his father.
Photo courtesy: Major and Mrs Wyndham Knight

Megiddo was one of the best-planned and executed British battles of the First
World War, and had the most dramatic results. The towns the 5th Cavalry Division
occupied included Nazareth, Haifa, Acre, Zahle, Mollaka, Homs, Hama and
Aleppo, at the very border of Turkey, a truly wonderful record. Night and day
since 19 September 1918, the Allies had relentlessly gone on in pursuit of the
Turkish soldiers. Hundreds of dead men, horses and even a flock of dead sheep
lay in between broken-down vehicles, abandoned guns, machinery and disabled
transport, blocking the path of the advancing horsemen.

The historical consequences of this campaign are hard to overestimate. The
immediate aftermath of Allenby's great victory saw the 600 year-old Ottoman
Empire stripped of its Arab lands and finally vanish into history.

The total number of casualties in action by the Jodhpur Lancers during the Great
War amounted to; three British Officers, five State Officers and 38 ORs killed,
one State Officer and 63 ORs died of disease and one British Officer, 10 State
Officers and 77 ORs wounded, and five ORs prisoners of war.

They won 93 Gallantry and Distinguished Service awards. Although the two
regiments formed a composite unit for the duration of the war, they still maintained
their own establishments, at least on paper, and these increased during the war –
1st Lancers rising from 604 in 1914 to 995 in 1915 and 2nd Lancers rising from
303 in 1914 to 815 in 1919. While the honours and awards given for overseas
service were gazetted simply to Jodhpur Lancers, those awarded for service in
India were gazetted to their respective regiments. In all, Jodhpur had despatched

A painting by James McBey, dated 10 November 1918. The Indian Cavalry encamped about
a mile from Aleppo town on the Alexandretta road. The tents are arranged in a long line with
the horses grazing behind and the citadel of Aleppo visible in the background.
Photo courtesy: © Imperial War Museum

to the field 1,369 combatants of all ranks. Besides this field service, which cost the
Marwar Durbar Rs 26,08,777 a total of 8,143 men were recruited from Marwar,
including both for Jodhpur Lancers and the Indian Army. Beside this 13 pound
gun shells were manufactured in the Jodhpur State Railway and the State also
supplied two ice machines for use in Iraq military hospitals.

News of the conclusion of the Armistice with Germany reached Jodhpur on
11 November 1918. The Government published the same by a special notification
and broadcast it all over the city. The news was everywhere received with great
enthusiasm but owing to state mourning due to the death of Maharaja Sumer
Singh on 03 October 1918 the festivities and public holiday were postponed to
07 December 1918.

On 12 November 1918, after the Armistice, Sir Pratap wrote a letter from Jodhpur
to Colonel Clive Wigram, Assistant Military Secretary to the King, expressing
the hope that he might be chosen as a representative of India to participate in the
Peace Conference. He wrote,

> I am glad to inform you that the Jodhpur Lancers played their part
> remarkably well in the Palestine Campaign. When the Turkish line was

first broken, I was with my cavalry for three days and nights on our horses, but in the subsequent charge (at Haifa) which has brightened the page of our history, I am sorry to say that fever prevented me from taking part in it. The dashing charge of our cavalry was splendid and worthy of the Rathores. Major Dalpat fell gallantly at the head of his cavalry in this memorable charge. To me it was highly gratifying and no more less elating.

Of all the soldier princes of India, I think I am the only soldier who has stuck to his post at the front throughout the war, and I hope it would be nothing but a fitting and gracious recognition of my loyal and humble services if I were to be honoured by being invited to partake in this august assembly.

Finally it was Maharaja Ganga Singh of Bikaner who was selected as Indian representative. Great as Sir Pratap's services were, probably his age and linguistic disabilities weighed against him.

For its contribution to the war effort, India gained independent representation at the Paris Peace Conference held in Versailles on 28 June 1919. The Peace Treaty of Versailles was signed by Mr Edwin Montague, the Secretary of State for India and Maharaja Ganga Singh of Bikaner. As a signatory of the Treaty of Versailles, India was granted automatic entry to the League of Nations on its formation in 1920 and later became one of the founding member-states of the United Nations Organisation in 1945.

At Aleppo during the Egyptian Rebellion 1919 and Return Home February 1920

To the great disappointment of all the Jodhpur Lancers' officers and men, when the war came to an end on 11 November 1918, the regiment did not return to Jodhpur at once, since it was decided to maintain 13 regiments of cavalry in Palestine, as part of the Army of occupation, and the Jodhpur Lancers along with the Hyderabad and Mysore Lancers were selected for the same, and they remained at Aleppo for one more year.

During this time the Jodhpur Lancers were stationed close to Aleppo town, taking over the barracks and vast stores and depots vacated by the Turks, whilst some units were pushed to Muslimie. After the 130 degrees F, or so, of heat in the Jordan valley, the cold in Syria, during the winter, seemed intense, and ice had frequently to be broken before the morning wash. On 31 December 1918

A rare propaganda postcard in Urdu with flags of Britain, America and France. The text reads:
'Final news of the European War—Germany surrenders and the war is over, 11 November 1918'.
The reverse contains a prayer for the safety of the King.
Photo courtesy: Professor K.C. Yadav

Lieutenant Colonel Pratap Singh assumed the command of the regiment after his leave from India.

At Aleppo race meetings were held regularly every alternate Saturday throughout the summer. The popular Aleppo race meetings were an attempt to pass the monotony of an enforced exile in a barren and dreamy land. The only beverages obtainable at this time were native wines and army rum, and as the former consisted chiefly of sweet alicante, ethylated cognac and arak, one became quite a connoisseur of the latter and the different methods of making rum punch.

In order to release men for leave, who have been overseas since the outbreak of war, it was decided to despatch a draft of 100 men from Jodhpur for the regiment in Aleppo in August 1919. All those who had served throughout the war, became entitled to five months of war leave (the entire leave had to be taken together, failing which the residual leave would lapse). Thus, during this period, the officers and men went on leave in batches through the Indian Transit Camp at Suez for further proceeding to India. The men also visited Cairo and Mecca on short leave. Few men were also sent on various courses of instructions to Haifa, Jaffa, Alexandria and Zeitoun. Sometimes the regiment was ordered out to help patrol the town and quell civil riots in Aleppo.

On 09 June 1919, six officers and 80 men proceeded to give a guard of honour to Emir Faisal (at the end of Turkish rule in October 1918, Emir Faisal helped set up an Arab government, under British protection, in Arab-controlled Greater Syria).

Finally the territory known as, 'Occupied Enemy Territory (East)', including Damascus, Homs, Hama, and Aleppo, was handed over to the Arab administration under Emir Faisal. And on 28 June 1919 Daffadar Zalim Singh, Daffadar Bir Singh and nine ORs proceeded to London to attend the peace celebrations after which they rejoined the regiment on 01 October 1919.

On 09 August 1919 newly promoted Major Aman Singh, having rejoined from leave, assumed command of the regiment, while Lieutenant Colonel Pratap Singh went on special leave to India.

On 23 September 1919 the GOC 15 I.S. Cavalry Brigade inspected the regiment on the first anniversary of the Haifa Day in Aleppo. It was decided that the Brigade's memorial be made at the spot where the last engagement of the Great War took place at Haritan, Aleppo. Thus on 05 November 1919 the Haritan, Aleppo Memorial to the 15 I.S. Cavalry Brigade was unveiled in the presence of all troops of the Brigade. The details of the unveiling ceremony of the memorial are covered in greater detail separately.

THE LIFE OF MEN AND HORSE IN PALESTINE DURING 1918-19

The campaign in the Palestine was intensely interesting, but at the same time there were many hardships—intense heat in the summer, along with dust and insects, and cold and heavy rains in the winter. The fortitude and endurance of the troops was beyond all praise, as the summer of 1918 spent by the Jodhpur Lancers in the Jordan Valley, at about 1,200 feet below sea-level, with temperatures varying from 110 to 125 degrees, was never forgotten by them. In parts of Palestine the flies, beetles, lizards, centipedes, scorpions, snakes, sand flies and mosquitoes were a few of many tortures.

The general daily routine when they were not involved in any marching was as follows: Reville 04:30; Parades 06:30 to 10:00; and 15:00 to 17:30 hours. Horses were watered twice and fed four times a day. The new regulations regarding rations and forage included 'Iron' and two days emergency-rations (in wallets) for the man, and one day's emergency-forage, in a 'sandbag' rolled in a ground-sheet and carried on the front arch of the saddle, for the horse, in addition to the two days forage carried in the nosebags; furthermore one day's rations and forage were carried on the wagons. In addition 100 rounds of ammunition, haversack, water bottle, mess tin, water bucket and a pair of wallets containing spare socks, underwear, shaving kit, grooming brushes, spare horseshoes and pouch and waterproof ground sheet. Including rifle bucket and blanket it all weighed five kgs.

A painting by Sir William Orpen, Signing of the Peace Treaty of Versailles on 28 June 1919.
Maharaja Ganga Singh of Bikaner is seen in the centre standing beside the right-hand pillar.
Photo courtesy: Wikimedia Commons and Lalgarh Palace, Bikaner

The following method of carrying kit in marching order was adopted by all mounted units of 15 I.S. Cavalry Brigade in Palestine:

1. On the man.
    (a) Over left shoulder on right side—bandolier (containing 90 rounds), field glasses and haversack with one day's mobile rations and unexpended portion of day's ration.
    (b) Over right shoulder on left side—water bottle
    (c) Over right shoulder and on back (except when in alert position) — S.B. respirator
    (d) Attached to belt, left side—bayonet, infantry entrenching tool (if carried) and wire cutter (small size).

2. On the saddle.
    (a) Front of saddle near wallet—toilet accessories including one pair of socks and hand towel.
    (b) Front of saddle off wallet—two days mobile rations and one tin dubbing.
    (c) Front of saddle over wallet—hay net, bivouac sheet (with bivouac pins in fold of sheet), wire-cutters (large size), bivouac mallet (one per section).
    (d) Rear of saddle—cornsack containing eight lbs grain, greatcoat, muzzle over rear end.

3. Attached to saddle near side.
    (a) On sword scabbard—surcingle pad, brush, picketting peg, bivouac pole (tied together and attached to scabbard)
    (b) Over sword hilt—steel helmet
    (c) Attached to rear arch—shoe case, containing one fore, one hind shoe, 12 nails and hoof pick, nose bag (to be emptied last).

4. Attached to saddle off side.

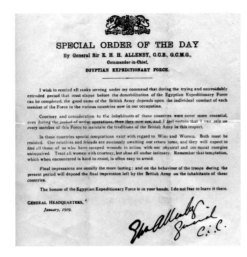

January 1919, Special Order of the Day by the C-in-C, EEF General Allenby. Excerpts: *'I wish to remind all ranks serving under my command that during the trying and unavoidably extended period that must elapse before the demobilization of the EEF can be completed, the good name of the British Army depends upon the individual conduct of each member of the force in the various countries now in our occupation... In these countries special temptations exist with regard to wine and women. Both must be resisted. Our relatives and friends are anxiously awaiting our return home, and they will expect to find all those of us who have escaped wounds in action with our physical and our moral energies unimpaired'.*
Photo Courtesy: Collection of Mrs B. Sutton

(a) Attached to rifle bucket—mess tin, water bucket containing *chagul* (leather waterbag made of goatskin).

(b) Attached to rear arch—nose bag (to be emptied first).

5.   Round horse's neck—bandolier containing 90 rounds, built-up rope, head chain or rope.

6.   Under saddle—one horse blanket and one man's blanket.

Each man was supplied with a bivy sheet, two of which lashed together with their rifles, for necessary support, could make a cover for two men. The officers had small calico bivy tents, open at one end. These made a light cover about three feet high, and there was just room for a person to crawl in. These tents were not rainproof. If time permitted, in these tents a trench, the length of the bivy and about one foot deep and one foot wide, was dug on one side. This enabled a person to sit down inside the cover. The Regiment carried three bell tents, one for the orderly room, one for the doctor, and one for the quarter-master's store. As soon as it was seen that there was going to be a stop at any place for more than a few days, cover was improvised if there was any material available. While in the oases, palm leaves were used for the purpose of making shacks. Forage bags were also used for this purpose. In a few cases, holes were dug in the ground and cover put over the holes.

They had to travel light. Surplus kit was dumped at divisional headquarters. Everything was done to spare the horses any extra weight, as the task of getting forage and water to such numbers of animals and men in an advance was a logistical nightmare. The logistical system was stretched as the men galloped ahead. Lagging miles behind, the camels carried gallons of water. The constant fear was that wells or waterholes might have been poisoned, tainted with camel's urine, or simply be brackish and unpalatable. The cisterns in the villages, insufficient for

Jodhpur Lancers Officers at Aleppo, February 1919. Seated fourth from left:
Lieutenant C.D.L. Clark, Captain Panne Singh, Lieutenant Colonel A.J. Reynolds, Lieutenant
Colonel Pratap Singh, Lieutenant A.B. Knight, Captain Anop Singh, Lieutenant Sagat Singh and
unknown. After Armistice, the regiment stayed on in Palestine and Syria for more than a year,
finally returning to India in February 1920 after six years of field service.
Photo courtesy: Major and Mrs Wyndham Knight

The War News was published regularly in Jodhpur, by the Marwar Publicity Board under Mr R.B.
Van Wart, the Principal of Rajput High School Chopasani. The ninth edition of this paper was
published on 01 March 1919. It carries a very smart looking photo of Major Dalpat Singh, MC. This
photo was taken a few months before he was killed in action at the head of the Jodhpur Lancers in
Haifa. He is wearing the 1911 Delhi Durbar ribbon on his uniform.
Photo Courtesy: Rajasthan State Archives Department, Bikaner and Mehrangarh Museum Trust Jodhpur

Captain Aman Singh, OBI, IOM (front camel) and Captain Anop Singh, OBI, IOM, MC (the 'B' and 'D' Squadron Commanders during the Battles of Jordan Valley, Haifa and Aleppo) take a 'joyride' in front of the Great Sphinx at Giza with the pyramid of Khafre in the background, in 1919. The Giza plateau was a popular tourist destination for the men while they were stationed at Aleppo.
Photo courtesy: Vasant Singh Rodla

the thousands of horses, were usually a disappointment. Some oases, too, were a source of frustration, while many waterholes were choked by waterweed or fouled by worms, if frogs were not present to eat them. A search for water while on the march in such places was not a very hopeful matter; at the most there might be two wells, from which water could be got up, a bucketful at a time—a hopeless look out, when there were hundreds of thirsty men and horses!

For weeks men were only given half a gallon of water a day for all purposes and the stench of unwashed men and clothes was constant. The shortage of water meant there was little to spare for washing clothes or bodies—the troops bathed naked whenever they could. So each man shared his pitiful water ration from his canvas water bottle with his drooping horse. Normally horses drink a bucket of water three times a day—more in hot weather or with heavy work. Along with the discomfort of the actual thirst, the dehydration caused indigestion, loss of condition and intestinal fermentation.

The cooking in standing camps was done usually regimentally or as per squadron, as it was found that there was not sufficient fuel to issue out to the men to enable them to do their own cooking. On the line of march, and during operations, the men arranged for their own cooking, usually in small parties of about four, the men collecting what fuel they could for that purpose. As a substitute for a table, it was found that the digging of a round trench about one foot wide and one foot deep, leaving the earth in the centre undisturbed, formed an excellent table.

Beside this the *khamsin* became very troublesome. This was a strong wind that blows, particularly in the afternoon. The soil being a mixture of fine sand and dust, the result can be better imagined than described; it was so bad that on few days the training would be entirely suspended! Though in this regard the Jodhpur men being accustomed to *loo* (strong hot and dry summer winds) in Marwar, were better suited than the rest of the troops!

In spite of lack of water, heat and dust the horsemen of Jodhpur were well fitted for the class of warfare they were called upon to undertake. They were accustomed to wide spaces and long days in the saddle, and were full of initiative, self-reliance and determination to overcome every obstacle in their way. The value of their work is best shown by the esteem in which they were held by the other troops. The long apprenticeship of the Jodhpur Lancers to the trench warfare of the Western front had robbed them of none of their dash and brilliancy in the open warfare to which they were so eminently fitted.

The wastage from malaria and other diseases was heavy as the advance of Jodhpur passed through one of the most malarious regions in the world. It was decided that a prophylactic dose of 10 grains of quinine daily, be given to all troops and it was recommended that mosquito nets would be used as far as possible. The infection had been brought from the Jordan Valley, the men went down by the score. Men, suddenly overcome, stuck to their saddles as long as they could, and then drew out from the column, and were helped into a shady place to await the ambulance men. By the time Jericho was reached there were hardly enough men left to lead all the riderless horses.

The horse nobly served the Jodhpur Lancers in the war, and never better than in the desert campaign. The gallant horses carried them over France and Palestine, they suffered wounds, thirst, hunger and weariness almost beyond endurance but they never failed. The soldier's lives regularly depended upon their horses, and the bond between man and animal was strong. The men regarded the horses, which endured so courageously, as comrades in arms, and treated them with self-sacrificing devotion.

But the parting of the men from their horses at the end of war was pathetic. The animals were divided into three classes—those of no further use which were to be shot, those to be sold, and those to be retained by the army of occupation. The

Lieutenant Colonel Holden, Reynolds, Knight and others in improvised 'officers mess', somewhere on the march in Palestine during 1918. The Jodhpur men were expert in raising such a shack in no time from local resources. The scorching heat coupled with lack of water, abrasive sand and masses of flies made life barely tolerable.
Photo courtesy: Major and Mrs Wyndham Knight

A mule driver is down with malaria. Disease was a far bigger threat than enemy action, with more than 10 times as many casualties caused by sickness. By 1918, only the worst cases were removed for treatment, with most men having to soldier on regardless. In short, the Jodhpur men who served in Palestine and Syria played a vital role in securing eventual victory, while facing appalling conditions and, for the most part, receiving little appreciation or recognition.
Photo courtesy: Paul Reed, Great War photos

men knew that horses sold to Egyptians probably would end their days in miserable slavery, and efforts were made, often successful, to have animals transferred to the class for the kindly bullet.

This campaign has been depicted in several films. The most famous is *Lawrence of Arabia*, a 1962 British epic film based on the life of T.E. Lawrence. Other films dealing with this topic include *Forty Thousand Horsemen*, a 1940 Australian war film directed by Charles Chauvel and *The Lighthorsemen* (1987). Perhaps the time is ripe to now make a grand film on the Jodhpur Lancers as well. Who knows, it may be a reality soon!

RETURN HOME TO JODHPUR

Those must have been difficult times for Jodhpur soldiers eager to return home after almost six years on foreign soils. All eyes were towards home.

Finally on 12 November 1919, the Jodhpur Lancers marched by easy stages and reached Beirut on 28 November. Embarking there on 07 December 1919, they

A group photo on the eve of Jodhpur's departure from Aleppo for Jodhpur! They had done their duty, and have left a record of service which will stand as an example for generations yet unborn, so parted a gallant company of friends.
Photo Courtesy: Major and Mrs Wyndham Knight

reached Kantara where they remained for three weeks. On 23 December 1919 at Kantara the C-in-C General Allenby inspected the regiment for one last time and bid them goodbye!

Eventually marching to Suez it embarked for India by, *S.S. Huntsend* on 09 January 1920 and reached Bombay on 23 January and Jodhpur on 02 February 1920, after an absence of five-and-a-half years' continuous service overseas. Later the fit animals of Jodhpur (510 horses and 131 mules) arrived at Bombay on 08 February 1920 by *S.S. Huntscastle*. On arrival at Jodhpur the Jodhpur Lancers Depot gave them a great reception and the next two days were given over to feasting and *tamasha* (a grand show).

On 10 January 1920 Lord Allenby sent the following message to the Durbars,

> On the Imperial Service Cavalry Brigade leaving EEF, I wish to express to you my admiration of the services performed by these units in the field which has been worthy of the finest fighting traditions of the races and of their discipline and spirit which has always been excellent. I wish them a safe return to the welcome they have so well earned and all success in the future.

BATTLE HONOURS

The successful action at Megiddo resulted in the Megiddo battle honour awarded to units that had participated in the battle. Two subsidiary battle honours, for the battles of Sharon and Nablus were also awarded. The Jodhpur Lancers received the following battle honours after their magnificent role during the Great

The original flag of Sardar Rissala in 1920.
Photo courtesy: 61st Cavalry Regiment

On return from war the men got busy to meet social obligations like marriages. While some men bought new gramophones to forget the horrors of the war quickly. For many Indian troops the war was an experience that broadened their horizons and increased their knowledge of the world.
Photo courtesy: The author

War: *Cambrai 1917, France and Flanders 1914–18, Megiddo, Sharon, Damascus, Palestine 1918.*

This, then, completes the account of the Jodhpur Lancers during the Great War of 1914–1918, and for subsequent service overseas, a total of five years and five months. This is a record of which the regiment may justly be proud, which had added lustre to the reputation enjoyed by the regiment since its inception.

What Happened to Soldiers on their Return Home

The story of soldier who returned from years of war often brutalised and suffering psychologically, is largely forgotten in the India today, but these soldiers and their war-time experiences did have an impact on post-war Indian society and politics. Perhaps the most significant outcome of the war was the very personal impacts it had on those Indians who experienced it firsthand. The war exposed the soldiers to new cultures, ideologies and ways of life that had a subtle impact on their life. Wherever the army men went, they saw with their own naked eyes the emerging forces of awakening. On their way back home they carried with them new ideas of progress.

The war years were difficult ones for Jodhpur men on the home front as well. Massive recruitment efforts, high taxes, war loans and a sharp rise in prices combined to impact the life of their families left behind.

After their return to Jodhpur the men quickly wanted to forget the horrors of the war and thus most of them got busy to get on to their lives. Those that returned also had to readjust to civilian life, often during periods of great political and social upheaval.

Many men found it difficult to talk about their experiences. Many also had to cope with physical trauma or the loss of family members and friends. The psychological consequences of the war continued to be felt for a generation or more.

However, many of the soldiers who were lucky to return to their villages after the war were now economically well off. They were able to buy land with their savings and build 'pucca' houses. Most men had to either marry off their children and some young soldiers got themselves married. They now wanted to send their children for school education, which had earlier been vehemently resisted.

Jodhpur during the Interwar Years— 1920 to 1939

The aftermath of the First World War saw many military, political, cultural and social changes taking place in Jodhpur. In recognition of the meritorious services rendered by the Jodhpur Lancers in the war the gun salute of the Maharaja of Jodhpur was raised from 17 to 19 guns in 1921. Also in 1921 the Imperial Service Troops Scheme was reviewed and revised.

Immediately on the return of the Jodhpur Lancers from the war, Viceroy Chelmsford visited Jodhpur from 20 to 22 November 1920. In his banquet speech the Viceroy said,

> ....The Jodhpur Lancers spent more than five years of distinguished service at the front and by their exploits at Haifa and in the Jordan Valley recalled the deeds of their ancestors who fought at Tunga, Merta and Pattan. The reputation which they have gained is well worthy of the glorious annals of Marwar. I may be permitted to pay a tribute to the dead and to mention the name of Major Dalpat Singh, MC, who met a soldier's death at Haifa while charging at the head of the regiment. I am confident that the welfare of those who went on active service will ever be an object of care and solicitude to the rulers of Jodhpur.

However, just before the arrival of the Viceroy there arose some serious discontentment amongst the troops of the Jodhpur Lancers, in July 1920, on

28 November 1921, the Jodhpur Lancers men posing with their medals acquired during the Great War. **Seated left to right:** Jemadar Sardar Singh (Senani), Rissaldar Sher Singh (Borunda), Captain Sagat Singh, MC (Jodhpur), Rissaldar Bhopal Singh (Sansri), Jemadar Bhopal Singh (Balada), Jemadar Jog Singh (Liliyan). **Standing:** Kot Daffadar Partap Singh (Ostran) and Kot Daffadar Jeevraj Singh (Guwalu). Interestingly two of them, Rissaldar Sher Singh and Jemadar Jog Singh are wearing the Turkish (Gallipolli Star) and German (Iron Cross) as war booty.
Photo courtesy: The author

account of pay, pension and conditions of service. Soon after their return from war, the men of the Jodhpur Lancers experienced a feeling of discontent, caused due to the reductions made after they returned from field service and the reversion from British Indian Army rates of pay (sanctioned for the duration of the war) to the old scale and suspension of free rations. In the latter stages of the war a large number of promotions were made and it was generally accepted that personnel so promoted would be permitted to retain the rank or anyhow retire with the pension of that rank.

The men complained in a detailed petition about their discharge, land grants and promotions:

> Our sepoys work is to give head in the war, and not to undertake the duty of a coolie but unfortunately for sometime we are compelled to do that...cutting 'pala' grass, trees, wood, carry them on our heads, and plucking 'sangris, 'kairs', carry earth from one place to another, ploughing, moving well and other big and small coolies work etc...

The men also complained bitterly about reduction of a complete squadron from the 2nd Regiment Sardar Rissala. Those who were likely to be discharged, mostly young people who had not been in the army for long, felt severely betrayed.

The men then went on a 'strike' demanding parity of pay, promotions, discharge and rations, like sepoys of the Indian Army. Major Aman Singh and Captain Anop Singh intervened and brought the situation under control.

A Court of Inquiry was held under Major R.W. Grimshaw, with Captain H. Hornsby and Lieutenant Colonel Sher Singh and Lieutenant Colonel Pratap Singh as members. The Regency Council under Sir Pratap Singh looked into the matter and accepted certain recommendations like restoration of free rations to the men and the situation was brought under satisfactory conclusion.

However, since certain defects in the organisation and system of the Imperial Service Troops movement had come to light during the Great War, a Committee of Ruling Princes assembled in Delhi on 10 November 1921 and discussed the question of a scheme for reorganisation. The result was the system of 'Indian States Forces' whereby all units of Indian States were included in the scheme for efficient training and armament. Thus, from January 1922, state units were no longer known as Imperial Service Troops, but as the Indian State Forces and graded according to a laid-down classification based upon their training and organisation.

The sanction of the Government of India for reorganisation from existing Jodhpur Imperial Service Troops to Jodhpur State Forces was received through letter No 845/174 Internal, dated 13 April 1922. The Jodhpur Durbar proposed reorganisation of his forces at total recurring expenditure of Rs 9,29,600 (approximately 10% of the state's revenue). It involved:

> 1. The conversion of the two regiments of Sardar Rissala into one regiment (Non-Silladar) with strength of 526 and one Reserve Squadron with strength of 131, fully equipped and fit for active service, and
> 2. One Headquarter Company and two Companies of Infantry (Half Battalion) as second line troops, which came to be known as Jodhpur Sardar Infantry (JSI) (It had 50% Jat troops).

The new scheme also involved re-organisation of the remaining irregular local military forces of the state, which involved an annual expenditure of approximately Five Lakhs of Rupees. It consisted of, Sumair Camel Corps; two Infantry Battalions and a small force of Fort Artillery. From 01 November 1922 the irregular local forces consisting of Sumair Camel Corps (869) and Sumair Infantry (338) were separated from the Military Department and were absorbed into the Police

A shoulder title badge of Jodhpur Fort Artillery.
Photo courtesy: Professor (Capt) Ashok Nath, FRGS, Nath Foundation, Sweden

and other departments of the state, while Fort Artillery was disbanded from 27 December 1924.

Major A.J. Reynolds was loaned as Military Adviser to Jodhpur Durbar from 28 December 1921. Later, he was succeeded by Captain A.H. Williams on 20 September 1924.

The Raising of the Jodhpur Sardar Infantry

On 28 August 1922 Major Aman Singh (Lieutenant Colonel from 18 February 1924) was made the first Commanding Officer of the Jodhpur Sardar Infantry. The JSI was organised as Indian States Forces, half battalion, on the Indian army

The two Haifa Squadron Commanders, Lieutenant Colonel Aman Singh and Lieutenant Colonel Anop Singh, were promoted and made the Commandants of Jodhpur Sardar Infantry and Jodhpur Sardar Rissala in 1922 and 1925 respectively.
Photo courtesy: the author and Vasant Singh Rodla

establishment on 1 October 1922, and was raised to a full battalion in March 1926. Its composition was two companies each of Rajputs and Jats and HQ Company mixed.

Though an infantry battalion with the name of Jodhpur Sardar Infantry (JSI) existed in Jodhpur, prior to this reorganisation of 1922, they were irregular troops. The Commanding Officers of JSI, before its reorganisation of 1922 were Maharaj Kishore Singh, Maharaj Bhopal Singh, Maharaj Colonel Rattan Singh and Colonel Raoraja Tej Singh.

The JSI was issued with short magazine Lee-Enfield (MLE) HV rifles, in accordance with sanction conveyed in the Foreign and Political Department letter No 267/174-Intl dated 16 February 1923. A total of 211 rifles in excess with the Jodhpur Lancers were transferred to the JSI. The JSI also took over the lines of the former 2nd Regiment of the Sardar Rissala.

On 27 December 1924 the Maharaja of Jodhpur ordered disbandment of the Fort Artillery and in lieu raised the strength of the Jodhpur Sardar Infantry from one headquarters company and two companies to that of full battalion on the Indian Army Establishment i.e. one headquarter company and four companies. The officers and men of the Fort Artillery who were willing to serve under the new terms in the Sardar Infantry were re-enlisted on their passing the required physical standards.

From then on, each of the four companies of the JSI would in turn provide garrison for the Jodhpur Fort and other forts in the state for a period not exceeding three months at a time. Thus, each company would spend nine months of the year at the headquarters and this period was considered sufficient for the purposes of training and for the maintenance of discipline and efficiency of the men.

On 22 April 1926 the JSI was classified as a Class 'A' unit organised on the Indian Army establishment, in view of strong recommendations given by General E.A. Fagan, the Military Advisor-in-Chief Indian State Forces who wrote, 'I have inspected this unit and it is well fitted to be considered as 'A' Class. It promises to be a fine Battalion'. The JSI was equipped with a total of 433 short MLE HV rifles. The officers and men were regularly sent on various courses of instruction to Indian State Forces Schools.

On 01 November 1939 the JSI was further reorganised according to the new War Establishment of an Indian State Forces Infantry 'Mixed' Battalion, and the raising of a Training company, designated as the 'Jodhpur Training Company'. Till the outbreak of World War II, the unit remained in the state on internal defence and guard duties. It was further reorganised in 1942.

17 February 1902: Sir Pratap seated right and Maharaj Rattan Singh seated left (Commanding Officer of the irregular JSI) on 17 February 1902.
Photo courtesy: Maharaj Dalpat Singh Bhopalgarh

The JSI in 1919. **From left:** Lieutenant Colonel Sujjan Singh and Colonel Tej Singh. Standing in the centre is Lieutenant Heer Singh (later CO of JSI) and on the extreme right is Daffadar Mool Singh Jodha.
Photo courtesy: Raoraja Vijay Singh

Perhaps the first JSI group photo after its reorganisation with Lieutenant Colonel Aman Singh (centre) and Major Sujjan Singh (seated third from left).
Photo courtesy: the author

A group of Jodhpur State Forces Officers in September 1924. Seated fourth from left Major Anop Singh, Captain Austin Henry Williams (he became ADC to King George VI in 1943), Lieutenant Colonel Pratap Singh, unknown, Lieutenant Colonel Aman Singh, unknown and Major Lachman Singh. Standing first row sixth from right is Captain Hem Singh (his son Major Shaitan Singh won the PVC in the 1962 War).
Photo courtesy: Chander Singh, Dhanari Kalan

Lieutenant Jawahir Singh of JSI, seated second from right, during the Second Preliminary Signalling Course (ISF) at Poona 1935–36.
Photo courtesy: Vikram Singh Rathore Pachranda

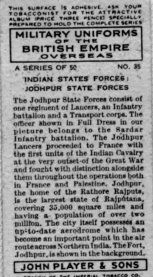

THIS SURFACE IS ADHESIVE. ASK YOUR TOBACCONIST FOR THE ATTRACTIVE ALBUM (PRICE THREE PENCE) SPECIALLY PREPARED TO HOLD THE COMPLETE SERIES

MILITARY UNIFORMS
OF THE
BRITISH EMPIRE
OVERSEAS

A SERIES OF 50   NO. 35

INDIAN STATES FORCES:
JODHPUR STATE FORCES

The Jodhpur State Forces consist of one regiment of Lancers, an Infantry battalion and a Transport corps. The officer shown in Full Dress in our picture belongs to the Sardar Infantry battalion. The Jodhpur Lancers proceeded to France with the first units of the Indian Cavalry at the very outset of the Great War and fought with distinction alongside them throughout the operations both in France and Palestine. Jodhpur, the home of the Rathore Rajputs, is the largest state of Rajputana, covering 35,000 square miles and having a population of over two million. The city itself possesses an up-to-date aerodrome which has become an important point in the air route across Northern India. The Fort, Jodhpur, is shown in the background.

JOHN PLAYER & SONS
BRANCH OF THE IMPERIAL TOBACCO CO.
(OF GREAT BRITAIN & IRELAND) LTD.

Lieutenant Colonel Raoraja Sujjan Singh, Officer Commanding JSI against the backdrop of the Jodhpur Fort in 1937. Sujjan Singh was the representative of the Jodhpur State Forces in the London Coronation Contingent in 1937. Photo card by John Player and Sons.
Photo courtesy: Mehrangarh Museum Trust

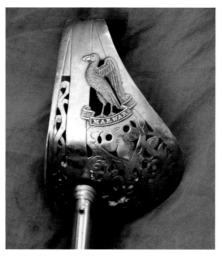

The JSI sword hilt was beautifully crafted with the *cheel* (kite) facing left resting on a scroll with the inscription 'Marwar'.
Photo courtesy: The author

The Reorganisation of Sardar Rissala

On 01 February 1922, the two regiments of the Sardar Rissala were reorganised as one Indian State Forces Cavalry regiment and its title changed from **Sardar Rissala to Jodhpur Sardar Rissala**.

The JSI on parade in February 1914 during the visit of Viceroy Hardinge.
Photo courtesy: Mehrangarh Museum Trust

The title was later again changed to Jodhpur Lancers on 29 May 1943.

The class composition of the Sardar Rissala was more mixed than had been the case for either of the two individual regiments. The regiment continued to recruit wholly from within the State. In July 1935 the uniform of the Jodhpur Lancers was changed from white to khaki.

Between the two World Wars the Jodhpur Lancers were mostly at Jodhpur and were sometimes called for training exercises to Meerut and Risalpur alongwith

The 1922 to 1942 Jodhpur Sardar Rissala cap badge. The badge depicts the *cheel* (kite) in flight above a half spherical globe within the upper angle of crossed lances with pennons, and across the lances two scrolls inscribed with 'Jodhpur' on the upper and 'Sardar Risala' on the lower.
Photo courtesy: Professor (Capt) Ashok Nath, FRGS, Nath Foundation, Sweden

Types of brass cap badges of Jodhpur Lancers worn from 1943 to 1953. The design consists of the *cheel* (kite) facing left, side view with wings outstretched, crossed lances with pennons, and a two-part scroll with the inscription 'Jodhpur Lancers'. These badges were worn until 1953.
Photo courtesy: Professor (Capt) Ashok Nath, FRGS, Nath Foundation, Sweden

Brass shoulder titles of Jodhpur Lancers and Jodhpur Sardar Rissala (JSR) including the collar badges.
Photo courtesy:
Colonel Devpal Singh Rathore

the Indian and British Cavalry units. The regiment then under the command of Lieutenant Colonel Bahadur Singh (from 18 September 1936–18 September 1941) did very well in the exercises. The regiment was always well mounted on Australian imported Waler Horses. It was said by the other cavalry units that when the Jodhpur Lancers walked, the other units had to trot to keep up, and when the

Jodhpur Lancers changed to khaki uniform in July 1935.
Photo courtesy: Mehrangarh Museum Trust

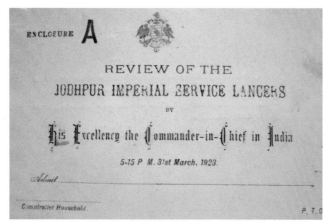

A Jodhpur Lancers invitation card and menu card for a State Banquet Jodhpur, 31 March 1923.
Photo courtesy: The author

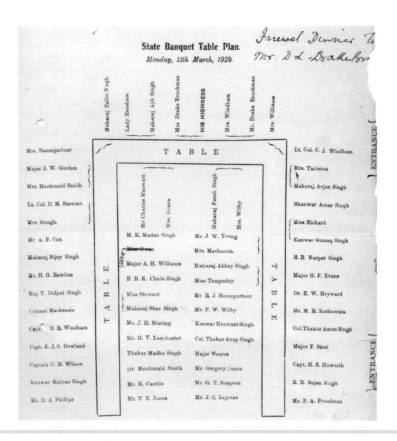

The high-life: Maharaja Umaid Singh enjoyed hosting lavish banquets with pomp and pageantry. A typical table plan of 11 March 1929 shows both the Commanding Officers of the Jodhpur Lancers and the Jodhpur Sardar Infantry in attendance on state banquets, held in honour of Mr Digby Livingstone Drake-Brockman, a Indian Civil Service Officer, who was Customs and Revenue Officer in Jodhpur State from 1921 to 1926.
Photo courtesy: The author

Jodhpur Lancers trotted, then others had to canter. The regiment also had a very fine Polo team and when stationed at both Risalpur and Meerut won all the Inter Regimental Polo Cups.

In addition the Jodhpur Durbar also maintained the following units as Class 'B' units with effect from 01 February 1922.

Jodhpur Transport Corps

When the Jodhpur Lancers was reorganised into a Non-Silladar Regiment in 1922, it was decided to form a Transport Corps consisting of two troops, the mules of the Jodhpur Lancers being utilised for the purpose. The corps came into

Jodhpur, 1935; **last row, left to right**: Risaldar Mangal Singh, Jemadar Sher Singh, Jemadar Achal Singh, Jemadar Sabal Singh, Jemadar Chhog Singh, Jemadar Dol Singh, Lieutenant Zabar Singh, Risaldar Bishan Singh, Risaldar Jodh Singh, Risaladar Madho Singh, Risaldar Prem Singh, Jemadar Girdhari Singh, Jemadar Bhopal Singh. **Middle row**: Jemadar Nathu Singh, 2/ Lieutenant Sangram Singh, Lieutenant Sultan Singh, Lieutenant Kesri Singh, State Officer Cadet (SOC) Chandan Singh, Lieutenant Surajbhan Singh, Lieutenant Shyam Singh, Jemadar Magan Singh, Lieutenant Mohbat Singh, Risaldar Indra Singh, Jemadar Baxu Khan. **Seated front row**: Lieutenant Chhotu Singh, Captain Kalyan Singh, Captain Bahadur Singh, Major E.H. Stead, Lieutenant Colonel Dalpat Singh Rohet, Colonel Prithi Singh Bera, Major Hem Singh, Captain Bahadur Singh and Lieutenant Bhoor Singh.

Photo courtesy: Jagat Singh Rodla

being on 1 February 1922, and Rissaldar Roop Singh, IDSM, a retired officer of Jodhpur Lancers was placed in-charge of it. Its strength was two Officers, 121 Non Commissioned Officers (NCOs) and men, seven followers and 288 mules. They also had 50 transport carts. The mules were mainly used for transporting grass from the railway station and Bisalpur 'Jorh' (grass farm) to the Rissala lines and also for the supply of water to the units. On 27 December 1924 the Transport Corps was placed under the Commanding Officer JSI. Its strength was reduced and reorganised as one Draught Troop. On 22 April 1926 it was classified as an 'A' Class unit. It was re-designated as the Mule Troop in February 1940.

There is a very interesting tale told about the functioning of this transport corps by Mr Peter Vacher, in his book on the Jodhpur Flying Club, during 1934, when Major Stead was Military Adviser to the Maharaja's troops. He writes,

> On inspecting the Transport Corps, Major Stead was horrified to find that more than half the carts were on permanent assignment unrelated to

The Camp Quarter Guard of Jodhpur Sardar Rissala during an outdoor exercise in 1936.
Photo courtesy: Dr Mahendra Singh Tanwar

Corps duties; ten at the Palace, five with Raja so-and-so, three with Raoraja so-and-so, and so on. How on earth could he run an efficient unit if he never saw it? He ordered that the carts return to lines after daily duties and none would be allocated permanently to anyone. At 2 AM that Saturday morning, he was called to the telephone. Raoraja Abhey Singh, Controller of the Household, said, 'Do you know, Sahib, that Her Highness was not able to have her bath last night?

'What has that to do with me?' replied Stead.

'I'm afraid it has a lot to do with you, he said. 'You see Her Highness by tradition can only bathe in water brought from a certain well in the city. One of our transport carts is fitted up as a water cart but I understand that all the carts have returned to the lines under your orders.'

The trivial matter reached the Maharaja who agreed to Major Stead's orders and all carts were relieved forthwith!

Military Station Hospital

It was established on 01 February 1922. Its strength was two Officers, four NCOs and men, 17 followers with 36 beds. It was intended to deal with all matters medical for the Jodhpur State Forces. The building was sanctioned to make a total of three beds for officers and 75 beds for NCOs and men. Today the modern Military Hospital of Jodhpur stands on this very location.

Jodhpur State Military Band

The band was first raised in 1906. Its strength was one British Band Master, 51 NCOs and men and five followers. It was part of the State Military Forces and attached to the JSI. On 01 June 1926 it was reorganised with Mr W.H. Ryman as the Band Master, being granted the honorary rank of Lieutenant. Unlike other Jodhpur units, its class composition was Muslims, Sikhs and Ghurkhas, about one-third of whom were drawn from state personnel. They played for the Infantry on the march and also once a week for the State Forces. The Jazz band with strength of seven men was also raised in 1927.

The Jodhpur State Military Band in action.
Photo courtesy: Colonel B.P. Singh

War Trophies and Decorations Awarded to States

After the war, between 1920 and 1924, various states—including Jodhpur—were allotted war trophies in recognition of the good services rendered by troops who took direct part in the war. The states which helped in other ways got saluting guns, but not the actual war trophies. The Quarter Master General's Branch in

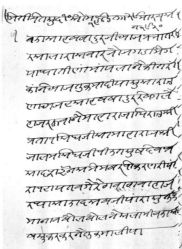

The Hakikat Bahi No 46 Samvat 1976 entry dated 29 March 1920 says that Great War medals were distributed to Jodhpur Lancers' men at residency bungalow, in the presence of Sir Pratap, Maharaj Zalim Singh, Pandit Sukhdeo Prasad, Finance Member and other prominent people.
Photo courtesy: Maharaja Man Singh Pusthak Prakash Jodhpur

Army HQs made the distribution as far as was possible from those parts where their troops served in, and in value according to the importance of the services rendered. All war trophies received from Kantara were distributed by Kirkee Arsenal Ordanance authorities. The trophies included 77mm guns, artillery shells, shell cases, gas masks, machine guns, rifles and bayonets, hand grenades, etc.

The Grant of Land Grants, *Jangi-Inams* and *Jagirs* to men of the Imperial Service Troops who had Rendered Distinguished Service during The Great War

The Indian Soldiers Board on 21 May 1919 at Delhi, laid down the procedures for bestowal of land rewards and special pensions to Indian Officers and Other Ranks for 'Distinguished Service' during the Great War. The Secretary of State had sanctioned only 20,000 such rewards for the whole of the Indian Army (9,000 in the form of Land Grants and 11,000 in the form of *Jangi-Inams*).

Land Grants were recognised as the most acceptable form of rewards but its limited availability necessitated an alternative method of reward, namely, *Jangi-Inam* taking the form of a money allowance payable monthly for two lives (Officer

Rs 10, Soldier Rs 5 and the Follower Rs 2-8-0 per mensem). As to land, the scale accepted in the Punjab was two Rectangles to Officers and one Rectangle to Combatants and ½ Rectangle to Non-Combatants (Followers). The Rectangle consisted of 25 acres.

In addition a distinct reward for 'Special Distinguished Service' in the form of 200 *jagir*s (grant of land for revenue) was earmarked for selected Indian Officers. The distribution of these rewards was based on comparison of the services of each unit during the war, based on which allotment was made to each unit and the Commanding Officers were to recommend the names of such individuals to the Indian Soldiers Board for final approval.

The Jodhpur Resident in his letter No 2 CB dated 6 January 1920 enquired as to how the Jodhpur Durbar would view an offer from the Government of India to defray the cost of *Jangi Inam*s or special pensions that the Darbar may decide to give to their men at the same rate and in the same proportion as that decided upon for officers and men of the Indian army. Thereupon the proposal was put up before the Jodhpur Council of Regency and it was resolved vide CR No. 1 dated 16 January 1920 that the Resident be informed that the Jodhpur Darbar will highly appreciate and gratefully accept any rewards which the Government of India may think fit to bestow on the officers and men of the Jodhpur Imperial Service Lancers and that the Jodhpur Darbar is also willing to grant rewards on the lines indicated in the above quoted letter of the Resident.

Later the 29 Meeting of the Indian Soldiers Board held at Delhi on 18 February 1920, laid down the principle that members of Imperial Service Troops should be rewarded for good service by the respective Ruling Princes. Based on which the Political and Judicial Member Jodhpur Regency Council, vide Note No 329 dated 21 February 1921 recommended grant of Land, Jangi Inams and Jagirs in Marwar to members of the Jodhpur Imperial Service Troops on the same scale as in British India. It was further resolved that the Military Department be asked to recommend names of officers and men who have rendered specially distinguished service during the war and to suggest rewards for them on the same lines and in the same proportion as is proposed by the British Government. Thus, the problem of deciding on the most deserving now confronted the two Commanding Officers of the Jodhpur Lancers.

Thereupon the Military Secretary Jodhpur received copies of letters from the Commanding Officers, 1st and 2nd Regiments Jodhpur Lancers, who had recommended the following officers and men for the grant of rewards:
1. Major Thakur Dalpat Singh of Deoli for *Jagir* to his brother Jagat Singh in Ajmer Merwara.
2. Captain Thakur Aman Singh, Bahadur, for suitable *Jagir*.
3. Trumpet Major Sher Singh for *Jangi Inam* to his son Amar Singh of Rs 10 per month for life.

Mr A.D.C. Barr, Rao Bahadur Mangal Singh Pokhran, Sir Pratap, Colonel R.A. Lyall and Rao Sahib
Shyam Behari Misra of Jodhpur Regency Council in 1914.
Photo courtesy: Mehrangarh Museum Trust

4. Dafedar Jor Singh (1029) for *Jangi Inam* in the form of Pension of Rs 5 per month for two lives.
5. Langri Sukhia for a Pension of Rs 2 and 8 Anna per month for two lives (Follower Sukhia was extremely popular among the men as he always found ingenious ways to cook up something to satisfy the cravings of the hungry men under adverse conditions).

The recommendations were then considered by the Regency Council which met at Jodhpur under the presidentship of Sir Pratap, on 01 March 1921 and granted the *Jagirs, Jangi Inams* and pension to the above mentioned officers and the men of the Jodhpur Lancers, who distinguished themselves during the Great War, based on the inputs provided by the Commanding Officer of the Jodhpur Lancers.

In addition, the Government of India had also approved grant of War Gratuities to Officers and Men of the Imperial Service Troops actually employed in the field during the Great War. The maximum gratuity payable to officers in respect of field service was as under:

Class I- Rs 600 (Commanding Officers)
Class II- Rs 542 (Squadron Commanders)

Class III- Rs 484 (Other Officers)
Class IV- Rs 426 (Other Ranks)

The Story of Major Dalpat Singh, MC

Major Dalpat Singh, MC, was born on 14 November 1892 in village Deoli near Jodhpur. He was the elder son of the renowned polo player and ADC to Sir Pratap, Major Hari Singh, popularly known as Hurjee (Hurjee was tall, handsome, talented and a great favourite of Sir Pratap).

Major Dalpat was educated at Eastbourne College along with Sir Pratap's son, Raoraja Narpat Singh under the guardianship of the Tudor family in England. He attended Wargrave and then Blackwater boarding houses in Eastbourne College between 1907 and 1911. He won his cricket colours as an opening bat and scored four centuries for the college, ending the 1911 season with an average of 61. He also played rugby for the First XV, winning second XV colours, and was awarded first Running 'strings', winning both the mile race and the steeplechase.

Commissioned on 18 October 1913, he was first appointed to the Jodhpur Lancers on 25 October 1914. Major Dalpat initially served as the Scout Officer and Adjutant of Jodhpur Lancers in France before being appointed as Squadron Commander.

On 14 July 1918, during the action at El Henu in the Jordan Valley, accompanied only by his trumpeter, No 1189 Trumpet-Major Sher Singh, (later both of them were killed in action at Haifa) he galloped a post containing an entrenched machine gun, killing and scattering the crew and capturing the gun. He also captured the

Major Dalpat Singh in 1917. His death is recorded on the Commonwealth War Dead Memorial at Heliopolis (Port Tewfik).
Photo courtesy: Raoraja Mahendra Singh, from the Archives of the late Raoraja Narpat Singh

Major Dalpat seated first from right in 1909; Blackwaters Cricket Team, Eastbourne College London.
Photo courtesy: Bill Bowden and Michael Partridge

commander of the 11 Turkish Regiment and another officer during the action. Major Dalpat Singh was awarded the Military Cross for his conspicuous gallantry and devotion to duty on this occasion (G of I No 316 of 8 February 1919).

Later, on the morning of 23 September 1918, Major Dalpat Singh gallantly led the Jodhpur Lancers in a mounted attack on Haifa. Dalpat Singh was only 26 years old when he valiantly fell in battle at the head of his regiment at Haifa. He was cremated next afternoon in an olive grove, at the south end of the Haifa city, looking out to the sea.

It is believed that the British government gave him the title of 'Hero of Haifa'. In his memory poet Kishore Dan Barhat, composed poems titled 'Dalpat Rasso' in the Marwari language.

A letter was written by Colonel C.O. Harvey to Mrs Tudor (She was Dalpat's guardian while he was studying at Eastbourne College) on 23 September 1918, describing the death of Major Dalpat Singh at Haifa,

> You will doubtless have heard by now that Dalpat Singh died in the early morning of September 24 from wounds he received, on the 23 when gallantly leading his regiment in a mounted attack on Haifa. We were the leading Brigade and had to take the place. There were over a thousand Turks with 15 guns and several machine guns defending it, and it is a naturally strong bastion. The only thing to do, was to hold them with gun fire, and send

a regiment in at the gallop. Jodhpur were selected for the ride; all went well until they got near the town when they were blocked by an impassable river.

Colonel Holden who was leading, jumped his horse into the river, to see if it was fordable, and it wasn't, so he shouted to Dalpat to wheel the regiment to the left. At the moment, Dalpat was hit in the spine by a machine gun bullet and fell. The machine gunners, did not live long, after firing that shot, the leading 'B' squadron galloped straight at them, and killed them in a second. The whole regiment was mad with rage, and took a lot of cooling down. They carried him into Haifa, but he died early next morning on the operating table. We buried him that afternoon, in an olive grove, at the south end of the city, looking out to sea.

He was a most gallant boy, and one of the few Indians, whom one would be really glad to see as an equal, holding the Kings Commission. He had complete power over the men, who would follow and obey him anywhere and in anything and also he was completely in with and saw eye to eye with us. The combination of these two qualities is very rare and I have never seen it so developed, in any other Indian, as it was in Dalpat. His death is a loss not only to Sir Pratap who adored him and to all the Jodhpurs, but to India and the whole of the British Empire. You must be proud to have brought him up, but may I be allowed, to offer you my deepest sympathy, at losing him, just when he was beginning to show you the fruits of your training ...

Colonel C. Harvey

On 01 April 1919, Sir Pratap wrote a confidential letter to General C.C. Monro, C-in-C in India, Delhi requesting for allotment of some irrigated land in Punjab based on a request received from Jagat Singh, the brother of Major Dalpat Singh.

In his reply, dated 10 April 1919, General C.C. Monro wrote to Lieutenant General Sir Pratap Singh, Maharaja Regent, Jodhpur Rajputana, as under

My Esteemed Friend,

I regret that my reply to your letter has been delayed owing to my being away from Army Headquarters on tour.

I fully sympathise with your anxiety regarding the position of Thakur Jagat Singh of Deoli, and you may rest assured I will give his case every consideration. At the present time however the general question of eligibility for grants of land in the Punjab is under consideration, and I am unable to give you any definite reply.

It is not customary to give a grant of land to the brother of a deceased soldier and this fact brings in one more point which has to be considered in cases such as that which you mention.

To
H.H. Maharaja Regent Sahib Bahadur
Jodhpur

May it please Your Highness,

I most respectfully beg to state that our family estate in Marwar is rather precarious as it depends on rains and I cannot expect to secure any irrigated lands in Marwar. It would therefore, be very kind of Your Highness to recommend me to his excellency the commander-in-chief for the grant of some rectangles on the Punjab canals, in recognition of the services of my late lamented brother Major Thakur Dalpat Singhji M.C. who lost his life in the Palestine. I enclose herewith copies of remarks made about his gallantry and also of the letter of His Majesty the King Emperor for favour of perusal. I trust my application would be favourably considered by the military authorities.

With humble mujro,

I beg to remain,

Your Highness' most obedient servant,

Jagat Singh of Deoli.

23.2.'19

My Esteemed Friend,

I herewith forward for your Excellency's kind consideration an application from Thakur Jagat Singh of Deoli, brother of the late Major Thakur Dalpat Singhji, M.C. who was killed in the action of Haifa in Palestine. I am very much interested in this family. These two boys are the sons of the late Thakur Hari - Singhji, the famous polo player of India and my A.D.C. After his death I have been bringing them up as my own boys and have educated them in England, and I am proud that one of them fell gloriously in the Service of His Imperial Majesty the King - Emperor.

Their family estate in Marwar depends on rains and brings in a very precarious yield and hence the Thakur's anxiety to get some irrigated land. I shall feel obliged if Your Excellency would favourably consider the claims of this family and grant Thakur Jagat Singh a number of rectangles on the Punjab Canals, where His Honour the Lieutenant Governor of the Punjab writes to me, a large area of 176000 acres has been reserved for Indian soldiers and their families.

With best wishes and kindest regards,

I remain,

Your most sincere friend,

Pratap Singh

Maharaja Regent, Jodhpur.

Letter from Jagat Singh, brother of Dalpat Singh, to Sir Pratap and further to General Monro for land grant in Punjab by Sir Pratap.
Letters courtesy: Mehrangarh Museum Trust

Hurjee in 1897 and Major Dalpat Singh, MC, in 1913.
Photos courtesy: Daulat Singh S/o Dr Rattan Singh, Panai Niwas

I am afraid some little time must elapse before the various doubtful points are finally decided.

With kindest regards and best wishes, I remain,
Your most sincere friend **C.C. Monro**

The Story behind the making of Teen Murti, New Delhi

On 15 July 1919 the Adjutant General's Branch, Army HQs, Shimla, issued a letter to all concerned that the Government of India has decided to proceed with the erection of War Memorials to commemorate the actions in which various Indian Expeditionary Forces have taken part during the Great War, in accordance with the recommendations of the Battle Exploits Memorial Committee in England. As per Army Order No VI, dated 12 April 1919, the main features of the scheme were:

(a) The erection of a Central War memorial at Delhi (India Gate. See box text).

(b) The erection of one memorial in each theatre of operations—France, Mesopotamia, Egypt (including Palestine), Gallipoli, and East Africa, in which the Indian Army has been represented. These memorials were to take the shape of a monument, on the plinth or base of which would be inscribed the names of all Divisions and other formations, as well as the name of all units, British, Indian and the Imperial Service Troops and the actions in which they had fought.

The Teen Murti is a reminder of the valour of the Jodhpur Lancers at Haifa. The iconic Teen Murti memorial at New Delhi pays homage to three unknown soldiers of Jodhpur, Mysore and Hyderabad Lancers, who carried out a victorious attack on Haifa on 23 September 1918.
Photo courtesy: The author

(c) The erection of commemoration tablets in all Indian villages which had contributed a high quota of recruits to the Army.

(d) The cost of each memorial was estimated at Pounds 2,500 to 3,000. The cost of all these will be borne by India.

INDIA GATE, NEW DELHI

On 11 February 1921, one officer and two men represented the Jodhpur Lancers at the foundation stone laying ceremony of the 'All India War Memorial' (India Gate) on the Kingsway (Rajpath) at Delhi by the Prince of Wales. A decade later on 12 February 1931 it was opened to the public by Viceroy Lord Irwin. The names of the fallen soldiers of the Jodhpur Lancers who died in the Great War are inscribed all along the walls of the arch of the India gate. The inscription on India Gate (designed by Edwin Lutyens), the largest war memorial in India, reads:

> To the dead of the Indian armies who fell honoured in France and Flanders, Mesopotamia and Persia, East Africa, Gallipoli and elsewhere in the near and the far-east and in sacred memory also of those whose names are recorded and who fell in India or the North-West Frontier and during the Third Afghan War.

Since the installation of the Amar Jawan Jyoti, in 1972, India Gate has served as a national memorial to India's fallen soldiers.

Simultaneously on 04 June 1919, Major General C.R. Harbord, GOC 15 Imperial Service Cavalry Brigade, Aleppo EEF, wrote a letter to Major General H.D. Watson, the Inspector General of IST in India regarding

(a) The erection of two War Memorials (at Haritan Aleppo and Port Tewfik) to commemorate the services of the 15 Imperial Service Cavalry Brigade in the EEF and

The inauguration of the War Memorial Arch (India Gate) was commemorated by the issue of a pictorial stamp. The value of this stamp was ½ anna.
Picture courtesy: The author

(b) The publication of a history of the war services of the three regiments composing the Brigade by Major E.M. Belcher, MC.

HISTORY OF THE 15th IMPERIAL SERVICE CAVALRY BRIGADE

Major E.M. Belcher, IARO, attached Mysore Lancers wrote the *History of the 15 Imperial Service Cavalry Brigade* from the date of their concentration at Deolali in October 1914 to 31 October 1918—the date of the armistice with Turkey. In 1919 General Harbord while proceeding on leave took away the script to England to print it in a book form. It was decided to print 1,000 copies of the book at total expenditure of 159 Pounds, of which Pounds 35 was borne by the Secretary of State for India and the balance expenditure was met by Brigadier Harbord. On 26 August 1920 the India Office, London despatched 950 copies to the Political Secretary, India, through *S.S. Nerbudda*. Out of these 240 copies each were distributed to Jodhpur, Mysore and Hyderabad states and 50 copies each to Alwar, Bhavnagar and Kathiawar states, 20 copies to Kashmir and the balance copies to each officer associated with the brigade.

THE TWO WAR MEMORIALS OF THE BRIGADE

The first and smaller memorial was sited about three miles NW of Aleppo on the Alexandretta road marking the site of the last engagement in the Middle East on 26 October 1918 between the British and Turkish Forces during the Great War. For this the necessary funds were collected from within the brigade to meet the cost of erection which was carried out locally. This memorial locally known as the *Qabr Inglizieh*, or the English Tomb, is a three-sided sandstone pillar, twelve feet high. The names of four British Officers and 17 Indian soldiers of the Jodhpur and Mysore Lancers are inscribed on its surface.

The Haritan Memorial was unveiled by Brigadier General Gregory, Commanding the 5 Cavalry Division, on 05 November 1919, in the presence of Brigadier General C.R. Harbord and Jaffa Pasha and officers of the Sherifian army witnessed the unveiling and marchpast by the troops of the brigade.

However, the Arabs—during the regime of the Feisal Government— destroyed this first memorial after the evacuation of Aleppo by the British. But the French authorities rebuilt this on the same site and an appropriate unveiling ceremony was held on 29 June 1922. General Gouraud, High Commissioner for Syria and

Memorial to 15 Imperial Service Cavalry Brigade at Aleppo, Haritan (Syria) was inaugurated on 05 November 1919. It is located near the 7th km stone from Aleppo on the north side of Aleppo-Alexandretta road near the village of Haritan. The Aleppo memorial has the following inscription. 'On this site was fought on 26 October 1918 between 15th Imperial Service Cavalry Brigade 5th Cavalry Division, Egyptian Expeditionary Force and the Turkish Forces the last engagement in the Middle East of the Great War 1914 -1918', and 'Roll of those who fell in this engagement or those who died of wounds received in it'. The Teen Murti memorial in Delhi was modelled from this very photograph.
Photo courtesy: Kunwar Karni Singh Jasol

Commander-in-Chief of the Army of the Levant, publically inaugurated this in the presence of large representatives of the French and British Armies, the Consular Officers of the Allied nations and the local Government officials of Aleppo. Colonel G.C. Grant, Colonel General Staff, and Captain Hinley, ADC to Field Marshal Allenby attended the unveiling ceremony to represent the EEF. A detachment of French troops consisting of Infantry, Cavalry and Artillery formed up in a large hollow square and a detachment of Indian Cavalry in Palestine from 31st Lancers furnished the Guard of Honour.

Later, on 18 January 1935, considering the bad state of its maintenance, the Imperial War Graves Commission, London agreed to assume responsibility for the maintenance of the Imperial Service Cavalry Brigade War Memorial at

Aleppo, provided that a capital donation of Pounds 65 or roughly Rs 900 is paid by those responsible for the memorial. The Government of India proposed that the above sum should be paid in equal proportions by the three Durbars, which they all paid up. It also emerged that this memorial was built on a private land belonging to Mr Abou Madiouin Ahmed Ben Cheikh Mohamed El Hedeily El Moughrabi, and the question of its acquisition was referred to three states. The Jodhpur Durbar readily agreed but the other two Durbars declined the offer to acquire the land and thus the Government of India on 03 February 1936 decided to drop the proposal. Till 2005 the memorial existed on the ground but the author has no idea if it has survived the current fighting in Syria.

The Second and larger memorial was initially to be erected as per the site given by the Egyptian Government at Port Tewfik, immediately south of the point where the sweet water canal emerges into the Suez Canal (on the West Bank of the Suez Canal near Kantara).

War Memorial to the honour of the Indian Army at Port Tewfik, Egypt, at the southern entrance of the Suez Canal. It was unveiled in May 1926 and part of its cost of Pounds 3,500 was paid for by the Chamber of Indian Princes. The Maharajas of Bikaner and Kapurthala sent representatives to the unveiling ceremony. The architect was Sir Joh James Burnet and the sculptor of the two superb tigers, crouching ready to spring, was Charles Sargent Jagger. Incidentally the Port Tewfik memorial built to commemorate the officers and men of the Indian Army who died in Sinai and Palestine campaigns of the Great War was destroyed during the Yom Kippur War of 1973. It was then relocated to the Heliopolis War Cemetery in Cairo in October 1980. A few remnants of Jagger's two tigers can still be seen in the gardens of the British War cemetery at Heliopolis, north of Cairo.
Photo Courtesy: Commonwealth War Graves Commission

Meanwhile, Major General C.R. Harbord, in end-1919, wrote privately to Sir Pratap Singh of Jodhpur, Sir Afsur-ul-Mulk of Hyderabad and Yuvraja of Mysore, sending them the design and giving them full particulars of the memorial that was proposed to be erected, and asking them if their states would each be willing to subscribe Pounds 3,000, the estimated cost of the memorial being Pounds 9,000. He further added that the erection of the memorial had been approved by the war office, which was necessary for erection of all such memorials and the sculptor was ready to put the work in hand on receipt of orders. Sir Pratap immediately responded by ordering his Financial Secretary to remit the amount to Messrs Cox and Co, London for the credit of the '15th I.S. Cavalry Brigade Memorial Fund', while the other two states decided to await the official request. On 1 July 1920 the Mysore and on 21 September 1920 the Hyderabad states also credited 3,000 Pounds each for the memorial fund and intimated the same to Major General Harbord, who was at the Cavalry Club, 127 Piccadily, London.

However, the authorities arranging for an Indian Army Memorial in Egypt asked for, and obtained, this site from Colonel Harbord, offering in exchange a site at Ismailia that had been given to them by the Suez Canal Company. This agreement for the exchange was signed by Army Department, India and Colonel Harbord on 30 June 1921.

Again there was another twist when the 15 Cavalry Brigade Memorial that had been in course of construction in London, by Leonard Jennings, was ready for shipment to Ismailia, but the Suez Canal Company now refused to allot the site at Ismailia to the 15 Cavalry Brigade!

Therefore, on 19 May 1922, on the recommendation of Gen Harbord, the Secretary of State for India, London, wrote to MA-in-C, Indian State Forces (ISF) asking whether the memorial could now be erected on a suitable site in New Delhi. Immediately PWD and the Chief Engineer Delhi were consulted as to whether a site in the new capital or the new cantonment area could be made available for this memorial and various locations at Parliament Street, opposite Kitchener College Memorial Hall and Princes Park at the end of the Central Vista near the War Arch (India Gate) were considered. On 16 August 1922 Mr H.T. Keeling, the Chief Engineer Delhi rejected the above sites and recommended that it may be left to Sir Edward Lutyens to advise the Viceroy regarding the location of the memorial, when he arrives in India in October 1923, after his leave from London.

However, on 22 January 1923, without awaiting for finalisation of the location, Major General C.R. Harbord wrote to Major General H.D. Watson, MA-in-Chief, ISF, that Messrs Coxs' Shipping Agency will ship the memorial to Bombay by *S.S. Caledonia* due to sail from London on 26 January 1923. He also enclosed

Two replica silver trophies of the Teen Murti cenotaph were made; one is now with the 61st Cavalry Regiment and another with the British Museum in England. They represent three unknown soldiers of Jodhpur, Mysore and Hyderabad Lancers mounting guard.
Photo courtesy: 61st Cavalry Regiment

'The Teen Murti' left to right—Maharaja Krishnaraja Wadiyar of Mysore, Nizam Osman Ali Khan of Hyderabad and Sir Pratap the Maharaja Regent of Jodhpur. They contributed 3,000 Pounds each for the construction of the 'Teen Murti' statue in New Delhi.
Photo courtesy: The author

the following necessary documents for the use of the PWD Officers-in-Charge, for the erection of the 15 I.S. Cavalry Brigade Memorial at Delhi.

(a) One photograph of the sketch model.
(b) Three copies of the drawings (blue prints).
(c) One diagram showing positions of statuary.
(d) One photograph of each of the statues.
(e) A list of the inscriptions on the shaft (for checking purposes only).
(f) A list of cases showing the stones contained therein.
(g) A list of cases showing the bronze work contained therein.
(h) Instruction for fixing the lances to the bronze figures of the 15 I.S. Cavalry Brigade Memorial.

Further on 05 March 1923 the Cox's Shipping Agency, Hornby Road, Bombay despatched 24 packages containing the war memorial to 'Store and Traffic Officer, Barakamba, Raisina, Delhi'.

The matter regarding the location of memorial could not be referred to Viceroy Lord Reading as, by the time the war memorial arrived in Delhi, the Government of India offices moved to Shimla and the decision was postponed till the arrival of Lutyens in October 1923. (in Imperial India all major decisions, tours, inaugurations, etc., were mostly made during the cold weather from October to March!).

Finally the site for erecting the memorial was approved by the Viceroy at Raisina near the Imperial Secretariat (South Block) in the new capital immediately in front of the gates to then Flagstaff House, the residence of the British C-in-C in India (after Independence the house was taken over as the residence of Pandit Jawaharlal Nehru, the first Prime Minister of India and rechristened as Teen Murti Bhawan). Simultaneously the consent of all three Chiefs of Mysore, Hyderabad and Jodhpur was also obtained, regarding the erection of the memorial at Delhi.

On 30th May 1923 the Chief Engineer PWD gave an estimate of Rs 6,771 for the cost of the erection of the memorial, including railway freight charges and 11% departmental charges. On 29 June 1923, Pounds 500 (which at that time's rate of exchange was Rs 7,500) was sent by Major General Harbord to Lloyds in Shimla, for the account to be operated by the MA-in-Chief, ISF, to meet the expenses in connection with the erection of the memorial. The cost of the three bronze statues was Pounds 7,500.

Meanwhile the Viceroy had consented to perform the unveiling ceremony on Thursday 06 March 1924. It was decided to invite only the Maharaja of Jodhpur for the unveiling ceremony but the Viceroy 'desired that all three Princes should be asked to be present, the invitation to do so being so couched that if they would rather not come up they may be able to make an excuse for not doing so without appearing to give offence anywhere'. In the end all three Princes regretted their inability to attend the ceremony.

The detachments of four Officers, four NCOs and 12 Sowars from Jodhpur, Hyderabad, Mysore, and one officer, one NCO and four Sowars each from Bhavnagar, Kashmir and Ratlam were invited. The accommodation for officers and other ranks was arranged in the new Body Guard Lines (PBG lines) Raisina close to the memorial (The Viceregal Lodge/Rashtrapati Bhawan was still under construction at that time). It was told that officers wishing to stay under their own arrangements may do so, but it may be noted that hotel accommodation in Delhi is limited and usually very difficult to obtain, as well as being expensive, with the normal charges being Rs 12 a day.

On 06 March 1924 at 1600 hrs the Viceroy arrived via South Avenue to the memorial, in the presence of a large and distinguished gathering. The route from the Secretariat to the site was lined by the 19 Lancers and the 2/13 Frontier Force furnished the Guard of Honour. The Indian State Forces detachments were drawn up in two lines facing inwards along radii from the memorial to the circumference of the circle on which the memorial had been erected, with bands and trumpeters in the rear. The Viceroy received an address of welcome from Major General Harry Watson, MA-in-Chief, ISF, who gave a brief history of the 15 I.S. Cavalry Brigade and he concluded that in the final defeat and pursuit of the Turks, from the Jeruslem line to Aleppo, a distance of some 400 miles, the brigade distinguished itself as the leading brigade of the 5 Cavalry Division. The casualties of the Brigade throughout the war amounted to 65 killed, 88 wounded and 12 missing, including five British Officers, seven Indian Officers killed and six British Officers and 16 Indian Officers wounded.

Viceroy Reading made the following speech at the Unveiling Ceremony:

> No ceremony can make a closer appeal to me than that which I have been invited to perform today. The distinguished services of the officers and men of the 15 I.S. Cavalry Brigade in the Great War are justly treasured in the Indian States and by the units represented here as among their noblest and most sacred traditions; and we are assembled to give to posterity a memorial to preserve and enshrine for future generations the moving story of the gallantry and sacrifice of those members of this Brigade who laid down their lives for the Empire.

> In company with the representatives of units who fought by their side and who shared with them the privations and dangers of long and arduous campaigns in foreign lands far from their homes, I pay my tribute to their memory.

The exploits of the Brigade, the distinction they won, the leading part they played in the protection of the highway from Britain to the East and in the rout and capture of the opposing forces in Palestine are pages of first importance in the annals of the Great War. They are of vivid interest as a record of human achievement and endeavour. There are few parallels in military history to the great advance movement, in which this Brigade took part, extending from the sea to the Hedjaz Railway and ending in complete success and victory at Aleppo. This campaign takes a highly honoured place among the great achievement of the armies of the Empire; and all praise is due to those who had a share in the successful issue of these operations. To their deeds this memorial will stand as an enduring testimony. It marks also, by the sacrifices it recalls, the strength of the ties of loyalty and devotion which bind the Indian Princes and their states and subjects to the person and throne of His Majesty the King Emperor. It proclaims that spirit of mutual trust, that high purpose, that sense of common attachment and endeavour which animates the different units of the Empire to work together for the common good of the Empire as a whole and for the gretaer happiness and peace of humanity.

Before I unveil the memorial, let me express my obligations to the Governments of Jodhpur, Mysore and Hyderabad for the munificence in erecting this memorial at Delhi. It will recall in after years the labours of the Indian States, in close co-operation and harmony with the Government of India, for the service of the Empire in the hour of her need.

The Viceroy then pressed the button and the drapery fell away disclosing the memorial. It was a three-sided stone obelisk with three unknown soldiers, collectively named Teen Murti, representing the three famous regiments of Jodhpur, Mysore and Hyderabad, mounting guard. The last post was sounded by trumpeters of the 19 Lancers and troops presented arms, the Viceroy inspected the State Forces detachments, viewed the memorial and departed.

Tributes are also laid at the Teen Murti memorial by the Indian Cavalry during the 'Armoured Corps Day' as well as on 'the Cavalry weekend' every year.
Photo courtesy: Director General Mechanised Forces

Finally, the actual cost incurred for the war memorial statues was Pounds 7,500. A sum of Rs 1,543 left unspent, after meeting all the expenses, was remitted back to all three Durbars through three drafts of Rs 514 each on 08 July 1930.

Today, the memorial stands proudly at a busy roundabout in New Delhi. One day I saw an old man going round and round the three statues and then he stood in front of one, oblivious of the honking and hooting of cars and buses. He must have seen a vision of his ancestor, an ordinary Lancer charging with his weapon at the Turks in the long chase right up to Haifa and Aleppo. His eyes were wet and soon tears streamed down his cheeks into his grey beard. Only soldiers with a tradition of valour and fighting in their veins or imaginative people can understand these feelings.

THE ERECTION OF COMMEMORATION TABLETS IN ALL INDIAN VILLAGES WHICH HAD CONTRIBUTED A HIGH QUOTA OF RECRUITS TO THE ARMY

On 12 February 1919, the Indian Soldiers Board had proposed to commemorate the war by erecting war memorial tablets throughout Indian villages which had supplied considerable number of recruits. In January 1920 a total of 27 tablets were alloted to Rajputana (Alwar—six, Bharatpur—four, Bikaner—two, Dholpur—one, Jaipur—seven, Ajmer Merwara—three and Jodhpur—four).

On 18 April 1923 a uniform design and inscription was decided by the Indian Soldiers Board for War Commemoration Tablets for whole of India. The uniform inscription was to be:

(NAME OF VILLAGE)
FROM
THIS VILLAGE
----- MEN
WENT TO THE
GREAT WAR
1914–1919
OF THESE ----
GAVE UP
THEIR LIVES.

However, the inscription proposed by the Marwar Darbar regarding their alloted 04 tablets was accepted as under:

OF THE MEN WHO WENT FROM SHERGARH/DIDWANA/
JODHPUR/SAMBHAR PARGANA
TO THE GREAT WAR 1914–1919, 79/77/54/47 GAVE UP
THEIR LIVES.

The tablets were made by the Principal School of Art, Jaipur. An average of 84 letters per tablet were allowed—each letter costing four annas to the Government.

In 1928 Lord Irwin, the Viceroy of India, visited Jodhpur from 23 January to 25 January. On 24 January 1928, there was a review of the state troops held under Maharaja Umaid Singh's immediate command. On the conclusion of the review, Maharaja presented the two Commanding Officers, Lieutenant Colonel Aman Singh, OBI, IOM, and Lieutenant Colonel Anop Singh, MC, OBI, IOM, to the Viceroy. The Commanding Officers then presented their own regimental officers. The Viceroy spoke after the review '...The honourable distinction won by Jodhpur Lancers in the Great War should make you all proud and I have no doubt that should occasion ever arise, the battalion of Sardar Infantry which Your Highness has lately raised under your personal supervision would give an equally good account of itself.'

Later Lord Goschen, the Viceroy and Acting Governor-General of India visited Jodhpur from 07 August to 09 August 1929. On 08 August 1929 at a dinner in Rai ka Bagh Palace the Viceroy presented awards to Lieutenant Colonel Aman Singh, Commanding Officer Sardar Infantry with the badge of Sardar Bahadur (OBI), Thakur Bakhtawar Singh, District Superintendent of Police (later IGP) with the King's Police Medal and badge of Rao Bahadur to Thakur Chain Singh of Pokhran.

A NEW PALACE BETWEEN THE TWO WORLD WARS

Maharaja Sumer Singh and later Maharaja Umaid Singh had felt the urgency and necessity of having a monumental, modern palace worthy of the Jodhpur State since long. Maharaja Umaid Singh felt that the palace structures scattered around Jodhpur were not imposing enough to convey an adequate sense of timeless Rathore power to either his fellow Rajputs in Jaipur, Bikaner and Udaipur, or the British bureaucrats. He felt his new palace was to be a cut above most, large and sumptuous in comparison even to Lutyen's grand design for New Delhi. Cost was a minor concern!

Thus, on 18 November 1929, Maharaja Umaid Singh laid the foundation of the magnificently conceived new Umaid Bhawan Palace (UBP) on the rocky Chittar hill south east of the city. The palace was designed by H.V. Lanchester of London and the construction was commissioned mainly to give employment to the people of Marwar during a severe draught that year (on the same day the Maharaja also laid the foundation of Windham hospital, now known as Gandhi Hospital). Named after the founder Maharaja Umaid Singh, this golden-yellow sandstone monument is an excellent example of the fashionable Art Deco style of that period. The pinkish-golden massive sandstone blocks were transported by special narrow gauge railway, 20 km long, to the palace site from Sursagar and Fidusar quarries. It took 3,000 artisans over 14 years to complete this 347-room palace and since 1943 it has served as the residence of the Jodhpur royal family.

On 18 November 1929, the following speech was made by Colonel Windham, Vice-President of the State Council on the occasion of the opening ceremony of the new palace

> The Astrologers having been consulted and the signs of the heavens having been declared favourable, we are assembled here today to perform the important ceremony of a new residence for Your Highness and the future rulers of Jodhpur. Striking, indeed, is the impression of romance and dignity which this occasion conveys. It conjures up both a retrospect of the past, and prospect of the future. Your Higness' ancestors have been kings from the dawn of history; and the panorama around us today recalls the time when drifting from Kanauj in the valley of the Ganges they invaded this desert, where they cut out their kingdom, and perched their fort on that rock opposite, some five centuries ago.

> But other times bring other manners, and that picturesque and noble fortress, which has been the residence of the rulers of Jodhpur all these centuries, has now, under the exigencies of the present age, out-lived its function as such, and can merely for the future brood over its ancient fame and history. It may frown with envious eyes on to-day's proceedings, and feel grievously supplanted; but in truth nothing that we modernists can do, can really rob it of its glory. The naked rock and hard-browed bastions will stand up, steadfast and indestructible for all time, proudly guarding the city at its feet. It will always be there, as a well-known writer has said of Jodhpur, 'The city may change, almost everything may pass away, but the fastness of the Rathores will endure for ever'.

> Facing that ancient fastness will stand here in future, on this site, incidentally associating it may be said, Past and Present, and East and West a stately modern Palace, a really magnificently-conceived building, the proud work

The visually stunning Umaid Bhawan Palace stands out for its size and magnificence and it dominates the Jodhpur skyline. Designed by architect Henry Vaughan Lanchester and commissioned by Maharaja Umaid Singh, the palace is a celebration of the art deco style on the grandest scale. Mr Henry Lanchester's only son Robbie had died in 1941 during the construction of Umaid Bhawan Palace and Mr Lanchester died in 1953.
Photo Courtesy: Umaid Bhawan Palace

of its talented architect Mr Lanchester of London. The construction has been entrusted to Rao Bahadur Shiv Ratan Mohatta, a contractor of considerable repute on this side of India, so that satisfactory results and a palace in keeping with the sentiments and traditions of the State, are assured. It is computed that the work will take about five years. It will provide employment on a large scale, and offer great educational opportunities to local labour in very varied places of building and construction, thereby contributing to the industrial benefit of the place.

This day and this hour have been chosen as propitious for this inauguration ceremony by the brahmins and they have found in the stars friendly assurances for the future. Your Highness' subjects regard this as a good omen; and it is their fervent prayer that the imposing 'Rajmahal' which will arise on these grounds hallowed by sacred mantras may be, for Your Highness, and Your Highness' successors an abode of unruffled bliss; and that the Providence, which has already attended you so bountifully, preserving you miraculously from danger and endowing you with a splendid family, will continue to guard and guide you, making you happy in the happiness of your people, and gaining for you that good name which is the best immortality of princes.

18 November 1929 Maharaja Umaid Singh laying the foundation stone of the Umaid Bhawan Palace. The cessation of warfare under British rule and exposure to the comforts of Western lifestyle prompted the maharajas to move from their medieval forts to modern palaces designed by British architects, culminating in the construction of the stately Umaid Bhawan.
Photo Courtesy: Umaid Bhawan Palace

Soon after its completion Maharaja Umaid Singh hosted large garden parties for Royal Air Force (RAF) personnel in Jodhpur and later for the Jodhpur State Forces men on their return from the war.

The entire palace complex was built with sandstone and marble and is set in an area of 26 acres of land, including 15 acres of well-tended gardens. The palace, magnificent in its lavish proportions, consists of a throne chamber, an exclusive private meeting hall, a Durbar Hall to meet the public, a vaulted banquet hall, private dining halls, a ball room, a library, an indoor swimming pool and spa, a billiards room, four tennis courts, two unique marble squash courts and long passages.

After independence the Maharaja of Jodhpur had agreed to give UBP to the Rajasthan Government if either Jodhpur was chosen as the capital of the new Rajasthan province or if Rajasthan University was located there. If either one or the other of these conditions materialised then the Rajasthan Government was to get the building on payment of Rs 18 lakhs to the Maharaja. However, the state government made Jaipur the state capital, so fortunately the deal fell through and the palace remained as the private property of the Maharaja of Jodhpur!

Today this, the last of the great palaces of India, is divided into three functional parts—the residence of the royal family, a luxury Taj Palace Hotel and a museum focusing on the 20th-century history of the Jodhpur royal family. As a tribute to its famous Jodhpur Sardar Rissala, the hotel has a restaurant named 'Rissala'. Recently, UBP was awarded the World's best hotel at the Traveller's choice award, for the second time.

AVIATION HISTORY OF JODHPUR— THE JODHPUR FLYING CLUB

Maharaja Umaid Singh was instrumental in establishing one of the first air bases in India when on 27 November 1924 the first aircraft landed in Jodhpur on a landing ground near the Chittar hill. Today that small airfield is one of the Indian Air Force's premier military bases. Maharaja Umaid Singh was in fact the first Indian Prince to earn an 'A' level flying licence after graduating at RAF Cranwell and was amongst the country's first licensed pilots.

It therefore came as no surprise that in 1931 Maharaja Umaid Singh announced that the JFC would be formed. Thus in 1931 a hangar was erected, the landing ground rebuilt and two Tiger Moth aircraft with Gipsy engines were bought and Flying Officer Geoff Godwin and Mr Samuel were hired as Pilot Instructor and Ground Engineer. With 12 flying members the JFC had a gala opening with an 'At Home' on 16 November 1931 in the presence of Air Vice Marshal Sir John Steel, the Officer Commanding the Royal Air Force in India. The JFC thus became the first flying club in an Indian State.

At the opening ceremony of the JFC, Maharaja Umaid Singh said,

> … We are ready, and anxious to co-operate, as far as possible with the authorities in the furtherance of Civil Aviation in India….You may be interested to know that some of my people, in the beginning, strongly objected to my flying. They forcibly stated their unwillingness to lose their ruler at an early age! I myself was somewhat diffident in the beginning but I can assure you all from the brief experience which I have so far gained, that flying is not only a healthy recreation, but it is as free from the ordinary risks of life as railway travelling, or, motor driving, or, may I add, polo!

By 1938, the JFC was at the forefront of civil aviation in India, with three trans-continental airlines (Imperial Airways, KLM and Air France) stopping at Jodhpur.

Maharaja Umaid Singh was a generous-hearted man who showed endless hospitality to the officers and all ranks of RAF personnel stationed at Jodhpur. The

Christmas 1943 supper menu at the Umaid Bhawan Palace for all ranks of the Royal Air Force.
Maharaja Umaid Singh's and Hanwant Singh's signatures can be seen top left.
Photo courtesy: Peter Vacher

The stunning sandstone edifice, built between 1929 and 1943 at a cost of Rs 94,51,565 awes
visitors with its immensity and muted golden hues made of desert sandstone. This was the
last of India's great palaces and one of the largest private residences in the world, now called
Umaid Bhawan Palace. It was formally opened on 25 May 1944. Seen here is Maharaja Umaid
Singh with the entire staff of RAF station Jodhpur on 09 September 1944.
Photo courtesy: Mehrangarh Museum Trust

The JFC in 1931. **Standing left to right:** Raoraja Hanut Singh, Lieutenant Mohan Singh, Hari Singh Kuchaman, Karan Singh Shyampura, unknown. **Seated:** Raoraja Narpat Singh, Geoff Godwin, Maharaja Umaid Singh, Mr Samuel, unknown. **On the ground:** Raoraja Abhey Singh and Sunder Singh.
Photo courtesy: Umaid Bhawan Palace

Christmas parties of 1943, 1944 and 1945 became legendary as Maharaja Umaid Singh had invited nearly 1,000 men of RAF base Jodhpur to his new palace. He famously enjoyed inviting his close friends for 'Sherry and Cocktails' in the sky!

In World War II, Jodhpur became a hub of air operations and the Jodhpur Air Training Centre maintained until 01 December 1943 was handed over to the No 2 EFTS, which had been functioning since 14 April 1941 for providing elementary flying training for pilots of the IAF. The Maharaja placed his personal aircraft—one Lockheed 12A, one Leopard Moth, two Tiger Moths and one Gull Glider—for the purpose of training.

On 02 March 1944 Maharaj Kumar Hanwant Singh, the heir apparent, announced a reward of Rs 1,000 to anyone on receiving a commission as a pilot officer, with a view to encourage recruitment to the Indian Air Force. In 1944 Maharaja Umaid Singh presented a Gold Sword to be awarded to the Pilot Officer who stood first at the Flying School in Ambala.

Jodhpur gained in importance as an airbase as the focus of the war shifted to Burma and the Far East. Maharaja Umaid Singh commanded the Allied Air Base in Jodhpur through World War II and was bestowed with the Honorary rank of Air Vice Marshal of the Royal IAF in 1945. 'I have no use for an honorary rank', he complained bitterly to the Viceroy as the Battle of Britain raged in Europe. Much

The fine Jodhpur Flying Club (JFC) logo still exists today on the erstwhile JFC hangars in the IAF station at Jodhpur.
Photo courtesy: AF Station Jodhpur

JFC was established on 16 November 1931 by Maharaja Umaid Singh. The JFC hangars guarded aloft by four stone *cheel*s or kites stand in the background.
Photo courtesy: Mehrangarh Museum Trust

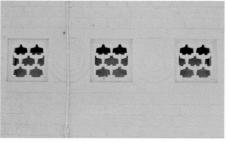

The splendid erstwhile JFC hangars still stand as a monument to aviation at Jodhpur. They have carved airplanes intact on its parapets that celebrate Maharaja Umaid Singh's passion for flying, the 'latest', as he used to say, 'of our recreations'.
Photo courtesy: Air Force Station Jodhpur

Maharaja Umaid Singh and others watching a flypast of Tiger Moths at No 2 Elementary Flying Training School (EFTS) from the control tower at Jodhpur.
Photo courtesy: Mehrangarh Museum Trust

to everyone's consternation, he had insisted on earning his fighting wings at the RAF station in Risalpur (now in Pakistan) in September 1940, but he could not be allowed to pilot Spitfires and Hurricanes in dogfights. From the end of war in 1945 until independence for India in 1947, the role of the RAF was an uncertain one. The Maharaja, meanwhile, lost no opportunity to fly friends around in his new Lockheed. He was a shareholder and major promoter of Tata airways, now renamed Air India.

In June 1947 after the death of Maharaja Umaid Singh, his son Maharaja Hanwant Singh decided to merge the JFC into a new body, State Aviation Jodhpur. Maharaja Hanwant Singh was himself a keen aviator, having gained his pilot's licence in 1943. He too acquired new aircraft, including five of the most popular machines, the Beech Bonanzas, by 1950. But tragically he was killed in Bonanza VT-CSE on 26 January 1952. His death marked the end of amateur flying at Jodhpur and the royal family decided to sell all their aeroplanes and close down the State Aviation Department. The price of aircraft remaining at State Aviation Jodhpur were depreciating every day and these were sold to pay off the liabilities.

Jodhpur Airfield became a key staging post for the great airlines like KLM, the Royal Dutch Airlines. Seen here with KLM's Fokker XVIII PH-AIP in 1933, second from right Maharaj Ajit Singh, Maharaja Hari Singh of Kashmir and Maharaja Umaid Singh of Jodhpur. Jodhpur became India's first international airport in the 1930s with English, French and Dutch aeronautical companies regularly stopping here.
Photo courtesy: Raoraja Vijay Singh

  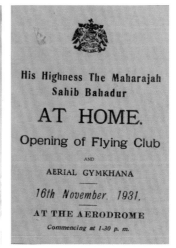

Left: A Indian National Airways poster with the Jodhpur Fort. Jodhpur's contact with the world also expanded dramatically in this period as its rulers began to travel widely by sea and air.
Centre: The JFC gave the state visitors and local dignitaries joy rides. This brought some revenue to the club's fortune. **Right:** Flyer announcing 'At Home', 16 November 1931.
Photos courtesy: Umaid Bhawan Palace

Maharaja Umaid Singh with Hawker Hart (India) K 2106 of No 39 Squadron at the RAF Risalpur station. He flew over three hours in this aircraft in September 1939.
Photo courtesy: Mehrangarh Museum Trust

Air Commodore Maharaja Umaid Singh presented a gold sword of honour to the IAF training school at RAF station Ambala in 1944. This was presented every six weeks at a passing out parade to the best all-round cadet officer on his obtaining wings; every such pupil who won this sword of honour received a silver replica of the sword in miniature. Air Commodore Hamidullah Khan, Nawab of Bhopal looks on.
Photo courtesy: The author

Seen here is Tiger Moth with registration number VT-CQX. This was built in March 1941 and it belonged to No 2 EFTS. Interestingly, although nearly half of the 99 tiger moths with EFTS crashed there is no evidence that anyone was killed.

Photo courtesy: Raoraja Lieutenant Colonel Sujjan Singh

Maharaja Hanwant Singh inspecting the cadets at passing out parade of Jodhpur Flying Training School in 1947. Jodhpur continued to remain home to the Air Force Flying College until the 1965 war.

Photo courtesy: UBP

The Jodhpur Railway

On 16 February 1881 the Jodhpur Railway commenced and in 1882 the first railway line in Marwar from Kharchi (now Marwar Junction) to Pali was constructed on the Rajputana-Malwa Railway, and further extended to Jodhpur in 1885. There was considerable delay in completing the last 20 miles to Jodhpur on account of the prejudices which then existed against railways. On 16 November 1885, just after the completion of the railway from Marwar Junction to Jodhpur, on the Rajputana-Malwa line, the Viceroy, Lord Dufferin, visited the state for the first time and had stayed at camp at Paota.

The Jodhpur Railway Jubilee was commemorated on 01 March 1932 on its completion of 50 years.

Further branches were constructed from Jodhpur to Punjab and from Luni to Hyderabad (Sind) in joint management with Bikaner from 1889 and it was known as Jodhpur-Bikaner Railway (till 1925). The Jodhpur Lancers often used the Rajputana-Malwa Railways for haulage of troops and horses, whenever moving out of Jodhpur from 1891 onwards.

During World War II the Jodhpur railways released 11 locomotives, four boilers, one railcar and 439 wagons for use overseas and seven heavy goods locomotives were lent to the Bengal Assam Railway. The Jodhpur railway also constructed war works costing over Rs 5,00,000 and laid 10 miles of track. In addition it helped in the making of 25 pounder shells, bayonets, pickaxe heads and wheelbarrows and in the assembly of 12,000 USA metre-gauge wagons at Hyderabad for war and railway departments.

With the coming of the railways to Jodhpur in November 1885, the Viceroy, Lord Dufferin, visited the state for the first time and likewise more than 50 years later on 17–18 March 1936 the Viceroy Lord Willingdon became the first Viceroy to visit Jodhpur by air. He inaugurated the museum and new public park then called Willingdon Gardens (now known as Umaid Gardens).

On 01 March 1932 the Jodhpur Railway Jubilee was celebrated. Jodhpur Railway employees received the commemoration plaques, made by the famous Regent street firm, 'The Goldsmiths and Silversmiths Company Ltd'.
Photo courtesy: Rishi Srivastava

As with the 1911 Coronation, the 12 May 1937 Coronation parade of King George VI also included Jodhpur Officers in London.

In January 1930 a very important visit of Field Marshal Allenby to Jodhpur took place. It rekindled the memories of the Great War where the Jodhpur Lancers had so gloriously distinguished themselves under his overall command in Palestine during 1918.

Visit of Field Marshal Allenby to Jodhpur in January 1930

Field Marshal Allenby, accompanied by his wife, visited Jodhpur from 26 to 29 January 1930. On the morning of 27 January 1930, the Field Marshal in company with the Maharaja inspected the state troops in their lines, where all serving and pensioned officers were personally presented to Allenby. On this occasion all the distinguished retired officers were also invited and were given the travelling allowance to Jodhpur from their respective places of residence.

On the night of 28 January 1930, Maharaja Umaid Singh gave a banquet at the Rai ka Bagh Palace, Jodhpur. His Highness proposed a toast to Lord and Lady Allenby in the following terms,

> I rise to propose the toast of my distinguished guests, Field Marshal Viscount Allenby and Lady Allenby. Field Marshal Allenby is, I feel, very closely associated with Jodhpur. The Jodhpur Lancers had the good fortune to serve under him in Palestine, and his name is a household word amongst them. He took the closest interest in them, inspiring them with the best military spirit and animating them to deeds of gallantry and sacrifice. His appreciative reports on them, from time to time, will ever be prized among the most treasured possessions of my state.

Field Marshal Allenby, in replying, paid a glowing tribute to the Jodhpur Lancers who served under him in the Great War, in the following terms,

> I am deeply moved and highly honoured by the kind words used by your Highness, about Lady Allenby and myself. You have said, sir, that I am closely associated with Jodhpur. It is true, and I take great pride in that association. I have seen and admired the Jodhpur troops, their skill, and endurance, their proud bearing in battle, their daring courage, and their loyalty—rare qualities, possessed by them in the highest degree, qualities which carried them to swift and glorious victory. When I was first associated

Left: Circa 1900, Maharaj Zalim Singh rides around the city with his private band of Rissala Guards. The arrival of the railway in Jodhpur (left corner of painting) caught the popular imagination of artists of the time.

Photo courtesy: Maharaj Hari Singh Zalim Niwas

Right: The managers of Jodhpur Railways: Mr W. Home 1882–1906, Mr R. Todd 1906–1910, Mr C.B. Latouche 1910–1921, Mr G.B. Warren 1921–1926, Mr J.W. Gordon 1926–1944; Mr H.G. Rawlins 1944–1946 and Mr C. Gregory Jones, MC 1946–1947, were the last two managers.

Photo courtesy: The author

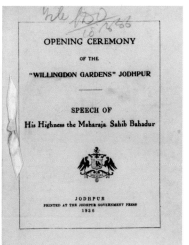

Left: Viceroy Willington along with Maharaja Umaid Singh inspecting the Jodhpur Lancers after they had converted to khaki uniform

Photo courtesy: Mehrangarh Museum Trust

Right: The opening of Willingdon Gardens Jodhpur on 17 March 1936.

Photo courtesy: The author

Officers of Indian State Forces taking part in the procession at Hampton Court during the coronation of King George VI on 12 May 1937. Lieutenant Colonel Raoraja Sujjan Singh (CO of JSI) is second and Colonel Bachan Singh of Nabha State Forces is fourth and Colonel Gurdial Singh Harika of Patiala State Forces is sixth from right in the front row.
Photo courtesy: Nagina Reddy

with the Jodhpur Lancers, long years of trench war in the west, had led some sour critics to declare that the cold steel was obsolete, that mobile cavalry was dead. Your Highness, the Jodhpur Lancers given the opportunity, soon silenced those croakers; and they showed that a bold rider, master of his weapon, clear vision, quick in mind, is as effective still as were the paladins of old.

The Jordan Valley, Haifa, Aleppo, will be names honoured in the annals of the Cavalry Arm. The torrid heat and tangled jungles of the Jordan Valley were disregarded; the massed machine guns of Haifa now decorate the Fort of Jodhpur. Haifa, the only town overtaken by a charge of Cavalry, where died gloriously that brilliant cavalry leader—Dalpat Singh, will ever in our minds recall that exploit unprecedented in war of the Jodhpur Lancers. And the final charge, outside Aleppo, where four squadrons of Indian Cavalry of which two were Your Highness' Lancers, rode through 3,000 Turks and

Travelling allowance bills of retired officers invited to Jodhpur to meet Field Marshal Allenby in January 1930.
Photo courtesy: The author

three batteries of guns, was a fitting climax in a brilliant campaign in which Your Highness' troops took a leading part.

The Baha'i Faith and The Jodhpur Lancers

While the strategic importance of Haifa is well understood, what is a lesser-known fact is that the Jodhpur Lancers, while capturing the city of Haifa in 1918, also secured the safety and freedom of Abdul-Baha, who was the spiritual head of the Bahai faith at that time and who the Turkish Commander-in-Chief, Jamal Pasha of the Ottoman Empire, had threatened to crucify on the slopes of Mount Carmel. Thus, the Battle of Haifa has a lasting historical connection with the Bahai faith.

In the summer of 1918, Major W. Tudor Pole, a British Intelligence Officer who was then serving in the Middle East, had sent the following telegraph message to an eminent British Bahai, Lady Blomfield, who was in London. 'Abdul-Baha in serious danger. Take immediate action'. At once, through her influence, the message was conveyed to British Foreign Minister Lord Balfour. That very evening a cable was sent to General Allenby with these instructions, 'Extend every protection and consideration to Abdul Baha...when the British march on Haifa'.

Thus on 23 September 1918, one of the objectives of Jodhpur Lancers after its entry into the town of Haifa through the German Street was to secure the safe

The guns captured at Haifa now decorate the Quarter Guard of the 61 Cavalry Regiment.
The regiment is now housed in the erstwhile lines of the Jaipur Lancers.
Photo courtesy: 61 Cavalry Regiment

release of Abdul-Baha. The leading 'B' Squadron of the Jodhpur Lancers, after clearing the defile, made its way along the lower slopes of Mount Carmel, and charged into the German Colony West of Haifa as its final objective. Jamal Pasha was forced to retreat in haste—thereby being rendered unable to carry out his cruel and unjustified threat. General Allenby then cabled London: 'Palestine was seized today. Inform the world that Abdul-Baha is alive.'

Therefore, as a direct result of the events of this battle, the threat to Abdul-Baha's life was lifted and he continued to serve and look after the population of Palestine till he passed away a few years later. This link between the Haifa charge and the Bahais, adds a fascinating dimension to this story.

Maharaja Gaj Singh of Jodhpur, in response to an invitation by the Bahai community to attend a function at the Bahai Lotus temple in New Delhi, to mark this unique connection between the Bahais and the events of the Battle of Haifa, wrote,

> The Jodhpur Lancers distinguished themselves with their equestrian and fighting skills and sheer courage...and the day is a very important one in our annals. The link between the Haifa Charge of 1918 and the life of Abdu'l-Baha is indeed interesting and adds a new dimension to the whole story of Haifa for us here at Jodhpur.

The administrative and spiritual centre of the Bahai Faith in 1918 and even today is located on the slopes of Mount Carmel in the city of Haifa. And while the Bahai

A visual panaromic view of the most beautiful city of Haifa, as it clings to the Mount Carmel range and spreads leisurely down towards the coast of the blue Mediterranean Sea, with the gold-leaf plated dome of Bahai shrines overlooking the German street and the Bay of Haifa. The Bahai faith, one of the youngest of the world's religions, had its birth in Persia. 'Baha' means radiance; and the faithful seek the radiance of the Lord in human relations, in friendship, amity and nature.

Photo courtesy: Alex Ringer

Faith today is a global religion, perhaps fittingly, the largest Bahai community anywhere in the world today calls India its home!

The First ever Haifa Day Commemoration in Israel in September 2010

In order to further reconnect with the historic city of Haifa, an Indian Army delegation visited Haifa, Israel, in September 2010 at the invitation of the Indian Embassy and the Mayor of Haifa. There is a very interesting incident behind re-establishment of the historic connection between Jodhpur and Haifa. An Israeli doctor, Professor Yitshak Kronzon, born in Haifa but living in New York, was flying to Mumbai after attending a medical conference in Delhi on 06 December 1992. But because of riots in Mumbai his aircraft was diverted to Jodhpur and, while there, he stayed at the majestic Umaid Bhawan Palace hotel. During his forced stay there, while dining in the Rissala restaurant, he saw a small statue of a soldier at the base of which was written Major Dalpat Singh, MC, 'Hero of Haifa'. He tried to find out the details of this 'Hero of Haifa', about whom he never heard of before, but could get no definite answer during his short halt at Jodhpur.

On his return home he wrote a small story on this incident in a local newspaper in April 1993. Later the story was picked up by members of the Haifa History Society, who, in 2010, finally approached the Indian Embassy in Tel Aviv to find out more about the history behind the statue.

The Indian Embassy in turn further enquired about it from Army Headquarters in New Delhi and finally the author was approached for more details. I, at once, not only provided the entire story (since I was already researching it) but also mentioned that this story can further strengthen Indo-Israel relations. Realising the importance of this unique First World War battle, it was at once decided to commemorate the Haifa Day in Israel for the very first time in September 2010. Thus the Haifa History Society and the Indian Embassy in Tel Aviv invited an Indian Army representation for the unique ceremony. A two-member delegation of the Indian Army was led by the author, where a moving ceremony commemorating the sacrifices of fallen Indian soldiers in the liberation of Haifa during the First World War was observed at the Haifa Cemetery on 22 September 2010.

The then Ambassador of India to Israel, Mr Navtej Sarna and representatives from Haifa City Council, Israeli Ministry of Defence, Haifa History Society, Representative of the Commonwealth War Graves Commission, Secretary General Bahai World Centre, Defence Attaches from several countries and a host of other dignitaries were present during the ceremony to honour those Indian brave-hearts.

The event was marked by a wreath laying ceremony by Ambassador Navtej Sarna and other dignitaries to remember and acknowledge the sacrifices made by those who lost their lives in the war. While speaking at the ceremony, Ambassador Sarna underlined the important role played by the Indian soldiers during the First World War and the valour shown by them in this theatre of war. He thanked the Haifa History Society for its untiring efforts to document India's role in this

Abdul-Baha, who is one of the central figures of the Baha'i Faith with Indian soldiers and
others, on the steps of his home in Haifa.
Photo courtesy: Ms Nazneen Rowhani, copyright held by the Bahai World Centre

important phase of history, which, unfortunately, is not known to many. He said
a large number of Indian soldiers sacrificed their lives in this region during the
First World War and nearly 900 are cremated / buried in cemeteries across Israel.

The Mayor of Haifa then said that, 'the residents of Haifa have learnt to appreciate
the contribution of the Indian soldiers and as a mark of recognition, the stories of
their brave deeds will be taught at schools here to preserve the city's history and
heritage'. The event since 2010 is now annually commemorated in Haifa and the

The first ever Haifa Day commemoration
ceremony in Haifa was held at the Indian
War Cemetery on 22 September 2010.
Photo courtesy: Alex Ringer

The first Haifa Day commemoration in September 2010 in Israel.
The invitation card carried the photographs of Major Dalpat Singh and Captain Aman Singh.
Photo courtesy: Alex Ringer

Haifa Municipality and Indian Embassy organised a centenary commemoration on 6 September 2018, which was attended by the author and Maharaja Gaj Singh of Jodhpur.

More importantly, 2018 not only marks the centenary year of the battle of Haifa but also coincides with the 25 years of establishment of full diplomatic relations between India and Israel. Both countries unburdened themselves of the yoke of British colonialism within a short span of nine months—while India gained independence on 15 August 1947, Israel did so on 14 May 1948. In a sense, India and Israel's rapprochement and development as functional democracies amidst varied security challenges emanating from their immediate neighbourhood can be considered as 'miracle stories' in the post-World War II scenario.

Visit by Prime Ministers to Haifa Memorials

On 06 July 2017 Indian Prime Minister Narendra Modi travelled all the way to Haifa and along with Prime Minister of Israel, Benjamin Nethanyahu, laid floral wreaths at the Indian Cemetery and paid homage to the gallant Indian soldiers. He wrote in the visitors' book at the Indian Cemetery in Haifa,

> I am deeply honoured to stand here today to salute the valiant soldiers, who laid down their lives for the liberation of Haifa during the First World War. Next year, the Centenary of the Battle of Haifa would present another opportunity to mark the enduring bond between India and Israel.

Mr Benjamin Nethanyahu wrote, 'In memory of the brave soldiers of India who helped liberate our land. In deepest respect'.

Later during his reciprocal visit on 14 January 2018, the Prime Minister of Israel Mr Netanyahu visited the Teen Murti memorial in New Delhi along with Prime

The story of 'Haifa Hero' published in Hebrew in Israel in April 1993 and on the right is the statue of Major Dalpat Singh, MC, in Umaid Bhawan Palace, Jodhpur.
Photo courtesy: Igal Graiver and UBP

Flanked by two Indian Officers on either side left to right the Author; Mr Igal Graiver, Haifa History Society; Ambassador Navtej Sarna; Lieutenant Colonel B.Y. Sharma and Group Captain Ajay Rathore, VM; at Haifa Indian Cemetery on 22 September 2010.
Photo courtesy: Alex Ringer

Minister Modi and paid floral tributes to the gallant soldiers who had liberated Haifa. During this solemn ceremony, as a symbolic gesture of friendship with Israel, the iconic Teen Murti roundabout was renamed as 'Teen Murti-Haifa Chowk'.

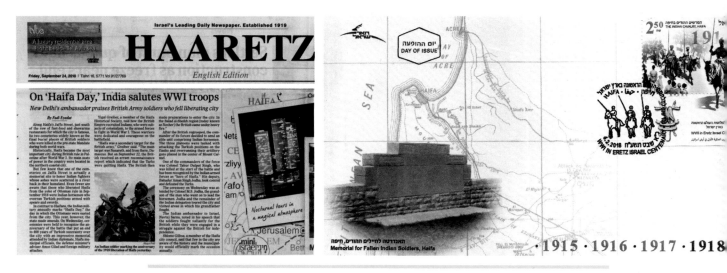

Left: The front page news carried in the Israeli newspaper *Haaretz* on the first commemoration of Haifa Day in September 2010. **Right:** Special stamp with a first day cover issued by Israel to mark the Centenary of the Liberation of Haifa, depicting a badge of the Jodhpur Lancers.
Photos courtesy: (left) Haaretz; (right) Design by Ronen Goldberg, Research by Society for the Heritage of Great War in Israel and the Israel Post

Left: A special cancellation seal with the crest of the Jodhpur Lancers. **Right:** To mark the centenary of the Battle of Haifa, Maharaja Gaj Singh issued a special first day cover.
Photos courtesy: Umaid Bhawan Palace and Rajasthan Circle, Department of Posts, India

Left: Together in homage to the fallen brave Indian soldiers, Prime Minister Narendra Modi and Benjamin Nethanyahu signing the visitors book at the Indian cemetery in Haifa. Mr Yona Yaha the Mayor of Haifa looks on. Incidentally the same visitors' book was carried by the author from Delhi in September 2010 for the first Haifa Day Commemoration! **Right:** 14 January 2018, Indian Prime Minister Narendra Modi with Israeli Prime Minister Benjamin Netanyahu during the formal renaming of the iconic Teen Murti roundabout as 'Teen Murti-Haifa Chowk' in New Delhi.
Photos courtesy: The author

Battle of Haifa Commemoration in UK in July 2018

To commemorate the centenary of the Battle of Haifa and the release of Abdul Baha from unjust captivity, the Bahai communities of India and the United Kingdom held a grand function in the House of Lords, London on 19 July 2018. This significant gathering was attended by over 150 distinguished guests including Lord Navneet Dholakia, Lord Karan Bilimoria, Mr Y.K. Sinha, the Indian High Commissioner and Maharaja of Mysore, the Maharaja Gaj Singh of Jodhpur had to return from London (due to the demise of his mother), Naznenc Rowhani, Secretary General of the Spiritual Assembly of the Bahais of India, members of the Bahai community from India and UK. The descendants of the Haifa heroes of 1918 including the author and the family members of erstwhile SSOs of Jodhpur Lancers like Lieutenant Colonel Hyla Holden, Major A.D. Strong, Lieutenant A.B. Knight, Major Tudor Pole and other distinguished guests attended the reception.

Messages from HE the President of India, HRH the Prince of Wales, HE Teresa May, the Prime Minister of UK and Maharaja Gaj Singh of Jodhpur and Maharaja YKC Wadiyar of Mysore were read out to the historic gathering. President Ram

Nath Kovind's message said, 'We remember with pride those Indian troops from Jodhpur, Mysore and Hyderabad who, one hundred years ago in Haifa, displayed valour, courage and heroism in the face of seemingly impossible odds.' Prime Minister Theresa May in her message hoped, 'that the Battle of Haifa, the last decisive cavalry action in the history of war, being commemorated in a function at the House of Lords would raise awareness on the vital contribution of the Indian army not only in this campaign but throughout the entire war.' And the message from HRH Prince Charles remarked that, 'the event offered a chance to honour, in particular, the courage and sacrifice of Indian service personnel at the Battle of Haifa and throughout the conflict—which made such an indelible mark on the shared history of Britain and India.'

Maharaja Gaj Singh of Jodhpur said in his message, 'it is a source of great satisfaction and pride for me that in India and abroad awareness has now been created about the gallant action of the Jodhpur and Mysore Lancers in this epic battle which many consider to be not only the last successful cavalry charge in the history of warfare but also the finest of all during the First World War. Rarely in the history of warfare have so few warriors achieved such a victory against overwhelming odds and that too when armed only with swords and lances against an enemy armed with modern weapons including machine guns and artillery.' And Maharaja YKC Wadiyar of Mysore said, 'On the occasion of the Centenary of the Battle of Haifa, it is my immense privilege to be part of the commemoration of the two brave Indian Cavalry Regiments that helped liberate the city of Haifa.'

The Sporting Jodhpur

A Rathore and an Englishman playing polo on the sandy plain at Jodhpore.
Photo courtesy: The author

In 1893 Colonel G.H. Trevor, the Agent to the Governor General in Rajputana wrote a song which he called 'The Song of Jodhpore':

> *THERE'S a place in Rajputana with a fort of old renown*
> *And a liberal-hearted fine old King,*
> *And the traveller who visits that most hospitable town*
> *Hears a lot about Sir Pratap Singh.*
> *He is Minister and Commandant of Cavalry in one,*
> *And his fellows, by Jove, can ride;*
> *You should go there for a 'Pig-stick' if you want to see some fun;*
> *There are pigs, sir, on every side.*

Hunting the gallant boar,
Englishman and Rathore,
Brothers in sport, ride o'er
The sandy plain at Jodhpore.

They won the Polo Tournament this year, the plucky team
Sir Pratap took to Poona t'other day;
And the liberal-hearted King, Maharaja Jaswant Singh,
Says his men can fight as well as play;
We shall find them by our side if we ever have to ride
On the frontier far away against the foe,
And we feel the brave Rathore, like his ancestor of yore,
Is an ally to be trusted, don't you know?

Over 100 years ago, Jodhpur was described as, 'the most sporting nation on this side of the Suez. In his book, *The House of Marwar*, Dhananajaya Singh mentions that in Jodhpore, Pig-Sticking (boar hunting) was the 'national sport' and Polo was the 'primary passion', but Horse Racing remained a favourite pastime'. There were six or seven racecourses around Jodhpur city, and these were in daily use to keep both horses and riders in condition. Polo was much played at the capital, where there were several polo grounds, made at considerable cost, regardless of the floating sands.

Marwar of yore was the land expressly designed for horses; and the people lived for nothing but the training and use of horses in war and sport. And nowhere in the world was the science of horse-training better understood or more perseveringly applied. Almost everyone, who could afford to keep a horse, took horse exercise and the Rathore was an accomplished horseman, whether born in the palace or in the village. Every morning at an early hour Sir Pratap and his ADC Hurjee would stand on a raised platform built near his house, and every horse in the stable was paraded for his inspection. He would examine them all critically; prescribe their exercise, food and work for the day, and then watch them go through their various trainings. Some were sent for slow gallops round the racecourse; others were practiced with stick and ball on the polo ground close by; and others were put through a course of correction for their various misdemeanours or bad habits. Sir Pratap had devised very peculiar and unsurpassed methods of breaking a horse. One of the methods he used to make a polo pony ball-shy was—a ball as big as a football was attached to a string and trailed about the ground by one man, while another rode the ball-shy pony at some distance behind it, for a considerable time. Gradually the distance between the pony and the ball would be decreased, until at last he came right up to it; and then the rider would tap the ball very gently with his stick. It was said to be a perfect cure.

Jodhpur, 1893: From left Colonel G.H. Trevor, Lady Trevor, Hurjee, Sir Pratap, unknown lady, Maharaj Kumar Sardar Singh and Major and Mrs Beatson.
Photo courtesy: Hemant Sharma Udaipur

In Marwar everyone was so attached to the equine species that he would often stint himself to feed his horse, which was housed under the same roof, and which, like the Arab's steed, was considered a member of the family from his birth. The Marwari horse was extensively bred in Marwar and the breed was celebrated for hardiness, beauty and ease of pace. Arab horses were used as chargers, troopers, polo ponies and pig-stickers and the imported Waler was principally used for driving, while the English horse was mainly used for racing and polo ponies. A pony was known to have fetched as much as Rs 3,000 in 1898. Sir Pratap's reputation as a player and trainer was so great that any pony known to have been ridden by him was certain to fetch a high price.

An English traveller wrote about Jodhpur of 1900,

> In Jodhpur when you raised your eyes to the sandy horizon, it was thick with horses on every side—young horses and old, Walers and Arabs and country-breds, racers and pig-stickers and polo-ponies, Hackneys and even a pair of Shetlands, Greys, Chestnuts, and Blacks, the whole country was a whirl of horses wherever the eye could see and as far as the eye could reach. Briefly, Jodhpur spells horse. Maharaja Sardar Singh loves to live at Rai ka Bagh Palace, among his four hundred or more horses. All Jodhpur is

horse-mad by the way, and it behoves anyone who wishes to be anyone to keep his own racecourse. No horses were shot in the Jodhpur stables, and when one dies, his funeral is an event. He is wrapped in a white sheet, which is strewn with flowers, and, amid the weeping of the 'saises', is borne away to the burial ground. Pillars were erected in the memory of the favourite horses and prayers were offered at these places!

In fact, racing preceded polo as far as Jodhpur was concerned since racing, rather than polo, remained the favoured sport of Sir Pratap's elder brother, Maharaja Jaswant Singh (1873–95), and he was one of the first Maharajas to maintain a fabulous racing stable in Calcutta, then the centre of the Indian turf scene. The area where they were quartered in the former Indian capital is still known as Jodha or Jodhpur Park. He was very fond of horses, a great patron of turf, and any broken-down jockey or needy racing man, who came to Jodhpur in his time, could rely on his sympathy and assistance.

But it was Maharaja Jaswant Singh's son, Maharaja Sardar Singh (1895–1911), who took Jodhpur racing to the very top. And in his time the *Panchranga*, the five colours of the Jodhpur flag, became a familiar sight in winners' enclosures from

1899, Jodhpur Gymkhana Races at Ratanada Palace. Often the Jodhpur Lancers men took part in the weekly races. The race meetings helped develop the soldiers' horsemanship and allowed them to compete, as well as providing entertainment for the military and public.
Photo courtesy: Mehrangarh Museum Trust

Sir Pratap Singh winning the Calcutta Derby. After the race Sir Pratap typically remarked,
'I riding ninety-seven, English jockey-boy riding sixty stone; I beating him'. Sir Pratap and Hurjee
both entered for the Jubilee races held at Ranelagh in 1887, but Sir Pratap was debarred on
account of being overweight. But the legendary Hurjee, was the hero of the day, winning six races.
Photo Courtesy: Umaid Bhawan Palace

*Maharaja Sardar Singh in his matching Westminster blazer from his school days wearing a safa
(turban). He was extremely fond of horses and dogs. In Jodhpur, colonialism brought a wave of
Anglicisation that left a lasting impact on its art and architecture, and on the lifestyle, cuisine and
sartorial choices of the Rathores.*
Photo courtesy: Mehrangarh MuseumTrust

Maharaja Sardar Singh wearing Jodhpur *panchranga* colours on the racecourse in Poona in 1902.
Photo courtesy: Umaid Bhawan Palace

Bombay to Bangalore, Poona to Ootacamund... Much racing silver was added to polo sterling...The Maharaja, who was also a competent polo player, himself raced often. Indeed, he won the Calcutta Derby; perhaps the only reigning monarch to taste victory in a major league race; and, it is said, he was dissuaded with great difficulty from taking part in the Grand National in England.

Maharaja Sardar Singh started a racing stable in Calcutta, a stable at Newmarket, stud-farm in Australia, and, of course, everything conceivable at Jodhpur. It was also Maharaja Sardar Singh who built the elegant red sandstone Racing Pavilion in the centre of his Race Course on the Ratanada Palace grounds in Jodhpur. Today, a hundred years later, now the property of the Indian Army, it ironically provides the perfect background to the new Polo ground in Jodhpur...

There was a time, coinciding with the high noon of the Empire—from the coronation of Queen Victoria to the declaration of the Second World War—when pig-sticking, along with polo and horse-racing, became the sport of princes, if only for the starkly practical reason that, to be able to participate in it you either had to own a horse or belong to a cavalry regiment and also, if you could, with impunity, ride across the country without hindrance, which only a 'sahib' could do anywhere on the subcontinent and a maharaja in his domain.

The elegant red sandstone racecourse pavilion at Jodhpur was built by Maharaja Sardar Singh in the centre of his race course.
Photo courtesy: Mehrangarh Museum Trust

However, the principal sport at Jodhpur was pig-sticking and it was famous over the length and breadth of India. Pig-sticking, the hunting of wild pig by mounted spearmen, was a popular, exciting and sometimes dangerous pastime of cavalrymen. In Jodhpur the 'sport' was encouraged by authorities as good cavalry training because, 'a startled or angry wild boar was a desperate fighter and therefore the pig-sticker must possess a good eye, a steady hand, a firm seat, a cool head and a courageous heart'.

In Jodhpur a typical pig-sticking party will drive off in a barouche to the ground very early in the morning. There were men posted all over the country on the watch for sounders of pig, and a squadron of camels scattered about acted as towers of observation under a Daffadar In-charge Pig-sticking! The camel scout will warn the party with a shout as soon as a sounder is sighted. The pig-sticker then goes over the rough and hillocky ground, with lots of bushes and trees, after a fast travelling sounder. Then a big boar is separated from the main lot by the rider. There is no sensation in the world like that of riding over bad ground after a pig. In pig-sticking concentration of mind on any one object except the pig is

The last pig stuck in 1951. This huge brute with bristly chine and curling tushes was done in by Thakur Aidan Singh of Pal during a typical morning round of pig-sticking. Wild pigs were found in great numbers in the low hills adjacent to Jodhpur, where they were carefully preserved.
Photo courtesy: The author

Sir Pratap (standing in centre with hat) with his day's bag in 1888 at Jodhpur—the paradise of pig-stickers. Wild pigs were found in great numbers in the low hills adjacent to Jodhpur and the pig-sticking here was far-famed sport. Sir Pratap had named his old steed 'Tirah', because he had carried Sir Pratap all through the Tirah campaign. Tirah was the most popular pig-sticker horse in Jodhpur from 1898 to 1901.
Photo courtesy: Raoraja Daljit Singh ji

impossible, for every second brings its new problem, requiring instant decision. You are no sooner out of a hole safely than you are down the bank of a *nullah*; you are no sooner out of the *nullah* than you are making straight for a tree. Practically, you leave everything to your horse. The whirl-like succession of sensations; the necessity for instantaneous decision; the confidence between man and horse which leaves to the latter the responsibility of deciding what the rider cannot pretend to decide; the fierce, undulating rush; the culminating intoxication of the final thrust—all these combine to make pig-sticking, for men of eager temperament, the finest sport in the world. After the sun has risen and all the available pigs are disposed off, the party gives up spears to the syces and ride back over the plain towards the distant towering fort of the Jodhpur. That was how the warrior clans of Rajasthan foraged for meat. They chased wild pigs on horseback and speared them to death. They then indulged in orgies of meat eating since there was no way of preserving meat — they hogged on hogs, as it were.

The Rajput nobles of Jodhpur were notable exponents of the far-famed but dangerous sport of pig sticking. No year passed in Jodhpur without a number of accidents in the pig-sticking field to both men and horses, and the wounds were often severe, as the boars charge with great courage, frequently overturning

Maharaja Man Singh pig-sticking at Jodhpur in 1827.
Photo courtesy: Mehrangarh Museum Trust

both horse and rider, and following up with a most determined attack upon the horseman who has been unseated. It was a blood sport of the Raj—blood sport at its bloodiest; a one-to-one contest, if that is the word, between the hunter and his quarry. The hunter was an able-bodied man riding a trained horse and carrying a nine-foot long spear. He hunted a pig—terrified, squealing, running for its life, and, often, turning around to make a blind charge at its pursuer. When closely pursued, the pig becomes extremely fierce, and rarely fails to make an obstinate defence. One very ugly trick the animal has, is that of suddenly stopping short, letting the horseman pass, and then making an impetuous rush at the horse's hind quarters (a practice known as 'jinking'). The ultimate skill for the rider was to take on the charge of a pig, which has turned around in its tracks and came to attack the rider.

The British, who ruled India, took to pig-sticking like ducks to water, and in no time at all, transformed it into a 'sport', which means that they framed rules for competition. There were pig-sticking 'meets' at which teams competed. There were 'umpires' to ensure that the rules were observed. There was even a 'Lords' and 'Wimbledon' of pig-sticking! The annual Kadir Cup meet at Meerut. The Kadir cup for pig-sticking was one of the principal sporting trophies of India. This tremendously exciting sport, in which a single man on horseback with a spear was pitted against boars, had been very popular among the Rathores since long and continued under the British. As in tiger shooting, a pig-sticking 'kill' was credited to the 'spear', meaning the rider who had drawn first blood, or inflicted a wound.

When the Prince of Wales (the future Edward VIII who abdicated in 1937) visited Jodhpur from 28 to 30 November 1921, he was taken out for pig-sticking, where he speared his first pig. Young Louis Mountbatten was also on the Prince of Wales's staff during this tour. Both the Prince and Mountbatten stuck their first pigs on the 'sandy plain at Jodhpur' as they both went out two mornings before breakfast, accompanied by Sir Pratap, who, despite his 77 years was as keen as a boy. The Prince speared the first pig on the first morning, and the total bag was five on the first day, and 11 on the second.

Before leaving Jodhpur he reviewed the Jodhpur Lancers who were the last Imperial Service Troops to leave France during the Great War. Six squadrons went past in magnificent style, and the Prince shook hands with the officers, and distributed decorations. In his banquet speech the prince mentioned that, 'he much enjoyed seeing the famous Rissala this afternoon'.

Excerpts from *The House of Marwar* by Dhananajaya Singh says 'Miniature paintings in the Mehrangarh Museum reveal that the Rathores first played polo with the Mughals but it did not become a passion with them till much later, in the 19th century.' In Mehrangarh Fort Jodhpur the 16th century paintings reveal

Going pig-sticking in a car! Armed with Enfield rifles and bayonets, lances, knives, swords, pistol and gun, Raoraja Sujjan Singh, later commanding officer JSI, stands in front of a car, while Colonel Raoraja Tej Singh, the CO of JSI, sits in the car in 1919! Going pig-sticking was a very special occasion that included a photo shoot before and after the game, as excited men gather around posing for the camera. The photo below is after the hog was speared.

Photos courtesy: Raoraja Vijay Singh and Dharmendra Singh

A pig-sticking competition under way with umpires on elephants! Hunting the wild boar on horseback was known as pig-sticking—a dangerous sport. The spear, a bamboo of some 8 or 9 feet in length, weighted with lead at the butt, is carried by the rider close to his knee, the point being depressed by thrusting into pigs' sides while chasing them at full gallop. The boar came armed with curved tusks up to 9 inches long. When unable to outrun its pursuer, the boar turned and charged.
Photo courtesy: Mehrangarh Museum Trust

polo was a popular sport, patronised by the Maharaja and played with enthusiasm throughout Rajputana.

Though polo had become very popular in British India, it had not yet caught on in the Indian Princely States. Sir 'P' was the first to introduce this game in Jodhpur, from where it spread to the other states in Rajasthan and thence to the other Princely States. The British referred to Sir 'P' as the father of modern polo. He was an excellent judge of the game and when watching, he could recount each stroke made by each player. He was unquestionably the best teacher of the game in his time. The Maharajas and their extended families who prized horses, horsemanship and valour in battle, took to polo with gusto, as polo offered a ritual substitute for mounted warfare—a test of warrior skills and horsemanship, tactics, teamwork, leadership, speed, danger and courage.

Sir Pratap and Major Beatson had started polo in Jodhpur in 1889, and in four years' time had got together a dream team. And it was with the Englishman that polo came to Jodhpur in its modern form and Jodhpur became the 'home of polo' in India. The Rathores took to it like fish to water; here was a splendid substitute for war. The Jodhpur Lancers saw the sport as ideal training for their riders and, socially, polo provided a vital link between the British Raj and the Indian nobility. The blood-rushing charges, the all-or-nothing riding-off, the frantic change of horses…it was all there.

In Jodhpur the world lies at the feet of the man who excels on the polo ground. It does not matter whether a man is a sweeper, and the son of a sweeper; if he can play polo well enough to make his inclusion in the first team a matter of policy, his future is assured. Naturally, when a man plays polo so well that his presence on the ground every evening is essential to the happiness of the Maharaja and his nobles, it was necessary to give him a definite status befitting his dignity as a mighty polo player.

The Indian Polo Association was formed in the year 1892, a time when there were many clubs, patronised and endorsed by the princes of modern India. From the beginning of the golden age of Indian Polo from 1890, one or another of the Rajput states dominated Indian Polo. Jodhpur first held sway, followed by Alwar, which was then eclipsed by Patiala. At the time among the most prominent teams were those of Jodhpur, Jaipur, Alwar, Bhopal, Bikaner, Hyderabad, Patiala, Kishangarh and Kashmir. Some of the well-known army teams were those of the Indian and British cavalry Regiments like the 15 Lancers, Central India Horse, PAVO Cavalry, Inniskilling Dragon Guards, 17/21 Lancers and the 10 Royal Hussars. In the early years of the last century the greatest contribution towards raising the standard of the game came from Rajputs and Sikhs. Superb horsemen, the members of these teams were also noted for excellence of their stick-work and horse control.

The year 1893 saw the Jodhpur polo team as the acknowledged champions of India, when they brought home their first trophy, 'The Rajputana Challenge Cup', with one of the finest teams ever seen there. The team consisted of Sir Pratap, Major Beatson, Hurjee and Dhonkal Singh, the last rated by many as one of the finest exponents of the sport ever.

As Amar Singh, wrote in his diary in 1900, 'Here in Jodhpur, and especially with Sir 'P', we have next to nothing to talk about but only polo! Polo! We play polo, we talk polo, and we even dream polo'. The result was that Jodhpur produced a galaxy of polo players. The polo grounds at Jodhpur were considered the best in India and attracted players keen to train. By the turn of the century Jodhpur had become an important polo centre, and it would remain so till 1949 (when the city boasted no less than six polo fields); rivaling Calcutta, the oldest polo club in the world, by the sheer number of players.

A few years later in 1897, Sir Pratap caused a sensation when he arrived with the Jodhpur polo team in London, amongst the earliest of foreign teams to invade

30 November 1921, the Prince of Wales and Maharaja Umaid Singh inspecting the Jodhpur Lancers at Jodhpur. The Jodhpur Imperial Service Lancers were as smart a tent-pegging corps as existed in the world.
Photo courtesy: Mehrangarh Museum Trust

Maharaja Man Singh playing polo with royal women at Jodhpur in 1827. Royal women actively participated in sports such as hunting and polo. They ride on majestic Marwari horses identifiable by their distinctive upturned ears. Rajput fearlessness in the saddle and a Marwari horse underneath proved to be an unbeatable combination.
Photo courtesy: Mehrangarh Museum Trust

England, for Queen Victoria's Diamond Jubilee. The Jodhpur team led by Sir 'P' challenged and defeated the English teams on their home ground at Hurlingham and Ranelagh.

Sir Pratap's breeches—designed with a unique wing shape for greater riding comfort—became almost as celebrated as the great man himself. 'Jodhpurs', as they would later be named, became de rigueur for equestrian sports. Sir Pratap returned to India victorious, with Jodhpur's reputation as the epicentre of polo in India assured.

In the Indian Army during the high noon of the British Empire, polo was more than just a game—it became an entire way of life. The powers-that-be recognised the potential of the sport in promoting the qualities essential in the making of a good soldier and extended full official support to its development at all stages of military life. Cavalry regiments denoted most of their spare time and energies to polo, as the close interaction of officers and men on the polo field fostered strong bonds between them and contributed immensely to the cohesiveness of the regiment as a fighting unit. One of those who recorded the atmosphere of those days was Lieutenant Winston Churchill of the 4 Hussars, newly arrived in India,

> We paid an equal contribution into the pot; and thus freed from mundane cares, devoted ourselves to the serious purpose of life. This was expressed in one word—Polo. It was upon this, apart from duty, that all our interest was concentrated. We nipped across to luncheon at half-past one, in the blistering heat and returned to sleep till five O'clock. Now the station begins to live again. It is the hour of Polo. It is the hour for which we have been living all day long. I was accustomed in those days to play every chukka I could get into. The whole system was elaborately organised for the garrison during the morning; and a smart little peon collected the names of all the officers together with the numbers of Chukkas they wished to play. These were averaged out so as to secure 'the greatest good of the greatest number.' I very rarely played less than eight more often ten or twelve.

The four leading teams in 1890s were the 7 Hussars, Jodhpur, Central India and Patiala. The Jodhpur polo team has beaten most in India, and no cavalry regiment thought itself quite ready for a big tournament till it had put in a fortnight's practice at Jodhpur. It was not surprising then that the 4 Hussars' Regimental Team, determined to win the prestigious Inter-Regimental Cup of February 1899 at Meerut, decided to spend a week's training in Jodhpur before the tournament, where they were royally hosted by the Regent, Sir Pratap. Playing at the No. 1 position for the 4 Hussars was Lieutenant Winston S. Churchill who wrote excitedly to his mother on 11 January, 1899 from his regimental headquarters in Bangalore, '...I am going next week to Madras to play polo...the week after that to Jodhpur where we all stay practising for the tournament with Sir Pratap Singh...'

We play polo, talk polo and dream polo. Amar Singh wrote in his diary on 27 September 1898, 'from morning till evening and….even in dreams at night Sir Pratap has nothing in his head except polo! The polo is "all in all" at Jodhpur and we have nothing to talk but only polo! Polo!' **Left to right:** Zalim Singh, Hurjee, Captain G.A. Cookson (16 Bengal Cavalry, was assistant inspecting officer, Rajputana Cavalry), Sir Pratap and Dhonkal Singh in 1897.
Photo Courtesy: Thakur Narendra Singh Gorau

The Jodhpur, Kota, Alwar and 7 Hussars teams at Mount Abu in 1897. **Seated from left:** unknown, unknown, Maharaja Jai Singh, Alwar; Maharaja Sardar Singh, Jodhpur; Maharaja Umed Singh, Kotah; unknown, Dhonkal Singh (then CO of 2 Sardar Rissala), unknown, Raoraja Amar Singh. Standing third from right is Moti Lal. Both Amar Singh and Moti Lal were Jodhpur players, but played for Alwar.
Photo courtesy: The author

Jodhpur, winners of the Central India Club trophy at Indore. **Left to right:** Maharaja Sardar Singh, Maharaj Akhey Singh, Maharaj Sher Singh and Dhonkal Singh in November 1907.
Photo courtesy: The author

The team practised with a group of noblemen under the watchful eye of Sir Partap, who, noted Churchill, 'loved polo next to war more than anything in the world and he used to stop the game repeatedly and point out faults or possible improvements in our play and combination'. 'Faster, faster, same like fly,' he would shout to increase the speed of the game. The Jodhpur polo field where they played consisted of thick red dust that billowed from the horse's hooves and became a dangerous place, particularly when 'Turbanned figures emerged at full gallop from the dust-cloud, or the ball whistled out of it unexpectedly . . . often one had to play to avoid the dust-cloud."

But misfortune struck in Jodhpur. The night before departing for Meerut, Churchill fell on the stone stairs of the Sir Pratap's home, spraining both ankles and re-injuring his chronic right shoulder, leaving his arm virtually useless. On the 9 of February, Churchill wrote to his brother Jack (John Strange) from the Rose-Red House of Sir Pratap, nearly in tears, 'I am staying with Sir Pratap Singh. All the rest of our team are here and everything smiled till last night; when I fell downstairs and sprained both my ankles and dislocated my right shoulder…'. Such was Sir Pratap's and Dhonkal's instruction, however, that the 4 Hussars did in fact go on to win the tournament, the injured young Winston (with the elbow strapped tight to his side) scoring two goals of four in a hard-fought contest that was not decided until the final seconds of the last chukka, when the 4 Hussars survived a ferocious onslaught to emerge as the champions of all India. Churchill never played the game again as his right shoulder had caused him a lifelong impairment.

After the death of Maharaja Sardar Singh in 1911, the sport in Jodhpur did suffer in the next decade, what with Sir Pratap and the Jodhpur Lancers away during the Great War for so many years. During the First World War period of 1914–19,

Idar Challenge Polo Cup, Mount Abu, 1911. Teams from Jodhpur, Kishangarh, Bikaner and Mount Abu Club participated. **Seated on chairs from right:** Maharaja Madan Singh, Kishangarh; Maharaja Ganga Singh, Bikaner; Sir Pratap; Colonel Windham; Major Dhonkal Singh; Mr Keen; Captain Maharaj Akhey Singh and last two unknown. **Standing:** unknown, Dalpat Singh (hero of Haifa), Fathe Singh, unknown, Kishore Singh, Lieutenant Colonel Maharaj Sher Singh (CO of Jodhpur Lancers in France), Bhoor Singh, Bheroon Singh, Ranjit Singh and Bakhtawar Singh. **Seated on ground from left:** Raoraja Shivdan Singh, Colonel Paney Singh (CO of Sumer Camel Corps), Captain Gaj Singh (Squadron Commander in France), Ratan Singh, Bane Singh (Jodhpur player who played for Kishangarh) and Ratan Singh. Standing on steps first left is Raoraja Narpat Singh (son of Sir Pratap Singh).

Photo courtesy: Daulat Singh Panehniwas

polo was at a standstill. Sadly many a good polo player was never again to be seen on the polo grounds, having fallen on different fields, in France, Belgium and Mesopotamia.

However, after the Great War, many talented Jodhpur players found places in all the prominent teams of the late 1920s and 1930s; among them the royal teams of Bhopal, Kashmir, Kishengarh and Alwar. Indeed, it was a hallowed tradition; the all-conquering Maharaja of Alwar's quartet that took home the magnificent Delhi Durbar Cup in 1911 had two Jodhpur players, Raoraja Amar Singh and Moti Lal. The famous Kishengarh team was powered by another Jodhpur player, Baney Singh. It was Jodhpur everywhere. So much so that a Nawab from Hyderabad was heard complaining one sunny afternoon in Delhi, 'Polo players seem to spring up like bloody mushrooms in Jodhpur!'

On 01 December 1921, however, when young Lord Mountbatten galloped on to the Chammi polo Ground for his first game he was amazed at the standard of play. A member of the Prince of Wales' Staff, he wrote in his diary,

Sir Pratap coached Lieutenant Winston Churchill of 4 Hussars at Jodhpur in January 1899. In this rare photo seated third and fourth from left are Sir Pratap and Lieutenant Winston Churchill.
Photo courtesy: Raoraja Daljit SinghJi

Lieutenant Winston Churchill practised polo on this thick red dusty ground of Ratanada Palace, Jodhpur, under the watchful eyes of Sir Pratap. The Racing Pavilion is seen in the background. British and Indian soldiers have long loved the game of polo, said to be the oldest team sport in the world.
Photo courtesy: Mehrangarh Museum Trust

The Jodhpur of yore boasted of polo teams from different localities of the capital town. Seen here is the Zalim Vilas Polo Team of 1910. **Standing left to right:** Hanwant Singh, Guman Singh, Panneh Lal Singh (ADC to Maharaj Zalim Singh) and Gajsingh (all three sons of Maharaj Zalim Singh). The players are wearing green jerseys with orange borders.
Photo courtesy: Daulat Singh Panehniwas

Raoraja Abhey Singh (seated left) and Captain Raoraja Abhey Singh (seated right) of Jodhpur formed part of the Kashmir team. Seen here along with Maharaja Hari Singh of Kashmir (standing left) and Major General Nawab Khusru Jung in 1934.
Photo Courtesy: Raoraja Vijay Singh

Some polo jerseys more than 100 years old still survive in erstwhile Jodhpur royal families!
Photo courtesy: Maharaj Hari Singh

'Jodhpur, Thursday 01 December…It was one of the best mornings I have spent anywhere…This day is a red letter one for me, as besides getting my first pig; I played in my first game of polo. I was playing on the Maharaja Umaid Singh's side against the Prince of Wales…In the last chucker, to my own intense surprise, I actually hit the ball three or four times! Anyway I loved it…'

He went on to record, 'The average handicap of the other players must have worked out at something over 5 and there was certainly some of the best polo in India being played here this afternoon…'

Mountbatten never forgot this 'Red letter day' and as Supreme Commander in South-East Asia towards the end of the Second World War, he named one of his major military campaigns in Burma 'Operation Pig Stick'. (It remains a mystery, though, as to who named the Hyderabad Police Action in 1948, 'Operation Polo'. It could well have been Mountbatten, then independent India's first Governor General). In 1947 Mountbatten had returned to India, the last British Viceroy. In the few, frantic months leading to, and following, Independence, he made sure he found time to visit Jodhpur one last time. There was no pig-sticking, but he was able to play polo on the new grass grounds at Paota.

After the Great War, the last four years of Sir Pratap's polo activities in Jodhpur, when his match playing days were over, were spent in building up a young side which might grow to be worthy of its forerunner; he had his reward when, in February 1922, at Delhi, in the presence of the Prince of Wales, he watched Jodhpur beat Patiala in the final of the Prince of Wales's Tournament, after a brilliant and thrilling struggle (the two best teams at that time, Jodhpur and Patiala were selected to play this exhibition polo match). It was a match often described as the finest ever. The game was watched by the Prince of Wales and his

The Ship House built in 1885 acted as polo pavilion overlooking Polo ground in Jodhpur.
Photo courtesy: Mehrangarh Museum Trust

06 May 1948, Lord Mountbatten and Maharaja Hanwant Singh at Rajput High School, Chopasani, Jodhpur. Mountbatten wrote in the school visitors' book, 'I was very much impressed by what I saw today'.
Photo courtesy: The author

entourage, the whole assemblage of Indian Princes and the elite of Indian society and the Raj establishment. Naturally, excitement ran high and both the teams were exhorted to 'do or die' to win this match.

For this prestigious match, Sir 'P' selected four promising youngsters, all in their early twenties, and personally trained them. The Patiala team on the other had comprised highly experienced veterans. It was here, in this game, that Raoraja Hanut Singh, the son of Sir 'P', made his debut. The Jodhpur team won the game and the Patiala team was so incensed by their defeat that they burnt their polo sticks on the ground itself. It had been a thrilling and exciting game which had kept the spectators enthralled, bringing them to their feet many times to applaud some outstanding play. But Sir 'P' had sat impassively through the match, watching the game without any emotion showing on his face. He had full confidence in his boys and they lived upto his expectations. When the Jodhpur team, after their victory, presented themselves before Sir 'P', he greeted them with a curt: 'Well done.' Coming from Sir 'P', this was high praise.

The epic match is described in detail by the doyen of Indian polo, the late Raoraja Hanut Singh himself:

> Imagine the scene in Delhi – a crowd of over a hundred and fifty thousand people, which included the future King-Emperor, the Viceroy, Sir Pratap himself, some fifty Maharajas and Princes, dozens of Generals and high government officials and all the ladies dressed in their finest attire watched spellbound. Such an atmosphere naturally added to our determination to win. The Jodhpur team consisted of Thakur Prithi Singh of Bera (Sir Pratap's daughter's son), Thakur Dalpat Singh of Rohet, Ram Singh and self (Sir Pratap's third son). My father had set his heart on this game and we had a string of 150 ponies from which to choose. Patiala had even greater resources, including a style of polo that I can only describe as a chess game, a wonderful control of the ball from all corners of the field. We knew the only way to beat them was the game of speed, always playing the ball to an imaginary line straight down the centre of the field from one game to another. That is the way we played, but Patiala was still leading 4-0 in the third chukker.
>
> I finally scored just before the interval, and after the interval we caught fire, drawing even with Patiala and in the final minute of the match, passing them. The roars from the crowd were so deafening that none of us heard the final bugle and we knew the game was over only when thousands of spectators began pouring into the field. As my No 1 Prithvi Singh rode past the VIP pavilion, he swung his stick round and round his head and threw it high in the air. Dignitaries from the pavilion rushed out into the field to try to capture the stick as a souvenir. It was a scene I will never forget,

Left: The 1923 Jodhpur polo team, wearing the Jodhpur *cheel* or kite on their jerseys. **Seated left to right:** Maharaja Umaid Singh and Raoraja Hanut Singh. **Standing** behind Maharaja is Raoraja Sagat Singh who won a Military Cross at Haifa. **Right:** Pirthi Singh Bera, Captain A.H. Williams, Raoraja Hanut Singh and Ram Singh winners of IPA Cup-1925. Three of these players (except Captain Williams) were part of the team that won the Prince of Wales Cup 1922.
Photos courtesy: Raoraja Daljit Singh ji

but what I remember most was the reaction of my father, who died later that year. I think Sir H. Perry Robinson, writing in 'The Times' of London, described the end of the game better than I can; 'Halfway through the chukker Jodhpur scored and drew even at five-all. Three more minutes to go, and through those minutes, men, important Generals and personages in high political office stood up in the grandstand waving their hats and shouting themselves hoarse, and women screamed. Only one figure it seems sat motionless. In front of the stands sat Sir Pratap Singh, Regent of Jodhpur and grand polo player, 78 years old and sits on his horse still beautifully. And all India knows that the Jodhpur team is the very apple of his eye, his darling and his pride, and he had coaxed and nursed it for this fight. Through all this game he sat immovable, not a muscle, not an eyelid or finger moving. Not even in the last demonical minute when Jodhpur scored its sixth goal and won. He was a figure carved out of wood. Then as the horn sounded, people from all sides broke, cheering and tumultuous, to congratulate him, the Prince among the first. And as the old man stood up, tears poured down his cheeks.

Jodhpur thus avenged in style their defeat years earlier at the hands of Patiala (Since 1900, the states of Jodhpur and Patiala had developed an intense polo rivalry). The magnificent Bhupinder Singh, Maharaja of Patiala, let his horses loose in the crowded by-lanes of the capital and ordered his team to burn their sticks.

They never entered the field again. Taking the defeat badly, Patiala abandoned polo while Jodhpur went on to greater glory. The game marked the eclipse of the famous Patiala team, for in 1924 it ceased to exist, and the ascendancy of the star of Jodhpur, which reigned supreme and unmatched for the next decade and more.

That victory of February 1922 was only the beginning. In early 1925 Maharaja Umaid Singh visited England with his extremely talented polo team, which included Raoraja Hanut Singh, Thakur Prithi Singh, Thakur Dalpat Singh, Ram Singh and an Englishman, Captain A.H. Bill Williams. Described in the *Tatler* as, 'Hot as Mustard', the Jodhpur team had a most wonderful season, beating every team there was to beat, including the US Army; and winning the Hurlingham Champion Polo Cup and the Roehampton Open Polo Cup, among many other lesser trophies. Before returning to Jodhpur, the Maharaja donated a new pavilion to the West Somerset Polo Club.

Only the Indian summer of 1933 was hotter than that of 1925, as Raoraja Hanut Singh returned to England with his younger brother, Raoraja Abhey Singh, in the Jaipur Team that year. Polo was, in fact, Jodhpur's gift to the Maharaja of Jaipur, the suave Sawai Man Singh II, popularly known as the dashing Jai. Many years earlier, after ensuring Jai's succession to the *Gaddi* of Jaipur, Sir Pratap had dispatched Dhonkal Singh to Jaipur to teach him polo. The old man had done well, but it was only after the young Maharaja's double marriage in Jodhpur (Man Singh II married Umaid Singh's sister and niece, many years before he married the beautiful Gayatri Devi of Cooch Behar) that Jaipur polo really took off.

The British took their games with them wherever they went. Sport was their chief spiritual export and was to prove among their more resilient memorials. The British introduced cricket, racquets, tennis, football, billiards, croquet and golf in

Maharaj Zalim Singh with his high wheel penny-farthing cycle at Jodhpur in 1887. He is wearing a racing cyclist's uniform of peaked cap, tight jackets and knee-length breeches, with leather shoes. This cycle was popular in the 1870s and 1880s, with its large front wheel providing high speeds and comfort. Although the trend was short-lived, the penny-farthing became a symbol of the late Victorian era. Its popularity also coincided with the birth of cycling as a sport.
Photo courtesy: Maharaj Hari Singh Zalimniwas

The Hurlingham Polo Championship Cup 1925 won by Jodhpur.
Photo Courtesy: The author

Jodhpur. Cricket was in much favour, and schoolboys could be seen practising in various places on the sand. There was a cricket ground at the palace and Maharaja Sardar Singh was proficient at this game, as at polo. Most of the Rathores were keen on guns and field-sports, when they could afford to shoot and hunt. They all took readily to games, whether of the East or West.

Besides polo and pig-sticking the unquestionable favourite pastime of the Rajputs was the blood sport of game hunting, tiger shooting and goat cutting (where a goat is suspended by its hind legs from a pole and the object is to sever its head with a single sword stroke). Such was the importance given to the hunting as a sport in Jodhpur that it had an office of hunting (*Shikar Khana*).

Encouraged from early adulthood to hunt as a form of physical exercise and training for the handling of arms, the soldiers were all very keen sportsmen, and were keen to shoot and hunt the small game of the country both for sport and for the table.

The small game like black buck, chinkara, hare, and game birds like partridges, quail, duck, bustard and that most delicious of birds, the imperial sandgrouse, were much shot, and available plentifully throughout the state. Of course, the imperial sandgrouse shooting at the Gajner palace in Bikaner, during the Christmas season, was the most sought-after invitation in the Indian social calendar during the reign of Maharaja Ganga Singh.

The hunting of big cats—tiger, lion, panther and bear, wild boar and crocodile, in that time, was a pretext for ostentatious demonstration of pomp and at the same time an occasion for the king to exhibit his grandeur when he set out to bring down a big cat and, particularly, a tiger, the hunting of which was an exclusive privilege of the Maharaja.

1933, The Invincibles! **Left to right:** Maharaja Sawai Man Singh Jaipur, Raoraja Hanut Singh, Raoraja Abhey Singh and Colonel Prithvi Singh Baria. In 1933, the Jaipur team had three Jodhpur players–they won all the open tournaments in England and India from 1930 to 1938.
Photo courtesy: Raoraja Daljit Singhji

Much polo silver was added during the time of Maharaja Umaid Singh, who himself was a good polo player. Maharaja Umaid Singh, Raoraja Hanut Singh, Raoraja Abhey Singh and Maharaj Ajit Singh posing at the Ratanada Palace Jodhpur with their Polo trophy in 1927.
Photo courtesy: Raoraja Daljit Singh

Jodhpur Cricket—1892. Maharaja Sardar Singh, seated in the centre wearing turban and pads.
The British introduced cricket in India in the 18th century and the game had acquired popular
appeal by the late 19th century.
Photo courtesy: Thakur Praduman Singh Chandelao

The Jodhpur Sardar Infantry Football team in 1919. Football continued to be a very popular game
in Jodhpur.
Photo Courtesy: Raoraja Vijay Singh

Maharaja Umaid Singh was a keen *shikari* (hunter). Seen here with gigantic elephant tusks weighing 117 and 114 pounds each, measuring 7 feet and 9 inches long that he shot during his successful big game hunting expedition to Kenya in June 1933. The safari method of trophy hunting was a development of sport hunting that saw elaborate travel in pursuit of trophies that required skillful tracking and acquisition of an elusive target. The above elephant tusks are now displayed in Rissala Restaurant in Umaid Bhawan Palace Jodhpur.

Photo courtesy: The author

For the pot, 1939. **Standing from left:** unknown, Lieutenant Colonel Sujjan Singh, Lieutenant Colonel F.D. Clarke and Lieutenant P.W.J. Crossland and men during the sandgrouse and partridges shoot in Jodhpur. Both Clarke and Crossland went as SSO with JSI during the War.

Photo courtesy: Nagina Reddy

Rounding off the day's bird shoot of Imperial Sand Grouse with the rather laborious method of count of the bag for the record. A great deal of skill and steady aim was required to down the birds because sportsmen had to shoot them precisely in the head or breast. These were the best-flavoured game birds in India and were much shot.

Photo courtesy: Mehrangarh Museum Trust

The Royal Hunts: Maharaja Umaid Singh seated first on right after a panther shoot. Jodhpur was also famous for big game like panther, crocodile and bear.

Photo courtesy: Mehrangarh Museum Trust

The camel is among the most useful of the domestic animals of Marwar. They are often very swift and can cover a hundred miles in a night without difficulty when the situation demands. November 1902, during the visit of Viceroy Curzon, trained camels were employed to carry back the pigs after the pig-sticking in Jodhpur. At least three pigs can be seen hanging from these 'shikar' camels.

Photo courtesy: Thakur Praduman Singh Chandelao

Maharaja Umaid Singh escaped the heat and dust of Marwar during the summer months by heading to his sumptuous estate 'Arranmore' in the southern hill station of Ooty. A gathering before Ootacamund hunt is pictured ready for action outside Arranmore Estate.

Photo courtesy: Mehrangarh Museum Trust

Wearing colourful gifted jerseys and jackets, the Jodhpur Polo stick makers pose for the camera
in style. The man on the left wears the Jodhpur Lancers sleeve badge on his chest!
Photo courtesy: The author

During Maharaja Umaid Singh's time (1923 to 1947) he would often spend his
summers at his beautiful Estate 'Arranmore' in Ooty in South India, famous for
his numerous fox hunts.

But the times were such. State affairs were not neglected, but the cavalry and
the polo, the racing and the pig-sticking, remained the serious business of life at
the Jodhpur of yore. During the day it was the shoots for the *shikaris* and polo
or pig-sticking for the riders. In the evenings the *Burra Sahibs* drank their 'Chota
whisky and soda' at the 'Jodhpur Sardar Club' with gouty old Majors sitting at the
bar regaling their audiences with war-time stories—for the war had now receded
into a dim past and all that was left were memories. Those were the great days of
peacetime soldiering in Jodhpur and life generally moved at a leisurely pleasant
pace. Sadly it all ended with the outbreak of the Second World War...The Jodhpur
Lancers, however, stubbornly continued to play while waiting to be mechanised
at Risalpur in 1940 (now in Pakistan) and won the Championship there, beating
well-known teams like Probyn's Horse. Finally Jodhpur's demise as a force in
polo and pig-sticking began in 1939 when the Jodhpur Lancers were mechanised.
Polo was suspended in India, as elsewhere, for the duration of World War II. From
1947 Jodhpur polo became a shadow of its former self.

Maharaja Gaj Singh with his son Yuvraj Shivraj Singh of Jodhpur.
Photo courtesy: Pradeepji Soni

Today, almost hundred years later, Maharaja Gaj Singh and his polo-playing son Yuvraj Shivraj Singh (till his promising career was cruelly cut short due to a severe head injury, while playing polo in 2005) have ushered a new era in the revival of Jodhpur Polo, and—to their credit—Jodhpur has again become India's leading polo destination.

The Jodhpur Lancers in the Second World War– 1939 to 1946

The year 1939 saw war clouds gather and the war jitters in England took no time to filter to dominions around the world. Viceroy Linlithgow made a hurried visit to Jodhpur in March 1939 and inspected the Jodhpur State Forces.

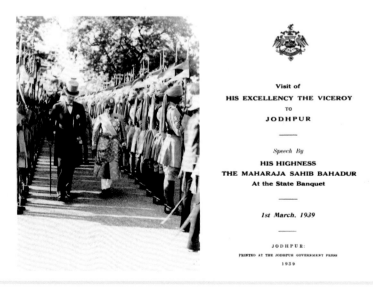

Left: 01 March 1939, Viceroy Linlithgow and Maharaja Umaid Singh inspect the guard of honour by the Jodhpur Lancers, **Right:** The banquet speech.
Photos courtesy: Mehrangarh Museum Trust

The Viceroy departs from Ratanada Palace, Jodhpur, as the men of Jodhpur Lancers (on left)
and Sardar Infantry (on right) stand guard on the eve of the Second World War.
Photo courtesy: Mehrangarh Museum Trust

01 March 1939 the Jodhpur Lancers awaiting the arrival of the Viceroy Linlithgow as the Marwar
and British bunting fly over them.
Photo courtesy: Mehrangarh Museum Trust

In May 1939, with the threat of war looming ever larger, it was decided to discontinue
the 1920 scheme and introduce a new 1939 scheme. The categorisation changes
of this new scheme, which came into effect on 01 December 1939 were:

1920 Scheme	1939 Scheme	Role
Class A (Earmarked)	Field Service Units (FSU)	Units placed at the disposal of the Crown in an emergency—*Jodhpur Sardar Rissala*
Class A (Non-Earmarked)	General Service Units (GSU)	Units which may be offered for service—*Jodhpur Sardar Infantry and Jodhpur Training Squadron*
Class B	State Service Units (SSU)	Units for internal security of the State—*Jodhpur Mule Troop*

Further concessions of the 1939 scheme included free distribution of a large numbers of horses from Indian Cavalry regiments, the opening of Kitchener College, Nowgong and Staff College, Quetta to personnel of the State Forces, and later in the war, the allocation of vacancies at various schools which had been established for training officers for the war, such as the Officers Training Schools at Mhow and Belgaum, and the Junior Commanders Course at Poona.

The Jodhpur Lancers was an 'earmarked unit', or, in other words, a unit, which could be demanded for service outside the state in the event of an emergency, while the role of Jodhpur Sardar Infantry at the commencement of war was for service in the state. However, the Jodhpur Sardar Infantry was not to be left very long at Jodhpur after the commencement of the war and the story of its adventures during the years to come make for good reading.

As with the First World War, so with the commencement of the Second World War, virtually all the rulers offered their State Forces for employment and 40 units were incorporated into the Indian State Forces (ISF) order of battle. Within a very short time 20 of the units were employed outside of their State territories and by the end of the war State Forces had served with distinction in every theatre of operation, with a total strength of 50,290.

On 09 November 1939 the Jodhpur Durbar offered placing of the Sardar Rissala and the Sardar Infantry at the disposal of the Government of India for service outside Jodhpur. On 16 November 1939 the Sardar Rissala was ordered to hold

Seated fourth from right, Lieutenant Colonel Sujjan Singh and standing second from right,
Captain Jawahar Singh of JSI attending the Senior Officers Course at Jaipur 1939.
Photo courtesy: Durgesh Nandini

itself in readiness to move from Jodhpur, not before 15 December 1939, for
incorporation with the 1 Risalpur Cavalry Brigade.

The biggest challenge faced was to meet the increasing demand of expansion
and training of Jodhpur State Forces. At the outbreak of war on 3 September
1939, the Jodhpur State Forces numbered just over 1,700 men. That number was
to be increased more than four times during the grim years of war. In 1945 due
to raising of the 2 and 3 Jodhpur Infantry, Demo Company, Infantry Training
Centre and the Durga Horse, the total strength went up to 6,462. After the war,
in August 1947, the Jodhpur State Forces numbered just 3,375.

During World War II the Jodhpur State Forces consisted of the following units: -

• The Jodhpur Sardar Rissala (Since 1889)
• Jodhpur Sardar Rissala Training Centre (Since 1922)
• The Jodhpur Sardar Infantry (Since 1922)
• Jodhpur Infantry Training Centre (From 01 Nov 1939)
• The Jodhpur Mule Troop (Since 1922)
• The Jodhpur Military Hospital (Since 1922)
• The Fort Guard (Since Oct 1935)
• The Durga Horse (From 16 May 1941)
• No 54 Jodhpur RIASC Company (From 17 Oct 1940)

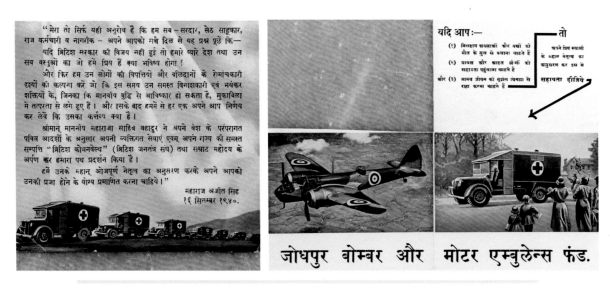

"मेरा तो सिर्फ यही अनुरोध है कि हम सब – सरदार, सेठ साहुकार, राज कर्मचारी व नागरिक – अपने आपको मंझे दिल से यह प्रश्न पूछें कि–
यदि ब्रिटिश सरकार की विजय नहीं हुई तो हमारे प्यारे देश तथा उन सब वस्तुओं का जो हमें प्रिय हैं क्या भविष्य होगा !
और फिर हम उन लोगों की विपत्तियों और बलिदानों के रोमांचकारी दृश्यों की कल्पना करें जो कि इस समय उन समस्त विनाशकारी एवं भयंकर शक्तियों के, जिनका कि मानवीय बुद्धि से आविष्कार हो सकता है, मुकाबिला में तत्परता से लगे हुए हैं । और इसके बाद हममें से हर एक अपने आप निर्णय कर लेवे कि उसका कर्त्तव्य क्या है ।
श्रीमान् माननीय महाराज साहिब बहादुर ने अपने वंश के परंपरागत पवित्र आदर्शों के अनुसार अपनी व्यक्तिगत सेवाएं एवम् अपने राज्य की समस्त सम्पत्ति "ब्रिटिश कोमनवेल्थ" (ब्रिटिश जनतंत्र संघ) तथा सम्राट महोदय के अर्पण कर हमारा पथ प्रदर्शन किया है ।
हमें उनके महान् ओजपूर्ण नेतृत्व का अनुसरण करके अपने आपको उनकी प्रजा होने के योग्य प्रमाणित करना चाहिये ।"

महाराज अजीत सिंह
१६ सितम्बर १९४०.

यदि आप :– → तो
(१) निस्सहाय स्त्रियों और बच्चों को मौत के मुख से बचाना चाहते हैं
(२) घायल और आहत लोगों को सहायता पहुंचाना चाहते हैं
और (३) मानव जीवन की बृहंस विनाश से रक्षा करना चाहते हैं

अपने प्रिय स्वामी के महान नेतृत्व का अनुसरण कर इस में सहायता दीजिये

जोधपुर बोम्बर और मोटर एम्बुलेन्स फंड.

An emotional appeal by Maharaj Ajit Singh for financial support to the 'Jodhpur Bomber and Motor Ambulance Fund'. During the war the posters were effectively used to reach and influence the people, conveying information while attempting to affect their behaviour.
Photo courtesy: Dr Mahendra Singh Nagar

Jodhpur Infantry Training Centre

It was raised at Jodhpur on 1 November 1939, as the Jodhpur Training Company. It later became Jodhpur Sardar Infantry Training Company in October 1941 and in April 1942 it became Jodhpur Training Battalion. Finally in May 1944 it became Jodhpur Infantry Training Centre. It consisted of Rajputs, Jats and Kaimkhanis.

Lieutenant Colonel Jawahar Singh became its Commanding Officer in March 1942.

The Bren gun replaced the lance and sabre. General Claude Auchinleck (fifth from right), the last British C-in-C in India and Maharaja Umaid Singh (in Air Force uniform), inspecting the Jodhpur Infantry Training Battalion on 09 July 1942. Brig R.C. Duncan (fourth from right), Lieutenant Colonel Sujjan Singh (sixth from right) and Lieutenant Colonel Zabar Singh (second from right) looks on.
Photo courtesy: The author

Jodhpur Sardar Rissala Training Centre

A Jodhpur Sardar Rissala Training Centre Logo.
Photo courtesy: Professor (Capt) Ashok Nath, FRGS,
Nath Foundation, Sweden

It was originally established in 1922, and was known as the Jodhpur Sardar Rissala Reserve Squadron. In February 1939, it was reorganised and was called Jodhpur Training Squadron. Until February 1939 the unit was an integral part of the Jodhpur Lancers, then it was separated.

On orders being received in February 1941, for the reorganisation of the Horsed Training Squadron to that of a Mechanised Training Centre, Brigadier R.C. Duncan and Lieutenant Colonel Zabar Singh and some officers and non-commissioned officers proceeded on a visit to No 1 Indian Armoured Corps Training Centre, Ferozepur, to see the general organisation and methods of training.

The result of mechanisation in 1941 led to a major conversion and construction with a few garages, workshops, model rooms, crew control room, signalling rooms, education rooms, a washing platform and a ramp being constructed at a heavy cost to the state. With the mechanisation of the Jodhpur Lancers, the squadron became the Jodhpur Sardar Rissala Training Centre in October 1941 and the Jodhpur Lancers Training Centre on 29 May 1943.

09 July 1942, inspection of Jodhpur Lancers Training Centre by C-in-C.
Left to right: Lieutenant Colonel Zabar Singh, General Auchinleck, Maharaja Umaid Singh and Brigadier R.C. Duncan.
Photo courtesy: The author

Shortly after orders for re-organisation, a few service vehicles were received to augment some of the state lorries, and this number was later increased; four non-commissioned officers of the Indian Armoured Corps were lent for a few months to help start off the training; automatic weapons were received gradually from arsenals; vacancies for officers and non-commissioned officers to attend courses at the Fighting Vehicles School, Ahmednagar, were given, and a considerable number of officers and non-commissioned officers passed through that school. After training in the Jodhpur Sardar Rissala Training Centre the recruits were sent for trade testing to the Indian States Forces Wing and Indian Armoured Car School, Ferozepur.

The strength of the unit was 147 and the class composition was Rajputs and Kaimkhanis and the uniform was khaki. Lieutenant Colonel Zabar Singh remained as Commandant of the Centre throughout the war and was awarded a Member of British Empire (MBE) in June 1943.

The Jodhpur Body Guard Squadron (Durga Horse)

A button, cap badge and shoulder title badge of the Durga Horse. The badge in gilding metal incorporated the *cheel* with Shiva's trident on its breast, crossed lances with pennants, and a two-part scroll below the *cheel* inscribed Durga Horse on the upper part and Jodhpur on the lower part.
Photo courtesy: Professor (Capt) Ashok Nath, FRGS, Nath Foundation Sweden

With the mechanisation of the Jodhpur Lancers in February 1941, it left the state with a decision as to the disposal of the horses. Permission was sought from Delhi, and granted, that a number of the horses could be returned to the state from Risalpur in order to create a new horsed unit. The unit was raised on 16 May 1941, in order to maintain the cavalry tradition in Jodhpur and designated the Jodhpur Body Guard Squadron with three troops of Rajputs and one troop of Kaimkhanis, a total authorised strength of 131. Personnel for the unit were drawn primarily from pensioners or discharged men of the Jodhpur Lancers and from pensioners of Indian cavalry regiments, which enlisted men from Jodhpur, namely the 2 Lancers, 16 Cavalry, Poona Horse and 18 KEO Cavalry.

A total of 180 selected horses were sent from Risalpur to the Body Guard Squadron and the rest of the horses were disposed off, on receipt of orders for mechanisation by the Jodhpur Lancers. Given the very careful selection of the best horses from the Lancers, the unit was probably the best mounted unit in India at that time.

The unit was initially commanded by Captain Mangal Singh and later by Captain Achal Singh, when Mangal Singh retired to command the Fort Guards in 1943. In addition to providing guards for the palaces, the squadron was also available for internal security duties and as such it was categorised State Service Unit. On 25 October 1945 it was re-designated as Body Guard Squadron and subsequently became the Durga Horse, with effect from 12 December 1946. It was still in existence at the time of Independence.

Major Shaitan Singh, PVC, served with this unit as officer cadet in 1947. Details of his career appear in the next chapter.

Jodhpur Fort Guards

©Nath Foundation, Sweden

A Jodhpur Fort Guard Belt, Cap and Shoulder title badges.
Photo courtesy: Professor (Capt) Ashok Nath, FRGS, Nath Foundation, Sweden

The Fort Guards were raised in October 1935 and it comprised of military pensioners, to relieve the Sardar Infantry of the Fort garrison duties. Till then the JSI was doing the guard duties in various forts of the state.

The unit consisted of a headquarters and two platoons. Personnel were armed with muskets, but were also responsible for firing salute guns from the fort. Maharaj Ratan Singh was appointed as *Quiledar* (Fortress Commander) of the Jodhpur Fort establishment in 1935.

The 54 (Jodhpur) General Purpose Transport Company, Royal Indian Army Service Corps—1940 to 1945

At the outbreak of the war there were only about 40 Mechanical Transport (MT) Sections in the RIASC and obviously the transport companies were in short supply, particularly in the Middle East where convoys of supplies to Russia were being organised during the Second World War. As the tempo of war increased, the states were asked to provide assistance by helping to raise such units for the Indian Army from within the States. One of the earliest acceptance of this scheme came from Jodhpur when, in the autumn of 1940, the Government of India accepted

March 1941: Lorries of Jodhpur RIASC Company with Jodhpur Fort in the background. The Jodhpur 'panchranga' colour bunting fly overhead.
Photo courtesy: Lieutenant Colonel B.P. Singh

its offer to raise a complete M.T. Company for the RIASC. The scheme was an ambitious one and bristled with difficulties, but the situation was serious and warranted unusual methods.

Left: The No 54 (Jodhpur) GPT Company RIASC Champion Section Challenge Shield presented by Maharaja in March 1941. The shield has the Jodhpur and RIASC logo on it. **Right:** December 1945, Officers of 54 (Jodhpur) Royal Indian Army Service Corps (RIASC) General Purpose Transport (GPT) Company. **Standing:** Lieutenant Durjan Singh (left) and Lieutenant Ram Singh. **Seated left to right:** Major Mod Singh, Lieutenant Colonel A.J.B. Sinker and Captain Sultan Singh. **On the ground:** Captain Chand Singh.

Photos courtesy: (left) Lieutenant Colonel B.P. Singh; (right) Colonel Devapal Singh Rathore (Retd)

General Claude Auchinleck, C-in-C, inspecting 54 RIASC GPT Company (Jodhpur) recruits undergoing mechanised training on 09 July 1942.

Photo courtesy: The author

The men of Jodhpur RIASC Company wearing dungarees in Basra Iraq in July 1941.
Major Mod Singh is seated in the centre (without headgear).
Photo courtesy: Lieutenant Colonel B.P. Singh

With the Jodhpur *panchranga* flag flying high, the drivers of No 54 (Jodhpur) GPT Company
RIASC, wearing khakhi dungarees, pray in front of adhoc unit *mandir* (temple) before taking off
for a convoy to Syria in 1941.
Photo courtesy: Lieutenant Colonel B.P. Singh

Major A.J.B. Sinker, was selected to raise and command the new company with Lieutenant Mod Singh, 2 Lieutenant Harvey James, Sub-Inspector Sultan Singh of Jodhpur Police (Later Captain and IGP in Jodhpur Police from 1968–74) and Lieutenant Chand Singh as officers. The raising of this company commenced at Jodhpur on 17 October 1940 and within two months was up to full strength of 460 men with class sections of Rajputs, Jats and Kaimkhanis. It was composed entirely of officers and men from the Jodhpur State, except the Commanding Officer and one other British Officer. On its formation some NCOs were transferred from the Jodhpur Lancers and JSI, but the sepoy drivers were mainly raw recruits with a small proportion of pensioners. It was accommodated in a part of the Jodhpur Lancers barracks, and it carried out its training at Jodhpur. It was soon found that though the Marwari had never before seen a mechanical contrivance such as a lorry or car, he could be trained on old 'crocks' into a first-class military driver.

The company was equipped with three-tonne trucks and moved to Loralai in Baluchistan, on the North West Frontier, in March 1941. During this time Captain Sultan Singh and few men were detailed for a three-month course at RIASC School, Kakul.

In April 1941 it provided a convoy of 25 vehicles, which carried out a round trip of 1,500 miles at an average speed of 12 miles per hour to the Persian Gulf at Jiwani. After a short period at Loralai where Lieutenant Woolmer joined, it moved overseas for active service to Basra, Iraq, in July 1941 and was engaged in the operations in Persia.

Seated on chairs left to right: Unknown, Major Sinker, Captain Mod Singh, Captain Sultan Singh, unknown, with Jodhpur RIASC Company football team in December 1945. They are wearing the Jodhpur *cheel* on their jerseys.
Photo courtesy: Lieutenant Colonel B.P. Singh

Here it took part in the Iran operations and later carried out a remarkable trip from Basra to North Iraq, into Syria, then into Palestine, and down to Jerusalem, Tel Aviv and Haifa (here all men visited the site of the gallant charge by the Jodhpur Lancers in the Great War) and back, a distance over 2,500 miles, during which it did not lose a single man or vehicle. Except for one vehicle that Lieutenant Mod Singh had to leave behind in an Australian workshop in Palestine, but he managed to obtain a certificate from the Warrant Officer in Charge that its condition was due to fair wear and tear; nor was it ever been substantiated that this cost him a bottle of whiskey, or 'Assa' (the Jodhpur special liquor)! All that is known is that he regularly carried a stock of such liquid 'currency' for any kind of emergency! On arrival in Baghdad in November 1941 the unit was inspected by Lieutenant General Hodgen, the Director of Supplies and Transport (DST) from General Headquarters, India, who was most appreciative of this unit's work.

Great interest was shown by everyone in the Jodhpur *cheel*, which was painted on the front and rear of each vehicle; this had also proved quite a factor in the growth of the unit's morale. In July 1942 Captain Woolmer left the unit on promotion to command the first Tank Transport Company of the RIASC in Iraq.

The company remained in Iraq and Persia providing transport for the Aid to Russia convoys, carrying stores and equipment to the Russians, journeying many times from Khanikin to Tabriz (the Russian rail head) for nine months, from June 1943 to March 1944, operating under HQ 16 Line of Control (L of C) Transport Column. The treacherous 730-miles-long one-way route required both skill and nerve. The time schedule for the turn round of 1,400 miles was 18 days, but this

Persia and Iraq (PAI) Force—Aid to Russia Convoy map.
Photo courtesy: AS3C Museum, Bengaluru

The Jodhpur RIASC men arrive by Bombay, Baroda and Central India (BBCI) railway at Rai ka Bagh
railway station, Jodhpur, while the Marwar and British bunting fly overhead, in July 1945.
Photo courtesy: Colonel Devpal Singh Rathore (Retd)

was often exceeded due to severe weather conditions. The men experienced
snowfall for the first time in their lives on this route.

The Company thus had a share in their task, 'Aid to Russia', three words that spelt
not only great victories in the field, but one of the greatest supply achievements
in the history of warfare. Official figures released by GHQ PAI (Persia And
Iraq) Command, show that over three and three-quarter million tons of Aid
to Russia material had been delivered to the Russians through the Persia-Iraq
Command. It would be of interest to know that a '16 Column Club' was formed in
'PAI FORCE' in April 1944 when the Column ceased operating on the 'Aid to
Russia' assignment.

Towards the end of March 1944 work on the 'Aid to Russia' convoys ceased,
and the unit was sent to Syria, the sixth country that they had served in since
leaving India in July 1941, the others being Persia, Iraq, Trans-Jordan, Palestine
and Egypt.

While in Syria, orders were received for moving to Italy in May 1944 where they
did excellent work for over a year after they were re-equipped with new Dodge

21 December 1945: The No 54 (Jodhpur) Company, RIASC marches past General
Claude Auchinleck, C-in-C at Delhi.
Photo courtesy: Lieutenant Colonel B.P. Singh

three-tonners, until the cessation of hostilities in Europe. During this time the
unit was billeted in a large Italian naval barrack at Brindisi, which was visited by
Maharaja Umaid Singh. While in Italy they would sometimes meet the Jodhpur
Sardar Infantry troops as well. Finally on 07 June 1945 while at Venice, the unit
received orders to return to India. The unit personnel took time off to visit the
city of Venice in gondolas, as well as Rome and the Vatican, with some of them
meeting the Pope! They arrived back in Bombay on 09 July 1945, almost exactly
four years since leaving India. The total battle casualties suffered by the unit
was 11 men. Shortly after landing they moved to Delhi where they joined 'B'
Mechanical Transport Mobilisation and Retraining Centre, RIASC.

Most of the men had not been on leave to their homes for the past four years. The
men were given two months special leave and they left for Jodhpur in a special
train. They were given a splendid reception at the Railway Station and later on
a large sumptuous dinner was given for them by the Maharaja at his new Chittar
Palace (UBP) that was completed during the time the unit was overseas.

After their return from leave they all came under the command of Major Mod Singh now appointed as Officer Commanding unit and joined 'B' M.T. Mobilisation and Retraining Centre, RIASC, at Delhi, commanded by Lieutenant Colonel A.J.B. Sinker. The unit finally moved to Jhansi.

The Jodhpur Lancers in World War II

With the outbreak of the Second World War the Jodhpur Lancers was the first Indian State Cavalry or Infantry unit to leave its state to join an Indian army formation, and was the first state cavalry regiment to be selected for mechanisation. Four officers of the Indian Army arrived at Jodhpur early in September 1939 for attachment with the Jodhpur Lancers—Lieutenant Colonel G.G. Collyns, 3 Cavalry; Major W.H.L. Spurgin, 19 K.G.O. Lancers; Captain A.G.S. Alexander, Central India Horse and Captain G.D.G Garforth Bles, Guides Cavalry. These

Viceroy Linlithgow with officers of the Jodhpur Lancers in 1939 at Jodhpur.
Seated left to right: Major Surajbhan Singh (he died during the war), Major Shyam Singh, unknown, Brigadier Duncan, Viceroy Linlithgow, Maharaja Umaid Singh, unknown, Lieutenant Colonel Bahadur Singh, Major Arjun Singh (father of Lieutenant General Hanut Singh, PVSM, MVC). **Standing from left:** Lieutenant Ramdan Singh, Captain Kesri Singh, Lieutenant Kheem Singh, unknown, Major Zabar Singh, Captain Kalyan Singh, Lieutenant Mohan Singh, Captain Sultan Singh, Lieutenant Bhopal Singh, Lieutenant Sardar Singh and Lieutenant Chandan Singh.
Photo courtesy: Kunwar Karni Singh Jasol

Viceroy Linlithgow being introduced to Commanding Officers Lieutenant Colonel Bahadur Singh of Jodhpur Lancers and Sujjan Singh of JSI.
Photo courtesy: Mehrangarh Museum Trust

officers were designated Special Service Officers (SSO), and their duties were purely advisory.

In November 1939, warning orders were received for the Jodhpur Lancers to move into British India to join the 1 Indian Cavalry Brigade at Risalpur under Brigadier A.A.E. Filose on the North-West Frontier, and the regiment left Jodhpur and arrived at Risalpur on 8 January 1940. The following officers were with the regiment—Lieutenant Colonel Bahadur Singh, CO; Major Shyam Singh, 2nd-in-Command; Captains: Arjun Singh, Surajbhan Singh, Kalyan Singh, Lieutenants: Keshri Singh, Sultan Singh, Chandan Singh, Jagat Singh, Dhonkal Singh, Bhopal Singh, Sardar Singh, Mohan Singh and 2nd Lieutenants Ramdan Singh, Prem Singh, Mod Singh, Kheem Singh and Tej Singh (Medical Officer). Cadet Pirthi Singh and Jabdi Khan were the State Officer Cadets (SOC) and Risaldar Major Chhog Singh. The total strength of the regiment was 17 State Officers, two SOC, 21 Indian Officers (JCO's), 486 Other Ranks (ORs), 383 followers and 521 horses. The Training Squadron left behind at Jodhpur was under the Command of Captain Zabar Singh with Lieutenant Mangal Singh as Adjutant and consisted of 5 Indian Officers, 134 Indian Other Ranks, 10 followers and 134 horses.

Left to right: Lieutenant Sardar Singh (father of Major Jaswant Singh, former Foreign and Defence Minister), Lieutenant Dhonkal Singh (later commanded 61 Cavalry), Captain Kalyan Singh (later Commandant Jodhpur Lancers 1946–1949), Lieutenant Jagat Singh Bera, Major Shyam Singh Rodla (later Commandant Jodhpur Lancers), Maharaja Umaid Singh, Major Surajbhan Singh Mayapur, Captain Sultan Singh, Lieutenant Ramdan Singh Ghantiya, Lieutenant Maharaj Prem Singh (6 handicap polo player), and Lieutenant Colonel Bahadur Singh, OBI (Commandant Jodhpur Lancers 1935–1941) during an outdoor exercise at Soorsagar in 1939.
Photo courtesy: Kunwar Karni Singh Jasol

The Jodhpur Lancers remained at Risalpur as part of the brigade for about 18 months. The regiment relieved the 16/5 Lancers there and was accommodated in the British Cavalry barracks, while the officers occupied the British Cavalry Mess. The regiment thoroughly enjoyed its time at Risalpur and benefitted greatly by working with the brigade and alongside other regiments. The unit was most popular there with everyone. The regimental Polo team consisting of Lieutenant Prem Singh, Captain Mohan Singh, Captain Jagat Singh, Lieutenant Sardar Singh and Risaldar Hanut Singh particularly distinguished itself. During this time Maharaja Umaid Singh, while on ten weeks RAF Cadets course at Risalpur, visited the unit.

When World War II started it was decided to keep the four best cavalry units of the Indian Army horsed. Jodhpur Lancers was among the four with 5 Probyn Horse, 9 Royal Deccan Horse and the 11 PAVO. Finally in February 1941 it was decided

The 1940-41 season was in fact the last hurrah on the polo fields for the Jodhpur Sardar Rissala players. Seen here is the Jodhpur Sardar Rissala team as winners of the Frontier Cup Polo in Peshawar 1940; 13/18 Royal Hussars (QMO) Challenge Cup Mardan 1940 and the Peshawar Club Cup Polo tournament 1940–41. Standing left to right is Risaldar Hanut Singh, Captain Jagat Singh, Lieutenant Sardar Singh, Captain Mohan Singh and Lieutenant Prem Singh.
Photo courtesy: Manvendra Singh Jasol (who is still preserving his grandfather
Major Sardar Singh's polo jersey made by the famous London sports shop, Lillywhites).

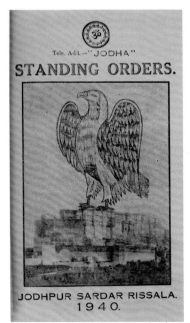

The Jodhpur Sardar Rissala revised its Standard Operating Procedures in 1940 while at Risalpur.
Photo courtesy: Colonel Kheem Singh Dakhan

there was no possible role for a cavalry unit in modern warfare and so even these last four best cavalry regiments had their horses stabled and were mechanised.

On 10 February 1941, the C-in-C had selected the Jodhpur Lancers for mechanisation, first with motor transport, but eventually being equipped as an armoured car regiment with the South African Marmon Harrington Armoured Cars. The entire cost being borne by the Government of India. This was a great honour, as it was the first Indian States Forces Cavalry Regiment to be chosen for mechanisation.

On 23 April 1941 orders were issued by Army Headquarters to relieve the Jodhpur Sardar Rissala of all its horses. The last mounted parade was held at Risalpur, where the Commanding Officer gave his final order: 'Make much of your horses!' All the riders simultaneously patted the proudly-arched necks of their deserving steeds for one last time.

It was decided to return 150 horses to Jodhpur and to cast all horses above 15 years of age and the balance of the horses were to be returned to the Remount Depot, Sargodha.

The last mounted parade of the Jodhpur Lancers at Risalpur. 'Make much of your horses' was the final order by the Jodhpur Sardar Rissala Commanding Officer during the last mounted parade held in Risalpur.
Photo courtesy: Kunwar Karni Singh Jasol

1935, Outdoor Exercise Jodhpur. **Last row left to right:** Jemadar Achal Singh, Jemadar Chhogh Singh, Risaldar Indra Singh, Risaldar Prem Singh, Risaldar Bishan Singh, Risaldar Jodh Singh, Risaldar Madho Singh, Risaldar Magan Singh, Jemadar Baxu Khan, Jemadar Amar Singh, Jemadar Madan Singh, Jemadar Bhopal Singh. **Middle row:** SOC Sardar Singh Jasol, 2/Lieutenant Kalyan Singh, Lieutenant Surajbhan Singh Mayapur, Captain Kalyan Singh Sankhwas, Major Hem Singh, Colonel Prithi Singh Bera, Captain Bahadur Singh, Captain Bir Singh, Lieutenant Kesri Singh. **Front row:** SOC Mohan Singh Osian, 2/Lieutenant Sultan Singh, Lieutenant Shyam Singh Rodla, Lieutenant Arjun Singh Jasol, Lieutenant Zabar Singh Bera, SOC Chandan Singh Galthani, SOC Bhopal Singh Bisalpur, SOC Sangram Singh.
Photo courtesy: Karni Singh Jasol

The beginning of mechanisation also saw command of the regiment transfer on 07 July 1941 from Lieutenant Colonel Bahadur Singh, who had almost completed his full term in command and was proceeding on retirement, to Lieutenant Colonel G.G. Collyns, 3 Cavalry, who had until that time been attached to the Jodhpur Lancers as SSO.

There began a very busy time for the regiment and for the Training Centre at Jodhpur. It was a complete change, training, tactics and organisation were all different. Many new things had to be learnt and much of what had been learnt had to be forgotten. All ranks that had learnt to ride and look after a horse had now to learn to drive a motor vehicle and to maintain it.

During this process of mechanisation in 1941 the Jodhpur men grudgingly sang, *'Once we learnt to slash with curling Sabres (Tulwar), then they made us thrust with pointing Swords. We have fought the mighty Sirkar's battles from China to France,*

Left: Lieutenant Colonel Bahadur Singh, Commanding Officer Jodhpur Lancers (September 1936 to July 1941). **Right:** A poem written by poet Kishandan in praise of Jodhpur Sardar Rissala while they were serving in Risalpur. The poet says, 'May you go forward and fight for the righteous cause and add fresh lustre to Marwar State and the British Empire'.

Photos courtesy: (left) Shyam Singh Sajjada; (right) Dr Mahendra Singh Nagar

Flanders and the Palestine. We travelled on our horses in a lordly tribal fashion....but all that's changed....and now we play with oil, our fingers sticky, dissecting Carburretor, Cam and Shaft. We find the Garage lingo rather tricky, for Zemindari's been our age-long craft......'

At this time the regiment was inspected by General Sir Archibald Wavell, the newly appointed C-in-C in India.

The process of mechanisation had not been fully completed when, on 20 October 1941, the Regiment was ordered to proceed to Bolarum, Secunderabad, to join the

A silver model of Jodhpur Lancers, Daimler Armoured Car Mk II, presented by Jodhpur Lancers Training Centre to Maharaj Kumar Hanwant Singh on his marriage on 14 February 1943.

Photo courtesy: Umaid Bhawan Palace

Brigadier Zabbar Singh, MBE.
Photo courtesy: Thakur Manohar Singh Bera

19 Indian Division commanded by Major General Smyth, VC, MC, as Divisional Reconnaissance Regiment. It remained at Bolarum for eight months when in July 1942 the regiment was transferred to 20 Division at Trichinopoly, though it was almost immediately transferred again to come directly under Headquarters, Madras District. In August 1942 it was again transferred, this time to the newly formed 25 Indian Division as Divisional Armoured Car Reconnaissance Regiment and was located at Attur at Chinna Salem. Shortly after it got to Chinna Salem, there was some danger of Japanese raids against the south of India, so two squadrons of the regiment were sent to the East Coast watching duty from Cuddalore to Porto Novo (Dhanuskhodi) while the third squadron was moved to Trichinopoly and later also carried out coast watching. In December 1942 the regiment left Poonainallu, where it then was and proceeded to Nanjangud in Mysore State for jungle warfare training. The Squadrons were moved around a number of locations in Southern India and took part in several exercises.

In April 1943 Lieutenant Colonel W.W.A. Loring, 15 Lancers, assumed command of the regiment at the same time as the Marmon Harrington Armoured Cars were exchanged for Humber IIIs and Daimlers.

In January 1944 the 25 Division was ordered to the Arakan under the command of Lord Louis Mountbatten. However, the Jodhpur Lancers were ordered to remain behind at Bangalore as there was no possible role for an Armoured Car Regiment in Jungle warfare. Everybody was very disappointed and Maharaja Umaid Singh of Jodhpur appealed to both Lord Louis and the Viceroy Lord Linlithgow to find an active role for the regiment. Coming under command of 19 Division again, the regiment was ordered to Madras where rumours of a Japanese invasion were rife, but nothing came of it and finally in March 1944 the regiment was ordered to join 'Persia and Iraq Force' (PAI Force).

At this time, Major Shyam Singh was second-in-command, Captain Dhonkal Singh was adjutant and the squadron commanders were Major Kalyan Singh, Major Arjun Singh, Major Surajbhan Singh, and Major Chandan Singh, while Major Sultan Singh was Liaison Officer, 25 Division. Major Shyam Singh later left for Jodhpur to take up a new appointment of Chief Liaison Officer, while Captain Prem Singh and Lieutenant Chhog Singh went back to join the Jodhpur Lancers Training Centre.

On 20 March 1944 the Command of the regiment changed from Lieutenant Colonel Loring to Lieutenant Colonel R.G. Hanmer. On 21 March 1944 orders were received for the Regiment to go overseas. After availing some leave on 11 May 1944 the regiment sailed from Bombay in *H.T. Ekma* and reached Basra on 19 May where it was equipped with Humbers IIIs and IVs, Carriers I.P. and Scout Cars and was detailed to relieve the Poona Horse guarding the Anglo Iranian oilfields.

The handover between the Poona Horse and the Jodhpur Lancers provided an occasion for a reunion amongst the Rajputs and Kaimkhanis of each regiment, as the Poona Horse recruit the majority of their men from Jodhpur state. The regiment joined the PAI Force under the command of General Henry Wilson and later under General Arthur Smith at Bagdad. The PAI Force was a British Army Command established in September 1942 in Baghdad. Its primary role was to secure from land and air attack the oilfields and oil installations in Persia (modern day Iran) and Iraq. Its further role was to ensure the transportation of supplies from Persian Gulf ports through Iraq and Persia to the Soviet Union. The Jodhpur Lancers was the only Armoured Car Recce unit in Iran and it had to cover and guard all the Southern Iranian oil fields and the Russian supply route from Bashra upto Kasvlu. The area extended as far East as Shiraz and Isfahan and the port of Shahpur Bander.

During one training exercise on 08 August 1944 the Jodhpur Lancers lost their senior officer, Major Surajbhan Singh, killed when a vehicle overturned. In August 1944 Lieutenant Colonel Hanmer was invalided to England. At the end of November 1944 the regiment left the Anglo-Iranian oilfields and, at the same time, Lieutenant Colonel E.J.R. Emtage, 6 D.C.O. Lancers, arrived from Italy to assume command, which he then held until the end of the war.

On 28 December 1944 Maharaja Umaid Singh accompanied by Colonel Maharaj Ajit Singh and Captain Hari Singh Kuchaman as ADC visited the unit, interacted with the men and had lunch in the mess with the officers.

During one stay of the unit at Diwaniya on 8 March 1945, the Sheikh gave a dinner party. The mass of food was unbelievable, and included whole sheep,

28 December 1944, Maharaja Umaid Singh with Jodhpur Lancers. Some officers and men are mounted on Daimler armoured cars.
Photo courtesy: Kunwar Aditya Singh Galthani

chickens and fish up to three or four feet in length. The Army Liaison Officer had previously warned officers how to behave at such ceremonies as the Arab Sheikh might take mortal offence at some comparatively trivial act. The regiment served in North Iraq until 20 October 1945, when it left Kermanshah, on transfer to the Middle East Force and served in Palestine, Syria and Lebanon.

Maharaja Umaid Singh having lunch in the Officers Mess.
Photo courtesy Major Sumer Singh Naila (Retd)

The Jodhpur Lancers in Haifa again, in December 1945! But this time they came mounted on their Daimler Recce Cars instead of horses.
Photo courtesy: Karni Singh Jasol

In Palestine, the Israelis were fighting for their independence and were giving the British a lot of trouble. Jodhpur Lancers were moved to a place called Afule on the oil pipeline half way between Haifa and the Jordan River crossing. During this time the Regiment had the opportunity to visit Haifa and it was, of course, of the greatest interest to all ranks of the Regiment to see this place, as it was at Haifa during the Great War of 1914–19 that the Jodhpur Lancers made an undying name for itself, when it carried out a historic mounted charge against the strongly defended Turkish position.

The Jodhpur Lancers relieved the 15/19 Hussars and were attached to the 1 British Division. Their duty was to guard the oil pipeline. The pipeline had been damaged about three to four times in the last six months. The earlier troops had the reputation of being rather ruthless but the Israelis left the Rajput troops, who were neither British nor Muslims, alone in peace! The divisional commander inspected the Jodhpurs about six months later and was very happy that the oil pipeline had not been attacked or damaged in this period. He was shocked to hear that the men were only getting sleep for two nights a week and the balance being spent on night patrol duties. The commander promised to move the Regiment to Beirut for one month's rest.

However, en route to Beirut the regiment was ordered to move further north to Tripoli to evacuate the French troops and French civilians out of Syria. The

Lieutenant Kalyan Singh Ustran, Commanding Officer
Jodhpur Lancers 1946 to 1949.
Photo courtesy: Dr Daulat Singh

Jodhpurs was tasked to cover the coastal road from Latakaria and Northern Syria
to Tripoli and to escort all French convoys. The Syrians were attacking the French
convoys unless protected by the allied troops. This job was completed and the
Jodhpur Lancers were ordered back to India for movement to the Far Eastern
Zone. However, before the Jodhpurs landed back at Bombay the Japanese had
surrendered and the war was over.

The regiment having served in North Iraq, Palestine, Syria and Lebanon, then
returned to its home base at Jodhpur on 21 June 1946, having been out since
1940. The total casualties suffered by the regiment were 15 killed.

21 June 1946 at Rai ka Bagh Railway Station, Jodhpur Lancers inspected by Maharaja Umaid
Singh, along with Lieutenant Colonel Kalyan Singh, on their arrival back from the War.
Photo courtesy: Dr Mahendra Singh Tanwar

Maharaja Umaid Singh taking the salute, as large crowds gather to watch the Jodhpur Lancers march-past at Teejamajis Temple Jodhpur on 21 June 1946. The regiment passed through the town in a festive mood, mounted on Daimler armoured cars, as Jodhpur and British bunting flew overhead.
Photo courtesy: Dr Mahendra Singh Tanwar

21 June 1946: Another view of the Jodhpur Lancers passing through the city, as large crowds gather around them.
Photo Courtesy: Dr Mahendra Singh Tanwar

The General Service Medal 1916 with clasp 'Palestine 1945–48' was awarded to the unit personnel. Captain Girdhari Singh was awarded the MBE on 1 January 1946.

The Victory Medal 1939–45 with a bust of Maharaja Umaid Singh and on the reverse a scene of Mehrangarh Fort with the inscription 'V.E. May 8. V.J. Aug:15 1945' was designed by John Pinches. Similarly Great War Service Medal 1919 with State Coat of Arms and on reverse inscription awarded for services rendered during the Great War 1914–1918 were struck. But both these medals were not issued, perhaps due to the fact that the Britishers discouraged the states from instituting their own medals. The stipulation was that 'the grant of war medals is the exclusive prerogative of the Crown. Should any ruler desire to grant war medals, the proposal will be considered on its merits and if necessary his Majesty's pleasure will be taken.'
Photo courtesy: The author

The Jodhpur Sardar Infantry in the Second World War

The JSI flag.
Photo courtesy:
Mehrangarh Museum Trust

The JSI remained at Jodhpur for the first year of the war. A training company was created for the training of recruits in November 1939. Hard training was the order of the day as occasional rumours did the rounds that the battalion will be sent out of the state, but, like most rumours, they came to nought. However, on 25 September 1940, orders were received for the movement of the battalion to Nowshera, to undergo a period of training before being employed elsewhere. On 26 October 1940 Maharaja Umaid Singh inspected the battalion and gave

Lieutenant Colonel Raoraja Sujjan Singh CO JSI from 09 August 1929 to 30 January 1941 and on the right the Cap badge of JSI, the *cheel* (kite) facing right over the scroll 'Marwar'.
Photos courtesy: Nagina Reddy and Rajat Singh Bhati

a farewell address to all ranks. The regiment left Jodhpur, by two special trains, on 31 October 1940.

The following officers left with the Battalion: Lieutenant Colonel Raoraja Sujjan Singh, CO; Major Jawahir Singh, 2nd-in-Command; Captain Ram Singh; Captain Lajpat Rai; Captain Dhonkal Singh; Lieutenant Umed Ram; Lieutenant Chattar Singh; Lieutenant Gulab Singh; Lieutenant Magni Ram; Lieutenant

The JSI Commandant's epaulette and swagger stick.
Photos courtesy: Rajat Singh Bhati

Left: The JSI shoulder title badge. Right: The collar badges of JSI.
Photos courtesy: (left) Professor (Capt) Ashok Nath, FRGS, Nath Foundation, Sweden; (right) The author

Dungar Singh; 2nd Lieutenant Deep Singh; 2nd Lieutenant Laxman Singh; 2nd Lieutenant Ram Singh (Medical Officer); SCO Gopal and Pehap Singh and Subedar Major Sultan Singh. Lieutenant Colonel F.D. Clarke, 8 Gurkha Rifles, and 2nd Lieutenant P.W.J. Crossland, 15 Punjab, went along as SSOs. The total strength of the battalion was 12 State Officers, two SSOs, two SOCs, 21 Indian Officers, 628 ORs, 56 followers, 10 horses and 32 mules.

The battalion arrived at Nowshera on 03 November 1940 and went into a camp where it was inspected by GOC Peshawar District. On 31 January 1941 Lieutenant Colonel Jawahar Singh assumed the Command of the Regiment vice Lieutenant Colonel Sujjan Singh who proceeded to Jodhpur as Staff Officer to Brigadier R.C. Duncan, Commandant Jodhpur State Forces. On 18 April 1941 the battalion left for Quetta. On 06 June 1941 it entrained and proceeded to Karachi, prior to proceeding overseas.

On 10 June 1941 the battalion embarked at Karachi in two ships *S.S. Devonshire* and *S.S. Neuralia*. It was, of course, the first time most of the men had ever seen the sea, and there was great excitement, and all ranks wondered what adventures lay ahead. The sea was rough soon after leaving port, and the men, unaccustomed to this form of travel, felt the motion badly, and a great number suffered from the seasickness. The ship was sailing under sealed orders, and it was known five days after leaving Karachi that they were on their way to Africa.

On 22 June 1941 they arrived at Massawa in Eritrea, which at this point in time was abominably hot. From Massawa, the battalion travelled in M.T. Lorries to Gura some 40 miles from Massawa and stayed there for three weeks. While here, Maharaja Sawai Man of Jaipur visited the battalion, and dined with the officers and saw the men. From Gura the battalion went to Asmara, the capital of Eritrea, where it was almost entirely employed on guard duties, which were very heavy.

On 08 August Maharaja Umaid Singh accompanied by Colonel Ajit Singh and Major Bishan Singh inspected the battalion. He dined with the men and visited all the installations guarded by men of the battalion, and also saw the other state battalions in the brigade—the Jaipur Guards, the Gwalior Infantry, the Alwar Jai Paltan and the Nabha Akal Infantry. On 29 November 1941 the battalion went back to Massawa where it was involved in guarding about 6,000 Italian Prisoners of War (POWs).

Maharaja Umaid Singh arriving and inspecting JSI at Gura near Massawa, on 08 August 1941.
Photo courtesy: Major Sumer Singh Naila (Retd)

On 02 March 1942 Lieutenant Colonel H.B. Rogers, 5 Maratha Light Infantry assumed the command of the battalion vice Lieutenant Colonel Jawahar Singh who went back to Jodhpur to command the Jodhpur Infantry Training Centre. The battalion held a farewell parade on 02 March 1942 and the men lined the road on either side and heartily cheered Lieutenant Colonel Jawahar Singh as he slowly passed by, while the pipe band played a slow march.

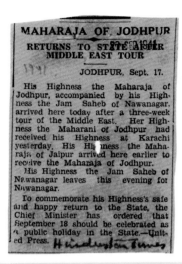

Hindustan Times, 17 September 1941, Maharaja Umaid Singh returns to Jodhpur after a three-weeks tour of the Middle East.
Photo courtesy: The author and Major Sumer Singh Naila (Retd)

Left: Lieutenant Colonel Jawahar Singh, CO JSI from 31 March 1941 to 01 March 1942. Right: Lieutenant Colonel Dhonkal Singh, Commandant 2nd Jodhpur Infantry during 1947–48 and later the last Commandant of JSI from 1950–51.
Photos courtesy: (left) Vikram Singh Rathore Pachranda; (right) Ravi Rathore

On 07 April 1942, after spending 10 months in Eritrea, the battalion (strength of 591 all ranks) embarked by *Prince Badauin* for Egypt. After three weeks stay at Qassassin, near Suez, the battalion moved to Faiyid, close to the Great Bitter Lake. From then on, for the next 13 months the battalion guarded a large (7,000 to 15,000) Italian and later German POW Camp, including guarding of a large Base Ordnance and Supply Depots both at Faiyid and at Tel-el-Kebir and a detachment guarding the airfield at Devasoir. There were many instances

War Bonds were debt securities issued by Government to finance military operations in times of war. Exhortations to buy war loan posters appeared often in Jodhpur accompanied by appeals to patriotism and conscience.
Photo courtesy: Sunilji Laghate

of Germans attempting to escape, but either being caught by our sentries or shot by them. In December 1942 the American troops relieved the battalion from the guard duties at Devasoir airfield. During this time many Indian films like 'Sanskar', 'Shadi', 'Holi', 'Anjan', 'Nirdosh', 'Padosi', 'Garib' and 'Musafir' were shown to all ranks by mobile cinema and were much appreciated by all.

On 24 December 1942, 2nd Lieutenants Madho Singh, Moti Singh, Kishan Singh and Guman Singh joined the battalion from India.

On 12 May 1943 the long period of apprenticeship for the battalion suddenly ended and it was transferred to Syria. The battalion was chosen for an important operational role, and seven independent companies were to be formed immediately, each with two officers and three platoons with a Liaison Officer to accompany these companies. Adventure and excitement lay ahead.

The seven companies had to be ready in less than a fortnight and it involved a lot of training and work. Four companies existed, of course, and the remaining three were formed from the HQ Company and reinforcements. The seven companies of the JSI were numbered from 83 to 89 as under:

- 83 Company— Captain Deep Singh and Lieutenant Moti Singh
- 84 Company— Captain Magni Ram and Lieutenant Nanu Ram
- 85 Company— Captain Dungar Singh and 2nd Lieutenant Guman Singh
- 86 Company— Captain Mohan Ram and Lieutenant Gopal Ram
- 87 Company— Lieutenant Pehap Singh and 2nd Lieutenant Sawai Singh
- 88 Company— Captain Ramcharan Singh and Lieutenant Kishan Singh
- 89 Company— Captain Raiwat Singh and Lieutenant Madho Singh

The JSI men on board a Steamer.
Photo courtesy: Major Sumer Singh Naila (Retd)

Lieutenant Colonel H.B. Rogers, Commanding Officer with Captain Jaithu Singh and Lieutenant Hamir Singh remained at Faiyid, later moving to a camp at Mina just outside Cairo. On 02 June 1943 the companies moved by rail from Faiyid to Aartouz, Syria. Major Ram Singh left with them as liaison officer to form part of No 35 Beach Group commanded by Colonel J.A.E. Ralston. No 35 Beach Group was composed of a small detachment from the Royal Navy, a battalion of the Durham Light Infantry, units of the Royal Army Service Corps and Royal Army Ordnance Corps and a Medical unit. A Beach Group is a very complex formation whose sole aim is to supply and feed an invading force and enable it to fight, until such time as it has been able to capture a port and get it working. The work is highly technical and the preliminary training was carried out in Syria and the final training was completed at the Combined Training Centre at Kabreet in Egypt, and the men learned to handle the actual craft and apparatus that had been designed and produced for this job.

In mid-July the battalion went to a rest camp near Alexandria for three days, and then embarked on the *S.S. Talma* where the battalion disembarked after five days to reach Sfax in Tunisia. From Sfax, it went by train to the North African Combined Training Centre near Bougie in Algeria where Brigadier Duncan and Lieutenant Colonel H.B. Rogers flew in by air and inspected the battalion and wished them luck in the great adventure before them. The battalion again trained for a couple of weeks and was moved to divisional concentration area in Bizerta. The battalion was still in the dark as to its destination, the beaches of Salerno in Italy. The battalion had its first experience of a heavy air raid here, which lasted for two hours, and the battalion was lucky to escape with only three casualties. The battalion then marched to the assembly area where the companies were attached to the various brigades of the division, which formed part of the landing force.

They eventually found themselves in eight different Landing Ship Tanks (L.S.T's) and Landing Craft Tanks (L.C.T's) in which they were to sail to Italy. On the third day after embarkation the impressive convoy marched in waves. The ships were American-manned and neither side understood the other's language, but smiles sufficed. On 08 September 1943 the convoy was attacked by an air raid and U-boats where one ship sank and one U-boat was destroyed by us. The battalion arrived in Salerno Bay just after midnight on the night of September 8/9, the naval bombardment started according to plan and the assaulting troops went off and landed at 0330 hours, and a quarter of an hour later, the first success signal went up indicating that they held the beach. There was a lot of shelling, chiefly 88mm and machine gun fire from the ground, but almost all of it went just over the heads of troops on the actual beach, 'Red Beach', as it was called. Beach Group HQ and some other elements went ashore before dawn and at 0645 hours Major Ram Singh with Major Blakeman who commanded the Forward Maintenance Centre, set foot on the shores of Europe's mainland. Despite shelling, machine gun fire from ground and air, and bombing, the JSI landed safely without any casualties. Major Ram Singh was awarded the DSO.

For the next 17 days, all companies were working at top pressure and the tonnage put through the beaches was nearly three times what had been estimated could be cleared. Captain Dungar Singh and 60 of his men took ammunition, supplies and water to forward companies in some particularly steep and difficult country and brought back casualties and so on for 48 hours, with little food and water and no rest, under constant fire. The divisional and brigade commander both wrote thanking the battalion for the valuable work that party had done. Captain Dungar Singh was awarded the MC. By 27 September 1943, Salerno had been captured and was beginning to function as a port when the JSI companies were moved to Salerno town. So ended the historic landing of the Fifth Army at Salerno. The JSI had played its part and a not unimportant one, and it is believed that the men of the battalion were the first Indian troops to land on the mainland of Europe. The Fifth Army continued to advance, and the Beach Group, which had helped to put it ashore and maintain it there, was left behind.

The C-in-C in India sent the following letter to Maharaja Umaid Singh in Jodhpur, on 17 November 1943: 'I have just read the most stirring account of the behaviour in action at Salerno of the Jodhpur Infantry. I know you must be as proud as I was to read of their courage and endurance. Please accept my congratulations and best wishes for their future.'

No-SF/3552 Major Ram Singh, DSO, CO, JSI from 06 March 1946 to 28 May 1949 and No-SF/3555 Captain Dungar Singh, MC, CO, JSI from 29 May 1949 to 31 March 1950 (both DSO and MC gazetted on 24 August 1944). Major Ram Singh became the first State Officer to have received this distinction. Dungar Singh's father Rissaldar Mohabat Singh served Jodhpur Lancers in China and the Great War. He was rewarded with a *Jagir* at the village of Utamber and a big bungalow at Jodhpur.
Photos courtesy: Ajit Singh Hariadana and Rajat Singh Bhati

Maharaja Umaid Singh replied as under:

> I am in receipt of your kind letter of congratulations of 17 November 1943, about the Jodhpur Infantry's baptism of fire on European soil. I am naturally very proud to learn that they have upheld the traditions of my State Forces, and I hope they will continue to maintain this standard. On behalf of myself and my Forces, I take this opportunity of expressing our thanks for the interest Your Excellency has always taken in my troops and I will, on the first opportunity, convey the contents of your letter to the Jodhpur Infantry.

One DSO, one MC, one MBE, three Military Medals (MM) and 17 Mentions-in-Despatches were approved to Officers and Indian Other Ranks of the battalion for gallantry during the landing at Salerno. Major Ram Singh became the first man ever to receive a DSO amongst the ISF troops.

Citation of Major Ram Singh—DSO
Salerno Beaches 09–27 September 1943

He was Liaison Officer in Command, of temporary Corps of this unit in 35 Beach, and he performed exceptionally fine work throughout the whole of this difficult period. His cool courage, and his constant cheerfulness were a wonderful example to all and were unquestionably largely responsible for the excellent work of the corps. In particular he was untiring in visiting troops who were under heavier fire than usual, regardless of his personal safety and he thus maintained cheerfulness of troops, which is so much appreciated by Indian troops.

Citation of Captain Dungar Singh—MC
Salerno. 22-25 September 1943

With 60 men of his company, he was sent to carry ammunition and supplies from Battalion Headquarters to the forward companies of a British unit, which was closely engaged. The country was precipitous, and was mostly under enemy observation and mortar and machine gun fire. This officer himself reconnoitred routes for his parties, and throughout displayed great personal courage and fine leadership, earning praise from Corps, Division and Brigade Commanders for his own and his company's work in exceptionally difficult circumstances.

During October 1943, the seven companies of the JSI remained at Salerno, guarding the docks, the railway station, prisoners of war cage and the 'Banka da Italia'. Early in November, however, all companies were transferred to Eastern Italy. All this time, HQ's and the remnants of the battalion had remained in Egypt but on 09 December 1943 they joined the rest at Barletta. About a month later, battalion HQ moved from Barletta to a large five-storied country house near Andria, which was particularly well furnished—long mirrors, dressing tables, canopied beds, sofas etc, were there in abundance. A long avenue lined by poplar trees led to the house, and there was a beautiful garden. The whole place was most comfortable. It was at once named 'Jodhpur House' and the battalion flag was hoisted on the roof. Here the officers used to entertain the Area HQ nearby, and on Saturday evenings the battalion pipe band played outside.

Towards the end of May 1944, the battalion left Italy and by 01 June 1944, it was collected in Sicily under the orders of the Commander 56 Area, No 1 District. On 02 June 1944 Lieutenant Colonel H.B. Rogers handed over the command of the battalion to Lieutenant Colonel C.A.S. Melville, 6 Rajputana Rifles and left Sicily for Egypt to return to India. The officers and the men had the most enjoyable time here with plenty of *Shikar* and visit to clubs in the evenings and many learnt to dance with Italian girls. As one officer put it, 'some of the men were living in an age of romance, and many of them had Italian girlfriends, who used to mend and wash their clothes; in fact they were living in a land of dreams.'

In October 1944 a warning order was received for the battalion to return to Italy and in end of November 1944 the battalion left Sicily to join the 10 Indian Division. Unfortunately Lieutenant Colonel C.A.S. Melville had to go into hospital at this time and he was unable to accompany the battalion and Major Ram Singh, DSO officiated as CO. On 01 December 1944 the battalion finally joined 10 Indian Infantry Brigade under the 10 Indian Division at Forli, a small town on the Adriatic coastal plain. On 10 December Maharaja Umaid Singh flew in to see the battalion and the 54 (Jodhpur) GPT Company, RIASC. During the whole of December 1944 there was heavy snowfall and severe winter conditions prevailed. During this time the battalion occupied the forward frontage of the brigade. On 11 February 1945 the battalion moved to area near Florence on the edge of the Sillaro Valley and remained here till relieved by the 2/4 Gurkha Rifles on 22 March. Enemy shelling during the period became an everyday experience. A considerable amount of patrolling was done by all companies, bringing back useful information and prisoners as the German patrolling in the sector was very active. The battalion received a letter of congratulations from the divisional and brigade commander for dealing with enemy patrols resulting in a good bag of POWs.

On 22 March 1945 the battalion moved out of the front line to the small town of Castel Del Rio in Firenzuola valley for a rest period, where an Indian film was screened and hot baths and change of clothing were produced by the Divisional Bath unit. On couple of occasions, the pipe band, now only five pipers and three drummers strong, played Retreat in the square. On 27 March Lieutenant Colonel Ram Singh, DSO, was given a warm send off when he left the battalion for India, having handed over the command to Major G.A.C. Maunsell.

On 02 April 1945 the battalion relieved the 1 Durham Light Infantry in the La Strada position and became responsible for the patrolling of the brigade sector. Officers took out fighting patrols and there were a number of clashes, both with enemy patrols and with the enemy in battle positions. Jemadar Parbhu Singh while carrying Platoon raid on Point 362 was awarded the MC for his leadership on 06 April 1945.

Citation of Jemadar Parbhu Singh–MC

On the night of 5/6 April 1945, Jemadar Parbhu Singh was in Command of the No 2 Platoon, 'A' Company, detailed to raid the enemy position on Point-362. In accordance with the orders, he led his platoon through the forward base established by No 1 Platoon towards the enemy position, across ground previously unreconnoitred by him. Owing to the skill with which Jemadar Parbhu Singh led his platoon, it arrived within 25–30 yards of the enemy position before it was discovered. Owing to the difficult nature of the ground, the advance of the platoon had been considerably delayed, nevertheless, in full knowledge of the fact that the approach of daylight would make his withdrawal extremely difficult, this VCO [Viceroy Commissioned Officer] continued the advance until the platoon was discovered. During the ensuing fight, he maintained excellent control under extremely heavy fire, both from the flanks and front. When it became obvious that the position was strongly held by the enemy, he, in accordance with the orders, withdrew his platoon, taking with him three casualties, through heavy fire from artillery, mortars and automatic

SF-3778, Jemadar Parbhu Singh, MC.
On the right is the formation sign of 10
Indian Infantry Division—a black square
crossed by a saltire of red from bottom
left to top right, over blue as worn by
Jemadar Parbhu Singh on his left sleeve.
Photo courtesy: The author

*weapons. The successful conclusion of this raid, designed to test the enemy strength, was
due in a great measure to the coolness, courage and leadership of this VCO.*

On 02 May 1945 the announcement of the cessation of hostilities in Italy was
received. On 08 May a parade was held to announce Victory in Europe Day and
was followed by thanksgiving prayers and in the evening a *Bara Khana* was held.
On 09 May 1945 Major General D. Reid, DSO, MC, GOC 10 Indian Division
inspected the battalion on parade and said that the battalion had gained an
excellent name for itself in the division. On 10 May the battalion left for Taranto
and, on reaching there, further moved to Middle East Force on 20 May as POW
escorts for a large party of German prisoners. On 25 May the battalion was

*Maharaja Umaid Singh, Maharaj Kunwar Hanwant Singh, Brigadier Duncan and Donald Field on
the arrival of the JSI at Jodhpur on 2 August 1945.*
Photo courtesy: The author

02 August 1945, Maharaja Umaid Singh welcoming his troops back to Jodhpur.
Photo courtesy: The author

concentrated at 'F' Camp Mina near Cairo, awaiting its turn to return to India.

On 19 July 1945 the battalion left camp and it embarked for India in *HMT Orduna* on 20 July 1945, in company with the Sawai Man Guards of the Jaipur Sate Forces. The battalion arrived in Bombay on 29 July 1945. The battalion arrived in two batches in Jodhpur, on 2 and 5 August 1945, and they received a rousing reception. The station was specially decorated for the occasion and Maharaja Umaid Singh; Maharaj Kumar Hanwant Singh; Lieutenant Colonel G.V.B. Williams, Political Agent, Western Rajputana States; Lieutenant Colonel Sir Donald Field, the Chief Minister; Brigadier R.C. Duncan; the State Ministers and all the senior civil officers were at the station to welcome the battalion on its arrival. A strong detachment of the RAF was drawn up on the platform and the state band played incidental music. After the battalion had detrained, His Highness shook hands with all the officers and then he, accompanied by Brigadier Duncan, walked down the line of the whole battalion. (Lieutenant Colonel Donald Field took office as Chief Minister of Jodhpur on 02 May 1935 and was the last of the British Raj officials to leave Jodhpur in 1947).

Later Maharaja Umaid Singh took the salute from an armoured carrier outside the station as the battalion marched past him with the battalion pipe band in

The JSI men marching to the camp.
Photo courtesy: The author

front. The whole route from the station to the camp, a distance of about 3 miles was lined by troops of the Jodhpur Lancers Training Centre, Jodhpur Infantry Training Centre and the 3 Jodhpur Infantry.

A special camp with electric lights and all facilities had been prepared for the battalion and on its arrival it was entertained to a sumptuous meal by the Jodhpur Infantry Training Centre and the following day by the Jodhpur Lancers Training Centre.

After an absence of over four years, the JSI had returned home covered with honour. The unit had been to many countries—Eritrea, Egypt, Syria, Algeria, Tunisia, Sicily and Italy. It had fought alongside British, Canadian, American, Polish and Italian troops. Wherever they had been, the officers and men had made friends and were liked and respected. They had seen the beautiful cities of Rome, Florence, and Naples and enjoyed the lovely countryside of Italy, Sicily, and Algeria. They had experienced the bitter cold of Italy in the winter and the intense heat of Massawa in the summer. During this long period of absence the JSI had gained a splendid name for itself and worthily upheld the great military traditions of the Jodhpur State.

The Maharaja entertained the whole battalion to a meal at the Umaid Bhawan palace on two nights, with half the battalion coming each night. On their arrival, Maharaja Umaid Singh shook hands with every man in the battalion and later

The men of the JSI were invited to Umaid Bhawan Palace for dinner after their arrival from the war. Maharaja Umaid Singh (extreme right) and Brigadier Duncan (in uniform) next to him are seen.
Photo courtesy: Colonel Devpal Singh Rathore (Retd)

walked among them and chatted with the men and wished them all a happy leave, which they all so richly deserved.

In connection with the celebrations of the V-J Day, 16 and 17 August 1945 were observed as public holidays throughout the state as the news of the Japanese surrender reached the public in Jodhpur. On 09 September 1945 Brigadier R.C. Duncan, Commandant of the Jodhpur State Forces was promoted to the rank of Major General in the Jodhpur State Forces.

The total battle casualties suffered by the battalion were—killed 75 and wounded 84, including five officers (including 2 and 3 Jodhpur Infantry).

2 Jodhpur Infantry

The unit was organised as a half battalion in June 1940 for internal security duty so that the JSI could be free for duty outside the state. It was raised to full battalion strength in September 1940 and designated as the 2 Jodhpur Infantry and it comprised of an HQs, two companies of Rajputs and one each of Jats

Left: 2 Jodhpur Infantry shoulder title badge. **Right:** Lieutenant Colonel S.F. Martin commanded the battalion for over three years from 1942 to 1945.
Photo courtesy: (left) Professor (Capt) Ashok Nath, FRGS, Nath Foundation, Sweden; (right) The author

and Kaimkhanis. Major Heer Singh was appointed the Commandant of the battalion and a nucleus of officers obtained from the Sardar Infantry and a few retired officers. Subedar Moti Singh who won a IOM and IDSM with the Jodhpur Lancers in the Great War took re-employment with the unit after retirement from the Lancers. There was no difficulty in obtaining recruits as men and boys poured into Jodhpur from the countryside to enlist in the new battalion. Captain Madho Singh, Birma Ram and Mamdu Khan were the Company Commanders and 2nd Lieutenant Mohan Ram was the Adjutant of the battalion.

Training continued without interruption in the first half of 1941 and in autumn 1941 Maharaja Umaid Singh offered the services of the battalion in British India and also offered to raise another battalion to take its place as a state service unit. The Viceroy gratefully accepted the offer, and on 11 December 1941 orders were received for the move of the battalion to Allahabad, United Provinces, for internal security duty. Lieutenant Colonel S.F. Martin, 15 Punjab, was appointed to Command the battalion on its arrival at Allahabad.

On 29 December 1941 the 2 Jodhpur Infantry was inspected by Maharaja Umaid Singh before its departure and he gave an inspiring farewell address. The following officers were on the strength of the battalion on its arrival at Allahabad:
Lieutenant Colonel S.F. Martin—CO, Captain Birma Ram, Captain Madho Singh, Captain Mamdu Khan, Captain Chhattar Singh, Captain Madan Singh, Lieutenant Daulat Singh and 2nd Lieutenant Karim Khan. Captain D.J.H. Roche, 9 Jat regiment, was the SSO while the Subedar Major was Sheodana Ram.

Brigadier Magnay, the Area Commander, visited the battalion on 13 January 1942

Group Photo of 2nd Jodhpur Infantry 1942. Seated left to right on chairs Captain Moti Singh, Lieutenant Khanji, Captain Mamdu Khan, Major Beerma Ram, Brigadier R.C. Duncan, Lieutenant Colonel Heer Singh, Major Mohan Ram, Captain Madho Singh (son of Lieutenant Colonel Aman Singh Jodha), Captain Daulat Singh, Captain Malam Singh. Standing 2 and 5 from right Subedar Achal Singh and Subedar Sher Singh.
Photo courtesy: Lakh Singh Hapa

and Brigadier Duncan too visited the battalion from Jodhpur during this time. In end-February 1942 orders were received for the move of the battalion to Yol POW camp, Kangra Valley, Punjab, and the battalion left Allahabad by troop special train on 11 March and took over guard duties at No 28 Italian prisoners of war camp, Yol. About this time Captain Madho Singh, Chhatter Singh and Birma Ram and 2nd Lieutenant Karim Khan returned to the State and were replaced by Major Gulab Singh and 2nd Lieutenant Doodha Ram.

The battalion carried out excellent work while at Yol and several unsuccessful attempts at escape made by the Italian POWs were foiled. Various officers inspected the battalion during October–November 1942 including Lieutenant General H.B.D. Wilcox, GOC-in-Chief, Central Command, Lieutenant General Sir F. Gwatkin, Military Adviser-in-Chief, Indian States Forces and Major General H.T.D. Hickman, Commanding Lahore District.

On 10 January 1943 orders were received for the move of the battalion to Barrackpore, near Calcutta. The battalion proceeded to Pathankot on 04 February 1943 and entrained there for Barrackpore, arriving at its destination on 09 February in relief of the 4/3 Madras Regiment. On arrival at its destination the battalion was spread over Western Bengal where US airfields were located from which bombers flew to and from Burma on operations. After few months in October 1943 the battalion was assigned the work of escort duty, which it continued to do for the next few years. Parties of the battalion travelled all over India to places as far apart as Karachi, Colombo, Manipur and Lahore and this did much to improve their education and broaden their outlook. The battalion experienced its first air raid on 05 December 1943 when about 43 Japanese planes raided Calcutta and dropped bombs, mainly in the dock area where a detachment from the battalion was stationed.

During February 1944 the battalion was inspected by Lieutenant General Sir A.G.O.M. Mayne, GOC-in-Chief, Eastern Command. In April 1944 Major Dhonkal Singh joined the battalion on permanent transfer from the JSI as 2-in-Command and on 16 April 1944 Brigadier Duncan visited the battalion from Jodhpur. At this time the battalion had the good fortune of receiving a large quantity of 'Victory Liquor' from Jodhpur.

On 03 November 1944 the C-in-C, General Sir Claude Auchinleck, inspected the battalion and he expressed his satisfaction with all that he saw. During 1945 the battalion was given the duty of supplying escorts to parties of Japanese POWs on their way to Central India.

On 04 July 1945 Lieutenant Colonel Ram Singh, DSO was appointed as Commanding Officer on the posting out of Lieutenant Colonel S.F. Martin who had been appointed as Commandant, Canteen Stores Depot, Delhi. The battalion finally returned to the state on 06 March 1946.

3 Jodhpur Infantry

The unit was raised on 01 December 1941 when Maharaja Umaid Singh's offer to deploy 2 Jodhpur Infantry to British India was accepted. Lieutenant Colonel Heer Singh, who had handed over command of 2 Infantry when it left the state,

Lieutenant Colonel Rao Bahadur Heer Singh who Commanded 3 Jodhpur Infantry from 1941 to 1946.
Photo courtesy: Major J.S. Deora

was appointed to raise and command the new battalion.

As with the 2 Jodhpur Infantry it comprised of a headquarter, two companies of Rajputs and one each of Jats and Kaimkhanis. In April 1942 serious disturbances broke out in neighbouring Sind Province when Hur rebels attacked the railway. In May, detachments of 3 Jodhpur Infantry were detailed to guard the railway and its associated stations, and to post armed guards on the trains running from Jodhpur to Hyderabad. These detachments remained on railway duty until March 1944. Meanwhile, in August 1942, an RAF station was opened at Jodhpur and 3 Jodhpur Infantry was given the job of guarding it. In January 1945 this duty was extended to another airfield at Salawas. The battalion was disbanded with effect from 15 August 1946.

JSI in Hongkong 1945-1947

A few days after the arrival of the JSI from the War in August 1945, all men of the battalion dispersed for their homes on some well-deserved leave. While they were enjoying their well-earned war leave, information was received at Jodhpur that the battalion had been selected to join the 150 Infantry Brigade for overseas assignment to Hong Kong, China. In 1945, the 150 Infantry Brigade was re-formed from a training brigade that included three state battalions and served as

The JSI in Hong Kong, December 1946.Standing left to right: Captain Megh Singh, Major Jethu Singh, Captain Sawai Singh, Captain Dr Ram Singh, Major Bush, Major Ramcharan Singh, Captain Ganesh Ram, Lieutenant Gumana Ram. Seated: Major Deep Singh, Maharaj Ajit Singh, Lieutenant Colonel Gillan, Maharaja Umaid Singh, Major Dungar Singh, Major Keshri Singh and Hari Singh Kuchaman.
Photo courtesy: Rajat Singh Bhati

Maharaja Sawai Man Singh of Jaipur (standing centre with cap in hand) with JSI officers in Hongkong 1946.
Photo courtesy: Rajat Singh Bhati

the garrison of Hong Kong.

On 13 October 1945 the battalion was again seen off on parade by Maharaja Umaid Singh and he later presented 'Mentioned-in-Dispatches' certificates to all those who had been awarded for their distinguished service while in Italy.

The JSI under the command of Lieutenant Colonel G.A.C. Maunsell left Jodhpur by special train on the night of 25 October 1945 and it detrained at Bowringpet, near Bangalore, and joined the 150 Infantry Brigade. Training was taken in hand almost at once and a large part of the battalion proceeded to Cuddalore for jungle warfare training. On 02 December 1945 the battalion with the 150 Infantry Brigade left Bowringpet for overseas. It embarked at Madras and sailed via Singapore for Hong Kong, China.

While in Hong Kong they were visited by Maharaja Umaid Singh as also by Maharaja Sawai Man Singh of Jaipur. The unit was mostly involved in garrison duties.

The JSI finally returned to Jodhpur on 02 February 1947. Incidentally the Jodhpur Lancers too had returned to Jodhpur on the same date, 02 February 1920, after the Great War. However, after its return to Jodhpur, on 18 May 1947 all Jat Personnel (three officers and 500 men) were arbitrarily discharged, without the usual Court of Inquiry and Court Martial proceedings, on some grievances. However they were subsequently taken back in July 1947.

On 28 January 1946 Maharaja Umaid Singh was created as an Honorary ADC to

King George VI. He also received the 1939–45 Burma, Africa and Italy Stars and the Defence Medal.

1946: The Army Cup and 150 Indian Infantry Brigade Hockey Tournament winners JSI, in Hongkong. Standing extreme right is Major Dungar Singh, MC, the team Captain. The players wear the Jodhpur logo of double *cheel* on their shirts.
Photo courtesy: Dr Jagat Singh Bhati

Jodhpur's contribution to the Victory. The booklet lists some of the contributions by the Jodhpur State Forces in the Second World War.
Photo courtesy: Mehrangarh Museum Trust

09 June 1947—Death of Maharaja Umaid Singh

Maharaja Umaid Singh, father of modern Jodhpur, died on 09 June 1947 of a ruptured appendix. On 06 June he went for a tiger shoot to Danta (near Mount Abu) but had to rush back to Mount Abu on 07 June suffering from severe abdominal pains. Colonel Hayward, the Principal Medical Officer Jodhpur, was immediately summoned over the telephone to Abu from Jodhpur. On 08 June early in the morning Colonel Hayward with Maharaj Kumar Hanwant Singh arrived at Mount Abu. Colonel Hayward diagnosed inflammation of the gall bladder and ordered penicillin treatment. The Maharaja's condition did not noticeably improve and on the evening of 8 June Colonel Hayward said that an emergency operation would probably have to be performed that night and that His Highness was unlikely to survive it. The operation was performed at 5 AM on 09 June and although His Highness rallied well, he died suddenly about midday; the cause of death, according to Colonel Hayward, being 'general peritonitis following perforation'.

He was 44 years old.

The remains of His Highness reached Jodhpur by special train at 11:30 PM on 9 June. At 06:30 AM on 10 June the cortege left the Palace with full military ceremony and proceeded via the Secretariat and Paota to Deokund near the fort, where the cremation ceremony was performed at a spot adjoining his ancestors' tombs. All offices and shops were closed as a mark of respect and a large crowd joined the procession and the troops of Jodhpur State Forces lined up the city streets for one last time.

It was only three days before his death, that the Viceroy Lord Mountbatten had announced India would become independent at midnight on 14 August 1947.

The End Game—Integration of the Jodhpur State Forces with the Indian Army

With the merger of the Princely States with the Indian Union after independence, the future of numerous state forces hung in the balance. All the princes were rewarded with privy purses and token marks of sovereignty. Maharaja Man Singh of Jaipur became Rajpramukh (ceremonial head of state) of the newly formed state of Rajasthan, and Jaipur city was selected as its capital.

According to the terms of the individual instruments of accession signed, in August 1947, by the rulers of the different states of Rajputana, their respective States

Maharaja Umaid Singh in Jodhpur Lancers khakhi uniform with his horse in 1939 during a outdoor exercise in Jodhpur.
Photo Courtesy: Mehrangarh Museum Trust

Forces had been excluded from the scope of the term 'Defence', which along with Foreign Affairs and Communication, had been handed over by the princely states to the new Government of India. As such, the various State Forces had remained under the authority of their respective rulers. The authority to raise, maintain and administer such State Forces was vested exclusively in the Rajpramukh, subject to any directions or instructions that might be given by the Government of India. The charge of commanding the integrated states forces was to be given to an officer of the Indian Army, specifically lent to the Rajpramukh for this purpose.

The new designations came into force with effect from 26 January 1950, when HQ Rajasthan Command became HQ Rajasthan Force; HQ Jaipur Area became HQ Jaipur Brigade; HQ Jodhpur Area became HQ Jodhpur Brigade and HQ Bikaner Area became HQ Bikaner Brigade.

In view of financial stringency, the princely states started retrenchment of their employees of various departments, including their armies for the 1948–49 Budget. Thus Marwar practically halved its army-related budget from Rs 65 lakhs to Rs 35 lakhs, retrenching 1,600 of its army personnel (1,000 Rajputs and 600 Jats). The Government of India was asked to consider absorbing the retrenched 1,600 soldiers in the Indian Army.

Officers of the Jodhpur Brigade February 1950. **Seated left to right:** Major Bhopal Singh, Lieutenant Colonel Dhonkal Singh, Lieutenant Colonel Zorawar Singh, Brigadier Bagh Singh, MBE, Major General U.C. Dubey, Lieutenant Colonel Dungar Singh, MC, Major Mod Singh, Major Ramdan Singh, Major P.R. Badve. **Standing 1st row:** Captain Narendra Bahadur, Captain S.K. Banerjee, Captain Prem Singh, Captain K. Sanwat Singh, Major Shyam Singh, Captain Baxu Khan, CaptainTej Singh, Major Raghuvendra Singh, Captain Ram Singh, Captain Megh Singh, Major Mohan Singh **Standing 2 row:** 2nd Lieutenant Partap Singh, 2nd Lieutenant Hari Singh, 2nd Lieutenant Kalu Singh, Lieutenant Chhatar Singh, Captain Sanwat Singh, 2nd Lieutenant Anop Singh, Lieutenant Ramsurat Singh and Major Kheem Singh.
Photo Courtesy: Colonel Devpal Singh Rathore (Retd)

However, in 1949 the Government of India took over all the military forces of the erstwhile Princely States and it framed a complicated 60-point system regarding the absorption of the officers from the States Forces into the Indian Army, and deciding their individual seniority, rank and regiment. In due course the entire procedure of either, retrenchment and pensioning off, or integration into the Indian Army, was complete and 69 selected ISF units were transferred to become part the Indian Army in April 1951.

The problems in merging and amalgamating armies that had their own long traditions was complex. Many issues like dealing with seniority, matters relating to pension and allowances to ex-soldiers, merging commands and posting troops and officers to other units, disbanding some state units and transferring the soldiers elsewhere and so forth. It was a tedious process that required meticulous attention. In the end, the war experience with their old, formidable, reputation saw several officers of the various former State Forces attain positions of seniority and authority in India's armed forces. Two of its officers Major Shaitan Singh and Lieutenant Colonel Tarapore of the Jodhpur and the Hyderabad State Forces respectively went on to win the Param Vir Chakra while serving with the 13 Kumaon and the 17 Poona Horse respectively after Independence.

Major Shaitan Singh, PVC, started his military career in 1947, when he joined the Durga Horse of the earstwhile Jodhpur State as officer cadet after finishing his schooling from Chopasani School and graduation from Jaswant College, Jodhpur, in 1947. He was an outstanding football player.

He was commissioned after passing out from Officers Training School, Poona, where he underwent training from 26 August 1947 to 31 July 1949. He then served with Umed Kotah Infantry from 01 August 1949 to 31 March 1951 and 20 Rajput (JSI) from 01 April 1951 to 24 May 1954. On 25 May 1954, after receiving his permanent regular commission in the Indian Army, he joined

Shaitan Singh standing second from left with winners of Labh Shankar All India Football Challenge Cup in 1942 with boys of Chopasani School, Jodhpur. Seated in the centre is the Principal Mr A.P. Cox, from New Zealand. He was Principal of Chopasni School from 1927 to 1947. He never married and died in 1972. Football continued to be a very popular game in Jodhpur till the 1950s.
Photo courtesy: Narpat Singh Bhati, Son of Major Shaitan Singh, PVC

Major Shaitan Singh, PVC, was born on 01 December 1924, at Banasar, near Phalodi in Jodhpur District. His father Lieutenant Colonel Hem Singh, OBI, served with the Jodhpur Lancers in the Great War, where he was wounded.
Photo Courtesy: Narpat Singh Bhati

13 Kumaon Regiment where he was killed in action on 18 November 1962 and was awarded the Param Vir Chakra (Posthumously).

However, aspects like the criteria for deciding the seniority created unrest among the officers, for the Government of India considered the Indian Army superior to the State Forces in the matters of training and equipment, and many of those absorbed into the Indian Army were downgraded. Thus they were aggrieved at the manner in which they were downgraded. The matter was taken to heart by both, the states which were integrated and the personnel thus affected. Many officers and the men from the Jodhpur State Forces were thus resigned to their fate but felt content that they had done their duty and been faithful to their salt.

State Forces Colours on Parade

All the King's Colours, which till 26 January 1950 were carried on parade by units of the Indian Army, were laid up with great ceremony at the National Defence Academy, Dehradun, and General K.M. Cariappa similarly insisted on laying up of the Colours of Indian State Forces as well, with effect from 01 April 1951, when all the Indian State Forces were completely integrated with the Indian Army. These colours now proudly decorate the hallowed Chetwode hall of the Indian Military Academy at Dehradun.

April 1951, the Jodhpur Lancers men proceeding on premature retirement!
Photo Courtesy: The author

Appeal to Prime Minister Nehru by Raj Pramukh Maharana Bhopal Singh of Udaipur Regarding Marwar and Mewar State Forces

On 12 April 1951 the Maharana of Udaipur, as Raj Pramukh, made an emotional appeal to Mr N. Gopalaswami Ayyangar, Minister of States and to Prime Minister Jawaharlal Nehru that, '...if some unit bearing the name of Mewar be kept in the Indian Army of the future.' He also conveyed that Maharaja of Jodhpur has conveyed their heartfelt anxiety over the disbandment of all the units of Jodhpur Forces.

> To now have no regular unit bearing the name of Marwar or Jodhpur or any connection with the State seems to me almost a sacrilege.

> To mention only one unit, of all the Indian State Forces Units, the Sardar Rissala has a history second to none. Therefore, it will be in the fitness of

things if at least the identity of this unit is kept up in our Armoured Corps. I hope the above points will be settled in keeping with our sentiments. In this connection I have also spoken to General Cariappa during his recent visit here.

On 13 May 1951, Prime Minister Nehru wrote to Sardar Baldev Singh, Defence Minister,

'What have you finally decided about Mewar and Jodhpur? In order to remind you of this matter, I am sending in original the letter of the Maharana of Udaipur written to me. I should like to know what has been done in regard to the various points he has raised. I hope that you will be able to go, as far as possible, to meet his wishes.

On 17 May 1951, in reply to Prime Minister Nehru, the Defence Minister Sardar Baldev Singh wrote,

We have already decided to retain the Mewar Infantry about which the Maharana was very anxious. According to strict principles the Mewar Infantry would have disappeared, but because of the traditions we decided to make an exception in its favour. We have also decided to retain the Jodhpur Sardar Infantry. The result of this is that Jaipur, Jodhpur, Udaipur and Bikaner will each have one Infantry unit in the integrated army and it cannot be stated that any particular state has been unfavorably treated.

As regards Jodhpur, as I have already mentioned, we are retaining the Jodhpur Infantry. The only other unit about whose reduction the Maharaja of Jodhpur was anxious is Jodhpur Lancers. I understand that the Maharaja of Jodhpur had a discussion in the matter with the Chief of the General Staff and he is now satisfied that it is not possible to retain this unit as it is. It is a Mechanised unit trained on an obsolete type of armoured car known as 'Stag hound' and there would be no justification for retaining such a unit. The personnel belonging to the unit who are suitable will, however, all be absorbed in other units. We have been considering also a suggestion that the name of Jodhpur Lancers may be retained, by amalgamating it with the 'Kacchawa Horse' and calling the amalgamated unit as Jodhpur/ Kachawa Lancers. I understand that the Maharaja of Jodhpur would be happy with this arrangement. The suggestion is now being formally put to the Raj Pramukh.

As a result of screening of personnel by Selection Boards, etc., and the decision to reduce the strength of the army by 50,000 during 1951, it was impossible to retain all the old state forces units. In Rajasthan the number of men who had been declared as fit for absorption could make only four Infantry Units. Strictly

An officer of Jodhpur Fort Guard stands behind Maharajkumar Gaj Singh seated on the left with his father Maharaja Hanwant Singh, for the very last time on 22 March 1951 during the Holi festival in Jodhpur Fort. As after 01 April 1951 the Jodhpur State Forces ceased to exist. Maharaja Hanwant Singh died in an air crash on 26 January 1952.
Photo Courtesy: The author

according to some suitable principles it was decided that in Rajasthan the following 4 units could be retained—The Jaipur Infantry, Sadul Infantry (Bikaner), Jodhpur Sardar Infantry and the Kotah Umed Infantry. But in view of the past history of the Mewar state it was decided that one unit of the Mewar State Forces should be retained in place of the Kotah Infantry.

The Story of the Unfinished Memorial to the Jodhpur Lancers

In October 1951 the Jodhpur Lancers under process of closing down were attached with Staff Duties Directorate in Army HQs at New Delhi. During this time a proposal was mooted by the Officers and men of the Jodhpur Lancers vide a Demi Official (DO) letter No. 197006A(SD), dated 15 October 1951, for raising of a memorial in the memory of the Jodhpur Lancers. The DO letter read,

> 'The brightest historical phase where the Regiment distinguished its name with all battle glory and valour in conquering the HAIFA Fort in PALESTINE should be revealed in a memorial of stone/metal to this effect

be erected giving the shape of the memorial which is in PALESTINE and in front of the residential mansion of the Prime Minister of our country. This is the heart felt desire of all the serving and ex-officers and men of the Regiment.

The photo on p. 294 will give a better idea and pictorial view for this purpose. The DO letter further says that,

> the selection of a site for such a memorial is NOT an easy task. It will NOT only reveal and commemorate the history of the Regiment but will also serve as an ideal symbol of deeds in the country for the coming generations of all castes and creeds. This unique memorial will be seen and venerated by millions. Therefore the members of different committees and all others who are interested in this are requested to spare no effort in a cause so noble, dear and fascinating to the hearts of all of us.

The likely sites for this memorial as proposed by the Regimental Durbar were listed as under:
1. Near Sir Pratap Singh Ji's statue in the courts
2. Sojati Gate
3. Railway Station
4. Umaid Garden
5. In front of Jodhpur Lancers Mess
6. Cross road Jodha Squadron
7. In front of Mahatma Gandhi Hospital

In addition the DO letter also proposed subscription in the Regimental Durbar for the memorial of the Jodhpur Lancers as under:

1. Serving Officers and Men.
   (a) Lieutenant Colonel—Rs 251
   (b) Major—Rs 151
   (c) Captain—Rs 101
   (d) Lieutenant – Rs 51
   (e) Rissaldar—Rs 21
   (f) Jemadar—Rs 15
   (g) Daffadar—Rs 11
   (h) Lance Daffadar—Rs 7
   (i) Sowar—Rs 5
   (j) Non Combatants and Civilians etc—Rs 2

2. Ex-Officers and Men. Since their income has been restricted to certain limits the option of choice has been proposed by all ranks. However all are requested to collect the subscription by whatever sources of love

they can and forward the same accordingly. Unless the fund is swollen it will be NOT possible to achieve the object in view. All are therefore kindly requested to do their best to collect the money to construct and erect a really good memorial so as to make it an ideal for the coming generations of the country.

3. Those who are interested and have love for this Regiment, whoever they may be, are also requested to subscribe whatever they deem proper.

4. Royal family members, '*Seth Sahukars*' (business men), *Jagirdars* and rich personalities of the town and the rural areas are being approached and requested separately to help in this commitment and noble cause.'

For this purpose three committees were proposed unanimously by the personnel of the regiment during the Regimental Durbar as under:

1. Main Committee
    (a) Chairman— Maharaja Hanwant Singh
    (b) Members— Thakur Bhawani Singh of Pokhran; Raja Hari Singh of Kuchaman; Thakur Bhairon Singh of Kherjala; Brigadier Zabar Singh of Bera; Colonel Shyam Singh of Rodla and Shri Gordhan Lall Kabra.
    (c) Secretary— Shri Narayan Das
    (d) Under Secretary and Cashier— Captain Rewat Singh

2. Regimental Committee.
    (a) President—Major Jagat Singh Bera
    (b) Members—Captain Bijay Singh, Jemadar Gulab Singh and Daffadar Bajrang Singh

3. Independent Committee. For site selection and shape choosing. It consisted of the following:
    (a) Chairman—Maharao of Bundi
    (b) Vice Chairman— Maharaj Ajit Singh
    (c) Members   Maharaj Himmat Singh, Maharaj Hari Singh, Maharaj Narayan Singh, Raoraja Narpat Singh, Raoraja Hanut Singh, Shri Moti Lall Sanghi, Shri Ganpat Singh Bengani, Shri Heera Nand, Shri Kishori Lall, Colonel Kalyan Singh, Lieutenant Colonel Arjun Singh, Lieutenant Colonel Sultan Singh, Lieutenant Colonel Dhonkal Singh, Major Barkat Ullah Khan, Major Uma Shankar, Captain Manohar Singh, Captain Ratan Singh and Captain D.A. Rajhansa.

However, in spite of the formation of such high-powered committees, why the memorial to the Jodhpur Lancers could never be made remains a mystery.

The only reason that could be inferred may be that soon after these committees were formed, then the chairman and the main inspiration Maharaja Hanwant Singh died in a tragic air crash on 26 January 1952. Thus, till date, Jodhpur continues to wait for a memorial to its heroes of Haifa.

Death of Maharaja Hanwant Singh in a Tragic Air Crash on 26 January 1952

On 26 January 1952, the Maharaja took off in a two-seater Beechcraft Bonanza series 35, VT-CSE aircraft, registered in his own name, with Zubeida. The aircraft flying dangerously low crashed on the dry bed of the Jawai River, at Erinpura, about 80 miles south of Jodhpur. Both the pilot and the passenger were killed and the aircraft was destroyed.

The Maharaja had obtained a pilot's 'A' licence No 1485 on 1 February 1943 and till then had total flying experience of 268 hours and 05 minutes. According to official investigation report (by Mr J. Sen, Deputy Director of Aeronautical Inspection), the aircraft took off at 1610 hours and the clock recovered from the wreckage of the aircraft showed the time as 1657 hours and on that basis the aircraft had flown for about 50 minutes after its takeoff from Jodhpur.

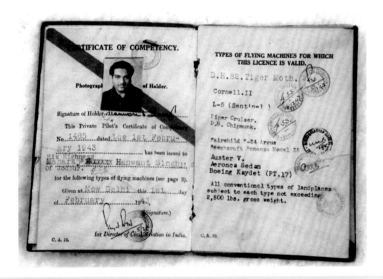

Maharaja Hanwant Singh's flying licence was issued on 1 February 1943. The licence last renewed from 14 December 1951 was valid till 11 October 1952. The licence was endorsed for quite a few types of interesting flying machines.
Photo courtesy: Umaid Bhawan Palace, Jodhpur

On the fateful day the aircraft was inspected by Mr Griffin, the Chief Engineer, and engine was started by Mr Godwin, Chief Flying Instructor and Officer-in-charge, State Aviation, and after carrying out the necessary checks he handed over the aircraft to the Maharaja, who before entering the aircraft informed Mr Godwin that he would fly over Sardarsamand lake and over a village on the bank of Jawai river near Jalore, where his election count was proceeding and he would be back before sunset.

While flying at a very low height over the Jawai river bed near Shivganj the aircraft appeared to dive past a *tonga* (horse-driven cart) which was trotting across the riverbed on its way to Sumerpur. It flew past the *tonga* at a height of about 15 feet, keeping the *tonga* on to its left. Immediately after this, the aircraft was seen gradually gaining height and in doing so it struck against the telegraph cables approximately 1,000 feet ahead. Four out of six telegraph cables, which were running across the river at a height of 40 feet, were broken. This happened at 16:57 hrs. The aircraft then advanced a distance of about 300 feet against the pull of the cables and struck the ground on its nose and the starboard wing tip and swung to the left before finally settling down on the riverbed. Immediately on impact the fuel tanks exploded and the aircraft caught fire. Both the occupants were thrown out of the aircraft in the forward direction and were instantaneously killed. Their clothes also had caught fire, which was subsequently extinguished by people who arrived at the spot immediately after the accident. The pilot and the passenger received first-degree burns on the posterior lower part of their bodies.

The centre section and the front half of the fuselage upto the luggage compartment were completely gutted by fire. The rear half of the fuselage was found unburnt but extensively damaged.

The readings on the instruments recovered from the wreckage, the position of the throttle, the actual nature of break of the propeller blades as well as the evidence from the witnesses, all conclusively indicated that the engine was under full power and was functioning normally when the aircraft hit the telegraph wires and dived on to the river bed. The findings of the investigation were that the accident was due to low flying and was not in any way due to engine failure.

Jodhpur town was filled with grief when at about 9 PM on 26 January 1952, news spread like wild fire in the city that HH Jodhpur who had gone for a test flight in his own plane was missing. Later on, news came that his plane had crashed while forced landing in the bed of Jawai River and the Maharaja along with Vidya Rani (Zubeida) who were the sole occupants of the plane had died on the spot. The news of the plane crash was communicated over telephone by the Railway Control to Jodhpur authorities and the DIG Range with the Commissioner and army ambulances, etc., rushed to the scene of the crash. Both the dead bodies, which were charred, were brought to Jodhpur early in the morning of 27 January.

Maharaja Hanwant Singh's election poster of 1952. The Maharaja's independent party had won a landslide victory taking 31 of 35 seats. But tragically he did not live to hear the results as he died in an air crash on 26 January 1952.
Photo courtesy: The author

On the morning of 27 January 1952, a wave of grief-stricken people swept towards Umaid Bhawan Palace where the dead body of the Maharaja was kept and was to be taken to the royal cremation ground. As relations from Jaipur, Baroda, Patiala and Rewa were expected by air, the funeral procession was delayed and it started about 1.30 PM from Umaid Bhawan Palace and contained besides thousands of civilian mourners, Indian Air Force Officers, Army and Police contingents. The

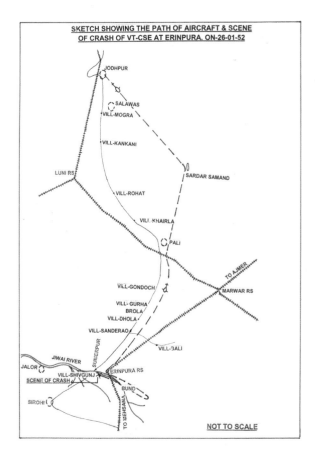

The sketch showing the path of the aircraft flown by Maharaja Hanwant Singh and scene of the crash of VT-CSE on Jawai riverbed at Erinpura, about 80 miles south of Jodhpur, on 26 January 1952.
Photo Courtesy: The author

On 26 January 1952 Group Captain Maharaja Hanwant Singh died in a tragic air accident in his Beechcraft Bonanza aircraft.

Photo courtesy: Indian Air Force Museum Jodhpur

Government of Rajasthan had ordered all flags to fly at half-mast throughout Rajasthan and declared Monday, 28 January, as a public holiday.

The funeral procession, about one lakh strong, reached the Fort area at about 5 PM when the dead body was cremated. The entire markets in Jodhpur were spontaneously closed on 27 January, as well as on 28 January in memory of the Maharaja who was very popular in his state.

So with the tragic death of Maharaja Hanwant Singh the saga of the Jodhpur State Forces came to an abrupt end.

The Jodhpur Lancers Today

At the time of the merger the Indian Army wished to take the complete Jodhpur Lancers into the Indian Armoured Corps but could not retain the same class composition (i.e. Rajputs and Kaimkhanis) and due to its obsolete equipment, it did not fit into the scheme of overall defence organisation. In August 1951 two Squadrons went to the 7 Light Cavalry on a special WE roll from which was raised 'D' Squadron 7 Light Cavalry (Later in 1956 it was split up and transferred to 20 Lancers and 8 Cavalry) and one Squadron went to the Armoured Corps Centre at Ahmednagar as Rajput reinforcement/replacements for Rajput Squadrons, and a balance of about 150/200 men were retired.

However, it was Prime Minister Jawaharlal Nehru who wished that a horse-based cavalry regiment be preserved in Independent India. Thus, as per minutes of a conference held at HQ Rajasthan Force on 10 January 1950, it was decided to add a Squadron to the Kachhawa Horse (Jaipur) which till then had only a HQ Squadron and two Sabre Squadrons. This Squadron was added to it after

Maharaja Gaj Singh (extreme right) gifted
the erstwhile flag of Jodhpur Lancers in
1977 to Colonel Govind Singh (in uniform),
Commandant of 61 Cavalry and Brigadier
Hari Singh, AVSM, (holding the flag—he
was first commissioned in Jodhpur Lancers).
Rear extreme right is Lieutenant Colonel
Parbhu Singh (son of Lieutenant Colonel
Heer Singh of JSI).
Photo courtesy: Aditya Singh Galthani

merging Dungar Lancers (Bikaner), Mewar Lancers (Udaipur) and the Durga
Horse (Jodhpur). On 01 October 1953 the combined regiment was further
amalgamated with 13 other state forces cavalry elements of ancient lineage to
form the 61 Cavalry Regiment of the Indian Army.

Today the 61 Cavalry holds the unique distinction of being the only horsed cavalry
regiment and is known world over for its contribution to the Equestrian sport.
Its boast to Equestrian glory is backed with an unmatched record of awards and
performance in the field with one Padma Shri and 10 Arjuna Awards, coupled
with many other equestrian victories in Olympic Games, Asian Games and World
Cup Polo Championships. After Independence, when the lustre of the erstwhile
princely states faded, the 61 Cavalry continued to carry the torch of Indian Polo.
There is not a single Polo tournament in the country that it has not won.

Traditionally the 61 Cavalry is the only regiment of the Indian Army that has
the Chief of Army Staff as its Colonel of the regiment. The regiment also has the
special honour to lead the Republic Day and Army Day parades each year.

The Regiment continues to carry the legacy that it imbibed from its ancestral units
with pride and elan. Every year 23 September is commemorated by the 61 Cavalry
as their battle honour day. But more than that, by honouring and celebrating one
of the greatest cavalry charges by the Jodhpur Lancers at Haifa on 23 September

1918, the 61 Cavalry has ensured that the Jodhpur Lancers finest hour will not be forgotten. The Jodhpur Lancers have gone but the 61 Cavalry still remembers them.

The Jodhpur Sardar Infantry Today

The regiment is considered the oldest Battalion of the Indian Army, tracing their origins to 1212 AD. The Jodhpur Sardar Infantry was reorganised in August 1922 and Lieutenant Colonel Aman Singh Jodha, OBI, IOM, was its first Commanding Officer. During World War II, the battalion had the proud distinction to operate and see action in the deserts of East Africa, Italy, Egypt and Hong Kong from June 1941 to January 1947. The unit was in the forefront in establishing a beach head at Salerno, Italy, as part of 5 American Army on 09 September 1943, against the German defence.

The Jodhpur Sardar Infantry was absorbed into the Indian Army on 01 April 1951 and re-designated as the 20th (Jodhpur) Battalion, The Rajput Regiment on 26 January 1954. The Battalion was converted to a Motorised Battalion on 01 April 1974. On 15 April 1993, it was converted to a Recce and Support Battalion and designated as 24 Mechanised Infantry (20 Rajput) (Recce and Support). Further in April 1994 the Battalion was converted to Recce and Support (Tracked) and was re-designated as 24 Mechanised Infantry (20 Rajput) (Recce and Support) (Tracked) on 30 October 1994.

The Regiment since Independence has actively participated in the liberation of Diu from Portuguese occupation and it captured Diu Fort on 18 December 1961. The Battalion participated in Operation Riddle (Indo-Pak War 1965), in Sialkot Sector and in Operation Cactus Lily (Indo-Pak War 1971) in Barmer Sector, wherein it was awarded Battle Honour 'Khinsar' and Theatre Honour 'Sindh'. The Battalion participated in Operation Vijay from 29 May 1999 to 05 January 2000 and in Operation Parakram from 19 December 2001 to 18 December 2002 and remained operationally deployed.

The Regiment has operated in the high altitude areas of Sikkim. It also served in UN Peacekeeping Operations in Lebanon and Sudan.

This then is the story of the Jodhpur State Forces, and of the officers and men who by their valour, dedication and sacrifices, much beyond the call of duty, made it great and famous. My aim was to tell the tale again, lest we forget the sacrifices they made a hundred years ago. Their forgotten faces needed to be seen again and their courage remembered and commemorated. Hopefully this book brings them to life again. I wish this story is made into a movie in days to come.

The Battle Honours

'HAZARA 1891', 'NORTH WEST FRONTIER OF INDIA 1897–98', 'CHINA 1900', THE GREAT WAR 1914–19—'CAMBRAI 1917', 'FRANCE AND FLANDERS 1914–18', 'MEGIDDO', 'SHARON', 'DAMASCUS', 'PALESTINE 1918'

COMMANDING OFFICERS OF THE JODHPUR LANCERS

Lieutenant Colonel Sir Pratap—CO 1st Regiment Sardar Rissala, 1889 to 1899

Lieutenant Colonel Hari Singh (Hurjee)—CO 2nd Regiment Sardar Rissala, 1893 to 1898

Major Jus Singh—CO 1st Regiment Sardar Rissala, 1899 to 1907

Maj Dhonkal Singh—CO 2nd Regiment Sardar Rissala, 1899 to 1901

Lieutenant Colonel Maharaj Sher Singh—CO 2nd Regiment Sardar Rissala, 20 August 1901 to 1921

Lieutenant Colonel Pratap Singh of Sankhwas, CBE, OBI—CO 1st Regiment Sardar Rissala, 26 March 1908 to 15 December 1925

Lieutenant Colonel Anop Singh, MC, OBI, IOM—16 December 1925 to 05 August 1929

Lieutenant Colonel Rao Bahadur Dalpat Singh of Rohet—06 August 1929 to 1934

Lieutenant Colonel Rao Bahadur Pirthi Singh of Bera—1935 to 17 September 1936

Lieutenant Colonel Bahadur Singh, OBI—18 September 1936 to 06 July 1941

LieutenantColonel G.G. Collyns—07 July 1941 to March 1943

Lieutenant Colonel W.W.A. Loring—04 April 1943 to 20 March 1944

Lieutenant Colonel R.G. Hanmer—21 March 1944 to August 1944

Lieutenant Colonel E.J.R. Emtage—01 December 1944 to June 1946

Lieutenant Colonel Kalyan Singh of Ustaran—24 October 1946 to 30 April 1949

Lieutenant Colonel Zabar Singh—01 May 1949 to 01 April 1951

COMMANDING OFFICERS OF THE JODHPUR SARDAR INFANTRY

Prior to 01 February 1922 the Sardar Infantry regiment existed as an irregular unit. Its last four Commanding Officers prior to 1922 were: Maharaj Kishore Singh 1893 to 1898; Maharaj Bhopal Singh, till he died in September1899; later his son Maharaj Rattan Singh, till he died on 03 January 1917; and lastly Colonel Raoraja Tej Singh, till his death in 1921.

Lieutenant Colonel Aman Singh, Sardar Bahadur, OBI, IOM—28 August 1922 to 08 August 1929

Lieutenant Colonel Rao Bahadur Raoraja Sujjan Singh—09 August 1929 to 30 January 1941

Lieutenant Colonel Jawahar Singh, MBE—31 January 1941 to 01 March 1942

Lieutenant Colonel H.B. Rogers—02 March 1942 to 01 June 1944

Lieutenant Colonel C.A.S. Melville—02 June 1944 to 30 November 1944

Lieutenant Colonel Ram Singh—01 December 1944 to 26 March 1945

Lieutenant Colonel G.A.C. Maunsell—27 March 1945 to 04 March 1946

Lieutenant Colonel G.M. Gillan—05 March 1946 to 28 February 1947

Lieutenant Colonel Ram Singh, DSO—01 March 1947 to 28 May 1949

Lieutenant Colonel Dungar Singh, MC—29 May 1949 to 31 March 1950

Lieutenant Colonel Dhonkal Singh—01 April 1950 to 01 April 1951

COMMANDING OFFICERS OF THE 2nd JODHPUR INFANTRY

Lieutenant Colonel Heer Singh—1940 to 1941

Lieutenant Colonel S.F. Martin—1942 to 1945

Lieutenant Colonel Ram Singh, DSO—1945 to 1946

Lieutenant Colonel Dhonkal Singh—1947 to 1948

COMMANDING OFFICER OF THE 3rd JODHPUR INFANTRY

Lieutenant Colonel Rao Bahadur Heer Singh—1941 to 1946.

OFFICER COMMANDING OF THE DURGA HORSE

Captain Mangal Singh—1941 to 1943

Captain Achal Singh—1943 to 1946

Major Mohan Singh —1947 to 1951

OFFICER COMMANDING OF THE JODHPUR LANCERS TRAINING CENTRE

Lieutenant Colonel Zabar Singh, MBE—1939 to 1946

Major Ramdan Singh—1947 to 1948

OFFICER COMMANDING OF THE DEMONSTRATION COMPANY

Major Keshri Singh—1942 to 1943

Captain A.C. Hobbs, 15th Punjab Regiment—1943 to 1945

Captain C.J. Olliffe—1945

Captain Raiwat Singh—1945 to 1946

OFFICER COMMANDING OF THE JODHPUR INFANTRY TRAINING CENTRE

Captain Gulab Singh—1941 to 1942

Lieutenant Colonel Jawahar Singh, MBE—1942 to 1947

Lieutenant Colonel Dungar Singh, MC—18 May 1947 to 28 May 1949

OFFICER COMMANDING OF THE JODHPUR TRANSPORT CORPS

Major A.J. Reynolds—1922 to 1923

Subedar Roop Singh, IDSM—1923 to 1934

Lieutenant Nag Singh—1934 to 1942

Captain Chatter Singh—1942 to 1946

Captain Dar Singh—1948

OFFICER COMMANDING OF THE STATE MILITARY BAND

Captain W.H. Ryman—1929 to 1938

Lieutenant W. Nichols—1938 to 1940

OFFICER COMMANDING OF THE JODHPUR FORT GUARDS

Major Umed Singh (Galthani)—1935 to 1943

Major Mangal Singh—1943 to 1948

Major Maharaj Himmat Singh—1949 to 1951

OFFICER COMMANDING OF THE MILITARY HOSPITAL

Lieutenant Colonel Rai Sahib S.N. Parnaik—1932 to 1939 (Grand Uncle of Lieutenant General S.N. Parnaik, who retired as Northern Army Commander in 2013)

Lieutenant P.R. Badve—1939 to 46

OFFICER COMMANDING OF THE 54th (JODHPUR) GENERAL PURPOSE TRANSPORT COMPANY RIASC

Major A.B. Sinker 1941

Major A.R. Harvey James 1942

Major G.V. Brooks—1942 to1943

Major C.T.M. Fowler—1944 to 1946

Major Mod Singh—1946 till its merger with the Indian Army

BRITISH OFFICERS WHO SERVED WITH THE JODHPUR LANCERS DURING THE BOXER REBELLION, CHINA 1900–1901

Major James Gibbon Turner, 4th Bengal Lancers. He was appointed the inspecting officer of IST and stationed at Jodhpur from 23 July 1898 to 09 January 1902. He died 20 October 1950.

Captain E.M. Hughes, 14th Bengal Lancers. He was with the Jodhpur Lancers from 1898. He later served as inspecting officer IST Rajputana 1904–05. He died on 11 September 1916, in Basra, Mesopotamia.

Captain E.M. Hewess.

Lieutenant Alexander, 6th Bombay Cavalry (Attached)

Lieutenant G.R.Gaussen, 3rd Bengal Cavalry (Attached)

Captain Pinchard.

Captain Jay Gould, IMS.

BRITISH OFFICERS WHO SERVED WITH THE JODHPUR LANCERS DURING THE GREAT WAR 1914–1918

Major H.N. Holden, 5 Cavalry (Killed in action, at Aleppo, on 26 October 1918).

Major A.D. Strong, 10 Hodsons Horse (Wounded on 21 December 1914 France. He died on 17 June 1930).

Captain E.L. Maxwell, 11 Probin's Horse (Killed in action, in France, on 20 July 1916).

Lieutenant Colonel P.F. Gell, 14 Lancers (Died in 1938).

Lieutenant Daji Raj, 27 Light Cavalry (Killed in action, in France, on 23 September 1917).

Major J.A. Fergusson, 15 Lancers (He was Vice Principal Chopasani School Jodhpur from 1921).

Lieutenant William Chubb, 36 Jacob's Horse.

Major A.J. Reynolds, 37 Lancers (Died on 06 September 1930, while Commanding the Hodsons Horse in Srinagar).

Lieutenant A.B. Knight, 4 Cavalry (Died in 1976).

Captain H.F.P. Hornsby, 5 Cavalry (Wounded at Aleppo. Died on 21 September 1925).

Lieutenant C.D.L.G. Clarke, 34 Cavalry (He was P.W. Camp Commandant in Borneo, where he was murdered by the Japanese on 06 July 1945).

Captain Claude Ernest Pert, 37 Lancers (Died on 14 March 1982).

Major Alexander Baird Skinner, 5 Cavalry (Died on 17 September 1951).

Major Guy Rutherford Prescott Wheatly, 27 Light Cavalry (Died on 02 December 1952).

Major Robert George Antony Trail, Guides Cavalry (Killed in Action, at Cambrai, France, on 01 December 1917).

Captain Frederick Owen Maynard, RAVC (Veterinary Officer. Died on 12 January 1920).

BRITISH OFFICERS WHO SERVED WITH THE JODHPUR LANCERS DURING THE SECOND WORLD WAR 1939–1945

Lieutenant Colonel G.G. Collyns, 3rd Cavalry

Captain A.G.S. Alexander, CIH

Major W.H.L. Spurgin, 19th KGO Lancers

Captain G.D. Garforth Bles, The Guides Cavalry F.F.

Captain J.B. Hampson 10/12th F.F. Regiment

Captain G.H. Hariman, 43rd Cavalry

Lieutenant Colonel W.W.A. Loring, 48th Cavalry

Major R.G. Hanmer, IAC

Captain R.J. Cooper, IAC

Lieutenant J.D. Pearson, 47th Cavalry

Lieutenant C.J. Allman, IAC

Major H.M. Bromillow, Hudsons Horse

Lieutenant J.A. Hislop, 43rd Cavalry

Captain G. Mck Davidson, Guides Cavalry

Lieutenant Colonel E.J.R. Emtage, 6th DCO Lancers

BRITISH OFFICERS WHO SERVED WITH JODHPUR SARDAR INFANTRY DURING THE SECOND WORLD WAR, 1939–1945

Lieutenant Colonel Frank Dennis Clarke, 8th Gurkha Rifles

Lieutenant Philip William John Crossland, 15th Punjab Regiment (He worked in India after 1947 as a journalist with The Statesman in Delhi from 1955 to 1967. He died in 2007).

Lieutenant Colonel T.G.L.E. Grant, 2nd Punjab Regiment

Major L.H.W. Axtel, 18th Royal Garhwal Rifles

Major D.A. Wharton Brown, 8/14th Punjab Regiment

Lieutenant Colonel Harry Buston Rogers, 5th Mahratta Light Infantry

Lieutenant Colonel Cecil Alan Swinton Melville, 6th Rajputana Rifles (Died 01 Dec 1956)

Major George Arthur Cecil Maunsell, 2/14 Punjab Regiment

Major L.M. Duncan, Kolhapur Rajaram Rifles

Captain J.T.H. Macaulay 7/17th Dogra Regiment

Lieutenant P.W. Stoolman, 5/4th Bombay Grenadiers

Lieutenant Colonel J.O. Ingham, 9th Jat Regiment

BRITISH OFFICERS WHO SERVED WITH 2nd JODHPUR INFANTRY DURING THE SECOND WORLD WAR 1939–1945

Lieutenant Colonel S.F. Martin, 15th Punjab Regiment

Major D.J.H. Rochs, 9th Jat Regiment

Major D.A.W. Brown, 8/14th Punjab Regiment

Captain J.C.P. Beloe, 14th Punjab Regiment

Captain R.M. Williams, 14/12th F.F. Regiment

Major E.A.G. McComas, 16/14th Punjab Regiment

Major H.G. Boulter, 6th Rajputana Rifles

LIST OF MILITARY ADVISERS OF JODHPUR STATE FORCES

Major Stuart Beatson	07 August 1889 to 19 July 1894
Captain H.R. Tate	August 1894 to June 1900
Major J.G. Turner	July 1900 to August 1901
Major A.D. Strong	March 1911 to June 1914

Major Hyla Holden	08 July 1914 to 26 October 1918
Major A.J. Reynolds	28 December 1921 to 19 September 1924
Major A.H. Williams, MC	20 September 1924 to 20 September 1929
Major E.A. Stead, MC	24 May 1934 to 29 February 1936
Brigadier R.C. Duncan, MVO, OBE	01 March 1936 to 03 January 1939

(From 04 January 1939 to September1947 as Commandant Jodhpur State Forces. He died on 30 June 1963)

| Brigadier Zabbar Singh, MBE | September1947 to April 1951 |

LIST OF INDIVIDUALS AWARDED THE KING'S SILVER JUBILEE MEDAL 1910–1935 IN JODHPUR STATE

A total of 52 Kings Silver Jubilee medals were approved for Marwar State on 06 May 1935, including 32 medals for Jodhpur State Forces. It was decided that all holders of the Order of British India, whether serving or retired, would receive the Jubilee medal.

1. Lieutenant Colonel Maharaja Umaid Singh, Maharaja of Jodhpur
2. Raoraja Abhey Singh, Comptroller of Household and ADC to Maharaja
3. Maharaj Ajit Singh, Director of Veterinary Department and Brother of Maharaja
4. Lieutenant Colonel Aman Singh, Sardar Bahadur, OBI, IOM, (Retd) Commandant Sardar Infantry
5. Captain Bahadur Singh Champawat, Squadron Commander Sardar Rissala
6. Captain Bir Singh, Squadron Commander Sardar Rissala
7. No 230 Daffadar Bhiv Singh, Sardar Rissala
8. Rao Bahadur Chain Singh, Judicial Member, Thakur of Pokhran
9. Jemadar Chhog Singh, Sardar Rissala
10. Lieutenant Chhotu Singh, Quarter Master, Sardar Rissala
11. A.P. Cox, I.E.S., Director of Education and Principal Chopasani School
12. Mr Tehmuras Gustadji Dalal, Foreign and Political Secretary of Jodhpur
13. No 204 Daffadar Major Dolat Singh, Sardar Rissala
14. Rao Bahadur Fateh Singh, Thakur of Asop
15. No 205 Daffadar Major Gambhir Singh, Sardar Rissala
16. Maharaj Guman Singh, A.D.C. to Maharaja
17. Raoraja Major Hanut Singh, A.D.C. to Maharaja and Comptroller Stables
18. Maharaj Kumar Hanawant Singh, Heir Apparent
19. E.W. Hayward, FRCS, Principal Medical Officer
20. Major Heer Singh, Second-in-Command Sardar Infantry
21. Major Hem Singh, Second-in-Command Sardar Rissala
22. Captain Hukma Ram, Company Commander, Sardar Infantry
23. Rao Bahadur Jey Singh, Thakur of Umednagar
24. No 204 Havildar Jivan Singh, Sardar Infantry
25. No 190 Daffadar Major Jor Singh, Sardar Rissala
26. Captain Kalyan Singh, Squadron Commander, Sardar Rissala
27. No 227 Daffedar Major Kanu Singh, Sardar Rissala

28. Havildar Kishore Singh, Sardar Infantry
29. Khan Bahadur M.R. Kothawala, MBE, Inspector General of Police
30. Madho Singh, Thakur of Sankhwas and Home Minister
31. Rissaldar Madho Singh, Sardar Rissala
32. Jamadar Magan Singh, Sardar Rissala
33. No 276 Daffadar Malu Khan, Sardar Rissala
34. Rissaldar Mamdu Khan, Sardar Rissala
35. Risaldar Mangal Singh, Sardar Rissala
36. Captain Moti Singh, Company Commander, Sardar Infantry
37. Captain Pane Singh, OBI, (Retd) Squadron Commander, Sardar Rissala
38. Rai Sahib Lieutenant Colonel S.N. Parnaik, Officer Commanding Military Hospital
39. Colonel Pirthi Singh, Commandant Sardar Rissala and Jagirdar of Bera
40. Risaldar Prem Singh, Sardar Rissala
41. Captain W.H. Ryman, Band Master, State Military Band
42. Jamadar Sabal Singh, Sardar Rissala
43. No 321 Regimental Daffadar Major Sadul Singh, Sardar Rissala
44. No 70 Battalion Havildar Major Sang Singh, Sardar Infantry
45. Subedar Shivdan Ram, Sardar Infantry
46. Maj Steel Frank, OBE, Assistant to Finance Minister and State Auditor
47. Raoraja Lieutenant Colonel Sujjan Singh, Commandant Sardar Infantry
48. Rai Sahib Topan Ram, Chief Judge
49. Rissaldar Udai Singh I, OBI, (Retd) Sardar Rissala
50. No 306 Daffadar Ugam Singh, Sardar Rissala
51. C.W. Waddington, CIE, MVO, Guardian and Tutor to Maharaj Kumar
52. Mr C.H. Wilson, Electrical Engineer

LIST OF INDIVIDUALS WHO RECEIVED THE CORONATION MEDAL 1937 IN JODHPUR STATE

1. Subedar Alidas Singh, Sardar Infantry
2. Sowar Bachan Singh, Sardar Rissala
3. Lieutenant Colonel Bahadur Singh, Commandant Sardar Rissala
4. Lieutenant Bahadur Singh, Sardar Infantry
5. Rissaldar Baxu Khan, Sardar Rissala
6. No 733 Naik Bijey Singh, Sardar Infantry
7. Captain Birma Ram, Company Commander, Sardar Infantry
8. Captain Chhotu Singh, Squadron Commander, Sardar Rissala
9. No 362 Regimental Daffadar Major Dhan Singh, Sardar Rissala
10. Brigadier R.C. Duncan, MVO, OBE, Military Adviser Jodhpur State Forces
11. Major Heer Singh, Second-in-Command, Sardar Infantry
12. Lieutenant Jawahar Singh, Adjutant Sardar Infantry
13. Lieutenant Kalyan Singh, Adjutant Sardar Rissala
14. Captain Lajpat Rai, Company Commander, Sardar Infantry
15. No 877 Lance Daffadar Lal Singh, Sardar Rissala

16. No 755 Regimental Quarter Master Daffadar Madho Singh, Sardar Rissala
17. Lieutenant Mamdu Khan, Sardar Rissala
18. Lieutenant Mangal Singh, Sardar Rissala
19. 2nd Lieutenant Mohan Singh, Sardar Rissala
20. Captain Moti Singh, Second-in-Command, Fort Guard
21. Subedar Nag Singh, Regimental Transport Corps Jodhpur
22. Raghunath Roop Rai, P.A. to Military Adviser Jodhpur State Forces
23. Lieutenant Ram Singh, Quarter Master, Sardar Infantry
24. Captain W.H. Ryman, Director of Music, Military State Band
25. No 70 Battalion Havildar Major Sang Singh, Sardar Infantry
26. Rai Sahib Lieutenant Colonel S.N. Parnaik, Officer Commanding Military Station Hospital, Jodhpur
27. Raoraja Sujjan Singh, Commandant Sardar Infantry
28. Major Umed Singh Galthani, Commandant Fort Guard
29. Lieutenant Zabar Singh, Quarter Master, Sardar Rissala

Sixteen medals each were also presented to Civil and Jodhpur Railways personnel by the Maharaja at a Durbar on 26 July 1937.

LIST OF MILITARY PERSONNEL GRANTED HONOURS ON THE AUSPICIOUS OCCASION OF THE BIRTH OF MAHARAJA GAJ SINGH ON 23 JANUARY 1948

TAZIM, GOLD AND HATHI SAROPAO

Lieutenant Colonel Aman Singh Jodha, OBI, IOM (Digarana)—Jodhpur Sardar Infantry

Lieutenant Colonel Bahadur Singh, OBI (Bagawas)—Jodhpur Lancers

Lieutenant Colonel Rao Bahadur Raoraja Sujjan Singh (Jodhpur)—Jodhpur Sardar Infantry (Jodhpur)

Lieutenant Colonel Hem Singh, OBI (Banasar, Phalodi)—Jodhpur Lancers

Lieutenant Colonel Rao Bahadur Heer Singh (Jipasani)—Jodhpur Sardar Infantry

Lieutenant Colonel Anop Singh, OBI, IOM, MC (Rodla)—Jodhpur Lancers

Lieutenant Colonel Jawahar Singh, MBE (Pachranda)—Jodhpur Sardar Infantry

Lieutenant Colonel Rao Bahadur Dalpat Singh (Rohet)—Jodhpur Lancers

Lieutenant Colonel Shyam Singh (Rodla)—Jodhpur Lancers

Lieutenant Colonel Arjun Singh (Jasol)—Jodhpur Lancers

Lieutenant Colonel Kalyan Singh (Ustran)—Jodhpur Lancers

Lieutenant Colonel Dhonkal Singh (Mamdoli)—2nd Jodhpur Sardar Infantry

Lieutenat Colonel Sultan Singh (Kisari)—Jodhpur Lancers Training Centre

Lieutenant Colonel Mohan Singh (Osian)—Jodhpur Lancers

Lieutenant Colonel Maharaj Prem Singh (Raoti)—Jodhpur Lancers Training Centre

Lieutenant Colonel Dungar Singh, MC (Awai, Jaisalmer)—Jodhpur Sardar Infantry

HATHI SAROPAO

Major Dhonkal Singh (Chuntisara)—HQ Jodhpur State Forces

Major Chandan Singh (Galthani)—Jodhpur Lancers

Major Jagat Singh (Bera)—Jodhpur Lancers

Major Bhopal Singh (Bisalpur)—Jodhpur Lancers

Major Ramdan Singh (Ghantiya)—Jodhpur Lancers Training Centre

Major Deep Singh (Indroka)—Jodhpur Sardar Infantry

Major Jethu Singh—Jodhpur Sardar Infantry

Captain Maharaj Dan Singh—Jodhpur Sardar Infantry

Major Raiwat Singh (Kasari)—2nd Jodhpur Infantry

Major P.R. Badve—Military Hospital

PALKI SAROPAO

Captain Hari Singh (Galthani)—HQ Jodhpur State Forces

Captain D.A. Rajhansa—HQ Jodhpur State Forces

Captain Kheem Singh (Dankha)—Jodhpur Lancers

Captain Girdhari Singh, MBE—Jodhpur Lancers

Captain Umaid Singh—Jodhpur Lancers Training Centre

Captain S.K. Banerjee—Jodhpur Lancers Training Centre

Captain Pehap Singh—2nd Jodhpur Infantry

Captain Karim Khan—2nd Jodhpur Infantry

Captain Madho Singh (Digarana)—2nd Jodhpur Infantry

Captain Magan Singh—Jodhpur Infantry Training Centre

Captain Prem Singh—Durga Horse

Captain Raoraja Devi Singh—Durga Horse

Captain Raiwat Singh—Fort Guard

Captain Sawai Singh—Jodhpur Sardar Infantry

GHORA SAROPAO

Lieutenant Durjan Singh—Jodhpur Infantry Training Centre

2nd Lieutenant Gulab Singh—Jodhpur Sardar Infantry

2nd Lieutenant Magan Singh—Forts Guard

TOTAL CASUALTIES OF JODHPUR LANCERS DURING THE GREAT WAR

	Officers	Other Ranks
Killed in Action	7	37
Died of Disease	1	63
Wounded	14	82

HONOURS AND AWARDS

The Order of British India (OBI) was instituted in 1837 and consisted of two classes. The First Class carried with it the title 'Sardar Bahadur' (literally meaning 'Heroic leader') and the Second Class carried the title 'Bahadur' (Hero). Both awards brought with them a small increase in pay. The Indian Order of Merit (IOM), also instituted in 1837, was traditionally considered to be 'The Indian VC'. It consisted of three classes initially, was open to any Indian officer or soldier, regardless of rank and was awarded for an act of conspicuous gallantry in the face of the enemy. All three classes included an increase in pay. In 1911, Indian Officers and Other ranks became eligible for the award of the Victoria Cross (VC) and accordingly the First Class IOM was abolished. In January 1915, Indian officers became eligible for the Military Cross (MC). The Indian Distinguished Service Medal (IDSM) was instituted in 1907 as a reward for Indian officers and other ranks on occasions when the gallant deed was below the standard required for the IOM. The Indian Meritorious Service Medal (IMSM) was established in 1888 and was granted, with a small annuity, to soldiers with 18 or more years of meritorious service.

DISTINGUISHED SERVICE ORDER (DSO)

Major A.D. Strong—France 14 January 1916

Lieutenant Colonel Hyla N. Holden—Haifa 23 September 1918 and Aleppo 26 October 1918

Major P.F. Gell—Jordan valley 14 July 1918

Major Ram Singh (SF3552)—Italy 24 August 1944

MILITARY CROSS (MC)

Major Dalpat Singh	Egypt, Jordan Valley, 14 July 1918
Captain Anop Singh	Egypt, Haifa, 23 September 1918
Captain H.F.P. Hornsby	Egypt, Aleppo, 26 October 1918
Lieutenant A.B. Knight	Egypt, Haifa, 23 September 1918
2/Lieutenant Sagat Singh	Egypt, Haifa, 23 September 1918
Captain Dungar Singh	Italy, 24 August 1944
Jemadar Parbhu (3778)	Italy, 06 April 1945

INDIAN ORDER OF MERIT (IOM) 2nd CLASS

Daffadar Dal Singh (3rd Class)	China, 12 January 1901
1470 Sowar Moti Singh	France, 29 July 1916
1392 Sowar Gulab Singh (Netiyas, Nagore)	France, 17 February 1917
1296 Sowar Dhonkal Singh	France, 18 January 1918
Captain Anop Singh, Bahadur	Jordan Valley, 14 July 1918
Risaldar Shaitan Singh	Jordan Valley, 14 July 1918
1444 Daffadar Amar Singh	Jordan Valley, 14 July 1918
Jemadar Asoo Singh (Posthumously)	Jordan Valley, 14 July 1918
Jemadar Khang Singh (Posthumously)	Jordan Valley, 14 July 1918
1189 Trumpet Major Sher Singh	Jordan Valley, 14 July 1918
Captain Aman Singh, Bahadur	Haifa, Egypt, 23 September 1918
1029 Daffadar Jor Singh	Haifa, Egypt, 23 September 1918

Rissaldar Keshri Singh   Haifa, Egypt, 23 September 1918
(Alwar Lancers attached Jodhpur Lancers)

ORDER OF BRITISH INDIA (OBI) 2nd CLASS

Maj Jus Singh	China, 16 May 1902
Lieutenant Colonel Pratap Singh	In India, 12 December 1911
Captain Aman Singh	In France, 20 April 1917
Captain Anop Singh	In France, 28 July 1917
Captain Paney Singh	Egypt, 19 June 1918
Risaldar Agar Singh	In France, 20 April 1917
1118 Risaldar Udai Singh	In India, 03 June 1922
Major Kishore Singh	In India, November 1920
Lieutenant Bhagwant Singh Jodha	In India, 30 November 1921
Major Hem Singh	In India, 03 June 1935
Lieutenant Colonel Bahadur Singh	In India, 08 June 1939
Subedar Major Sultan Singh, Sardar Infantry	In India, 08 June 1944
Subedar Achal Singh (SF 9709), 3rd Jodhpur Infantry	In India, 01 January 1946
Risaldar Baxu Khan (SF 12704), Body Guard Squadron	In India, 01 January 1946

ORDER OF BRITISH INDIA (OBI) 1st CLASS

Major Jus Singh	India, 01 January 1903
Colonel Pratap Singh	France, 28 July 1917
Lieutenant Colonel Anop Singh	In India, 03 June 1928
Lieutenant Colonel Aman Singh Jodha, JSI	In India, 02 November 1928
SF 3560 Subedar Major Sultan Singh, JSI	In India, 01 January 1946

KNIGHT COMMANDER OF THE MOST EXCELLENT ORDER OF THE BRITISH EMPIRE (KBE)

Maharaja Sumer Singh, 1918

COMMANDER OF THE MOST EXCELLENT ORDER OF THE BRITISH EMPIRE (CBE)

Colonel Pratap Singh of Sankhwas—30 December 1919.

OFFICER OF THE MOST EXCELLENT ORDER OF THE BRITISH EMPIRE (OBE)

Rai Bahadur Dhonkal Singh of Gorau—03 June 1919.

MEMBER OF THE MOST EXCELLENT ORDER OF THE BRITISH EMPIRE (MBE)

Captain Girdhari Singh—16 February 1946
Lieutenant Colonel Zabar Singh, Jodhpur Lancers Training Centre—India, 28 May 1943.

Lieutenant Colonel Jawahar Singh, Jodhpur Infantry Training Centre—14 June 1945.

No SF 3723 Jemadar Ganga Ram, Jodhpur Sardar Infantry—Italy, 24 August 1944.

ORDER OF THE LEGION OF HONOUR (GRAND OFFICER)

Maharaja Sir Pratap Singh—France, January 1918

GRAND CORDON OF THE ORDER OF THE NILE

Major Maharaja Sumer Singh— Egypt, May 1918

Lieutenant General Maharaja Sir Pratap Singh— Egypt, May 1918

CROIX-DE-GUERRE, FRANCE

1097 Jamedar Anop Singh—In France, 01 February 1918

RAO BAHADUR/RAI SAHIB

Lieutenant Colonel Raoraja Sujan Singh, Jodhpur Sardar Infantry—01 January 1941

Lieutenant Colonel Heer Singh, Jodhpur Sardar Infantry—08 June 1944

Major Dhonkal Singh of Gorau, Rao Bahadur—February 1914

Guman Singh Khichi, Rao Bahadur—February 1914

Shivnath Singh of Bera

Baba Bihari Singh, Head Clerk Jodhpur Lancers, Rai Sahib—01 January 1919.

Captain S.N. Parnaik, Medical Officer Jodhpur Lancers, Rai Sahib—01 January 1921.

Major Dalpat Singh Rohet, Military Secretaty to Maharaja, Rao Bahadur—03 June 1921.

Colonel Prithvi Singh Bera, Jodhpur Lancers, Rao Bahadur—01 January 1936.

Captain Raoraja Hanut Singh, Jodhpur Lancers, Rao Bahadur—12 May 1937.

MILITARY MEDAL (MM) WORLD WAR II

1783 Havildar Bhura Ram, Jodhpur Sardar Infantry—Italy, 24 August 1944

1811 Lance Naik Kishore Singh, Jodhpur Sardar Infantry—Italy, 24 August 1944

1503 Naik Shaitan Singh, Jodhpur Sardar Infantry—Italy, 24 August 1944

INDIAN DISTINGUISHED SERVICE MEDAL (IDSM)

151	Daffadar Chiman Singh	France, 29 July 1916
1121	Daffadar Bhur Singh (Later Lieutenant)	France, 17 February 1917
1263	Daffadar Roop Singh (Later Lieutenant)	France, 17 February 1917
1485	Lance Daffadar Zalim Singh	France, 17 February 1917
1086	Sowar Bahadur Singh	France, 20 July 1918
1186	Daffadar Aidan Singh (Died 22 September 1918)	France, 20 July 1918
	Jemadar Jawar Singh	Jordan Valley, 14 July 1918
1564	Sowar Guman Singh	Jordan Valley, 14 July 1918
1119	Daffadar Jog Singh (Liliyan)	Jordan Valley, 14 July 1918
1889	Sowar Jagat Singh	Jordan Valley, 14 July 1918

1361	Lance Daffadar Dhonkal Singh	Jordan Valley, 14 July 1918
1604	Lance Daffadar Bijai Singh	Jordan Valley, 14 July 1918
1316	Lance Daffadar Khang Singh	Jordan Valley, 14 July 1918
1678	Sowar Man Singh	France, 20 July 1918
1595	Sowar Mool Singh	France, 20 July 1918
1342	Daffadar Bhoor Singh	France, 20 July 1918
1216	Jemadar Bishen Singh Sajjada	Haifa, Egypt, 09 November 1918
1288	Daffadar Mobhat Singh (Later Lieutenant)	Haifa, Egypt, 09 November 1918
	Jemadar Bahadur Singh	Haifa, Egypt, 09 November 1918

(Later CO Jodhpur Lancers and Father of AVM Chandan Singh, MVC, AVSM, VrC)

1049	Daffadar Doong Singh	Haifa, Egypt, 09 November 1918
1321	Lance Daffadar Bhairon Singh	Haifa, Egypt, 09 November 1918
1630	Sowar Bagh Singh	Haifa, Egypt, 09 November 1918
1427	Sowar Ganpat Singh	Haifa, Egypt, 09 November 1918
1559	Sowar Padam Singh	Haifa, Egypt, 09 November 1918
1109	Sowar Bhoor Singh	Haifa, Egypt, 09 November 1918
1538	Sowar Bhim Singh	Haifa, Egypt, 09 November 1918
1353	Sowar Amar Singh	Haifa, Egypt, 09 November 1918
1151	Sowar Bishen Singh	Haifa, Egypt, 09 November 1918
1470	Daffadar Moti Singh, IOM	Egypt, 03 May 1919

(Later Subedar in JSI in World War II)

1327	Sowar Sanwat Singh	Egypt, 03 May 1919

INDIAN MERITORIOUS SERVICE MEDAL (IMSM)

1273	Daffadar Udai Singh	France, 20 July 1918
1226	Sowar Pabudan Singh	France, 20 July 1918
1316	Sowar Khang Singh	France, 20 July 1918
1034	Lance Daffadar Megh Singh	France, 20 July 1918
1089	Kot Daffadar Pith Singh	France, 20 July 1918
1216	Kot Daffadar Bishen Singh, IDSM(Sajjada)	France, 20 July 1918
1177	Kot Daffadar Berisal Singh	France, 20 July 1918
1078	Sowar Mool Singh	France, 21 September 1918
1163	Daffadar Sultan Singh	France, 21 September 1918
1431	Daffadar Samel Singh	France, 21 September 1918
1397	Daffadar Suraj Baksh Singh (Later Jemmadar)	France, 21 September 1918
1334	Daffadar Jog Singh	France, 21 September 1918
1119	Daffadar Jog Singh, IDSM(Later Risaldar)	France, 21 September 1918
1373	Daffadar Arjun Singh	France, 21 September 1918

(Father of Lt Gen Hanut Singh, PVSM, MVC)

968	Farrier Mukan Singh	France, 21 September 1918
1050	Sowar Ashraf Khan	France, 21 September 1918
999	Farrier Khum Singh	France, 21 September 1918
1378	Daffadar Balwant Singh	France, 21 September 1918

155	Daffadar Bage Khan	India, 17 April 1920
1160	Daffadar Magan Singh (Later Risaldar)	India, 17 April 1920
1186	Lance Daffadar Deo Singh	India, 17 April 1920
1354	Lance Daffadar Gobind Singh	Egypt, 27 November 1920
993	Farrier Jagat Singh	Egypt, 27 November 1920
1130	Daffadar Mod Singh	Egypt, 27 November 1920
1076	Daffadar Baney Singh	Egypt, 27 November 1920
1116	Daffadar Geegai Singh	Egypt, 27 November 1920
1141	Daffadar Gain Singh	Egypt, 27 November 1920
1090	Sowar Pith Singh	Egypt, 27 November 1920
1103	Sowar Dan Singh	Egypt, 27 November 1920
1050	Sowar Gain Singh	Egypt, 27 November 1920
1200	Sowar Rawat Singh	Egypt, 27 November 1920
1315	Sowar Megh Singh	Egypt, 27 November 1920
1131	Sowar Magh Singh	Egypt, 27 November 1920
1351	Sowar Gokul Singh	Egypt, 27 November 1920
1391	Sowar Birad Singh	Egypt, 27 November 1920
1575	Sowar Bakshu Singh Khan	Egypt, 27 November 1920
1588	Sowar Daulat Khan	Egypt, 27 November 1920
1540	Kot Daffadar Kan Singh	Egypt, 27 November 1920
1165	Daffadar Kannu Singh	Egypt, 27 November 1920
1151	Sowar Rudh Singh	Egypt, 27 November 1920
1204	Sowar Tej Singh	Egypt, 27 November 1920
1430	Sowar Bakhtawar Singh	Egypt, 27 November 1920
1084	Daffadar Kalyan Singh	Egypt, 27 November 1920
1013	Daffadar Bakhtawar Singh	Egypt, 27 November 1920
1279	Sowar Kalu Singh	Egypt, 27 November 1920
1052	Daffadar Doong Singh	Egypt, 27 November 1920
1232	Sowar Jawar Singh	Egypt, 27 November 1920

MENTIONED IN DESPATCHES (MID)

Major Jus Singh	China, 06 July 1901
Lieutenant Colonel H.N. Holden	France, 15 June 1916 and Egypt, 17 July 1920
Major P.F. Gell	Egypt, 19 July 1919
Major A.J. Reynolds	Egypt, 05 June 1919
Major A.D. Strong	France, 14 January 1915
Major General Sir Pratap	France, 14 January 1915
Lieuteant Maharaja Sumer Singh	France, 14 January 1915
Lieutenant Colonel Maharaj Sher Singh	France, 15 June 1916
No 360 Risaldar Anop Singh	France, 15 June 1916
470 Daffadar Alim Khan	France, 15 June 1916
Colonel Partap Singh	Egypt, 17 July 1920

Captain Khem Singh	Egypt, 08 March 1919
Captain Sankar Narain Parnaik	Egypt, 08 March 1919
1090 Daffadar Khayn Singh	Egypt, 08 March 1919
Risaldar Udai Singh	Egypt, 17 July 1920

MENTIONED IN DESPATCHES (MID)-JODHPUR SARDAR INFANTRY-WORLD WAR II

SF 3556 Captain Magni Ram	Italy, 24 August 1944
SF 3717 Jemadar Dungar Singh	Italy, 24 August 1944
SF 3766 Jemadar Kishna Ram	Italy, 24 August 1944
1794 Naik Prahlad Singh	Italy, 24 August 1944
1775 Naik Shivnarayan Singh	Italy, 24 August 1944
1668 Lance Naik Narana Ram	Italy, 24 August 1944
2117 Sepoy Bagh Singh	Italy, 24 August 1944
2149 Sepoy Jawahir Singh	Italy, 24 August 1944
1926 Sepoy Mod Singh	Italy, 24 August 1944
SF 3591 Lieutenant Moti Singh	Italy, 24 August 1944
SF 3709 Jemadar Jodha Ram	Italy, 24 August 1944
1698 Havildar Major Thakur Ram	Italy, 24 August 1944
1925 Naik Khet Singh	Italy, 24 August 1944
1788 Naik Magha Ram	Italy, 24 August 1944
1689 Naik Pusa Ram	Italy, 24 August 1944
1415 Lance Naik Kishna Ram	Italy, 24 August 1944
1512 Sepoy Amara Ram	Italy, 24 August 1944
IEC 9230 Major Ram Singh, DSO	Italy, 29 November 1945
IEC 9317 Captain Ram Charan Singh	Italy, 29 November 1945
Lieutenant Colonel A.J. R. Emtage	Italy, 29 November 1945
4225/1839 Havaldar Madan Singh	Italy, 29 November 1945
4168/1768 Naik Purkha Ram	Italy, 29 November 1945
Lieutenant Colonel G.A.C. Maunshel	Mediterranean, 23 May 1946
3573 Subedar Basti Ram	Mediterranean, 23 May 1946
3724 Jemadar Bega Ram	Mediterranean, 23 May 1946
3816 Jemadar Hanuman Singh	Mediterranean, 23 May 1946
4276 Jemadar Parbhu Ram	Mediterranean, 23 May 1946
4660/2257 Naik Jaisha Ram	Mediterranean, 23 May 1946
4223/1837 Naik Lakha Ram	Mediterranean, 23 May 1946
4381/1973 Lance Naik Padam Singh	Mediterranean, 23 May 1946
4890/2490 Lance Naik Punjraj Singh	Mediterranean, 23 May 1946
5185/2798 Lance Naik Punjraj Singh	Mediterranean, 23 May 1946
4584/2177 Sepoy Lalla Ram	Mediterranean, 23 May 1946
4920/2521 Sepoy Roopla Ram	Mediterranean, 23 May 1946

'JANGI INAMS' AND 'JAGIRS'

Major Dalapat Singh, MC—Jagir to his brother Jagat Singh

Captain Aman Singh Jodha, OBI, IOM—Jagir

Trumpet Major Sher Singh, IOM—Jangi Inam to his son Amar Singh

Daffadar Jor Singh, IOM—Jangi Inam

Langri Sukhia—Pension

RECRUITING BADGES FOR THE FIRST WORLD WAR

Maharaj Zalim Singh

Thakur Ugam Singh Chandelao

Major Dhonkal Singh Gorau

RECRUITING BADGES FOR THE SECOND WORLD WAR

Mool Chand Vyas, Vyasji building, Oswal Neyat ka Nohra, Jodhpur—17 March 1944

Man Mohan Singh, Parbatsar, Jodhpur—17 March 1944

Johri Mal, Manak Chowk, Jodhpur—27 January 1945

Bhopal Chand, Tobacco Lane, Jodhpur—27 January 1945

Kuber Singh, C/O Tehsildar Sendra, Jodhpur—27 January 1945

Rai Sahib Shah Gordhan Lal Kabra, S/O Barmanand Lal Kabra, Bankar Hatro, Jodhpur—13 May 1946

Kazi Zahoor Ahmed S/O Qazi Sardar Bux, Ashraf Manzil, Udaimandir, Jodhpur—13 May 1946

INDIAN SOLDIERS, SAILORS AND AIRMEN'S BOARD SANAD

Thakur Madho Singh Sankhwai, Hakim of Jodhpur in August 1946.

'GALLANT WERE THEIR DEEDS, UNDYING BE THEIR MEMORIES'

ROLL OF HONOUR OF OFFICERS AND MEN OF THE JODHPUR LANCERS IN THE FIRST WORLD WAR

MAZARGUES WAR CEMETERY, MARSEILLES-BOUCHES-DU-RHONE

1551 Sowar Bhopal Singh. 13 December 1917. Son of Swarup Singh, of Kherwo, Pali, Jodhpur.

1325 Sowar Bhur Singh. 20 June 1917. Son of Khem Singh, of Dhanari Badi, Jodhpur.

1524 Sowar Dal Singh. 28 July 1916. Son of Mug Singh, of Mithari, Samphar, Jodhpur.

1415 Sowar Dul Singh. 02 January 1918. Son of Kishan Singh, of Atambar, Shergarh, Jodhpur.

1523 Lance Daffadar Ful Singh. 20 July 1917. Son of Lakh Singh, of De, Nagaur, Jodhpur.

1342 Sowar Lal Singh. 10 December 1916. Son of Mesdan Singh, of Asawari, Nagaur, Jodhpur.

Author at a Cemetery of the Great War in France, where Jodhpur Lancers troops were laid to rest.
Photo courtesy: The author

1383 Sowar Mul Singh. 02 October 1917. Son of Khuman Singh, of Harsolao, Merta, Jodhpur.

1535 Sowar Sardar Singh. 09 October 1917. Son of Bahadur Singh, of Roino, Nagaur, Jodhpur.

No 2 Follower Tejia, 24 October 1914.

No 1540 Sowar Sheonath Singh, 27 November 1916.

No 1777 Sowar Nathu Khan, 24 May 1917, Son of Shamdi Khan of Alakpura, Didwana, Jodhpur.

MEERUT MILITARY CEMETERY, ST MARTIN-LES-BOULOGNE-PAS-DE-CALAIS

1148 Sowar Hari Singh. (Died of Bronchitis) 04 April 1915. Son of Jawand Singh, of Dechhu Shergarh, Jodhpur.

381 Sowar Deo Singh. 18 March 1915. Son of Madho Singh of Lunavo, Jodhpur.

Captain Thakur Ragunath Singh, 15 Jul 1915 (Died of Pneumonia)

No 104, Follower Bhooria, 21 February 1915.

No 1421, Sowar Chatar Singh, 02 February 1915, Son of Rawat Singh of Rabarias, Jaitaran, Jodhpur.

No 31, Follower Chhailio, 08 April 1915.

Follower Ganglio, 26 March 1915.

No 1004 Lance Daffadar Jawal Singh, 17 March 1915.

No 1203 Sowar Khem Singh, 22 December 1914, Son of Chain Singh of Babaro, Jaitaran, Jodhpur.

No 1247 Sowar Mul Singh, 26 April 1915, Son of Bishun Singh of Dero, Shergarh, Jodhpur.

NEUVE-CHAPELLE MEMORIAL-PAS-DE-CALAIS

1449 Daffadar Hamir Singh. 14 April 1917. Son of Kalyan Singh, of Pali, Phalodi, Jodhpur.

15 Sowar Hukam Singh. 21 May 1917. Son of Dhan Singh, of Khangar, Siwana, Jodhpur.

1125 Sowar Jatan Singh. 20 October 1917. Son of Debi Singh, of Thano, Didwana, Jodhpur.

1358 Sowar Jawand Singh. 21 September 1917. Son of Kalu Singh, of Rangao, Parbatsar, Jodhpur.

1267 Daffadar Khet Singh. 20 December 1914. Son of Sudha Singh, of Mokalsar, Jodhpur.

No 1346 Sowar Sardar Singh of Galthani. 20 December 1914. Son of Bhom Singh of Galthani, Bali, Jodhpur.

1659 Sowar Lun Singh. 23 May 1917. Son of Ajit Singh, of Jetiyas, Jodhpur.

1066 Sowar Magej Singh. 20 August 1916. Son of Chaman Singh, of Muwano, Jodhpur.

1235 Sowar Magh Singh. 21 December 1916. Son of Ranjit Singh, of Chaoo, Nagaur, Jodhpur.

1589 Sowar Makhan Singh. 24 April 1917. Son of Mul Singh, of Sardad, Phalodi, Jodhpur.

1217 Kot Daffadar Modh Singh. 28 July 1917. Son of Shanwat Singh, of Babaro, Jaitaran, Jodhpur.

1053 Sowar Mul Singh. 16 November 1917. Son of Pem Singh, of Sonei, Pali, Jodhpur.

991 Daffadar Nahar Singh. 20 July 1915. Son of Roicho, Siwana, Jodhpur.

905 Daffadar Daula Singh. 20 July 1915. Son of Gomad Singh of Kherapo, Parbatsar, Jodhpur.

1003 Sowar Samdar Singh. 20 April 1915. Son of Rirmal Singh of Mamrodo, Didwana, Jodhpur.

1648 Sowar Phul Singh. 08 March 1918. Son of Durjan Singh, of Lalano, Parbatsar, Jodhpur.

1259 Sowar Sohan Singh. 01 December 1917. Son of Jodh Singh, of Garo, Shergarth, Jodhpur.

No 1784, Sowar Bagh Khan. Son of Umar Khan of Beri, Didwana, Jodhpur.

No 1314 Sowar Bakhtawar Singh. 22 March 1916. Son of Kor Singh of Chheti Tantawas, Nagaur, Jodhpur.

No 1526 Kot Daffadar Bane Singh. 19 June 1916. Son of Udai Singh of Gagutaro (Gaguda), Merta, Jodhpur.

No 1530 Sowar Banne Singh. 09 May 1917. Son of Dan Singh of Bankali, Pali, Jodhpur.

No 1260 Sowar Bhairon Singh. Son of Shalam Singh of Chandawo Shergarh, Jodhpur.

No 1419 Sowar Bhawani Singh. 13 March 1917. Son of Ajit Singh of Digari, Jodhpur.

No 1376 Sowar Bhopal Singh. 13 September 1917. Son of Kalu Singh of Ranigao, Parbatsar, Jodhpur.

No 1569 Sowar Bhur Singh. 21 August 1916. Son of Mohobat Singh of Ketu, Shergarh, Jodhpur.

No 1522 Sowar Bijoi Singh. 13 June 1918. Son of Salam Singh of Barjasar, Phalodi, Jodhpur.

No 1627 Sowar Chand Singh. 30 November 1917. Son of Bhagwant Singh of Ratango, Nagaur, Jodhpur.

No 1730 Sowar Chatar Singh. 03 February 1917. Son of Jodh Singh of Isalu, Sojat, Jodhpur.

No 1358 Sowar Dhankol Singh. 20 February 1918. Son of Jagat Singh of Kinjaro, Jodhpur.

No 1408 Sowar Dul Singh. Son of Man Singh of Khiwaro, Desuri, Jodpur.

No 1416 Sowar Gulab Singh. 20 December 1914. Son of Shiunath Singh of Dewali, Pali, Jodhpur.

No 1537 Sowar Hamid Khan. Son of Annu Khan of Khario, Didwana, Jodhpur.

Follower Himativa. Son of Dhurio of Gigalo, Jodhpur.

No 1763 Sowar Ladu Khan. Son of Hamid Khan of Bawari, Didwana, Jodhpur.

No 1403 Sowar Moti Singh. 07 April 1915. Son of Bhopal Singh of Pemsingh, Sojat, Jodhpur.

No 1560 Sowar Raghunath Singh. 02 January 1918.

No 1027 Sowar Rewat Singh.

No 1768 Sowar Sagat Singh. 22 February 1918. Son of Kheta Singh of Solkotalo, Shergarh, Jodhpur.

NEUVILLE-SOUS-MONTREUIL INDIAN CEMETERY-PAS DE CALAIS

1298 Sowar Kehar Singh. Died of enteric 16 February 1915. Son of Gaya Singh, of Dechhu, Shergarh, Jodhpur.

SAINT HILAIRE CEMETERY, FREVENT

909 Lance Daffadar Bhur Singh. Died 19 June 1916. Husband of Jora of Gelasar, Parbatsar, Jodhpur.

VADENCOURT BRITISH CEMETERY, MAISSEMY

Lieutenant Kunwar Daji Raj, 27 Light Cavalry. Died 23 September 1917 (S/O K.S. Yadvendra Sinhji of Jamnagar, Kathiawar)

ST SEVER CEMETERY, ROUEN

No 1760 Sowar Jitu Khan. 30 March 1917.

ST RIQUIER BRITISH CEMETERY

No 57 Follower Shivram. 28 December 1916.

HELIOPOLIS MEMORIAL (PORT TEWFIK), EGYPT

No 1186 Daffadar Aidan Singh. 22 September 1918. Son of Ram Singh of Parhiyaee, Phalodi, Jodhpur.

No 1655 Sowar Aman Singh. 14 July 1918. Jordan Valley, Son of Bakhtawar Singh of Setorha, Jodhpur.

No 1218 Sowar Anand Singh. 26 October 1918. Son of Birad Singh of Mundeti, Siwana, Jodhpur.

No1545 Sowar Aneg Singh, 06 August 1915, Son of Man Singh of Jewalabas, Didwana, Jodhpur.

Jemadar Assu Singh, IOM. 14 July 1918. Jordan Valley.

No 1733 Sowar Azam Khan. 14 July 1918. Jordan Valley, Son of Himmat Khan of Kuchaman, Sambhar, Jodhpur.

No 1249 Sowar Balu Singh. 14 July 1918. Jordan Valley, Son of Gopal Singh of Gopali, Merta, Jodhpur.

No 107 Follower Bhagwana. 11 January 1920.

No 1390 Lance Daffadar Bhiron Singh. 14 July 1918. Jordan Valley, Son of Shiudan Singh of Meethapur, Parbatsar, Jodhpur (Missing Killed).

No 1664 Sowar Bharat Singh. 21 January 1920. Son of Bur Singh of Khirjan, Shergarh, Jodhpur.

No 1217 Sowar Bhur Singh. 14 July 1918.

No 1767 Sowar Bhur Singh. 16 February 1918. Son of Mohobat Singh of Gopalser, Shergarh, Jodhpur.

No 4, Driver Dalia. 04 September 1915. Son of Surja of Sambher, Jodhpur.

No 1296 Daffadar Dhonkal Singh. 23 September 1918. Haifa, Son of Dhan Singh of Gurha, Nagaur, Jodhpur. (Died on 27 Sept 1918).

No 1536 Sowar Dool Singh. 14 July 1918. Jordan Valley, Son of Sundar Singh of Hudeel, Sambhar, Jodhpur. (Missing Killed).

No 2052 Lance Daffadar Gaja Singh. 25 July 1919.

No 519 Driver Girdhari Khuman. 05 June 1918.

No 1449 Sowar Gopal Singh. 23 September 1918. Haifa, Son of Hanut Singh of Maroth, Sambhar, Jodhpur. (Died on 30 September 1918).

No 1381 Lance Daffadar Hamir Singh. 22 December 1918. Son of Gulab Singh of Nimbarontalao, Shergarh, Jodhpur.

No 1885 Sowar Hussain Khan. 14 July 1918. Jordan Valley.

No 1896 Sowar Janci Singh. 12 July 1918. Son of Sanwtt Singh of Balano, Bali, Jodhpur.

No 160 Follower Jawahir Singh. 20 January 1919.

No 1059 Jemadar Khang Singh, IOM. 14 July 1918. Jordan Valley, Son of Kan Singh of Mitharhi, Didwana, Jodhpur.

No 1775 Sowar Kan Singh, 14 July 1918. Jordan Valley. Son of Bhabhu Singh of Khudialo, Shergarh, Jodhpur. (Missing Killed).

No 32 Driver Kannu. 19 May 1916. Son of Chataru of Jodhpur.

No 1574 Sowar Kannu Singh. 14 July 1918. Jordan Valley, Son of Bahadur Singh of Shekalo, Shergarh, Jodhpur.

No 1871 Sowar Karan Singh. 09 November 1918.

No 162 Follower Karna. 25 August 1918.

No 1230 Lance Daffadar Khet Singh. 14 July 1918. Jordan Valley, Son of Asa Singh of Ketoo, Shergarh, Jodhpur.

No 1226 Daffadar Koom Singh. 14 July 1918. Jordan Valley, Son of Jaswant Singh of Dechoo, Shergarh, Jodhpur.

No 1702 Sowar Ladhoo Khan. 14 July 1918. Jordan Valley, Son of Hamir Khan of Ladnoo, Didwana, Jodhpur. (Missing killed).

No 1066 Sowar Magar Singh. 20 August 1916. Son of Chamman Singh of Mulana, Jodhpur.

No 1242 Daffadar Man Singh. 14 July 1918. Jordan Valley, Son of Ram Singh of Korto, Bali, Jodhpur.

No 38 Follower Mangalia. 09 August 1917. Son of Rawat Singh of Khojias, Jodhpur.

No 1241 Sowar Megh Singh. 22 September 1918 (Died 10 October 1918). Son of Dal Singh of Rathaser, Bikaner.

No 1204 Sowar Mul Singh. 26 August 1916.

No 1887 Sowar Musharraf Khan. 14 July 1918. Jordan Valley (Missing killed).

No 1749 Sowar Paney Singh. 14 July 1918. Jordan Valley, Son of Bhopal Singh of Ghura, Shergarh, Jodhpur.

No 1375 Lance Daffadar Rewat Singh. 14 July 1918. Jordan Valley, Son of Assa Singh of Borunda, Bilara, Jodhpur.

No 1308 Sowar Sabal Singh. 30 August 1916.

No 1049 Sowar Shazad Singh. 23 September 1918, Haifa.

No 1189 Trumpet Major Sher Singh, IOM. 23 September 1918. Haifa, Son of Simrath Singh of Borunda, Bilara, Jodhpur. (Died on 15 Nov 1918).

No 1536 Sowar Suhel Singh. 15 July 1918.

No 1616 Sowar Tagat Singh. 23 September 1918. Haifa, Son of Gen Singh of Suladnos, Merta, Jodhpur.

No 1188 Sowar Tej Singh. 02 December 1918. Son of Ishar Singh of Gigalo, Jodhpur.

Maj Dalpat Singh, MC. 23 September 1918 Haifa. Son of Hari (Hurjee) Singh of Deoli, Pali, Jodhpur.

No 1517 Sowar Bhoor Singh. 14 July 1918. Jordan valley.

No 1655 Sowar Aman Singh. 14 July 1918.

ALEPPO WAR CEMETERY, SYRIA

Lieutenant Colonel Hyla N. Holden. 26 October 1918. Alepo.

No 16 Sowar Amar Singh. 30 December 1918.

No 1730 Sowar Junjar Singh. 26 October 1918. Alepo.

No 1553 Sowar Jaswant Singh. 20 January 1919. Son of Onar Singh of Anwano, Jodhpur.

KANTARA INDIAN CEMETERY, EGYPT

1647 Sowar Mehirat Khan. 16 May 1919. Son of Kalu Singh of Daudsar, Didwana, Jodhpur. (Died of malaria in 41 Indian General Hospital).

No 1735 Sowar Mehrab Singh. 06 January 1920. Son of Debi Singh of Meriyo, Shergarh, Jodhpur.

TURKISH CEMETRY AT MARSA

Sowar Phul Mohd Khan. 27 October 1918.

RAMLEH WAR CEMETRY

No 1470 Sowar Sultan Singh. 23 September 1918. Haifa (Died 18 October 1918),
Son of Bira Singh of Deshnok, Phalodi Jodhpur.

ROLL OF HONOUR OF OFFICERS AND MEN OF THE JODHPUR STATE FORCES IN THE SECOND WORLD WAR

JODHPUR SARDAR INFANTRY

1. No 2896, Sepoy Anand Singh, 17 April 1945, 22 yrs, Cassino Memorial Italy, Son of Teep Kanwar of Davia, Shergarh, Jodhpur.
2. No 2300, Sepoy Badan Singh, 03 March 1945, 25 yrs, Cassino Memorial, Italy, Son of Ajan Kanwar of Roop Pura, Sambher, Jodhpur.

3. Havaldar Bagh Singh, No 4167, 11 June 1946, 25 yrs, Sai Wan Cremation Memorial Hongkong, Son of Mangal Singh and Hem Kanwar of Osian, Bikamkor, Jodhpur.

4. No 1808, Sepoy Bagtawar Singh, 08 December 1941, 22 yrs, Keren Cremation Memorial Eritrea, Son of Sultan Singh and Kishan Kanwar of Rainsar, Marwar.

5. No 2394, Sepoy Bhagirath Ram, 17 April 1945, 26 yrs, Cassino Memorial Italy, Son of Lachhuri of Mati, Parbatsar, Jodhpur.

6. Sepoy Bhagtawar Singh, No 6198, 13 November 1946, Sai Wan Cremation Memorial Hongkong.

7. Sepoy Binja Ram, No 2026, 16 October 1941, 19 yrs, Keren Cremation Memorial, Eritrea, Son of Bhagwana Ram and Pushi of Hansolaw, Marwar.

8. No 1466, Naik Chuna Ram, 07 August 1941, 25 yrs, Keren Cremation Memorial, Eritrea, Son of Sheo Karan Ram and Husband of Umali, of Ratan, Marwar.

9. No 839, Havaldar Fateh Singh, 23 May 1942, 41 yrs, Alamein Cremation Memorial, Egypt, Son of Bagh Singh and Laj Kanwar, Husband of Ugam Kanwar of Kadara, Marwar.

10. No 3357, Sepoy Ghisu Singh, 18 April 1945, 24 yrs, Cassino Memorial Italy, Son of Chhotu Singh and Meeran Kanwar, Husband of Jaith Kanwar, of Dayal Pura, Didwana, Jodhpur.

11. No 522, Havaldar Giana Ram, 39 yrs, Keren Cremation Memorial, Eritrea, Son of Sukh Ram and Jaiti, Husband of Kesar of Sinwa, Marwar.

12. Naik Hari Singh, No 4636/2232, 04 June 1946, 25 yrs, Sai Wan Cremation Memorial Hongkong, Son of Budhi Singh and Anop Kanwar, Husband of Biraj Kanwar of Hukampura of Badu, Jodhpur.

13. Sepoy Himta Ram, No 6596, 05 January 1946, 21 yrs, Sai Wan Cremation Memorial Hongkong, Son of Dungar Ram, Husband of Karku of Baithwasiya, Jodhpur.

14. No 3395, Sepoy Heera Ram, 17 April 1945, 25 yrs, Forli Indian Army War Cemetery, Italy, Son of Labu of Khangta, Bilasu.

15. Sepoy Jawahir Singh, No 4588, 23 yrs, Sai Wan Cremation Memorial Hongkong, Son of Tikam Singh and Jorawar Kanwar of Zaidarmair, Modra, Jaswantpura, Jodhpur.

16. No 2257, Naik Jaisa Ram, MID, 20 April 1945, 25 yrs, Cassino Memorial Italy.

17. No 1985, Sepoy Jor Singh, 14 July 1944, 24 yrs, Forli Indian Army War Cemetery, Italy, Son of Jagat Singh of Tapu, Teori, Jodhpur.

18. Sepoy Junjar Singh, No 5631/3256, 06 August 1945, 26 yrs, Alamein Cremation Memorial, Egypt.

19. No 1620, Sepoy Khet Singh, 25 June 1941, 26 yrs, Keren Cremation Memorial, Eritrea, Son of Moti Singh and Kanwar of Tapu, Jodhpur.

20. No 41, Water Carrier Mangu Ram, 15 August 1941, 26 yrs, Keren Cremation Memorial, Eritrea, Son of Dhana Ram of Nundra, Marwar.

21. No 3733, Sepoy Mohan Singh, 14 April 1945, 25 yrs, Cassino Memorial Italy, Son of Baldeo Singh, Husband of Sugan Kanwar of Lichara, Jodhpur.

22. No 3172, Sepoy Mohan Singh, 03 February 1944, 23 yrs, Sangro River Cremation Memorial Italy, Son of Sirdar Kanwar of Banwara, Merta City, Jodhpur.

23. Sepoy Mula Ram, No 5163/2774, 27 July 1945, 26 yrs, Forli Cremation Memorial, Italy, Son of Kola Ram of Kunehi, Asop, Jodhpur.

24. No 3586, Sepoy Nimba Ram, 12 April 1945, 26 yrs, Forli Cremation Memorial, Italy, Son of Mabai of Panchala Singh Ka, Teori, Jodhpur.

25. No 2651, Sepoy Padma Ram, 04 January 1945, 27 yrs, Forli Cremation Memorial, Italy, Son of Jori of Sirdarpura, Sambhar, Jodhpur.

26. Sepoy Prem Singh, No 2452, 04 June 1945, 28 yrs, Alamein Cremation Memorial, Egypt, Son of Mot Kanwar of Nathrau, Jodhpur.

27. No 2527, Sepoy Puran Singh, 24 November 1942, 21 yrs, Alamein Cremation Memorial, Egypt, Son of Bhur Singh and Ladan Kanwar, Husband of Rajan Kanwar of Sunthali, Jodhpur.

28. No 2077, Naik Rup Singh, 27 July 1944, 24 yrs, Alamein Cremation Memorial, Egypt, Husband of Sugan Kanwar of Kitalsar, Jodhpur.

29. No 2940, Sepoy Sawai Ram, 22 April 1945, 25 yrs, Cassino Memorial Italy, Son of Shiveji Ram and Anchi of Adani, Jodhpur.

30. No 1958, Sepoy Shera Ram, 17 April 1945, 24 yrs, Forli Indian Army War Cemetery, Italy, Son of Mota Ram of Khokrani, Didwana.

31. No 2383, Sepoy Sugan Singh, 17 April 1944, 26 yrs, Alamein Cremation Memorial, Egypt, Son of Mukam Singh, Husband of Mari of Dodoli.

32. No 2545, Sepoy Uma Ram, 17 April 1945, 25 yrs, Cassino Memorial, Italy, Son of Pema Ram of Marothio, Bikaner.

2nd JODHPUR INFANTRY

1. No 6816, Naik Aidan Singh, 09 September 1944, 23 yrs, Delhi/Karachi 1939–45 Memorials, Son of Aidan Singh and Aman Kanwar of Gogadezaro Garo, Jodhpur.

2. No 6366, Recruit Amar Singh, 22 January 1945, 18 yrs, Delhi/Karachi 1939–45 Memorials, Son of Bhoor Singh and Suraj Kanwar of Junjhunu, Jaipur.

3. No 234, Sowar Apuro, 05 November 1945, 48 yrs, Delhi/Karachi 1939–45 Memorials, Son of Dhura, Husband of Chunki of Rajlani, Jodhpur.

4. No 1759, Sepoy Balu Ram, 20 August 1944, Bengal, 25 yrs, Delhi/Karachi 1939–45 Memorials, Son of Bhuri of Bahara Kalan, Jodhpur.

5. No 4531, Jemadar Chatra Ram, 22 February 1945, 31 yrs, Delhi/Karachi 1939–45 Memorials, Son of China Ram, Husband of Kesuri, of Chhapalo, Jodhpur.

6. No 1387, Sepoy Dallu Ram, 13 August 1942, 31 yrs, Delhi/Karachi 1939–45 Memorials, Husband of Guli of Dewolo, Rajasthan.

7. No 1171, Sepoy Dewa Ram, 02 December 1943, 18 yrs, Kohima Cremation Memorial, Son of Lacha Ram of Maulasar, Didwana, India.

8. No 7044, Sepoy Dol Singh, 18 January 1946, 45 yrs, Delhi/Karachi 1939–45 Memorials, Son of Bhoor Kanwar of Hirawati, Marwar.

9. No 3650, Jemadar Durga Ram, 11 April 1945, Bengal.

10. No 1613, Sepoy Durga Ram, 27 November 1943, Delhi/Karachi 1939–45 Memorials.

11. No 1581, Hav Fateh Ram, 25 January 1945, 27 yrs, Delhi/Karachi 1939–45 Memorials, Son of Nani, Husband of Baluri of Khajwana, Jodhpur.

12. No 4540/1943, Naik Hanumana Ram, 07 November 1941, 22 yrs, Delhi/Karachi 1939–45 Memorials, Son of Bhoora Ram and Shoanki of Norangpura, Jodhpur.

13. No 6665, Recruit Hir Singh, 22 January 1945, 22 yrs, Delhi/Karachi 1939–45 Memorials, Son of Magej Singh and Saman Kanwar, Husband of Shirey Kanwar of Khojas, Jodhpur.

14. No 1544, Sepoy Hrid Singh, 08 October 1943, Bengal.

15. No 4770/2367, Naik Hukma Ram, 21 September 1943, 19 yrs, Delhi/Karachi 1939–45 Memorials, Son of Teja Ram and Tejan of Baimoth Kalan, Jodhpur.

16. No 4542, Sepoy Jawahir Singh, 01 September 1944/30 September 1944, Delhi/Karachi 1939–45 Memorials, Son of Amir Singh and Kesher Kanwar, Husband of Bhoor Kanwar of Bapani, Jodhpur.

17. No 13, Barber Jawahiro, 16 April 1946, 34 yrs, Delhi/Karachi 1939–45 Memorials, Husband of Sundari of Osiya, Jodhpur.

18. No 123, Bootmaker Joga, 28 September 1943, Delhi/Karachi 1939–45 Memorials.

19. No 304, Sepoy Keshar Singh, 03 September 1939/31 Dec 1947, Delhi/Karachi 1939–45 Memorials.

20. No 1631, Sepoy Khet Singh, 03 September 1939/31 Dec 1947, 24 yrs, Delhi/Karachi 1939–45 Memorials.

21. No 5912/3539, Recruit Kishan, 24 September 1944, 25 yrs, Delhi/Karachi 1939–45 Memorials, Son of Heer Singh and Mdhel of Jinjanyalo, Jodhpur.

22. No 6480, Recruit Kishan Singh, 25 June 1945, 20 yrs, Delhi/Karachi 1939–45 Memorials, Son of Chaitan Singh and Keshar Kanwar of Palwas, Jaipur.

23. No 6666, Recruit Kishna Ram, 23 January 1945, 23 yrs, Delhi/Karachi 1939–45 Memorials, Son of Dewa Ram and Beejan Bai, Husband of Mango Bai of Begsan, Jodhpur.

24. No 1358, Sepoy Ladu Ram, 07 September 1943, 31 yrs, Delhi/Karachi 1939–45 Memorials, Son of Dewa Ram and Husband of Pemli of Derwa, Jodhpur.

25. No 250, Sepoy Ladu Ram, 18 March 1943, Delhi/Karachi 1939–45 Memorials

26. No 186, Bootmaker Ladhio, 12 July 1945, 31 yrs, Delhi/Karachi 1939–45 Memorials, Husband of Teejhi of Kharia Bera, Jodhpur.

27. No 144, Water Carrier Mula Ram, 22 October 1943, 42 yrs, Delhi/Karachi 1939–45 Memorials, Son of Ramu Ram and Dhapu, Husband of Magani of Baldri, Jodhpur.

28. No 267, Naik Moti Singh, 26 June 1943, 17 yrs, Delhi/Karachi 1939–45 Memorials, Son of Hamir Singh and Lal Kanwar of Dewan Goada, Jodhpur.

29. No 1667, Sepoy Nenu Ram, 21 December 1943, Kohima Cremation Memorial.

30. No 6659, Recruit Natha Ram, 22 January 1945, 27 yrs, Delhi/Karachi 1939–45 Memorials, Son of Bala Ram and Panni Bai of Dikowo, Jodhpur.

31. No 332, Sowar Nawalio, 19 August 1945, 61 yrs, Delhi/Karachi 1939–45 Memorials, Son of Ral Chand, Husband of Jadawati of Gawalu, Jodhpur.

32. No 6669, Recruit Nazir Khan, 22 January 1945, 17 yrs, Delhi/Karachi 1939–45 Memorials, Son of Imandi Khan and Mahta Bi, Husband of Muneeran of Losal.

33. No 322, Naik Rekha Ram, 7 November 1943, 20 yrs, Delhi/Karachi 1939–45 Memorials, Son of Purkhi of Indokhel, Jodhpur.

34. No 1589, Sepoy Sanwal Ram, 25 April 1944, Bengal.

35. No 1474, Sepoy Shaitan Singh, 09 November 1944, 38 yrs, Delhi/Karachi 1939–45 Memorials, Son of Hem singh, Husband of Phool Kanwar of Dasana Katan, Marwar.

36. Recruit Awaz Khan, No 6667, 22 January 1945, 20 yrs, Delhi/Karachi 1939–45 Memorials, Son of Mahrab Khan and Nani Bai of Kildoli, Jaipur.

37. Recruit Girdhari Ram, No 5257/2872, 29 May 1942, 17 yrs, Delhi/Karachi 1939–45 Memorials, Son of Adu Ram and Meera Bai, Husband of Jamuna of Chanu, Jodhpur.

38. Recruit Govind Singh, No 5770/3396, 25 August 1943, 19 yrs, Delhi/Karachi 1939–45 Memorials, Son of Aidan Singh and Bhoor Kanwar of Sowaliya, Jodhpur.

39. Recruit Man Singh, No 5101/2709, 24 March 1942, 22 yrs, Delhi/Karachi 1939–45 Memorials, Son of Raghu Nath Singh and Surat Kanwar of Achina, Jodhpur.

40. Sepoy Mangal Singh, No 5635, 15 December 1945, 25 yrs, Delhi/Karachi 1939–45 Memorials, Son of Achal Singh and Mothan Kanwar of Bhinyar, Jodhpur.

41. Havaldar Mohan Singh, No 6153, 01 August 1947, 25 yrs, Delhi/Karachi 1939–45 Memorials, Son of Ganga Singh and Anand Kanwar, Husband of Bhanwar Kanwar of Natiash, Jodhpur.

42. Sowar Motia, No 215, 49 yrs, Delhi/Karachi 1939–45 Memorials, Son of Magho, Husband of Haturi of Mallana, Jodhpur.

43. Sepoy Rup Singh, No 3611, 19 September 1944, 25 yrs, Delhi/Karachi 1939–45 Memorials, Son of Agar Singh and Singar Kanwar of Basani, Jaipur.

JODHPUR LANCERS

1. No 1660, Sowar Ramzan Khan, 09 September 1944, 20 yrs, Son of Amani Khan and Pehpi, of Chawato, Mundwa, Alamein Memorial.

2. No 1899, Sowar Anup Singh, 04 August 1942, 19 yrs, Son of Karan Singh and Chiman Bai of Nuo, Bikaner, Delhi/Karachi 1939–45 War Memorials.

3. No 1616, Sowar Zalim Singh, 22 October 1941, 20 yrs, Son of Tej Singh, Husband of Ugam Kanwar, of Ratao, Jodhpur, Delhi/Karachi 1939–45 Memorials.

4. No 1399, Sowar Moti Singh, 03 June 1940, 19 yrs, Son of Mal Singh and Tej Kanwar, of Harsolao, Jodhpur, Delhi/Karachi 1939–45 Memorials.

5. No 257, Daffadar Khangar Singh, 28 January 1947, 23 yrs, Son of Jai Singh and Sugan Kanwar and Husband of Bhanwar Kanwar of Badi Khatu, Delhi/Karachi 1939–45 Memorials.

6. No 1233, Lance Daffadar Devi Singh, 26 July 1943, Husband of Mohan Kanwar of Balara, Jodhpur, Delhi/Karachi 1939–45 Memorials.

7. No 20, Squadron Daffadar Major Sujan Singh, 28 January 1945, 28 yrs, Son of Sanwat Singh and Bakhtawar Kunwar, Husband of Sugan Kunwar, of Basani Nikuban, Jodhpur, Basra Cremation Memorial, Iraq.

8. No 728, Sowar Moti Singh, 24 August 1946, 27 yrs, Son of Dal Singh and Sada Kanwar, of Lapundra, Jodhpur, Delhi/Karachi 1939–45 Memorials.

9. No 1026, Daffadar Tej Singh, 24 April 1942, 31 yrs, Son of Nahar Singh and Kan Kanwar, Husband of Magan Kanwar, of Bhagwanpura, Jodhpur, Delhi/Karachi 1939–45 Memorials.

10. No 1728, Sowar Sumer Singh, 26 September 1942, 20 yrs, Son of Berishal Singh and Salab Kanwar, of Koyal, Jodhpur, Delhi/Karachi 1939–45 Memorials.

11. No IEC/8551, Major Kanwar Surajbhan Singh, 08 August 1944, 37 yrs, Son of Thakur Devi Singh of Mayapur, Jodhpur, Basra Cremation Memorial, Iraq.

12. No 1138, Quartermaster Nathu Singh, 06 January 1944, Son of Sukh Singh, of Bhungra, Jodhpur, Delhi/Karachi 1939–45 Memorials.

13. No 1423, Sowar Ladia, 27 March 1945, Husband of Madki, of Beri, Jodhpur, Basra Cremation Memorial.

14. No 1718, Sowar Allah Din Khan, 29 December 1943, Son of Bhoore Khan and Nasi Bi, Husband of Gulab Banu of Dausar, Jodhpur. Delhi/Karachi 1939–45 Memorials.

15. No 76, Daffadar Major Kalyan Singh, 27 January 1946, 30 yrs, Son of Moti Singh and Antar Kanwar, Husband of Bagat Kanwar of Bhadana, Jodhpur, Beirut Cremation Memorial.

NO 54 (JODHPUR) GPT COMPANY, RIASC

1. IECO/1506 Lieutenant Magh Singh, 30 March 1944, Iraq.

2. MTN/912541 Lance Naik Chhotu Singh, 23 August 1941, Iraq.

3. MTN/912512 Lance Naik Bala Ram, 16 June 1942, Iraq.

4. MTN/912523 Lance Naik Sawai Singh, 17 February 1944, Iraq.

5. MTN/912549 Lance Naik Sajjan Singh, 30 March 1944, Iraq.

6.   MTN/912514 Sepoy Mool Singh, 8 December 1941, Iraq.

7.   MTN/912563 Sepoy Gorakh Singh, 9 April 1942, Iraq.

8.   MTN/941064 Sepoy Kishen Singh, 26 December 1942, Iraq.

9.   MTN/912734 Sepoy Dhul Singh, 8 June 1943, Iraq.

10. MTN/912562 Sepoy Sugan Singh, 30 March 1944, Iraq.

11. MTN/912490 Sepoy Shivkaran Singh, 30 March 1944, Iraq.

Bibliography

A Brief History of the Jodhpur State Railway 1882–1932. Bombay: The Times of India Press, 1933.

A List of English Records of the Jodhpur Mahakamakhas 1893 to 1950, Volume II. Bikaner Rajasthan State Archives, 25 August 1989.

Adams, Lt Col. Archibald. *The Western Rajputana States: A Medico-Topographical and General Account of Marwar, Sirohi, Jaisalmer.* London: Junior Army and Navy Stores, 1899.

Anglesey, The Marquess of. *A History of the British Cavalry Vol 5 1914-1919, Egypt, Palestine & Syria.* Barnsley: Pen & Sword Books Ltd, 1994.

Barker, A.J. *The Neglected War – Mesopotamia 1914–1918.* Faber and Faber, 1967.

Bibikoff, Massia. *Our Indians at Marseilles.* London: Smith, Elder and Co, 1915.

Diver, Maud. *Royal India.* London: Hodder and Stoughton 1942.

Duncan, Major General R.C. *History of the Jodhpur State Forces in the War 1939–45.* Jodhpur: Government Press, 1946.

Falls, Capt. Cyril. *Military Operations Egypt and Palestine Part II.* London: HMSO, 1930.

Gardner, Nora Beatrice Blyth. *Rifle and Spear with the Rajpoots.* London: Chatto and Windus, 1895.

Grimshaw, Captain Roly. *Indian Cavalry Officer 1914–15.* Tunbridge Wells: D J Costello Ltd, 1986.

Head, Richard and Tony McClenaghan. *The Maharajas' Paltans: History of the Indian State Forces.* New Delhi: United Services Institution of India of India, 2013.

History of the 15 Imperial Service Cavalry Brigade during the Great War 1914–1918. London: HMSO, 1920.

Hypher, P.P. *Deeds of Valour, Performed by Indian Officers and Soldiers, 1860 to 1925,* Shimla: Lidell's Press, 1927.

Keegan, John. *The First World War: An Illustrated History.* New York: Random House, 2002.

MacMunn, Lt General. *Sir George. The Indian States and Princes,* London: Jarrolds Publishers, 1936.

Man Singh, Maharaja of Jaipur. *A History of the Indian State Forces.* Bombay: Orient Longmans, 1967.

Mason, Philip. *A Matter of Honour: An Account of the Indian Army, Its Officers and Men.* London: Papermac, 1986.

Merewether, C.I.E, Lt Col. J.W.B. *The Indian Corps in France during the First World War.* London: John Murray, 1917.

Nath, Ashok. *Izzat, Historical Records and Iconography of Indian Cavalry Regiments 1750–2007,* New Delhi: Centre for Armed Forces Historical Research, United Service Institution of India, 2009.

Preston, DSO, Lieutenant Colonel R.M.P. *The Desert Mounted Corps 1917–18.* London: Constable and Company Ltd, 1921.

Radhakrishan, Shriman. *Maharaja Sir Pratap Singhji Sahib Ka Swalikhit Jivan-Charitr.* (Hindi), Mori Gate Lahore: Vir Milap Press, 1939.

Reu, Vishwanath. *Marwar Ka Itihas* (Hindi). Jodhpur: Government Press, 1938.

Richard, Aldington. *Lawrence of Arabia. A Biographical Enquiry.* Collins, London, 1955.

Rudolph, Susanne H. and Lloyd I. Rudolph. *Reversing the Gaze: Amar Singh's Diary.* New Delhi: Oxford University Press, 2000.

Sandhu, Maj. Gen. G.S. *History of the Indian Armoured Corps.* New Delhi: Vision Books, 1981.

Shah, P.R. *Raj Marwar during British Paramountcy.* Jodhpur: Sharda Publishing House, 1982.

Singh, Dhananajaya. *The House of Marwar: The Story of Jodhpur.* New Delhi: Roli Books, 1994.

Steevens, G.W. *In India.* Edinburgh: William Blackwood and Sons, 1900.

Tod, James. *Annals and Antiquities of Rajasthan.* Calcutta: Brojendro Lall Doss, 1884.

Trench, Charles Trevenix. *The Indian Army and the King's Enemies, 1900-47.* London: Thames and Hudson, 1988.

Trevor, CSI, Col. G.H. *Rhymes of Rajputana,* London: Macmillan and Co. 1894.

Vacher, Peter. *The History of the Jodhpur Flying Club in Princely India,* Apogee Books, 2008.

Van Wart, R.B. OBE, *The Life of Lieutenant General HH Sir Pratap Singh.* London: Oxford University Press, 1926.

Watson, Major General, Sir Harry. *A Short History of the Services rendered by the Imperial Service Troops during the Great War, 1914–18.* Calcutta: Government of India, 1930.

Wavell, Field Marshal, Earl. *The Palestine Campaign.* London: Constable, 1936.

Wavell, Sir Archibald. *Allenby: A Study in Greatness,* London: George G. Harrap, 1940.

ORIGINAL SOURCES:

Files, documents, diaries, letters, speeches, notes, memoranda, gazettes, albums, pertaining to Jodhpur State Forces (Mehrangarh Museum, The Fort, Jodhpur; Sumair Public Library, Jodhpur; The National Archives of India, New Delhi; The State Archives, Bikaner; and innumerable private collections)

Administrative Reports of the Jodhpur State from 1885 to 1946.

Hakikat Bahi, Maharaja Man Singh Pushtak Parakash Research Centre, Mehrangarh Fort Jodhpur.

Imperial Service Troops Army List Jul 1915, Jul 1916, Jul 1917, Jan 1918, Jan 1919, Jan 1920, Jan 1922.

Nagar, Dr Mahendra Singh. *Rajputane ke Ethihasik Letters,* Maharaja Man Singh Pustak Prakash Research Centre, Mehrangarh Fort, Jodhpur.

The Diaries and Photo Albums of General Amar Singh Kanota, Jaipur.

The Illustrated War News, 28 June 1916.

The Indian State Forces List Jan 1923, Jan 1924, Jul 1924, Jan 1926, Jan 1927, Jan 1929, Jan 1931, Oct 1933, Dec 1933, Jul 1939, Jan 1941, Jan 1942, Apr 1945, Jan 1946.

War Diary, The Jodhpur Lancers. 29 Aug 1914 to 17 Dec 1919, Public Record Office, Kew, WO 95/1158

SECONDARY SOURCES:

Interviews with numerous Officers, men and their descendants who had served with the Jodhpur State Forces.

Visits to France, Belgium and Haifa, Israel, where the Jodhpur Lancers fought during the Great War.

Photo courtesy: Mahendra Singh Rathore, RAS

Index

C